AFTER THE EDUCATION WARS

ALSO BY ANDREA GABOR

The Man Who Discovered Quality

Einstein's Wife

The Capitalist Philosophers

AFTER THE EDUCATION WARS

How Smart Schools Upend the Business of Reform

Andrea Gabor

THE NEW PRESS

NEW YORK
LONDON

Published in the United States by The New Press, New York, 2018
Distributed by Two Rivers Distribution

ISBN 978-1-62097-199-4 (hc)
ISBN 978-1-62097-200-7 (e-book)

CIP data is available

The New Press publishes books that promote and enrich public discussion and understanding of the issues vital to our democracy and to a more equitable world. These books are made possible by the enthusiasm of our readers; the support of a committed group of donors, large and small; the collaboration of our many partners in the independent media and the not-for-profit sector; booksellers, who often hand-sell New Press books; librarians; and above all by our authors.

www.thenewpress.com

Composition by dix!
This book was set in Minion

Printed in the United States of America

10 9 8 7 6 5 4 3 2 1

For Sarah, Annie, and Jose.
And in memory of Magda and Imre;
I think of you every day.

CONTENTS

AFTER THE EDUCATION WARS

INTRODUCTION

The Quiet Revolution

Detroit, 1979. U.S. auto companies were being threatened by foreign competition, and the Motor City became a symbol of American industrial decline. Chrysler would be subjected to its first (but not last) government bailout; the Ford Motor Co. was about to lose $1 billion for that fiscal year, and at least as much again in 1980; and GM's profits were expected to plunge by a breathtaking $2.5 billion. Meanwhile, Japanese automakers were gaining market share; Toyota would soon surpass GM as the world's largest car company. (A similar scenario played out in other industries too, especially consumer electronics and the copier industry.)

Then, as now, the convenient scapegoat was the rank-and-file employees—in Detroit's case, the unionized workers whose relatively high wages and ostensibly poor work ethic were initially blamed for the automakers' problems. Only as Japanese wage rates reached parity with those in the United States and Japanese automakers began hiring American workers for their U.S. plants did some Detroit auto executives begin rethinking the narrative of blue-collar failure.

In 1980, an NBC documentary, *If Japan Can, Why Can't We*, served as a wake-up call for American industry. The documentary introduced the methods of a little-known American quality expert by the name of W. Edwards Deming to an American audience. Deming, the subject of my first book, had helped Japanese companies rebuild following World War II, becoming a hero in Japan. The much-heralded Toyota production system grew out of a years-long dialogue between Deming and the automaker and, via its Kaizen methodology, formalized the way continuous improvement came to encompass Toyota's entire corporate culture and management philosophy.

Responding to an urgent appeal from the new president of Ford, Deming flew to Detroit and, during the next few years, proceeded to rip the lid off of the prevailing assumptions about the quality problems of U.S. companies. It is a testament to how desperate the auto executives were that they grudgingly embraced Deming's message, despite the fact that he laid the lion's share of the blame for quality problems on senior management instead of on labor.

Ford's then-president, Donald E. Petersen, alone among what were then the Big Three top executives, embraced Deming's message without reservation. At GM, executives in charge of Cadillac and Pontiac smuggled Deming in via the back door, fearful of how senior management would react. In the coming years, his ideas about a bottom-up, systems-oriented approach to management helped transform both automakers and became associated with, among others, the revival of Cadillac, the Saturn project, and the creation of Ford's highly successful Taurus and Sable automobiles.

Deming was a quintessential outsider. Raised in Wyoming, Deming was trained as an engineer and physicist but became a pioneer in statistical sampling methods. At the peak of his popularity, he worked out of the basement of his modest home in Washington, D.C. Driven by a messianic belief in his ideas, Deming would never be as wholeheartedly embraced as his contemporaries were, especially Peter Drucker, who never challenged the fundamental status quo and thus became the darling of twentieth-century CEOs.

At a time when American industry was becoming ever more siloed and finance focused, Deming advocated a collaborative, systems-focused, process-obsessed approach to management. While he was often derided as a mere statistician, Deming made a crucial breakthrough by linking the scientific (in particular, how to understand and manage the statistical variation that erodes the quality of all processes) and the humanistic (an intuitive feel for the organization as a social system and a collaborative, democratic vision of management).

Variation is as ubiquitous as air or water. But a cornerstone of Deming's teachings was that only the employees closest to a given process can identify the variation that invariably diminishes quality and develop ideas for improving quality. Ordinary employees—not senior management or hired consultants—are in the best position to see the cause-and-effect relationships in each process, Deming argued. The challenge for management is to tap into that knowledge on a consistent basis and to make that knowledge actionable. To do so, management must train its employees to identify problems and develop solutions. More controversially, Deming argued, management must also shake up the hierarchy (if not eliminate it entirely), drive fear out of the workplace, and foster intrinsic motivation if it is to make the most of employee potential.

What, readers may be wondering, does industrial improvement in the automotive industry have to do with the ongoing controversy and debates surrounding the quality of American education?

Since the beginning of the millennium, the story of education reform has been, in important respects, a business story. That's how I, a longtime management writer, first got hooked on the subject. What I aim to demonstrate in the pages that follow is that the corporate-reform industry that is gaining ever-increasing influence on how American schools educate children has largely ignored the successful examples and strategies for improving schools that are hiding in plain sight. These distinct examples together form something of a quiet revolution in education. By casting light on them, this book explores the cultural and organizational infrastructure that schools and districts need in order to achieve lasting improvement. Even as the generative, systems-oriented ideas were finding their way into companies, inspired by Deming and like-minded management thinkers, some schools and school districts around the country were following suit. They were resisting the mandates, the punitive teacher evaluations, and, in some cases, even the standardized tests and were searching for—and finding—an alternative path.

In 2004, near the start of what would be Michael Bloomberg's three terms as mayor of New York City, a management magazine asked me to write about the NYC Leadership Academy, the new administration's bid to recruit and train new principals for an armada of new schools it was hoping to open to help transform education in New York City.

The Leadership Academy was part of a new class of much-touted public–private partnerships that aimed to use business expertise and metrics to improve publicly funded institutions. It modeled itself on GE's famous Crotonville, New York, leadership development institute, which had recently been renamed the John F. Welch Leadership Development Center after the company's combative former CEO whose management practices had won him the moniker Neutron Jack.

I was intrigued. What could Neutron Jack teach educators? And how would those lessons be received?

Like many reform efforts around the country, the Leadership Academy represented a laudable effort to meet a vital challenge in new and better ways. The hierarchy and rules of the New York City education department made it difficult for principals to function as anything but compliance managers; beholden to the superintendents who controlled school budgets, the job often attracted educators eager to move up the salary scale and willing to do the bidding of their superiors. The Bloomberg administration, by contrast, was determined to infuse city schools with a new cadre of entrepreneurial leaders; principals would get more power, crucially over their own budgets, in exchange for increased accountability.

But what I learned—a lesson that I didn't fully absorb until I had explored many other efforts to apply business lessons to education, years after my original piece was published—is that the cultural blinders and received truths of the businessman mayor and others among what I will call the corporate-reform elite threatened to derail even their best ideas.

In Bloomberg's New York, some of the country's savviest business minds, their worldviews honed at Wharton and Harvard Business School, would encounter one of the most sophisticated education brain trusts, whose education philosophies were forged in the crucible of the civil rights movement in Selma and Chicago's South Side and in some of the neediest inner-city classrooms. New York's education innovators and Bloomberg's business people couldn't have been more different. Yet they shared one important thing in common: a determination not only to improve schools, but also to create smaller, leaner schools that would be more responsive to the needs of students and to shake up the education bureaucracy and the status quo.

It was a unique opportunity, but one that would never be fully realized.

Long before the Bloomberg era, in the depths of the fiscal crisis of the mid-1970s, New York City had experienced a "miracle in Harlem," one of the most sustained education-turnaround efforts in the nation. It was an effort led by an extraordinarily talented cadre of educators and one that would span one of the poorest districts, spread to other parts of the city, and would even briefly inspire education policy in Albany, the state capital, and for a time serve as a model for the Bill and Melinda Gates Foundation.

The Bloomberg administration recognized the know-how of these educators and would elevate many of them to positions of prominence in its Department of Education. The principals who were groomed in Harlem and in other districts inspired by Harlem's progressive reformers also would receive extraordinary protection under the Bloomberg regime.

But to be an educator in Bloomberg's New York was a little like being a Trotskyite in Bolshevik Russia—never fully trusted and ultimately sidelined, if not doomed.

The business reformers came to the education table with their truths: a belief in market competition and quantitative measures. They came with their prejudices—favoring ideas and expertise forged in corporate boardrooms over the knowledge and experience gleaned in the messy trenches of inner-city classrooms. They came with distrust of an education culture that values social justice over more practical considerations like wealth and position. They came with the arrogance that elevated polished, but often mediocre (or worse), technocrats over scruffy but knowledgeable educators. And, most of all, they came with their suspicion—even their hatred—of organized labor and their contempt for ordinary public school teachers.

At the start of the new millennium, the newly appointed head of the Bill and Melinda Gates Foundation's education efforts discovered one of New York City's most successful education transformations, what became known as the Julia Richman Education Complex, which long predated the Bloomberg education reforms. Once one of the city's most dysfunctional high schools—it housed three thousand students at its peak—Julia Richman had become the setting for a novel experiment, one that would involve taking over the failing high school, which in recent years hadn't graduated more than about 150 kids per year, phasing it out one graduating class at a time, and moving in a half dozen new small schools that had been incubated elsewhere by a group of New York's maverick educators (see chapter 1). One of the project's champions had sold the idea to then-chancellor of education Joseph Fernandez by saying: "Think of it as a condominium for schools."[1]

The founders of what would become the Julia Richman Education Complex would win one of the first major education grants from the Gates Foundation and would become one of the city's longest-surviving education success stories.

The Gates man spent a year trolling the halls of Julia Richman. When he offered the Julia Richman people another grant to replicate what they had done, one of the complex's founders warned: "Small is a necessary, but not sufficient" condition for school reform.

What she meant was that "small" was just the most obvious trait that the Julia Richman schools shared. Each school was actually quite distinct. More important was the cultural glue, virtually invisible to the casual observer, that had incubated, nurtured, and held together the schools. Julia Richman was a radical grassroots operation. Its leadership was bold and visionary. Its flagship schools were largely teacher run and student focused. Teacher training and mentoring was at the heart of what made many of its schools successful, as was a management approach that relied on consensus. For more than twenty years, virtually every decision that had allowed the six schools within Julia Richman to co-exist, share common facilities, and thrive had been driven by consensus—slow, tedious, often fraught consensus. As a group, they also had fought together to keep the barbarians of the bureaucracy—its mandates and even its standardized tests—at bay.

The Julia Richman Complex—like most of the examples in this book—are "traditional public schools."

The Gates man was smitten with Julia Richman, but he didn't see what was actually happening there. Instead of a carefully planned condominium—gathering a committed group of educators, investing in their vision, and relying on their expertise—the Gates Foundation threw up small schools like so many tract houses in the midst of a real estate bubble, and not just in New York City, but across the country. Some sold well. Many went bust. Eventually, the small-school strategy was deemed a failure.

The Bloomberg administration also fell in love with small schools. But like the Gates man, the Bloomberg administration never fully understood or trusted the cultural glue that held together the Julia Richman Complex and made its schools work.

Bloomberg's New York was one of the most sophisticated efforts at corporate-style reform in the country. It made huge strides in shaking up the education bureaucracy, creating fertile soil for innovative schools. But it was not enough.

One goal of this book is to understand what makes *real*, long-term education reform work—the ecosystem that nurtures it—and why so many efforts have failed. If small size, as the Gates Foundation would eventually learn, isn't the secret sauce, what is?

Real, meaningful education reform has been taking root in cities and counties and even states around the country for years, hiding in plain sight. This quiet revolution, of which Julia Richman is but one tiny example, is in fact a guerrilla movement that has, over the years, exploited the cracks in the cement of locally, state-, and federally imposed public-school bureaucracies. Almost every example in this book has taken root over the course of more than a decade and, in most cases, has survived at least two generations of management. In other words, the movement has proven to be lasting and sustainable in the medium-to-long term.

Nor is it confined to individual maverick schools. The warriors in this revolution have come to encompass districts and quasi-districts as large as a medium-sized American city. And, in at least one case, the ideas that characterize this quiet revolution suffused an entire state.

Often as not, the successful reforms began as grassroots movements and grew out of rank-and-file educators' passion for social justice, or out of the civil rights movement itself. The reforms are not confined to blue states or red states; the examples in this book span both. Some have taken root in union soil; some have thrived in "right-to-work" states. The reforms have suffused small schools but, contrary to the assumptions surrounding the Julia Richman experiment—that small is "necessary"—there are also giant schools with thousands of students that managed successful transformations. Nor are such reforms the product of a particular education ideology—among them are progressives and traditionalists, as well as those who would eschew such labels.

What they do share is a particular cultural and organizational DNA, which this book argues helps to explain their success. As diverse as these examples are, they share a number of traits in common—traits that would be familiar to the savviest business entrepreneurs:

- They are nurtured through a process of democratic collaboration and iterative improvement, in which grassroots participation is key.
- They are embraced by savvy leaders who have used participative management to foster deep wells of trust.
- They have often been protected from bureaucratic meddling by winning exemptions from specific regulations, often including union rules, and sometimes with the help of enlightened policymakers.
- They value data but understand its limits, knowing that the most important factors are often immeasurable.

What intrigued me is that this organizational DNA was wholly familiar and not at all unique to schools or educational institutions. It's at the heart of some of the most successful business organizations. In fact, it represents a renegade approach to management that has gained traction in the years since global competition, the Internet, and distributive processing put large hierarchical companies at a disadvantage to flatter, nimbler, often more democratic entrepreneurial organizations.

What has led the mainstream education establishment astray is that it has adopted the *wrong* lessons from American business. It has looked to the top-down, hierarchical world in which employees are directed from above, siloed into departments that never communicate with each other, and manipulated with carrot-and-stick incentives—an approach that, these days, seems about as successful as a Ford Pinto or a Deep Water Horizon drilling operation.

Improvement in education, as in all worthwhile endeavors, is critical. But in place of a top-down, carrot-and-stick hierarchy, this book argues for a look backward—and forward—to a more generative systems-oriented approach to improvement that harnesses both the energy and the knowledge of ordinary employees. It is based on the conviction that those most knowledgeable about problems—and solutions—are those closest to any given process. In the case of schools, that would be the teachers and even the students. Capturing that know-how requires the development and careful nurturing of a culture of continuous improvement, including systematic training, trust, iterative learning, and relentless commitment.

To understand why the Gates Foundation could spend a year at the Julia Richman complex and not "see" what made it work, let alone replicate its processes, it helps to understand the big battle that shaped American industry itself and that produced, especially toward the end of the twentieth century, some of its costliest mistakes.

The struggle over American industrialization and the American workplace—indeed, American life—was shaped a century ago by the larger-than-life men who were, in their day, every bit as iconic then as Bill Gates and Steve Jobs are today. They developed surprisingly divergent approaches to fostering productivity in the American workplace—a disagreement that is reflected in the conflicting approaches to education reform today.

The debate over scientific management would have far-reaching consequences not just for American companies, but also for men and women at all levels of the workplace and for society at large. It influenced not only the way companies are run, but the essence of labor-management relations as well. It was invoked in key Supreme Court decisions. It informed the way journalists viewed—and wrote about—industry. (Ida Tarbell, who helped break up the Rockefeller trust, was also an influential supporter of the scientific-management movement.)

Indeed, the winner of that managerial struggle—a man whose ideas have permeated the DNA of American industry and society—was Frederick Winslow Taylor, whose obsessive rationalism oversold the ability of science to improve productivity; undervalued the creative input of employees, especially hourly workers; and leveled its greatest ire against labor unions.

Taylorism even shaped public education. "[F]or better or for worse, Taylor's influence 'extended to all of American education from the elementary schools to the universities,'" writes Robert Kanigel, Taylor's biographer.[2]

While the success of Taylorism seems a foregone conclusion today, in his day there were powerful alternative ideas about fostering innovation and productivity with a more collaborative model of business—ideas that were pushed aside then but increasingly characterize some of the most successful twenty-first-century organizations. It has taken a century to begin to shed society's exoskeleton of Taylorism.

In schools and classrooms around the country, a much-needed break from the century-old legacy of Taylorism and its modern-day descendants in the corporate-reform movement is taking place. This break represents, in many ways, the road not taken in American industry. American industrialization diverged over a century ago, and, fatefully for both U.S. companies and society, America chose the Taylorite path. There are, of course, noteworthy outliers, including SAP Software; W.L. Gore, the maker of Gore-Tex; and Chobani, the yogurt company that recently promised employees a 10 percent ownership stake, if the company is sold or goes public, in acknowledgment of their contributions to the business; as well as dozens of companies such as Patagonia, Whole Foods (pre-Amazon), and the Container Store that pioneered "conscious capitalism," a movement that aims to "align" and "integrate" the interests of all of a company's major stakeholders, including employees and communities, not just shareholders.[3]

There is the open-source software movement, an entirely flat, self-motivated cadre of volunteer software engineers who have produced higher-quality software than the private sector has. Think Mozilla's Firefox Web browser versus Microsoft's Internet Explorer. These examples have bucked the Taylorite trend and thrived on a business model that eschews hierarchy and aims to empower and reward all of its constituencies—including employees—not just shareholders.

Educational institutions have profoundly different goals and cultures and constituencies than businesses do, which makes them much less suited either to a free market model or to Taylorism. Educators are much more driven by social justice and job security than by money. Good teaching is as much art as science. Good education also is seen, increasingly, as collaborative and interdisciplinary. Last but not least, children are more vulnerable than adult employees or consumers to Schumpeterian disruptions of the marketplace.[4]

By contrast, just as Taylor sought to eliminate the skilled crafts that dominated manufacturing and to dumb down and standardize production, Doug Lemov's carefully scripted gestures, shorthand (*SLANT*), and "taxonomy" were designed to help no-excuses charters function with inexperienced teachers.[5] Meanwhile, the education-reform prophets Terry Moe and John Chubb promoted an education vision in which kids would learn via computer with only occasional assistance from "asynchronous" instructors who worked out of centralized teacher warehouses.[6]

Indeed, this book argues that the Taylorite legacy is responsible for one of the most distorted and counterproductive received truths of the mainstream education-reform movement, one that blames teachers for the lion's share of the problems that ail schools and has turned teacher-bashing into a blood sport.

During the course of researching this book, I asked dozens of sources—business leaders and education reformers of all stripes—what percentage of teachers they would consider to be "bad teachers." When I asked Paul Vallas, the controversial standard-bearer of the corporate-reform movement and the former superintendent of both the now all-charter New Orleans schools and the Bridgeport, Connecticut, school system, his answer surprised me: "The vast majority are excellent when provided with the curriculum, instructional models and supports" they need.[7]

Vallas's answer mirrored, almost exactly, what Stephen Phillips, the New York City superintendent of alternative high schools who, for over a decade beginning in 1983, was known as the chief champion and protector of the city's best and most maverick progressive schools, said: "About 20 percent of teachers are exceptionally good, 60 percent are solid, dependable performers; 20 percent shouldn't be there in the first place."[8]

Phillips's estimate—that is, pegging the number of "bad" teachers at 20 percent—is on the high side of the estimates I heard. No one knows for sure.

Yet it's noteworthy that much of education policy over the last thirty years has been directed at identifying, punishing, and expelling a relatively small percentage of poor performers. In the process, the educational establishment has produced a set of policy mandates—including a constantly shifting round of punitive and ill-conceived performance appraisals that were linked to steadily shifting and often ill-conceived standardized tests—as well as canned curricula that have sucked the joy and creativity—and often the purpose—out of teaching and learning. They have not only subjected kids to round after round of testing and mind-numbing lessons; they have also proven deeply demoralizing for teachers—the vast majority of whom are capable educators who want nothing more than to *improve* their practice.

As the opt-out movement, the implosion of the Common Core State Standards, and stagnant test scores have shown, three decades of top-down, corporate-style education reforms have proven deeply unpopular and have reaped few benefits. (Importantly, the backlash against the Common Core has less to do with the standards themselves than with the haste with which they, and accompanying tests, were imposed from on high without any meaningful debate by states and the federal government.)

As Richard Kahlenberg and Halley Potter have shown in their insightful book *A Smarter Charter,* much of education reform has resulted in reducing the voice and input of teachers, with devastating effect. The animating idea behind charter schools was to give "teachers greater voice" than they had in traditional schools, and also to be a vehicle for integrating schools so they would promote "social mobility and social cohesion." Yet the entire charter school movement, conceived by the legendary labor leader Albert Shanker to give both parents and teachers a hand in innovating schools, has been upended. Instead, charter schools have come to be marked by a growing "hostility to teacher voice and teachers unions" and increased segregation. Moreover, an oligopoly of charter-management organizations has brought increasing uniformity to the charter sector, in many communities making a mockery of the idea of "choice" and closing the door on parent participation.

Instead of nurturing teachers to stay in the profession and improve their practice for the long term, the reform movement has focused on a Taylorite effort to standardize teaching so that teachers can be easily substituted like widgets on an assembly line. This despite the fact that, on average, "unions have a positive effect on student achievement" and the best charter schools are often the independent charters that give teachers voice, often via union contracts.[9] In this context, it's important to understand that behind the teacher-bashing is another Taylorite mantra that runs at cross-purposes with the aim of fostering an improved teaching corps: a unionized teaching force is a sure route to perdition. Better to maintain a revolving door than risk the possibility that teachers might join a union.

Thus, a laudable effort to provide young, temporary teachers for poor districts that had trouble recruiting teachers quickly turned into a teacher-substitution strategy. In New Orleans, young, inexperienced, mostly white outsiders quite literally replaced the mostly black teachers who were fired in the aftermath of Hurricane Katrina; as of 2013, eight years after the storm, 38 percent of teachers in the mostly black Recovery School District, which educated the vast majority of kids, including the neediest, had less than three years of teaching experience, according to Tulane University's Cowen Institute. Wisconsin met a growing teacher shortage with a proposal that would have allowed even those without a college degree to teach academic subjects. Meanwhile, Moe and Chubb's online-education vision produced, instead, a dystopian reality of failed virtual schools.[10]

The result of all these efforts has been an unsustainable level of teacher turnover in both traditional public schools and charters—and in many districts it is the best and most seasoned teachers who wind up throwing in the towel.

Even the conservative (and pro-charter) American Enterprise Institute recognizes that schools can't fire (and hire) their way to better results. The total number of college graduates from Barron's "highly competitive" or "most competitive" colleges is approximately 141,956 annually. If fully 10 percent entered into teaching for a two-year period before moving on to other careers, it would provide just 27,655 educators annually, 6 percent of the 438,914 teachers at work in the nation's largest school districts (as of 2008).[11]

Simply put, schools have no choice but to work with the teachers they've got.

Part of the problem is that there has never been a consensus about the nature of the public school "problem." One theory holds that American education has been "homogenized and diluted," that it lacks rigor, and that the teaching force is wholly inadequate to the task—"too many" drawn from the bottom of their high school and college classes, too few experts in science and math, and not enough money to attract better candidates. Another theory argues that schools in middle-class and affluent areas are doing just fine, and it is the poor schools that are getting short-changed. Yet another theory argues that the standardized tests that were intended to inject more rigor into education are, instead, "driving instruction *away* from the development of . . . skills and thinking abilities increasingly needed" both in the workplace and in academia (emphasis added).[12]

However you define "the problem," there is little doubt that a global marketplace, one characterized by exponential technological change, and an increasingly diverse democratic society demand an education system that is capable of systematic adaptation and constant improvement. Yet, as of this writing, there is a growing realization that many of the remedies that have been touted for the past three decades have at the very least fallen short and have done little to improve American education overall, especially in the poorest neighborhoods.

Moreover, there is a striking parallel between the failures of corporate reform and the near-fatal misdiagnosis of one of the last big Taylorite disasters in American management history—the competitiveness crisis that led to a wave of bankruptcies and near bankruptcies in the late 1970s and early 1980s.

The schools and districts that have bucked the corporate reforms of the education wars suggest that there is also a direct link between their approach to education improvement and the continuous-improvement strategy that was eventually, if grudgingly, embraced by American industry in the wake of that competitiveness crisis.

Amid the economic tumult of the late 1970s and 1980s, many policymakers came to believe that a failure in education was to blame for the country's poor economic growth and industrial failures. In 1983, just as Deming's ideas were transforming Detroit, a national bipartisan commission published *A Nation at Risk.* In its very first sentence, the report invoked the competitiveness crisis and economic malaise from which the country was suffering: "Our once unchallenged preeminence in commerce, industry, science, and technological innovation is being overtaken by competitors throughout the world." It continued:

> The risk is not only that the Japanese make automobiles more efficiently than Americans and have government subsidies for development and export. It is not just that the South Koreans recently built the world's most efficient steel mill, or that American machine tools, once the pride of the world, are being displaced by German products. It is also that these developments signify a redistribution of trained capability throughout the globe. Knowledge, learning, information, and skilled intelligence are the new raw materials of international commerce and are today spreading throughout the world as vigorously as miracle drugs, synthetic fertilizers, and blue jeans did earlier. If only to keep and improve on the slim competitive edge we still retain in world markets, we must dedicate ourselves to the reform of our educational system. . . . Learning is the indispensable investment required for success in the "information age" we are entering.[13]

What followed in the report was a litany of failures, many of them linked to student performance on both international and American standardized tests. At the time, and in the years since, scholars have criticized the report's use of data, arguing that it was "too pessimistic." Whatever the reality, *A Nation at Risk* hit a responsive note among both policymakers and the public and "helped launch the first wave of education reforms that focused on expanding requirements for high school graduation, establishing minimum competency tests, and providing merit pay for teachers."[14]

The message of public school failure also was amplified in the media and came to be widely accepted. A search of the phrase "failing schools" in the *New York Times* appeared just eleven times in 1990, but eighty times in 2010.[15]

Without a doubt, there are great public schools and miserable ones. Despite decades of education reform, there remains, for a variety of reasons, a clear correlation between income and school quality. The principal purpose of this book is not to identify specific resources and policies—laudable or deplorable though they may be—that need to be directed at schools. The purpose, rather, is to explore diverse regions that successfully bucked the trends in education reform by relying on a collaborative approach to continuous improvement. Which brings us back to Deming.

In parallel with some of the most heated debates in education reform, some of Deming's most controversial ideas were about pay incentives. One strategy that almost certainly does *not* promote collaboration, he argued, is individualized incentive pay, which Deming said "nourishes short-term performance, annihilates long-term planning, builds fear, demolishes teamwork, nourishes rivalry and politics."

Deming built on Abraham Maslow's ideas about intrinsic motivation and the hierarchy of needs. He believed that if you create the conditions that allow people to do their best work, most people will rise to the occasion. (The obverse is also true: a climate of fear and insecurity is the surest way to kill intrinsic motivation.)

Deming invoked the power of statistical theory: if management is doing its job correctly in terms of hiring, developing employees, and keeping the system stable, most people will do their best. Of course, there will always be fluctuations—human beings, after all, aren't automatons. Deming understood that an employee with a sick child, a toothache, or some other "special cause" problem may not function at peak performance all the time. However, in a well-designed system, most employees will perform around a mean.

There will also be outliers who perform above or below the mean, though well-run organizations will have the *fewest* outliers because their hiring and training practices will guarantee a consistent level of performance. The work of high performers, Deming believed, should be studied; their work can serve as a model for improving the system.

Low performers, Deming believed, represent a failure of management to perform one of its key functions. Deming believed that hiring represents a moral and contractual obligation. Once hired, it is management's responsibility to help every employee succeed whether via training or relocation. While it might occasionally be necessary to fire a poor performer, Deming believed this option should be a last resort.

Deming's opposition to merit pay made him so unpopular among business leaders that many shunned him, a key reason he is not better known today. Even at Ford, Petersen's immediate successors dismantled Deming's legacy, but when the company once again fell on hard times, his ideas were revived by a new CEO, Alan Mulally.

In education, the research on merit pay is clear. A 2010 Vanderbilt University study showed that the performance of teachers who were offered a bonus of up to $15,000 was no better than that of teachers who were offered no incentive. A more recent metastudy found that merit pay produced a very modest increase in math and ELA scores; significantly, by far the greatest impact was seen in schools that offered group, not individual, incentives. And a 2012 survey of 40,000 teachers funded by Scholastic and the Gates Foundation—five years after Bill Gates appeared before Congress and testified in favor of merit pay—found that only one-quarter of teachers felt that performance pay was likely to have a strong impact on student achievement; instead, what the teachers valued the most, according to the study, was "supportive leadership, family involvement in education, access to high quality curriculum and student resources, and time for collaboration with colleagues."[16]

Controversial though they might be, Deming's ideas were part of a growing systems-oriented view of management and leadership. Deming and like-minded thinkers like Peter Senge and Russell Ackoff argued that schools and school systems—like corporations—are complex social systems and living communities and must be treated as such.

A systems view requires an understanding of how all the parts fit together as a whole, as well as an intimate understanding of the parts themselves. The key challenge, according to Ackoff, is to design systems that can learn and adapt. "Experience is *not* the best teacher; it is not even a good teacher," he argued. "It is too slow, too imprecise, and too ambiguous." Organizations, Ackoff argued, would have to learn and adapt through experimentation.

And for experimentation to work, it has to be driven at the local level by knowledgeable experts with a hands-on understanding of the system's processes and constituent parts.

Each example in this book has pursued the same bottom-up strategy for more than a decade—in some cases for at least three decades—thus reaping meaningful improvements across a wide range of measures that have seen increasing numbers of students graduate high school, complete college, and, yes, show improved testing results.

Importantly, every example has relied on a participative, collaborative, *deeply democratic* approach to continuous improvement, drawing on diverse constituencies—including students, teachers, and local business leaders—in their efforts. In each case, the local leadership in the schools, districts, and the one state profiled here focused on creating a climate of trust and respect that was crucial to the improvement effort. In addition, each example won some cover from bureaucratic meddling, usually in the form of an explicit exemption from some government mandate.

This story begins in New York City in the 1970s, in the midst of the fiscal crisis and the civil rights movement, with a progressive grassroots movement in education. The schools were small and highly collaborative, and, although they were founded in some of the poorest neighborhoods in the city, which had a preponderance of poor, minority children, they soon far outperformed their neighbors. This progressive rebellion, led by a group of "lefty hippies" who happened to be extraordinarily gifted educators, marked the start of both the "choice" and the small-schools movements. In the 1990s, the success of dozens of schools like those in the Julia Richman Complex was such that they very nearly inspired state education policy to buck the standardized-testing trend that was sweeping the nation in the aftermath of *A Nation at Risk.*

The small New York City schools with their brave and independent educators would also become models for the Bloomberg-era reforms. In exchange for accountability, the Bloomberg administration would vest principals with important new powers—significantly, giving them control over their own budgets. However, as the Gates man discovered, small size alone is no guarantee of success. Chapter 2 will explore what the Bloomberg administration borrowed from the small-schools movement, as well as what, to its detriment, it failed to learn.

In the early 1990s, as the education standards movement was sweeping the country, Massachusetts was confronted with a crisis of its own making. A rigid tax cap combined with an economic downturn had gutted school budgets, with devastating results for both schools and kids.

Chapter 3 will explore how the Massachusetts education reforms that would make the Commonwealth's schools the nation's gold standard for education grew out of that crisis. It is a remarkable story of a bipartisan alliance between a Republican governor and Democratic state legislators. But it is also the story of a grassroots participative process that spanned the state and came to include local business leaders, teachers, families, and the teachers union. The chapter will also explore how this democratic process was mirrored in, and would ultimately transform, one of the largest, poorest, and most dysfunctional high schools in the state.

Brockton High School was neither small nor progressive; with over five thousand students at its peak enrollment, Brockton High's transformation would show that small size is not a prerequisite for continuous improvement. But like many other examples in this book, the changes at Brockton grew organically from the grassroots up, supported by local leadership and, in the Commonwealth of Massachusetts, at least for a while, by state education policy.

Far from the Democratic redoubts of New York and Massachusetts, another experiment in participative education reform was taking place in a deeply conservative district in central Texas.

The Leander district was a small, poor, struggling school district of 2,500 students when one administrator happened to watch the sequel to the documentary about W. Edwards Deming that had inspired the Ford Motor Co. Leander would become one of the first school districts in the country to explicitly adopt Deming's ideas of grassroots-driven quality and continuous improvement. Beginning in the mid-1980s, tiny Leander soaked up the Deming philosophy like a desert cactus drawing water from a deep vein of new ideas, carefully husbanding the moisture, distributing it when and where it was needed, and even developing a way of protecting itself from outside threats. Demingism quite literally became the Leander culture, which for three decades informed everything from the way the district trains its employees to the design of its school buildings; it's a culture that fosters experimentation and risk taking and taught everyone from its youngest students to seasoned teachers the value of constant improvement. Chapter 4 will explore how Leander successfully maintained its culture for three decades even as it grew exponentially into a district that now rivals New Orleans in size.

The example schools in this book have not only survived—they have flourished. They have grappled with the challenges of changing leadership, bureaucratic meddling, funding constraints, politics, and the fallout of challenges faced by students who live in poverty. But the biggest threat to their survival has been the headwinds of the corporate education-reform movement, with its tests and accountability systems that have imposed a tsunami of mandates, narrowed the curricula, and fomented distrust.

Chapter 5 will explore the logical outgrowth of these reforms as they have panned out in New Orleans, which was to be a showcase for the ability of free-market reforms, especially independent charter schools, to transform education. Corporate reformers, from the Gates Foundation to the Walton Family Foundation, poured tens of millions of dollars into the city's schools, reconstructing and refurbishing its buildings—only 16 of the city's 128 school buildings had survived the storm relatively unscathed. New Orleans became a magnet for social entrepreneurs and idealistic young teachers, who flocked to the city and launched dozens of charter schools.

Education reformers proclaimed New Orleans a miracle; U.S. Secretary of Education Arne Duncan even asked whether "Hurricane Katrina was the best thing that had happened to the education system in New Orleans." But as the proponents of democratic continuous improvement discovered in New York City and Massachusetts and Leander, education reform works best when it proceeds quietly, from the grassroots up. Noisy transformations are often more mirage than miracle.

More than a decade after Hurricane Katrina, the New Orleans elementary schools produce somewhat better test scores than the schools did before the storm. But New Orleans is also a cautionary tale of skewed incentives and rushed reforms that have often hurt the city's most vulnerable children. Chapter 5 will explore how the poorest, most disadvantaged students are as likely to slip between the cracks and land on the streets or in jail as they are to graduate. It describes a temporary teaching infrastructure that is, by most accounts, unsustainable.

Perhaps most troubling of all, the New Orleans transformation was a raucous, self-congratulatory experiment executed by a mostly white establishment that had, once again, failed to give the long-disenfranchised black community a meaningful role. Education reform in New Orleans was colonial. During a mostly celebratory meeting in New Orleans on the occasion of the tenth anniversary of Hurricane Katrina and the charter movement, Howard Fuller, the former school superintendent in Milwaukee and a leading African American advocate of charter schools, shocked his mostly white audience with the following impassioned lament:

> When black people came out of slavery they understood the connection between education and emancipation. Two groups of white people descended on us—the missionaries and the industrialists. They both had their view about what kind of education we needed to make our newborn freedom realized . . . I've said this to all my friends in TFA and to others. . . . What people haven't firmly grasped is that we wanted to be helped, [but] we wanted to be an integral part of defining what role education should play in our continuing struggle to truly realize freedom. That has unsettled my soul. How do I help make that happen when I'm swimming with sharks on the right and on the left? How do I chart a course that speaks to the pain that my people have experienced?[17]

For many of the schools that have defied the corporate-reform movement, choice—whether in public schools or charter schools—was focused on giving long-disenfranchised communities a voice in the education of their children. Integration also has been a key objective, as has imparting the values of democracy. The schools and districts that embrace a collaborative approach to continuous improvement take to heart the dictum of John Adams, who declared education to be "necessary for the preservation of their rights and liberties," declaring that democracy depends "on spreading the opportunities and advantages of education." Adams enshrined public education into the constitution of the Commonwealth of Massachusetts, the first colony to pass a law requiring that children be taught to read and write and to require every town to establish a public school.

Democratic control of education has long been seen as inefficient at best and corrupt at worst. For much of the last century, the trend has been toward consolidating districts—and schools—in the interest of streamlining and cost saving, thus creating ever greater distance between districts and their constituencies. Weldon Beckner, professor emeritus of education at Baylor University in Texas, estimates that the number of school districts shrank from 128,000 to 16,960 between 1930 and 1972; at the same time, the number of high schools fell by half even as enrollment tripled.[18]

Indeed, historically, local educational control served to "shelter" school districts from the ideological battles at the national level and "promoted close identification between local communities and public schools," argues Sarah Reckhow, a political scientist at Michigan State University and the author of *Follow the Money: How Foundation Dollars Change Public School Politics.*

By contrast, the corporate education-reform movement has deep antidemocratic roots. *After the Education Wars* will reveal that a well-designed, collaborative, trust-based approach to continuous improvement can work anywhere.

This book was conceived long before Donald Trump's victory, during a quaint past when a Trump presidency seemed fantastical. For over thirty years, ever since *A Nation at Risk*, education reformers have focused on the utilitarian concerns of American economic competitiveness and whether schools will produce young people who meet the demands of industry and a global economy. In the process, these reformers have created a boom in the educational testing and technology industry, narrowed curriculum, and eviscerated the teaching of non-tested subjects, especially history and civics.

In fact, Jal Mehta, at the Harvard Graduate School of Education and author of *The Allure of Order*, points out that for public-relations purposes, the "inflammatory rhetoric" of the published version of *A Nation at Risk* was far more negative than the authors had intended:

> Internal drafts do show that the report's inflammatory rhetoric about a system in crisis was a conscious choice made by some on the commission in order to increase impact. An outline of the final report that was approved in September 1982 reveals a version that would have been much longer and more complimentary, including . . . a

> "relatively brief, positive description of the size and scope of American education."[19]

It is time to reestablish the connection between education and local democracy, not just because it is good management practice to do so. In the aftermath of Trump's victory, during a period of "fake news," "alternative facts," Kompromat, demagoguery, bigotry, and hate—much of it now emanating from the highest office in the land—reviving that connection is also vital for our democracy.

Like Winston Churchill, the educators who are upending corporate reform reaffirm their belief in democracy as the *least* worst form of government. As Deborah Meier, MacArthur Award winner and leader of New York City's progressive movement, once said, a school should be "[a] community where kids could see the complexity of democracy, and fall in love with it."[20]

After the Education Wars documents a radical—but highly productive—departure from both the one-size-fits-all approach of traditional education bureaucracies as well as the corporate-reform establishment's search for its own One Best Way. The latter was informed by the convergence of growing federal control under President George W. Bush's No Child Left Behind program and President Barack Obama's Race to the Top initiative, as well as the growing influence of a tiny elite of business executives and venture philanthropists, creating what Sarah Reckhow calls a perfect storm. At the turn of the millennium, Bill Gates emerged as "the most influential individual in U.S. education policy." The Broad Foundation and Walton Family Foundation were also powerful, as were individuals such as Michael Bloomberg and Mark Zuckerberg.

But Gates's position was unique. The Gates Foundation was already the largest in the world when, in 2006, Warren Buffett, the CEO of Berkshire Hathaway, pledged more than $30 billion to the Gates Foundation, with the stipulation that the foundation spend *the total value of the gifts from the previous year.* This put enormous pressure on the Gates Foundation to disburse large sums of money at a record clip. The amount of grants paid out by the foundation more than doubled within five years to $3 billion in 2009.[21]

At the same time, Gates led a change in the very role of philanthropy. Notes Reckhow, "A living philanthropist can take positions on policy in ways that extend the work of the foundation as an institution. Bill Gates exemplified this trend."[22]

The search for One Best Way in education increasingly has become Bill Gates's way. The Gates Foundation favored cities with mayoral control, pouring money into New York City and Chicago, but virtually ignoring

Detroit. The Gates Foundation was the key mover behind shaping, funding, and promoting the Common Core State Standards. Arne Duncan, the U.S. secretary of education, hired Gates Foundation alumni for key positions at the Department of Education. Duncan named as his chief of staff Margot Rogers, a top Gates official whom he got to know when, in his previous job as the chief of Chicago Public Schools, the city received $20 million in Gates funding to turn large high schools into condominiums for small schools. He also hired James Shelton, a program officer at the foundation, to serve first as his head of innovation and later as the deputy secretary responsible for a wide array of federal policy decisions. And there was Joanne Weiss, director of the Race to the Top competition, who was a former partner at the New Schools Venture Fund, a major Gates grantee and an intermediary funder for charter-school management organizations. Lower-level education-department policymakers also received their imprimatur at the Gates Foundation.[23]

The influence of the Gates Foundation is so profound that when an education department official gave a talk on Obama's education policy at the Ford Foundation, he mistakenly referred to the "Gates administration," a slip of the tongue that had his audience in stitches. "The support that the foundation gave to the department either directly or indirectly, both financially and through intermediaries, greatly affected how some of the early Obama education initiatives were formulated and implemented."[24]

In his congressional testimony in 2007, while still chairman of Microsoft, Bill Gates made his priorities clear: better math and science education; better metrics for measuring both student and teacher performance; incentive pay for teachers. (Also, lifting a cap on immigrants with science and math skills.)

This is the point at which an eager student in the front row of the class, exercising her critical-thinking skills, waves her hand in the air and asks: but what would Steve Jobs make of the Gatesian One Best Way? The two technology pioneers were polar opposites, after all. The tension between their very different visions redefined not only the role of computing, but also the very essence of how we live our lives. Gates combined the heart of an engineer and the soul of a technocrat, developing software that was good enough—what economists call *satisficing*—and steadily built Microsoft into a software empire.[25]

By contrast, Jobs was a marketing magician, a perfectionist, an aficionado of Zen Buddhism and Italian design. He envisioned an appliance—a digital Cuisinart—that would, by its simplicity and elegance, transform almost every aspect of personal communication. More Michelangelo than mogul, Jobs cared first and foremost about the design of his products—their look and feel and how those qualities impacted functionality.

Both Gates and Jobs were college dropouts. But as Walter Isaacson, Jobs's biographer, points out, Gates dropped out to found a computer company; Jobs dropped out "to find enlightenment with an Indian guru."[26] Even after he had abandoned his degree at Reed College, Jobs studied Eastern meditation, Bauhaus architecture, and, famously, calligraphy, which would influence his approach to product design at Apple.

Although Apple's designs were "more innovative, imaginative, elegant in execution" and design, and even though "Microsoft created a crudely copied series of products," it was Microsoft Windows that became the PC operating standard. "This exposed an aesthetic flaw in how the universe worked: The best and most innovative products don't always win," writes Isaacson in his Jobs biography.[27]

Great ideas are almost always the product of more than one innovator and grow out of a zeitgeist as much as out of the creativity of a single great genius. Yet history usually rewards just one winner. Jobs's vision for Apple is a rare example of an alternative narrative that succeeded.

As the mainstream corporate education-reform movement falters, it's time to brush off and recover the road not taken, to explore exactly what—in the epic battles over American education—has been left undone. Our children, our schools, our economy, and our democracy depend on it.

1

BIG DREAMS, SMALL SCHOOLS

How Entrepreneurial Rebels Built a Movement in New York City

In 1968, at Seward Park High School, I faced the hardest challenge of my whole teaching career. I had the usual five classes: three English as a Second Language and two regular ninth-grade English classes. One of those ninth-grade classes consisted of twenty-nine black girls from an uptown feeder school and two Puerto Rican boys who sat in a corner, minding their own business, never saying a word. If they opened their mouths, the girls would turn on them. Who axed you? All the ingredients of difficulty were wrapped up in this one group: gender clash; generation clash; culture clash; racial clash.

—*Teacher Man*, Frank McCourt[1]

On the morning of October 29, 1975, New Yorkers woke up to the infamous headline in the *Daily News*: "FORD TO CITY: DROP DEAD." The night before, President Gerald Ford had given a speech denying federal assistance that would spare New York from bankruptcy.[2]

President Ford's rebuff was not as unilateral as the newspapers made it appear. Two months after the infamous headline, Ford signed legislation approving a federal loan for the strapped city.

But, for New York City, perhaps only September 11, 2001, marked a period more traumatic than the fiscal crisis of 1975. News of New York's impending default spurred its civic, business, and labor leaders into action and ultimately ushered in years of austerity that would hit schools, as well as services for the poor, particularly hard.[3]

The fiscal crisis was a final blow to what was already a school system in turmoil. Throughout the 1950s and 1960s, the New York school system had been roiled by teacher shortages, an incipient union movement, bureaucratic mismanagement, the staggering costs of replacing old buildings and accommodating an influx of new students—both migrants and baby boomers—following World War II, and finally seismic battles over civil rights and desegregation. As the middle class fled to the suburbs, New York City schools reached a tipping point in 1966, when the "minority" enrollment of black and Latino students in the city's schools surpassed the 50 percent mark.[4]

That was when, for the first time, New York City released school-by-school reading scores, which showed that a fifth of the city's children, most of them concentrated in the poorest neighborhoods, were two years behind grade level; schools in more affluent neighborhoods, by contrast, performed much better. But the disparities in test scores fueled deep racial and ethnic divisions, as well as suspicion that behind the students' poor performance was a pernicious combination of low expectations, poor teaching, and crass indifference on the part of the mostly white education bureaucracy.[5]

With the fiscal crisis, the plight of both the city's poor communities and the schools would be exacerbated. Six thousand teachers lost their jobs. Poverty soared. Libraries closed. Class sizes swelled. The building and maintenance of new schools came to a virtual halt.[6]

It was a period of "immense overcrowding, immense teacher shortage, immense shortage of materials and supplies and books," recalled Alice Seletsky, a longtime teacher at Central Park East in Harlem.[7]

Vasthi Acosta, who now runs Amber Charter School in Spanish Harlem, recalls the chaos she encountered when she got her first teaching job by a fluke right after the financial crisis; the spate of teacher layoffs meant there were no jobs for new graduates, and she had been forced, at one point, to take a job as an insurance underwriter. When she finally got a job in a school in Washington Heights, her alma mater, Acosta was put in charge of a fifth-grade class with forty-five students. "The overcrowding was crazy," she recalls. "Classes were immense."[8]

Nor did she get any help, recalls Acosta, who says she "never saw the principal."

Frank McCourt, who started teaching in New York City schools in 1958, actually dates the era of schoolhouse deprivation back to the 1950s. "In Eisenhower's America there is prosperity but it does not trickle down to the schools, especially to new teachers who need supplies for their classes," writes McCourt in his memoir *Teacher Man*.[9]

Yet, amidst the crowding and the shortages and the crises, a promising school movement was taking root, galvanized by the civil rights movement and enabled by the chaos of near-bankruptcy. It was led by a cadre of Chicagoans and New Yorkers, many of whom had first met as students and civil rights activists at the University of Chicago's South Side campus.

Through the civil rights movement, these young educators and activists had become involved with freedom schools, storefront schools that offered young black students the intellectual stimulation that was not available to them in traditional public schools. Then, too, the freedom schools, which met in churches, private homes, and even abandoned buildings, were the only educational option in many districts, especially ones that chose to close their schools rather than be forced to integrate them. While the freedom schools are mostly associated with the South, they also took root in New York City, Boston, and Chicago as a protest against de facto segregation.[10]

The development of an active democratic citizenry was front and center for the freedom schools, young education reformers, and civil rights activists. They sought to educate young people who would become robust participants "in the movement to transform the South's segregated society."[11]

Reaffirming education's role in developing a democratic citizenship *à la* John Adams was a key idea that would animate the leaders of what henceforth I will refer to as the progressive coalition. That democratic mission would become integral to the small, unofficial schools that flourished in New York City in the 1970s—the education equivalent of entrepreneurial skunk works, or bootleg projects, that would become the foundation of a successful small-schools movement.

Many Chicago-bred educational rebels found their way to New York City. They included Deborah Meier, who returned to the city of her girlhood after years in the Midwest and became one of the most important education reformers of the turn of the twenty-first century, as well as Ann Cook and Herb Mack, who helped found one of the most successful, and longest lasting, alternative education experiments in New York. Steeped in the progressive educational values championed by John Dewey and informed by the experience of the civil rights era, the progressive educators formed networks in New York and teamed up with like-minded school reformers nationwide. In particular, many became members of the Coalition of Essential Schools, which was founded by Ted Sizer in 1984.

While the progressive coalition was highly idealistic, it was also deeply practical. Their schools were so leanly staffed—often too leanly—that in the beginning they had virtually no hierarchy whatsoever. In the first year or two of Central Park East, its founder, and the small-school movement's most famous exponent, Meier, ran the school with fellow teachers after they had taught a full day of classes. Eventually, and only reluctantly, Meier realized that she needed to give up teaching in order to run the school.

As the progressive coalition matured, it developed a collaborative leadership approach that was rooted in democratic pluralism and a belief in pushing decision making down to the level closest to the child. It also emphasized teacher mentoring and training as the fulcrum for school improvement and new school development. Although its leaders had no training in management or mainstream organizational development, some had been active in 1960s grassroots organizing and had arrived at many of the key tenets of a continuous-improvement philosophy much like that of W. Edwards Deming. The New Yorkers discovered that a learning community, one that would inspire and engage both adults and children, must be built on deep reservoirs of trust. Explained Meier: "[T]he kind of trust that fosters productive collegiality is critical not just to schools like ours, but to any school that wants to learn from its own practices." [12]

With time, the progressive coalition came to be characterized by a pedagogical and management savvy that far outstripped its size and belied its rebellious roots. It developed a surprising degree of consistency among its management practices and outcomes:

> The extent to which the schools were able to develop sophisticated designs and practices and manage a range of difficult problems is unusual. This was supported by the fact that many of the new school "launchers" had been teachers in the older, successful schools and were mentored by expert veteran principals and teachers while belonging to an organization that could run interference as well as provide professional development.[13]

The movement flourished. By the start of the new millennium, the progressive coalition had come to include hundreds of schools nationwide. But New York City was its epicenter, with well over one hundred schools at its peak, nearly 10 percent of the city's schools.

The progressive network thrived on what is essentially a four-pronged strategy.

First, they relied on extensive teacher collaboration, including team teaching and multidisciplinary courses; for teachers, these approaches eased the onerous teaching load and provided more one-on-one time with individual students, as well as flexibility in how they approached core subject areas. This collaborative strategy also had the benefit of boosting both learning and engagement among kids and job satisfaction for teachers. Two decades before the Common Core State Standards, the progressive network encouraged much greater depth in curriculum and fostered a rich complement of academic skills from research and writing to analysis and critical thinking.

Second, the new school designs and management structures were created in partnership with the union—though many district union leaders thought small schools exploited teachers—and were premised on both trust and shared decision making among teachers, administrators, and the community. Teachers often worked beyond normal school hours—indeed that was a prerequisite for being hired at many schools—though they were compensated for their time either with money or with informal arrangements for time off. And teams of teachers were part of a rigorous hiring process, which helped promote teamwork among a cadre of like-minded professionals. "Teacher voice" was seen as a key asset at virtually every level of decision making.[14]

Third, a carefully embedded mentoring and professional-development process gave teachers vital training in a more engaging and thought-provoking "inquiry" approach to teaching, improved the rigor of the schools, and created a "birthing process" for new schools, as teachers nurtured in the system periodically set out to create their own small schools. At the same time, the schools' connection to like-minded networks, such as Sizer's Coalition of Essential Schools and Meier's Center for Collaborative Education, provided other important infrastructure, including training, funding, and political support.

Fourth, they developed a rigorous, sophisticated, and *iterative* accountability system—one wholly unrelated to standardized testing, but rather encompassing a wide range of student-performance indicators and data and focusing on improvement. In many cases, the schools were explicitly exempted from most standardized tests.

On the surface, these schools—and their networks—embody many of the hallmarks of the mainstream education-reform movement. They are entrepreneurial. They prize "choice" and accountability. They have attracted funding from a host of foundations, including the Bill and Melinda Gates Foundation and the Annenberg Foundation, and, indeed, helped inspire philanthropy's focus on small schools. They even catalyzed some key reforms promulgated by Michael Bloomberg, the businessman-turned-mayor, and thrived during his administration. But the parallels between the movements go only so far.

While some of the movement's proponents would go on to found charter schools, most remained deeply committed to reforming public education from within. Where choice has come to be synonymous with the no-excuses charter movement—a fundamentally paternalistic approach that families of color are invited to sign up for or to reject, but rarely to influence—among New York City's small-school rebels, "choice" had an entirely different connotation. Choice, in their context, was about empowering teachers, kids, and communities to work together on improving education. Whereas charter schools have increased racial segregation, the New York small-school rebels worked to integrate their classrooms. Where labor organizing is virtually anathema in the mainstream charter movement—especially in the leading charter-management organizations—the unions were partners in the development of the progressive coalition.

Last but not least, the founders of the small-school movement sought to create a culture that was the philosophical antithesis of the no-excuses charter movement's focus on behavioral conformity and control. Instead of silence and strict adherence to rules, the New York rebels prized argument, questioning, and independent thinking. In short, they sought to create the habits of mind necessary for nurturing a skeptical and engaged democratic citizenry. Operating in poor neighborhoods where few of the adults in the lives of schoolchildren were afforded any agency, the schools emphasized education in democratic values and action and sought to create a world in which children could see and feel that they had choices.

"Schools should be repositories of democratic control," explains Meier. "The governance piece is key in terms of what it means to be a public institution. I don't think you can serve well the purposes of public education, which is to create a democratic citizenry," in a system that nurtures children for twelve years "unless the adults in children's lives have real power."[15]

The small-school rebels took root long before the Bloomberg era of entrepreneurial government and Schumpeterian disruption. Their leaders were, for the most part, antiestablishment "lefty hippies"—the stylistic and political converse of the buttoned-down technocrats who ruled the DOE during the Bloomberg administration. Yet there was a surprising alignment between the discipline these educational rebels brought to their vision of small schools—their schools were virtually all lean and entrepreneurial and bent on systemic improvement—and the kinds of schools, and school leadership, that were promoted by the administration of the billionaire mayor. The progressive coalition understood an important lesson in organizational leadership—one that the most successful CEOs would readily recognize. This is how Eric Nadelstern, founder of the much-acclaimed, oft-replicated International High School at LaGuardia Community College, a charter member of the progressive coalition where a majority of students are English-language learners, put it years later: "When school leaders share their authority with teachers, parents and even the students themselves, they widen the circle of those who are responsible, and ultimately accountable, for student success. Just as important, they acknowledge that education is about developing the leadership potential of each student, and understand that each teacher is a classroom leader with the potential to become an effective school leader."[16]

Bloomberg's education department and the progressive coalition made for strange bedfellows. While denouncing the quantitative focus of the mayor's accountability system—the school grades and the obsession with test scores—a cadre of talented principals flourished and experimented with great abandon during the Bloomberg years. In an unprecedented move, Bloomberg gave principals control over their budgets in exchange for increased accountability. The Bloomberg administration also recruited some of the most talented educators in the city as policymakers (see chapter 2). Many of the city's principals would complain bitterly when, years later, Bloomberg's successor, Bill de Blasio, tightened controls and increased bureaucracy.

Bloomberg's education department was poised, for a brief time, to move some of the key lessons of the progressive coalition to the heart of the administration's education policy. Yet a fundamental misunderstanding of what made the best schools work, as well as a combination of hubris and what the management thinker Peter Senge would call entrenched mental models—the conceptual frameworks and assumptions that informed the education outlook of the businessman-mayor and his closest advisers, especially a bias in favor of corporate experience over educational expertise—would prove highly problematic and ultimately counterproductive.

SMALL SCHOOLS, BIG IDEAS

The intellectual roots of the progressive school movement go back to John Dewey, Jean Piaget, and Friedrich Froebel, all of whom emphasized the importance of hands-on learning, exploration, and creativity. But the catalyst and immediate antecedents of the New York City progressive coalition can be found in the civil rights movement and British open-education, which focused on child-centered learning. Lillian Weber, a City College professor who had studied for a time in England, brought open-education to the attention of New York's rebel educators. She also founded the Workshop Center at City College, a training center where teachers could develop hands-on curricula. In Harlem, Weber used an "open corridor" arrangement—an especially apt approach in schools that were gravely overcrowded and in which classes literally spilled into hallways—to link a handful of elementary classrooms. So doing, she mixed grades and age groups based on interests and abilities and provided professional development for teachers in how to create a more stimulating learning environment. She also promoted both planning and collaboration among educators, as well as closer relationships between adults and children, who spent two years with the same teacher.[17]

As Meier, a protégé of Weber, explained it, the hallways and lobbies of schools "work best if we think of them as the marketplaces in small communities—where gossip is exchanged, work displayed, birthdays taken note of; where clusters of kids and adults gather to talk, read and exchange ideas."[18]

Fostering collaboration and community—across classes and among teachers, adults, and children—was key to Weber's concept. So too was developing an environment in which teachers saw themselves as part of a "community of peers, rather than as individuals isolated in their classrooms."[19]

Weber mentored Meier, as well as Ann Cook and Herb Mack, who also traveled to London in the 1960s to see the open-education movement firsthand. Importantly, all these reform pioneers maintained a commitment to teacher development as a precondition both for implementing a progressive pedagogy and for school improvement. Weber "pointed to the loneliness of the teaching professional as a serious roadblock to good work with children," recalls Meier. "Weber argued that both children and adults needed to be part of a community of learning."[20]

Weber also reinforced the movement's subversive, and entrepreneurial, bent. "Lillian Weber had an expression: Find the cracks. She did, and everyone who followed in her footsteps . . . did," says Ann Cook, referring to Debbie Meier. "And we did."[21]

Like small plants threading their way through cracked concrete, these education reformers would become masters at building new schools in the spaces in between, often exploiting the chaos of the years that followed the civil rights battles and the financial crisis. In the process, they also perfected an essential strategy for working around the education bureaucracy, as well as the art of what Debbie Meier calls "creative non-compliance."

This schoolhouse insurgency mirrored the revolt by radical white and minority parents against the education bureaucracy, which led to the creation of thirty-two community school districts in 1970. While decentralization would spark infighting and dysfunction in many parts of the city, East Harlem emerged with a "unified, stable" school board.[22]

Led by Robert Rodriguez, the District Four board in 1973 selected Tony Alvarado as the superintendent for the poor, largely black and Latino district, which ran north from 96th Street to 125th Street and west from Fifth Avenue to the East River and had the lowest reading scores among the city's thirty-two school districts. Ten years later, the district had climbed to fifteenth place.

Years later, Alvarado accomplished a similar feat in District Two, which encompassed most of Manhattan below Harlem. When Alvarado became superintendent in 1988, the district ranked near the middle of New York's thirty-two school districts. By the time Alvarado left about a decade later, it was ranked number two.[23]

There was actually nothing very miraculous about the improvements in District Four or later in District Two. Put simply, Alvarado was a master at fostering both improvement from the grassroots up and creative noncompliance. He encouraged educators to start new schools and schools-within-schools that focused on the disparate needs and interests of kids. During his years at District Four, Alvarado created over twenty mini-schools, including ones that emphasized sports, the arts, and environment. Later, he developed an iterative, local, and highly successful approach to identifying, replicating, and improving best practices in teaching. And he created an in-house leadership-development strategy—a model the Bloomberg administration would later emulate, though not as successfully.

In short, Alvarado fostered an educator-driven approach to improvement, one that was "negotiated over time, not proclaimed from above." He also encouraged his teachers and principals to find, and to cultivate, the cracks in the system.[24]

Alvarado grew up playing stickball "sewer to sewer" in the South Bronx. But his parents—Puerto Rican and Cuban emigrant laborers—sent him to Catholic schools. Alvarado would become, briefly, the first Latino New York City schools chancellor. The qualities that led him to bend rules with abandon in the interest of education reform eventually led to ethically dubious decisions that would, for a time, be his undoing.[25] It is, however, a testament to Alvarado's enormous gifts as an educator and maverick bureaucrat that he was rehired to run District Two just a few years after a scandal had forced him out of the chancellorship. And, during a decade-long tenure at District Two, he fostered both leadership-development and teacher-centered curriculum-improvement efforts that would have wide-ranging impacts on the city in the years to come.[26]

Soon after taking the job in District Four, when he first became a superintendent during the financial crisis, Alvarado put out word that he was looking to build new small schools and was willing to entertain any "original vital idea." Alvarado had tried throwing money at the schools without much effect. Now, he was calling for *teachers* to act.[27]

"We do not have time to wait for Godot," Alvarado once famously told a group of teachers. "We get caught up in a cycle of all the reasons we can't do anything: The kids, the parents, the neighborhood, the union, the rotten politics, the budget. But we can stop the barbarians at the gate. The ones who want to dismantle the system, with one thing: Results." [28]

The teachers in District Four rose to the occasion—dozens of them.

At the time, Meier was working as a professional-development adviser at Weber's Workshop Center for Open Education, the research and training umbrella for her corridor schools. Meier came to Alvarado's attention when, eager to get back to more hands-on work in schools, she took a job at a new small school in the West Village.[29]

To help galvanize his reform efforts, Alvarado had recruited Bonnie Brownstein, a science teacher who had worked at Weber's Workshop Center, and asked her to create "open education" programs for District Four. Brownstein, in turn, recruited Meier. In the fall of 1974, Meier launched Central Park East on the second, third, and fourth floors of P.S. 171, a large, decades-old school building at 103rd Street between Fifth and Madison Avenues.[30]

Central Park East would be operated on the "open classroom" principles that Meier and Weber espoused—no fixed curriculum, but lots of learning-by-doing, art, music, and field trips. The school would be small. During its first year, Central Park East had only thirty-two students distributed among three classrooms: two kindergarten classes and one first grade. Soon, Meier added a combined second-and-third grade.

In keeping with Meier's aim, the children would be a diverse group—black, white, and Latino; educated liberals as well as poor immigrant families sent their children to Central Park East. In 1985, after over a decade of operation, 75 percent of the students were African American and Latino. Half the students had family incomes under $12,000; another 25 percent had incomes under $20,000.[31]

Meier handpicked a coterie of teachers who shared her educational philosophy and who also reflected the students who would enroll in Central Park East. Two of her first teachers were African American, and one was Latino. Central Park East's integrated staff would help allay neighborhood suspicions. And the school would be run democratically by the staff; there would be no hierarchy.[32]

Central Park East was to have an almost entirely flat organization, with teacher leaders who taught during the day and ran the school after the kids went home. An answering machine in the office informed parents who called before 3 p.m. that all the adults in the building were occupied with children, and that their calls would be returned in the afternoon.[33]

The guiding principles of the school were based on a conviction "[t]hat children—all human beings in fact—are capable of making responsible choices, being engaged by the things of this world, asking good questions, and becoming independent thinkers and learners."[34]

That conviction was built on trust—not just in the potential of children, but also in the self-actualization of adults—and a belief that by building "a trusting and trustworthy community" the schools could "help children learn in more efficient and natural ways." Meier herself organized her class around "New York City's Natural Environment," planning field trips to Central Park, where children could study rock formations and animals, and even to eastern Long Island, where they visited the seashore. There were classes focused on the study of the Middle Ages in which children not only read books on the subject but also built armor and castles, cooked food that was typical of the period, and visited the Cloisters and the Metropolitan Museum of Art. Soon there would be Shakespeare productions, daily "sings," and music lessons.[35]

The word about Central Park East spread quickly, and parents flocked to the school. In keeping with Meier's belief in the power of "choice," one of the school's few entry requirements was that families would have to visit the school before they could enroll. By the end of its first year, enrollment had nearly tripled to 85 students.[36]

Alvarado was so impressed by what he was hearing that he doubled the school's size the following year, adding grades two to five.[37]

Of course, Central Park East wasn't actually a school. It was a program within a large school. It didn't officially exist on paper. And Meier wasn't a real principal—she had neither the title nor the salary. Alvarado liked to compare the education system to a giant octopus; he would walk around the district with a metaphorical pair of shears in his back pocket. "Whenever I see a tentacle, I'll take them out," he liked to say. But creating schools like Central Park East was more like gardening—planting fragile saplings in what Weber called the cracks of the system—than battling octopi.[38]

By the autumn of its second year, the honeymoon at Central Park East was over; a powerful tentacle threatened to squeeze the life out of the school. Some locals—both educators and parents—began to view Central Park East with suspicion. "[T]hey regarded Meier's efforts with attitudes ranging from indifference to outright hostility," recalled Sy Fliegel, who was then the newly appointed head of the alternative-schools division in District Four.[39] (Fliegel was also part of a 1988 meeting with Al Shanker and several others who, in the wake of *A Nation at Risk*, would hash out the details of a proposal for establishing charter schools.[40])

The new school also ran into resistance from the local union representative, who was "somewhat hostile to Alvarado and his plans"—though Meier is quick to point out that citywide union leadership was very supportive. In the years to come, all of Meier's schools would have close working relationships with the union; in fact, they would help craft key contract innovations that would give schools more flexibility within rigid work rules.[41]

At the same time, the financial crisis made it difficult for Meier's selective hiring practices, which circumvented union seniority rules, to stay under the radar. "There was a system-wide reshuffling of teachers, as those 'excessed' from one school exercised their seniority rights and claimed positions in others," wrote Fliegel. He quotes Alvarado, who said: "We tried a number of creative ways to ensure the kind of teachers that were required to run a program like Debbie's, and it involved a lot of risk-taking."[42]

"Bending the rules when hundreds of teachers were defending their rights to their jobs was not always easy," recalls Fliegel.[43]

By then, Meier was also teaching a combined class of forty-two third, fourth, and fifth graders, most of whom were new to the school, while continuing to serve as director of Central Park East.

Things fell between the cracks. Some of the messages left on the school answering machine were not always returned promptly—a circumstance that would enrage parents under the best of circumstances. Just a few years after the teachers strike and the racial strife that had shaken both Harlem and Ocean Hill–Brownsville, where African American parents had been pitted against the mostly white teachers and their teachers union, a handful of Central Park East parents distrusted a "white Jewish lady" running their school.[44]

Meier, who still thinks of herself as a Social Democrat, had conceived of Central Park East as a "teachers' collective" and was distressed by the criticism.

"What I was seeking was the kind of ease, trust, and mutual respect that would permit us to avoid absolutely rigid distinctions and fully spelled-out roles," explained Meier. But with the exponential growth of the school and the external pressures, there wasn't always time to build consensus.[45]

At the same time, Meier encountered the limits of egalitarianism and collaboration. While she believed deeply in functioning democratically, Meier was held responsible for "solving big problems" and sometimes felt she had to be the decider. One teacher rebelled and fomented unrest among dissident parents. Meier lost an ally when Elsa Lurie, the principal of P.S. 171 when Central Park East first moved into the building, left and was replaced by a woman who enjoyed engaging in "time-consuming turf wars."[46]

The dissidents eventually appealed to Alvarado, demanding that he remove Meier. Alvarado sent Fliegel to investigate. This is how Fliegel recalls the situation he found at Central Park East:

> For the next week I made it my business to visit the school every day. I talked to Debbie Meier, to the teachers, to the students, and to the parents. I looked around the school. Whenever I go to a school I observe the children, and if they are involved and paying attention, I know that there is learning going on and that it's a good place for a kid to be. I was not disappointed with what I found at Central Park East.
>
> The truth is, after all my investigating, I determined that Debbie Meier was running a superior school. She regarded kids as individuals, an approach that my own teaching experience had convinced me was essential. She cared about youngsters, about learning, and had assembled a staff excited about education. There aren't enough people like that in the world, so when you find the Debbie Meiers, the people who really try to do something, you have to stand by them. They will make some mistakes, and they will always draw fire. But ultimately, people like Debbie and schools like Central Park East are always worth protecting.[47]

Fliegel told Alvarado, bluntly, that he should support Meier "to the hilt."

"You support good people, I told him, even when they make mistakes. That's what support is all about. And Alvarado agreed."

Fliegel met with the Central Park East parents to tell them his decision and to offer any family that wanted to leave help transferring to a school of their choice.

As Central Park East emerged from this crisis, Meier evolved from a reluctant teacher–leader into a strong and respected head-of-school—though it wasn't until about 1980 that new rules required that school "directors" like Meier at small schools like CPE become licensed principals. Meier had corralled a group of gifted teachers, and she was determined that they should be collaborators in her vision. That vision focused not only on the pedagogy of an open classroom, but also on creating a "democratic community with a 'small d,'" one that encompassed "a respect for diversity, a respect for the potential of each individual person, a respect for opposing points of view, and a respect for considerable intellectual vigor." And, of course, trust.[48]

Indeed, there were two key parts of Central Park East, which it turns out were deeply interlaced: the open-classroom pedagogy and democratic governance. Accountability was balanced at the intersection of both.

The foyer of the apartment in which Deborah Willen grew up, located in an elegant art deco building at the corner of Riverside Drive and 86th Street in Manhattan, was dominated by the giant Diego Rivera mural *Workers of the World Unite*. Stalin, with bloodshot eyes, stared menacingly from one corner of the mural, while Trotsky stood, "looking heroic," in the other corner.[49]

"The mural made everyone uncomfortable," says Meier, recalling her childhood impressions of the controversial mural.

How the famous mural had made its way to the Willens' foyer is a little murky. As Meier remembers it, Rivera gave the mural, a copy of one that hangs in Mexico City, to Jay Lovestone, a leader of the American Communist Party and an old City College friend of her father. (Like many Jewish intellectuals at the time, Meier's parents, Pearl Larner and Joseph Willen, were leftists; Willen was a prominent philanthropist and Larner was a political activist.) Lovestone had initially offered it to the ILGWU, the garment-workers union, which didn't want it. Eventually, after some misunderstandings about the size of the piece, the mural ended up in the Willen household, where it hung, initially in the dining room and eventually in the foyer. After the deaths of Joseph and Pearl, the mural was sold to an art museum in Nagoya, Japan.[50]

Whatever its origins, the mural helped to leaven the lively debates among the wide range of visitors who gathered regularly around the Willens' dining room table, including journalists, union leaders, and civil rights activists. (It was young Debbie's job to greet black visitors in the lobby so they wouldn't be sent up in the service elevator.) Debbie, who was not yet ten years old when the mural came into the family's possession, doesn't recall participating in those dinner-table debates. But she did find them mesmerizing.[51]

Years later, Meier realized, it was those adult dinner-table conversations, so many conducted beneath the disapproving gaze of Stalin, Lenin, and Trotsky, that she was trying to re-create at Central Park East. That and the freewheeling discussions and explorations that were an everyday activity at the progressive and elite Ethical Culture Fieldston School she had attended, a school that had been founded "for working men and women, to teach the arts of democracy in the interest of an egalitarian vision of society."

Meier savored the irony of such a vision for a private school that "not a single working man's child now attended"—an exaggeration, as a number of the school's students receive scholarships. Nevertheless, Meier wanted to re-create that vision for low-income kids in the city.[52]

At Central Park East and other schools that were part of the progressive coalition, the central office was conceived as a sort of family room, a place to which children were welcomed, not just condemned when they had "done something wrong." It was a place with computers for kids to use, and was where Meier kept the desk from which she ran the school's business—everything from ordering school supplies to arguing about school budgets with bureaucrats at the education department.[53]

This was the point, says Meier—to include kids "in the life of the school," in its larger arguments and in its minutiae. Meier wanted children to understand that they "belonged to a world that was both small and large." Children should be comfortable in both the private sphere of the family and the public sphere of local democracy.

Schools, the progressives argue, should be the last redoubt for local democracy. At a time when it becomes harder and harder for the average citizen to participate directly in government at either the local or national level, democratic decision making both inside schools and among local school boards is the last best opportunity to exercise the rights of democratic citizenship and to educate young people about participation in a democracy.[54]

Central Park East, and the progressive schools movement in general, sought to make that link between democracy and pedagogy explicit. In one highly successful large school building that would come to house a half dozen schools, a building's council made all decisions about shared spaces, schedules, and the like via consensus, a sometimes slow and cumbersome process, but one that allowed the students to become aware that the adults in the building had decision-making power over most of the major issues that affected them. The focus on democracy also was reflected in small-bore schoolhouse debates on whether students should have to request bathroom passes and, at one point, whether students should be forced to comply with an education-department directive banning popular headgear known as "do rags." Some of the schools voted to support the do-rag ban; others resisted. And it found expression in protests that were endorsed, explicitly or implicitly, by the staff. For example, students marched against police brutality, and parents, years before the opt-out movement, boycotted state tests.[55]

Small schools made it easier to foster both trust and democratic decision making, but they also posed special challenges with regard to accountability. Notes Meier:

> The kind of changes required by today's agenda can only be the work of thoughtful teachers. Either we acknowledge and create conditions based on this fact, conditions for teachers to work collectively and collaboratively and openly, or we create conditions that encourage resistance, secrecy and sabotage. Teachers who believe in spelling tests every Friday or are "hooked on phonics" sneak them in, even when they're taboo. And so do those who want good books or fewer workbooks, regardless of school regulations. The braver and more conscientious cheat the most, but even the timid can't practice well what they don't believe in.[56]

Within their classrooms, teachers encountered little interference. Yet, at the same time, there was constant collaboration among teachers and discussion of the needs of individual students.

Of course, thoughtful collaboration was time-consuming. And the smaller the school and the closer its teachers work together, the harder it is to tell "tough truths." The problem of accountability is one that Meier wrestled with, and continued to refine, for years, in both New York and Boston, where she founded the Mission Hill School in 1997 (see chapter 2). One solution involved a subtle shift from judging—and criticizing—teachers' work to establishing an adult learning culture in which the four or five adults who shared responsibility for each cohort of approximately eighty students met regularly; colleagues also observed each other's classes and focused their judgments on giving constructive feedback on student work and curriculum. The aim was to develop dispassionate professional judgments about pedagogical strategies and how to get through to specific students.

While Meier's schools often eschewed standardized tests, the teachers gathered a rich array of documentation and data. Data that "came largely not from tests but from observations and actual student work, from the notes teachers keep on a regular basis and the folders full of ongoing student work. We also have a substantial collection of student work in our school archive . . . sorted by student and year; we have five years of taped interviews of each and every student as a reader and their teacher's narrative reports."[57]

As with almost everything else in education, there was a constant tension between the values of collaboration and the need for strong leadership. Few exemplified that tension as clearly as Meier herself, who routinely tussled with the strong and strong-willed teachers she hired. For example, when some Central Park East teachers announced that they wanted to discuss whether kids with special needs should be admitted to the school, Meier "ruled the question as out of order," noting that "CPE was founded for the purpose of serving all kids and that as a public school we had no choice."[58]

"[B]y prohibiting the discussion, I had perhaps missed a way to bring the issues out of that subterranean underground. Still, it was also important to draw a line. A school that is always rethinking basic premises creates unacceptable intellectual and moral disorder for kids and families. Sometimes it's even worth sticking with the wrong consistencies for a while. In schools, as in classrooms and families, there are necessary routines and rituals."[59]

Of course, the tension between strong leadership and teacher voice was never fully resolved at Central Park East or elsewhere in the progressive network. And, like Central Park East during its first two years, many schools struggled, at one time or another, especially during changes of leadership. And not all survived.

But, by almost any measure, Meier's schools were highly successful. As many parents flocked to Central Park East, waiting lists ballooned. In 1980, Meier opened a second elementary school, Central Park East II, and, two years later, a third, River East. Wrote Sy Fliegel: "Out of the more than two hundred students who graduated from Central Park East in the years 1977 to 1984, only two are known to have dropped out of secondary school. (In the city as a whole, more than 40 percent drop out; more than 60 percent of minority children drop out.) Just as impressive, in Central Park East's first decade not a single student was suspended."[60]

Central Park East Secondary, also known as Central Park East High School, was founded in 1985 and would, for a time, join the movement to opt out of standardized testing. But during the eight years leading up to 1985, Central Park East sixth graders scored well above the city average on standardized reading tests, according to a study by David Bensman of Rutgers University. Curiously, in all but the last three of those eight years, the scores of its second graders fluctuated—some years scoring higher, and other years lower, than the city average—suggesting that the school's methods worked over time. Wrote Fliegel: "The data indicate that many Central Park East students caught up with and surpassed the national norm during their school years."[61]

Even more remarkable was what happened to the students who completed Central Park East elementary. Bensman conducted phone interviews with 88 percent of the school's graduates. Of those, 95 percent graduated high school. Of the high school graduates, 66 percent went on to college, some of them to elite schools like Brown University and Columbia

University. Moreover, the graduation- and college-attendance rates of the Latino and African American students were only slightly lower than those of the white students.[62]

In 1985, ten years after founding Central Park East, Meier opened Central Park East Secondary School. Among the high school's first two graduating classes, 90 percent of the students graduated, and 90 percent of those went to college; this was at a time when the dropout rate in the city was 50 percent.[63]

"Such statistics would be misleading if Central Park East had simply skimmed the cream of the community's students, selecting only the motivated and well-prepared children," explains Fliegel. "But this was not the case. Central Park East generally followed a first-come, first-served policy, from which it deviated only in two ways: it strove to be racially integrated, and it gave preference to the younger siblings of current students. Indeed, in many instances the opposite of skimming took place."

Two years after founding Central Park East Secondary School, in June 1987, Meier became the first teacher to be awarded the MacArthur Foundation's "genius" award. Meier celebrated with a party at her weekend home in Hillsdale, New York, a small brown clapboard farmhouse in a remote, down-at-the-heels town on the edge of the Berkshires to which, years later, she would retire.[64]

Meier's work—and, no doubt, her award—as well as the achievements of a burgeoning cadre of alternative schools, did not go unnoticed in New York City. Around 1989, Norm Fruchter, then education-program director of the Aaron Diamond Foundation and a board member of the Fund for New York City Public Education, contacted Stephen Phillips, who headed what was now the Alternative High Schools and Programs District, and suggested that they found a group of new small schools, patterned off of the alternative high schools that could serve all New York City students, not just those at risk of dropping out.[65]

Phillips likes to quip that he was the first out-of-town administrator hired in New York City since the board of education had been formed in 1896 (that, of course, would change under Bloomberg). Phillips had been the protégé of Sidney L. "Sid" Johnson, a maverick superintendent in Syracuse, New York—the first African American to hold that job. A product of Jim Crow Georgia, Johnson was a retired Air Force major when he became, first, a teacher of "business"—business arithmetic and bookkeeping—and, eventually, the top administrator in Syracuse, where he would help integrate the schools and sanction a slew of progressive experiments. For example, Johnson redistricted the selective high school where Phillips had taught—Central-Technical High School—to include kids from the housing project nearby, who until that point had been required to travel to inferior schools farther away. "When the assassinations of MLK and Bobby Kennedy blew the schools up, Sid was wise enough to know that something tangible had to be done, and I think that's what led to a number of us younger folks (I was only 26 in 1968) being given a lot of responsibility and room to operate in," recalls Phillips, who remembers setting up one of the first black history courses in Syracuse and adding not just "minorities" but also women authors to reading lists. The Syracuse schools also experimented with what is now called "credit recovery," block programming, schools within schools, and storefront schools. One of the latter was set up by Lionel "Skip" Meno, another Johnson protégé, who would become the first out-of-state schools chancellor in Texas, where he would play a pivotal part in a quiet revolution in central Texas (see chapter 4).[66]

In 1983, during his brief stint as chancellor, Alvarado recruited Phillips to head the new alternative high schools division. By creating an autonomous division for alternative high schools—which encompassed everything from transfer high schools for over-age, under-accredited kids and programs on Rikers Island, the notorious jail that housed incarcerated youth, to the surviving street academies and a small group of direct-application schools like Central Park East Secondary—Alvarado believed that he could keep the schools "on the perimeter" of the bureaucracy.[67]

Alvarado also thought an autonomous division could lay the groundwork necessary to both grow and sustain alternative high schools. Alvarado had three aims, according to Phillips. First, he wanted to create a network of schools that could learn from each other while preserving their unique identities; indeed, alternative-school principals often helped each other place students to ensure the best fit between school and child. Second, he wanted the district—and its leadership—to serve as a "locus of advocacy" for the schools. Third, he wanted to create new schools.[68]

Under Phillips, the Alternative High Schools and Programs District realized Alvarado's mission. The district grew to encompass fifty-nine schools and enrolled more than 47,500 students. Although many of its schools were "last chance" institutions for kids who failed elsewhere, the district's success in graduating kids would soon make it a model for an ambitious expansion of small alternative high schools. Also, over the course of his fourteen-year tenure as head of the district, Phillips did more than just win the trust of his principals—he became beloved. Ask almost any principal who worked with Phillips and they will regale you with stories of his fierce and adept advocacy for, and protection of, the alternative schools.[69]

Small experimental schools were hot. Beginning in about 1990, they began to be seen, even by some policymakers, as a possible answer to the drumbeat of criticism that had hammered public education throughout the 1980s.

It was about this time that Norm Fruchter told Phillips that the Fund for New York City Public Education was "interested in seeing if some of the underlying components in the alternative high schools . . . could serve REGULAR students, not just prior dropouts or at-risk students, better than the city's huge high schools (components such as interdisciplinary instruction; non-gradedness . . . blocked programming; teacher-developed curricula . . . and, most important, small size)." The fund, which later became New Visions, had already "funded a number of small grants for my superintendency," recalls Phillips.[70]

In the late 1980s, Phillips suggested they have the fund do a study of the performance of the schools in the district and mount a publicity campaign. "We hoped this would capture Green's attention," recalls Phillips, referring to Richard Green who served briefly as chancellor until he suddenly died of an asthma attack in 1989.[71]

Now the focus shifted to wooing Joseph A. Fernandez, the incoming schools chancellor. At the time, Fruchter also served as education adviser to the Diamond foundation; Fruchter told Phillips that the Diamond foundation would fund "'planning grants' for teams of individuals to develop concept papers for twenty, new, small schools."[72]

Thus began an effort to open dozens of new small schools as part of a joint venture between the alternative high schools division and New Visions (the Fund for New York City Public Education), one of several intermediary organizations that would, in the coming two decades, play a pivotal role in nurturing New York City's growing crop of small schools. Fernandez was so impressed with what he saw when he got to New York that he promised to match the funds put up by the Diamond foundation and double to sixty the original number of new small schools that Diamond expected to open. (Diamond would channel about $25,000 per new school for start-up costs via New Visions because the foundation had "a 'rule' that money would never be given directly" to the Department of Education because "it would vanish into a bottomless pit." Both the Diamond grant and Fernandez's matching funds were for start-up costs, not operational expenses.)[73]

New Visions hired Naomi Barber to "launch" the effort. Barber and Phillips held "grassroots meetings throughout the five boroughs," inviting "any group" to propose a school. They favored nontraditional arrangements—block scheduling, themed curricula, unorthodox grade arrangements, such as combined middle and high schools or schools that started in the tenth grade. One of the few requirements was that the proposal represent a *collaborative school community.* "We insisted that everyone have a planning team with students, teachers, parents, and at least one administrator," recalls Phillips.[74]

The proposals poured in—close to three hundred of them. At one time, there was even a plan to open a school in collaboration with Goldman Sachs, the investment bank.[75]

Even as this Diamond–New Visions alternative schools project was getting under way, Phillips and Debbie Meier became involved with two other major efforts to seed both small schools and the infrastructure for sustaining them. One project involved converting large failing schools into what Phillips called "condominiums" for new small schools. The other project, which would be funded by the Annenberg Foundation—in the years before the Gates Foundation, one of the key philanthropies supporting public-school education—was even more ambitious: it aimed to bring together four intermediary organizations, each of which would seed dozens of small autonomous schools.

These disparate small-school projects were interconnected and would help lay the groundwork for a distributed "network structure" that proved to be a promising vehicle not just for seeding schools, but also for bringing together communities of like-minded educators who could share professional practices and foster improvement, as well as bring a degree of oversight. The schools built on connections to local community and civic groups. Together, the three efforts, which all took root during the superintendency of Joe Fernandez, would spark about 140 new small schools.

With the $350,000 from her MacArthur genius award Meier had founded the Center for Collaborative Education (CCE) to work with, and help support, New York City schools that were part of Ted Sizer's Coalition of Essential Schools, which had evolved into a national support organization for progressive schools. Both organizations—Sizer's coalition and Meier's CCE—provided funding, teacher training, and other supports for a growing network of autonomous progressive schools.[76]

BEFORE TAKEOVERS TOOK OVER

In 1992, Meier also began working on what came to be called the Coalition Campus Schools Project (CCSP), which was aimed at gradually closing the city's large, factory-style high schools one grade at a time and replacing them with new schools that were "hot-housed" offsite. Thus, as the freshman class of a phase-out school became sophomores, a new class of kids would move in—though they belonged to a new school, with new teachers and new management. But instead of one giant class with several hundred students, there would be several small schools, each with its own management and culture, that would be the "condo" occupants. This approach also would become the model for Mayor Bloomberg's takeover strategy—a controversial one—for phasing out failing schools and foreshadowed the development of "a citywide office to manage the city's 'portfolio' of schools."[77]

The Coalition Campus Schools Project was a collaboration between Fernandez's education department and the CCE, and it targeted three large dysfunctional New York high schools—one in Manhattan, one in Brooklyn, and a third in the Bronx. Each high school had about three thousand students at peak enrollment. In total, eleven small schools would be incubated, though not all were moved directly into the new high schools.

The Brooklyn takeover would never fully come to fruition, and in the South Bronx only a few of the schools that were intended to replace the shuttered James Monroe High would become successful—and, of these, many were not physically located at the old James Monroe campus. For example, Fannie Lou Hamer Freedom School was located about a mile from Monroe, and Brooklyn International High School, as its name suggests, was in Brooklyn. Indeed, what came to be over a dozen international schools—small schools specifically designed to serve English language learners—would form their own collaborative mini-network within the alternative high schools division. Modeled after Nadelstern's LaGuardia International, they were among the most successful of the new small schools.

The Coalition Campus Schools Project's most ambitious—and most successful—turnaround effort took place at Julia Richman in Manhattan. Despite its location on East 68th Street, on the Upper East Side, the school had always served mostly poor kids from Harlem. At the time, Julia Richman had an official four-year graduation rate of under 40 percent—though, in the years before it closed, the old high school never graduated more than about 150 students.[78] With time, the schools affiliated with what became known as the Julia Richman Education Complex became so successful they inspired the Gates Foundation and successive New York City administrations—none more so than Bloomberg's.

The Julia Richman story actually began in the mid-1980s with a small entrepreneurial teacher-training and -mentoring effort that encompassed, at its peak, a dozen schools and followed the progressive "open-education" philosophy of Meier, Weber, and Sizer.

The project was midwifed by Ann Cook and Herb Mack, a husband-and-wife team who had met on the South Side of Chicago in the 1960s.

Mack was a teacher at the Hyde Park School, a largely black public school, when he met Cook, a civil rights activist who was developing tutoring programs for inner-city kids. Both Mack and Cook were members of SNCC, the radical Student Nonviolent Coordinating Committee. For their first date, they attended a lecture by Arthur Schlesinger, the historian and social critic and former speechwriter for Adlai Stevenson's presidential campaign. Cook is often described as the politically savvy, big-picture thinker and Mack as the quieter implementer who knew how to get things done inside schools. What's clear is that their personalities complemented each other. Cook possessed the determination and know-how needed to overcome bureaucratic obstacles, which would prove vital in helping to solidify the educational programs she and Mack developed. Mack, meanwhile, served for twenty years as the unassuming orchestra conductor who held together a diverse and sometimes cacophonous group of schools. (In fact, the combination of bureaucratic meddling and the lack of strong advocates would come to hamper the Monroe project.)

Cook grew up on the white edge of a black neighborhood on the sharply segregated South Side of Chicago and honed her political determination on the grindstone of the Daley machine. It was a time when a slew of urban-renewal projects—notably those affiliated with the expansions of the University of Chicago and the University of Illinois—threatened longtime communities on the South Side.[79] Cook was working at a South Side tutoring program when she personally ran up against the Daley machine. Although the program was funded by a Johnson administration antipoverty program, the disbursements were controlled by the Daley administration. One day a Daley auditor visited the program and found a student essay describing how, during a recent election, he and his uncle, a precinct captain for the Daley campaign, had spent the day taking down the opposition's campaign signs and "stomping" on them. "After that we had nothing but trouble" from the Daley administration, recalls Cook.[80]

Cook and Mack left Chicago in 1966 and, like Weber, traveled to England to observe open-education firsthand. Two years later, they moved to New York.[81]

By the late 1970s, Cook and Mack were running the Inquiry Demonstration Project at the City University of New York, a teacher-development program that worked in about a dozen New York City schools and was designed to help teachers get kids more engaged in both classroom and community problems. The project promoted an inquiry-based approach to education, described by its evaluators as "a student-centered process in which the student questions, analyzes and evaluates a body of material."[82]

This husband-and-wife teacher-training effort soon added a half-day program for at-risk teens who were in danger of dropping out. The goal of the program, which they called Urban Academy, was to inspire students, many of whom were "disenchanted or disengaged" from their schools, to develop their critical-thinking skills and to get them to finish their schooling. The program also worked on a host of inquiry-oriented "habits of mind," including finding and weighing evidence; making connections among and assessing the value of the ideas they had studied; and developing their writing skills.[83]

Urban began meeting with its students in the mid-1980s at a decrepit school building on East 96th Street. The students came to Urban in the morning and were supposed to go back to their "home" high schools in the afternoon.

One morning, the head of the education department's high school division came for a visit and asked the students to tell her about the program. She then asked them where they went in the afternoons. The kids hemmed and hawed.

"Oh," said the supervisor. "I get it; you don't go anywhere" in the afternoon.

The supervisor gave a green light to turn Urban into a full-time program. When in 1989 Urban ran out of space on East 96th Street, Cook and Mack moved the program downtown to the new High School for the Humanities on West 18th Street.

THE TRIUMPH OF ROOM 100

If you asked all the students in your five classes to write three hundred and fifty words each then you had 175 multiplied by 350 and that was 43,750 words you had to read, correct, evaluate and grade on evenings and weekends. That's if you were wise enough to give them only one assignment per week. You had to correct misspellings, faulty grammar, poor structure, transitions, sloppiness in general. You had to make suggestions on content and write a general comment explaining your grade. You reminded them there was no extra credit for papers adorned with ketchup, mayonnaise, coffee, Coke, tears, grease, dandruff. You suggested strongly they write their papers at desk or table and not on the train, bus, escalator or in the hub-bub of Joe's Original Pizza joint around the corner.

If you gave each paper a bare five minutes you'd spend, on this one set of papers, fourteen hours and thirty-five minutes. That would amount to more than two teaching days, and the end of the weekend.

You hesitate to assign book reports. They are longer and rich in plagiarism.

—*Teacher Man*, Frank McCourt[84]

In his legendary 1984 critique of the typical American high school, *Horace's Compromise*, Ted Sizer outlined the devastating compromises that even the most dedicated teachers must make. In the assembly line that was the American education system, a teacher in an urban school district would typically teach five classes, in fifty-or-so-minute increments, with a total of 175 students cycling through his classroom every day. There was no way a teacher could possibly respond to even the most cursory homework assignments, let alone meaningfully critique essays by so many students. Writes Sizer: "Horace is realistic. . . . He compromises, averaging five minutes for each student's work by cutting all but the most essential corners. . . . So, to check homework and to read and criticize one paragraph per week per student with the maximum feasible corner-cutting takes six hundred minutes, or ten hours, assuming no coffee breaks or flagging attention."[85]

At Central Park East Secondary School, Meier and her team had developed a solution to this problem by pursuing a "less-is-more" approach to education, creating larger blocks of time for interdisciplinary study. Instead of cycling five batches of students in fifty-minute increments throughout the day, teams of English-and-social studies or math-and-science teachers would work with at most eighty students per semester for blocks of time measured in hours, not minutes. Teachers focused on depth, not breadth, on teaching their students to wrestle with so-called essential questions—big, open-ended, important questions that don't necessarily have clear answers.[86]

The students also stayed with each teacher team for two years, allowing teachers to get to know their students well so as to cultivate relationships between teacher and students that are considered so vital to adolescent development. A structured advisory system also helped teachers stay on top of student needs and connect with families.[87]

Urban would follow a very similar playbook. Urban was a tiny transfer school, a last-chance stop for kids who had failed everywhere else.[88] Urban referred to them as kids who "march to their own drummer." Among the school's 160 or so students, some kids were homeless or in foster care, while some were "two steps away from juvie." Others had landed at Urban after leaving private schools or one of the city's elite public schools, such as Bronx Science. Most were minorities.[89]

The kids at Urban may have been unsuccessful at other schools, but as its reputation grew, the school attracted a number of intellectually gifted kids. Although Urban started in the tenth grade and accepted only students who had failed or dropped out of another school, Urban's admissions policy required students to visit classes, participate in an interview, and complete both an in-school assessment and a take-home application.[90]

At Urban, students would learn by conducting investigations and interviews, debating and listening to debates, writing reports, and completing research projects. And questioning—always questioning. The exact nature of each class differed depending on the subject matter and the participants. But "the constants were the student-centered approach, the in-depth study of each topic, the emphasis on critical thinking, and the emphasis on research."[91]

Often, teachers, with input from students, would pick a topic that interested them—a strategy designed to keep both teachers and students keen. A social studies class that began as a look at Puerto Rico evolved to include a comparative study of Puerto Rico, the Dominican Republic, and Cuba, as well as how U.S. policy impacted them all. In one English Language Arts (ELA) course, students would select much of what they read, with the expectation that some of the works would be "literature" and some "junk"; the students spent the semester analyzing and exploring the difference between the two. Discussions about social justice might include interviews with both the police and activists.

The curriculum was chock full of sometimes seemingly offbeat subjects that might seem suspect to traditionalists. But proponents of Urban's inquiry method point out that its students read a rich complement of classical texts. A years-long study by Linda Darling-Hammond and Jacqueline Ancess, which examined a sampling of students' portfolios, found that the students had studied works by Allende, Brecht, Ibsen, Chekhov, de Maupassant, Poe, Shakespeare, Tolkien, and Richard Wright, among others.[92]

Decades before the Common Core State Standards elevated critical thinking and the ability to develop and support arguments with evidence to a national obsession, Urban Academy was doing that and more. For example, should people be allowed to sell their organs because other kinds of uncomfortable or dangerous work, like digging the Second Avenue subway, are legal? That's the kind of question that Urban kids might grapple with in "Looking for an Argument," one of the school's most popular and enduring courses. A course on the civil rights movement asked: do heroes create movements, or do movements create heroes? Another course, on the United States Constitution, queried: is there any speech that can be censored under the Constitution? Why was the Bill of Rights not included in the original Constitution?[93]

Under Cook and Mack's leadership, democratic values were, from the beginning, deeply interlaced with Urban's culture. Urban was operated quite literally as a collective in which everything—from student discipline to selecting a new principal to head the school—is collaboratively decided by the entire faculty. Importantly, when Urban became the anchor school for the Julia Richman complex, its collaborative culture and democratic values—if not its pedagogical methods—seeped into the fabric of the half dozen neighboring schools with which it shared a building.

Local wags had dubbed the old giant high school Julia Rikers after the notorious New York City jail, Riker's Island. There were walk-through metal detectors at every entrance. A dozen security guards scanned kids with handheld metal detectors as they streamed in every morning. And a "cage," an eight-by-twelve-foot floor-to-ceiling wire enclosure, occupied part of the guidance counselor's office; that was where the school locked accused miscreants until the police arrived.[94]

Julia Richman's large 1920s-era brick building takes up much of the block that spans East 68th Street between Second and Third Avenues and, on the outside, it looks much like any other large New York City public school. Inside is a different story. Julia Richman is home to a crazy quilt of a half dozen schools that was carefully assembled by Cook and Mack, but that few traditional educators would have ever chosen to house together in one building. There are four small high schools, anchored by Urban Academy, two of them focused on recent immigrants who are English-language learners. One school specializes in low-achieving students. And defying the practice of keeping young children separated from the dubious influence of teenagers, Cook insisted on locating both a K–8 school and a day care center in the complex. There is also a school for autistic kids.[95] Like the Monroe cohort, several of the original Coalition Campus Schools that were affiliated with Julia Richman never actually moved into the Julia Richman complex; for example, Manhattan Village Academy is located on West 22nd Street. But it remains part of both formal—and informal—progressive-schools networks that continued to link the schools long after the Coalition Campus Schools project, as such, had ceased to be funded.

At the heart of the Julia Richman complex is a commitment to both choice and school autonomy. While the complex's schools share facilities and have developed an unusual governance structure designed to resolve common problems and disputes, each school is physically self-contained and controls its own admissions procedures.

Equally important, Julia Richman forged a series of unique agreements with the teachers union, the result of years of trust cultivated between Debbie Meier and other members of the progressive coalition, on the one hand, and Sandra Feldman, then-leader of the United Federation of Teachers.

First, Feldman had agreed to "call off the dogs"—i.e., to help deflect any objections on the part of its membership—regarding the takeover of Julia Richman High. Then, Feldman had agreed to let Julia Richman adopt a peer-led hiring process that Eric Nadelstern had pioneered a decade earlier when he launched LaGuardia International High School.

Like Meier, Nadelstern had been looking for like-minded teachers for his new school, a virtually impossible goal if he adhered to official education-department hiring procedures, which involved two bureaucrats—one from the board of education and one from the union—secreted in a room at the central division of human resources on Court Street in Brooklyn and divvying up the transfer requests virtually at random. Principals had no say. So Nadelstern persuaded two LaGuardia International teachers who were active in the United Federation of Teachers to propose a rule change that would permit them—the hiring school's teachers—to interview job candidates. "Essentially Eric's reasoning was: 'I don't have anything to do with the selection process, so I might as well at least get my teachers involved with the selection,'" recalls Phillips.[96]

Selling the idea—that, in order to build a common school culture, teachers could help pick their own colleagues—to the union leadership, he adds, was "a kind of revolution."[97]

Soon, the flexible options that had been developed inside the alternative high schools division at the international schools and at Julia Richman would be formalized in the so-called School Based Option, which, if 70 percent of teachers agreed, would allow schools greater flexibility in work rules and would become "one of the policy pillars of small-school development and stability in New York."[98] The School Based Option would, in turn, give rise to the PROSE agreement in the 2014 teachers contract, which emphasized *teacher-led transformation* and allowing schools and teachers "to alter some of the most basic parameters" by which schools function—"including the way teachers are hired, evaluated and supported; the way students and teachers are programmed; the handling of grievances; and certain city and state regulations." Randi Weingarten, the head of the American Federation of Teachers, noted that PROSE realized efforts dating back to Albert Shanker to put teachers at the center of school improvement; the new agreements, she said, were an "essential tool that builds trust and engenders collective responsibility."[99]

The Julia Richman complex would be a path breaker in other ways as well. The 68th Street campus became the epicenter of resistance to the standardized-testing regime that was embraced both at the state level and, soon, by the Bloomberg administration's education department. It was also the hub of an effort to develop alternative assessments, as well as a political movement to win legislative support for a more pluralistic approach to accountability.

With time, the schools in the Julia Richman complex also galvanized both the Gates Foundation's small-schools strategy and the Bloomberg administration's commitment to taking over large, struggling high schools. That's because the schools inside the Julia Richman fortress, with their "at-risk" kids—most of them poor, black, and brown—rebellious leaders, and lefty teachers, would become very, very successful. In fact, over the course of more than two decades and multiple education administrations, no high school takeover would surpass the results Julia Richman chalked up year after year—its graduation rates and the number of kids it sent to college, especially among the city's most disadvantaged kids.

By most accounts, what set the Julia Richman complex apart—as well as affiliated, nearby schools that had been part of the Coalition Campus Schools project—from its counterpart in the Bronx was both the campus's strong leadership and the *structures* it had put in place to share space, resolve disputes, and, importantly, keep the bureaucracy at bay. The Monroe Complex lacked a building council that could give voice to its individual schools. It was also the subject of constant meddling from the board of education. Thus, when Meier left New York City in the mid-1990s, her departure "left a huge education and political leadership vacuum."[100]

While Meier had been a brilliant founder of new schools, she was much less successful at creating the infrastructure that would be necessary to help both her schools and the CCE flourish in her absence. While a deep bench of Meier-trained or -inspired educators continue to run progressive schools in New York City to this day, some of her original schools—Central Park East Secondary, in particular—eventually abandoned their progressive roots and became indistinguishable from other city schools. The CCE, which had served as a buffer, a resource, and a cultural beacon for the progressive coalition, also fell apart shortly after Meier left New York City.

Instead, the key to developing the infrastructure that the burgeoning crop of small New York City schools needed would be the network structure that had its origins in the international schools and in the second major small-schools project, financed by the Annenberg Foundation, which sought to unite four intermediaries in the creation of new schools. The small-school infrastructure also continued to emanate from the Julia Richman pioneers. With their laser-like focus on teacher training and mentoring and their battle to develop alternative assessments of student work and definitions of school quality, they forged a blueprint for sustaining a progressive and collaborative outsider school agenda.

The first years of the Julia Richman takeover were difficult, however. For one thing, the teachers at the phase-out schools viewed the newcomers with suspicion. What remained of the old high school, at the time of the takeover, had dwindled to about eight hundred students who were "demoralized and largely abandoned," said Ann Cook. "'Now you are fixing the place,' they would say when they saw workers doing renovations. It was horrible." That experience would foreshadow the criticisms of big-school takeovers during the Bloomberg administration—a challenge that was never resolved.[101]

Once the new schools moved into the building, Cook and Mack were determined that each school should maintain its autonomy. Students applied to each school separately, and the building was divided so that, even when schools shared the same floor, each school remained physically self-contained, with neither students nor faculty wandering into each other's spaces.[102]

From the beginning, Cook and Mack had to fight off the Department of Education, which began by trying to install a centrally appointed bureaucrat to manage the building—by no means the greatest outside hurdle the complex would face. While co-locations would foment hostility and infighting in the years to come—especially when charter schools were co-located with public schools and were often given the most desirable real estate—the Julia Richman complex, especially after the difficult transition years, insisted on shaping and governing its own community. To help build a connection among the students, the four high schools established interscholastic sports teams and would compete against one another. Meanwhile, the adults in the building formed a building council that met regularly to work out schedules and problems. And every year, the council elected a building manager to run the complex; for close to twenty years, they kept reelecting Herb Mack. It was a job he conducted even as he served as co-director, with his wife, of Urban Academy.[103]

How the hodgepodge system of schools worked is best illustrated by the way Julia Richman resolved the tension between having little kids and big kids occupy the same spaces. Little kids in the elementary school would help to "civilize" the older kids, Cook believed, and would "create a different tone" in the building. Cook remembers a fire drill, when a gaggle of high school kids milling about outside unleashed a torrent of profanity. "It was f—— this and f—— that," recalls Cook. "I went up to them and said, 'There are little kids here, can you clean it up a bit?'"[104]

Cook got no pushback at all from the teenagers, she recalls, because "it made sense to them."

Another time, older kids on the playground hurtled themselves against the chain-link fence just as a row of kindergarteners was returning from a field trip. The bounce from the chain-link fence knocked over a few of the little kids. The teacher got so upset, she complained at the next building-council meeting.[105]

Together, the educators at the offending high school as well as the elementary school turned the incident into a teaching moment. "So five or six of these great big boys" visited the kindergarten class, where the little kids explained why their behavior had been "scary."

"The big kids got it and said, 'you need to come up and tell everybody,'" recalls Cook. "So the little kids went upstairs and talked to all the home rooms and advisories" of the high schools and asked the big kids to "'be careful because we're little.'"[106]

"It was delicious," recalls Cook, cracking a rare smile. The big kids responded because "it was organic . . . no one preached at them."[107]

Today, says Cook, she routinely sees high schoolers holding the door for elementary school kids. The tone, she says, has definitely shifted.

Not all disagreements were so easily resolved, especially as the Julia Richman council insisted on settling disputes via consensus, rather than majority rule. Unless you have consensus, "there will always be one or two schools left on the outside," explains Terry Weber, a recently retired long-time Urban Academy teacher.[108]

The problem with Room 100 is a case in point. Early on, all the Julia Richman schools agreed to share common facilities, including the two gyms, auditorium, cafeteria, and library. A majority of the schools wanted to turn most of the ground-floor facilities into common spaces. But what to do about Room 100, which doubled both as the principal's office for one of the schools, Talent Unlimited, and as a rehearsal space for the school chorus?

Talent Unlimited had been a program in the old Julia Richman high school before becoming a high school in the new complex. The school's principal, who also served as its chorus director, didn't want to relinquish Room 100, with its tiered seating that was ideal for choral practice. A battle raged for three years. Finally, the dispute was resolved when the other schools in the building each agreed to chip in money to buy tiered seats in an upstairs room for Talent Unlimited. (Talent Unlimited is also the only traditional high school in the Julia Richman Complex that still offers the full gamut of Regents examinations.)

Twenty years after Julia Richman's conversion, the building council is still the primary governing body for the six schools within the building. After Mack's retirement, the council voted to have Bill Klann, the principal of Vanguard, another high school in the building, replace him. At the time, Mack and Ann Cook were ceding their own roles as co-directors of Urban to two longtime teachers, Adam Grumbach and Becky Walzer. But, as always at Urban, the decision was made by the faculty as a whole; after months spent interviewing outside candidates, the faculty decided they needed to promote teachers from within. That, says Mack with a knowing smile, was a foregone conclusion—but one the faculty needed to figure out for themselves. At a school where teachers love to teach, the new heads were, in essence, drafted; both continue to teach, as had Mack and Cook when they were directors—though only Grumbach is recognized officially by the education department as the school "principal."

Most of the time, the unorthodox governance structure has worked for the Julia Richman Complex, even though, over the years, the building has faced repeated threats from the outside. Periodically, the Department of Education tries to impose hires on schools in the building—though, so far, the Richman schools have been able to resist most of these efforts. In one of the gravest threats to the building, just a few years after the establishment of the complex, a group of affluent white parents at a nearby elementary school—in a "confrontation where race and class were never far from the surface of the debate"—lobbied to have the building converted back into a high school, but this time as a zoned school for Upper East Side students. A few years later, the city threatened to let nearby Hunter College, part of the City University of New York system, take over the building in exchange for land the college held forty blocks south.[109]

The complex fought back with the help of hundreds of parents, teachers, and neighbors, often relying on the high-powered "board of advisers"—influential lawyers, corporate executives, and union leaders—Ann Cook had compiled early on. Cook had also cultivated relationships with foundations, academics, and civil rights leaders, whom she didn't hesitate to call on when necessary. "Like most bureaucracies, the New York board of education responds to outside pressure, not to middle management," says Cook.[110]

Cook prevailed in almost every instance. The white parents who wanted their own high school were given Eleanor Roosevelt High, a few blocks north of Julia Richman. Hunter got a building in Spanish Harlem. And, as became clear when Cook took on the state's standardized-testing establishment, if politicking and influence didn't work, Cook didn't shy away from taking more desperate measures.

Of course, Cook's lobbying efforts wouldn't have worked if the schools in the complex hadn't flourished academically. The complex graduated its first cohort of seniors during the 1997–1998 school year. That was also roughly when the Julia Richman complex gelled into its final form with four high schools, a K–8 school, a school for autistic kids, and a day care center. One of the original schools dropped out of the project because of "philosophical differences."

The remaining schools racked up college-attendance rates that far exceeded the city's average. Overall, 89 percent of students at Julia Richman schools enrolled in college, with Urban Academy and Manhattan International achieving matriculation rates of over 90 percent.[111]

Despite the fact that their student bodies were more "at risk" than those of the original Julia Richman high school, by 1995–96 the Coalition Campus schools had "established attendance rates well above those of the former school, and their average rates of student suspension, disciplinary incidents, and dropping out were far below the citywide and Julia Richman averages." The annual dropout rate at the surviving Coalition Campus schools was just 3.4 percent, significantly lower than the 20 percent city rate. Even Vanguard, a school that specifically targeted challenging students, had a dropout rate of only 4 percent.[112]

As of 2017, each of the Julia Richman high schools outperformed citywide averages on the "academic" portion of the surveys conducted by Insideschools.org, which provides independent analyses of New York City public schools. Only Talent Unlimited's scores were comparable to citywide averages on the website's questions about "engaging curriculum."[113]

TEACHING THE TEACHERS

Avram Barlowe was teaching in the South Bronx when he began training in Cook and Mack's inquiry method. As part of the training, Cook and Mack regularly observed participant teachers in their classrooms and offered input and mentoring. The teachers also attended summer seminars, where they would teach classes to high school kids using the approach while being observed and critiqued by other members of the seminar.

Those were the years when the Bronx was quite literally burning; the acrid smell of both smoke and despair filled the air. (To save money during the fiscal crisis, in the 1970s, Mayor John Lindsay had closed dozens of fire stations.) But the Bronx also nurtured a flowering of street art, especially graffiti and hip-hop. At the time, Barlowe, who grew up on Sedgwick Boulevard in the Bronx—later renamed Hip Hop Boulevard because it was also where one of hip-hop's founding fathers, DJ Kool Herc, and his sister held their first hip-hop party—was teaching a course on popular culture. Tall, rail-thin, and intense, Barlowe thought he might be able to use some of the new creative genres both to engage his students and to raise important social issues. Michael Jackson's newly released music video "Thriller," which some have interpreted as a date-rape fantasy, might help spark a conversation about misogyny, Barlowe thought. "My take was, they're obsessed with music," he recalls. "It's integral to their vocabulary. They're taking in all this stuff, this misogyny washes through them. I would show them."[114]

Barlowe no longer remembers the details of the lesson—only that it wasn't working as he had planned. Sitting at the back of the classroom that day, Herb Mack ventured a suggestion: "Why don't you ask them if the video is appropriate to show a four-year-old?"[115]

That question was "a revelation," says Barlowe. Every kid in that class had a younger sibling or cousin or some other young child he or she knew. They "began to ask questions about what that video meant. They had ownership."

Even though few of his students had excelled academically, "they were naturally inclined to be analytical."[116]

Barlowe decided to try a similar approach in his American history class. The challenge of the inquiry process would be to shift the focus from having Barlowe ask the questions to having the kids do the questioning. Under Mack and Cook's guidance, Barlowe gave his students a list of 150 names, ranging from Bill Gates to Sitting Bull. He instructed the students to eliminate the names they didn't know. Then, he divided his students into teams and had the teams identify the five they thought were the most important people and the five they considered to be the least important. In the process, the students would debate what makes someone "important"; they also were instructed to keep track of their criteria.[117]

Books and articles followed. Once he had hooked the kids on an argument or a provocative idea, Barlowe found it was easier to engage them in readings. "When you are encouraging voice" to be part of learning, says Barlowe, "you are also encouraging rigor." If the teacher doesn't have the answer, then you "create an environment in which evidence becomes important." It becomes part of the classroom culture.[118]

The focus on developing arguments, on analysis, on evidence would be familiar to proponents of the Common Core. But whereas the Common Core focuses on "author's choices," the Urban Academy approach is much more student focused. It seeks to draw out the students' own points of view. It is the key to getting kids engaged and to much deeper learning, argues Barlowe.[119]

Conducting an effective inquiry approach is "much more intellectually engaging" for both students and teacher, argues Barlowe. But it is also difficult.

It took Barlowe years to master the inquiry process, he says, including the sense for when to linger on a topic, when to digress, and when to move on. You also have to "learn how to shut up" and let the kids wrestle with a problem or idea. "You need to do more thinking on your feet" than you would in a typical classroom.[120]

Barlowe transferred to Urban in the fall of 1986.

Urban Academy would become a laboratory school where its teachers trained in the inquiry methods promulgated by Cook, Mack, Meier, and Sizer. At Urban, new hires, whether they were relatively new to teaching or veterans, go through a scaffolded, two-year mentoring process. During their first semester at the school, new teachers are asked to develop the first three weeks of a course and a timeline for the rest of the semester; the course is then fleshed out in collaboration with a mentor—a veteran Urban teacher. During the first semester in the classroom, the mentor sits in on every class, offering advice and assistance; the mentee also spends time visiting classes taught by his or her mentor. In the coming semesters, the new teacher picks up another class or two, often not reaching a full teaching load of three to four classes per semester until two years has passed, all the while meeting regularly with his or her mentor.[121]

Herb Mack sits at his desk in the crowded Urban Academy office, a room nearly the size of a basketball court. The office is a rabbit warren of filing cabinets and desks, one for every teacher and administrator at the school. Kids wander in and out, frequently climbing over an obstacle course of file folders and backpacks to reach the desk drawer in which Mack keeps a stash of gum for their masticating pleasure. A tall, gangly youth hovers, eavesdropping, near some desks where three grown-ups are chatting. This is the chaotic central office-cum-dining room of Meier's dreams—minus Stalin, Lenin, and Trotsky. This is also the room that, in the old days, housed the cage where the old Julia Richman miscreants were kept waiting for the police to take them away. A small sepia photo of Abraham Lincoln is pinned to the divider that separates Mack's desk from his neighbor's. Although Mack is dressed in a pale blue sweater over a faded blue polo shirt and is wearing black athletic shoes, he bears an uncanny resemblance to the former president—tall and thin, hollow cheeks, and jutting, though clean-shaven, chin, his gray hair swept away from his forehead.

Mack is working on the latest iteration of a course on current events that he and Barlowe are team teaching. (Though Mack retired a few years ago, he still comes by to teach for fun.) Called "Current Issues," the course evolved from "Looking for an Argument" and was intended to be a timely lead-up to the 2016 presidential elections. In an earlier iteration, Mack and Barlowe decided to build the course around *Losing Our Way*, a new book by Bob Herbert, the former op-ed columnist for the *New York Times.* But for students without enough background knowledge, Herbert's writing was difficult to understand.[122]

So Mack and Barlowe retooled the course, making a list of important issues in the lead-up to the presidential election, and arrived at the subject of housing and gentrification. Although they weren't getting much play in the 2016 presidential race, these issues were important in New York City. As with most inquiry classes, Mack and Barlowe brought in experts to speak to the class. They also organized a field trip to the Bedford-Stuyvesant section of Brooklyn, where Mack's daughter now lives; she helped corral African American neighbors to speak with the Urban students about their fears of gentrification, of being priced out of their neighborhoods.[123]

Then, the San Bernardino shooting happened, and the kids wanted to talk about gun control and terrorism. So, midstream, the course shifted. The students in "Current Issues" began to read about the Second Amendment, including Justice Antonin Scalia's 2008 opinion in *District of Columbia v. Heller*. Other students wandered further afield, researching the foster care system or women in sports. Throughout the course, the students were encouraged to read, to interview experts, to follow up, to figure out when they weren't getting the answers they needed. To dig deeper.

The students also wrote several papers. To facilitate the writing process, Barlowe and Mack arranged to meet one-on-one with each student three or four times during the course of the semester. It's the only way to meet the needs of students with a wide range of abilities, explains Mack.

But Mack and Barlowe still weren't satisfied with the course. So they set about preparing the next iteration. Some of their goals: to narrow the range of questions the students explore and to have more one-on-one meetings about writing. And to have less talking—that is, the teachers need to talk less.[124]

At Urban, such experimentation is routine. Mack figures that in the fifty-or-so semesters he's taught at Urban, the school has never taught exactly the same course twice. Curriculum development is an iterative process; it keeps the courses, and the teachers, fresh.[125]

Twice a year, at the beginning of the fall and spring semesters, the school teaches several two-week intensives. These can range from jewelry making to voter-registration drives, like the one that took a group of kids to Ohio in 2008, to a course on museums. And each semester there's also the option of working on a musical that is staged and produced in just thirteen days. Each student takes just one intensive, but every teacher has to participate in developing one of the offered courses. And every semester the courses are different. For the students at a transfer school, the two-week intensives serve as a bonding experience for new kids who arrive throughout the course of the four-year high school experience, including in January.

The two-week intensives, though, are just as important for the teachers, says Mack. Teachers need to decide on a topic, common experiences, and a concluding activity. The courses involve "planning curriculum outside each teacher's comfort zone," says Mack. "The teachers are knocked out of their ruts. It's an excellent curriculum thinking period." [126]

During a recent visit to Urban Academy late one afternoon, a group of students lingered after school, sprawled across the comfortable sofas that line the hallways. When asked by a visitor how they liked the school, the students called out in unison: "We love this place!" [127]

Amber Cedano, a former student who had to leave Urban when her parents moved out of town, wrote this about Urban Academy on a local education website: "i've never missed a school so much, Urban made me feel so comfortable and, yes the work was not easy but it challenged me intellectually and made me think in a different form. Urban was more than just a school for me. The people at urban became my family and Urban academy became my home. I am highly home sick and for my Senior year i have to spend it at a school that teaches for test rather to learn . . . so for that thank you Herb, Ann, Shiela, Avram, Adam . . . and every other staff member at urban academy." [128]

For Danyelle Gonzalez, Urban Academy has become something of a way of life. After dropping out of Bronx Science, she landed at Urban, where she found a community of students and teachers with whom she could "connect." Gonzalez did so well at Urban that she got into Northwestern University in Evanston, Illinois. In retrospect, having "failed" at a large high school, Gonzalez says she should never have chosen a large suburban college, especially one where, as a poor black girl from the Bronx and Brooklyn, she felt she couldn't fit in.

Gonzalez dropped out of Northwestern and returned to New York, where she eventually went to work for Deutschbank. Gonzalez later married and had two children, whom she sent to Ella Baker, the elementary school in the Julia Richman building. She now works in the office at Urban Academy and occasionally serves as an assistant teacher. Gonzalez completed college with a degree from Empire State College, a SUNY school for older students; at forty-four, she is about to enroll in a graduate degree program in education.[129]

THE POWER OF NETWORKING

> *Every June during my eight years at McKee [Vocational and Technical High School, Staten Island], the English department met in a classroom to read, evaluate, grade the New York State English Regents examination. Barely half the students at McKee passed the examination. The other half had to be helped. We tried to inflate the failure grades from high fifties to passing, the mandated sixty-five.*
>
> *We could do nothing about multiple-choice questions, the answers were right or wrong, but we helped with essays on literature and general topics. Give the kid credit for being there. . . . Three points for showing up, for selfless citizenship. Is his writing legible? Sure. Another two or three points . . .*
>
> *Does the student use paragraphs? Oh, yeah. Look how he indents. The kid is a master of indentation. There are definitely three paragraphs here . . .*
>
> *Why not raise him another three points? He's a nice kid and his brother, Stan, is in Vietnam. His father got polio when he was a kid. Spends his life in a wheelchair. Oh, give the boy another point for having a father in a wheelchair and a brother in Vietnam.*
>
> —*Teacher Man*, Frank McCourt[130]

In November of 1972, before the Inquiry Demonstration Project, before Urban Academy or Julia Richman, even before Central Park East, the New York rebels traveled to Grand Forks, North Dakota, for a meeting of the leading progressive educators from around the country. Debbie Meier and Lillian Weber were there. So were Ann Cook and Herb Mack. They had been gathered together by Vito Perrone, who later became director of teacher education at the Harvard Graduate School of Education and has been called the "conscience of the profession." They were there to discuss some "common concerns about the narrow accountability ethos that had begun to dominate schools and to share what many believed to be more sensible means of both documenting and assessing children's learning."[131]

The meeting proved to be the first for what became known as the North Dakota Study Group on Evaluation. Although the reference to "evaluation" was often omitted from the group's moniker, members of the NDSG soon became key voices in the debate about testing and evaluation.[132]

Cook and Mack wrote the following, somewhat prophetically, in one of the NDSG's first monographs:

> Without question, the problems in our schools require emergency attention. To act, however, on the premise that because a disastrous situation exists quick solutions can be found, only serves to

> compound the situation. The time has come to abandon the quest for "instant" answers, the "perfect" system, or the "teacher-proof" curriculum that can be measured and judged "successful" by some computer-scored, standardized test. It is time that we turn, instead, to the complex task of making the most of the resources available—specifically those human resources already existing in our schools, colleges and communities.[133]

The schools in New York's progressive coalition—those founded by Debbie Meier and the ones nurtured by Cook and Mack and myriad others they had inspired—were taking root against the clamor for more testing and accountability, which had already begun in the 1970s and picked up steam with the 1983 publication of *A Nation at Risk.*

A report produced by President Ronald Reagan's National Commission on Excellence in Education, *A Nation at Risk* appropriated the language of war and heralded a crisis in the country's schools and a threat to the nation's very security. To defend itself against the collectivism and uniformity of the communist dictatorships of Russia and China, the nation's education reformers would resort to a collectivist, standardized approach to transforming education. With time, they would promulgate a standardized menu of responses—including strict measurement, breaking down the component parts of instruction, and even, in some cases, dumbing down the work of teachers so that individual teachers could be more easily replaced. There were, of course, pockets of resistance to the pressure to create One Best Way in education. One such interregnum took place in New York State where, in 1991, then education secretary Tom Sobol recognized Urban Academy as "an exemplary school" and as a model for what became his Compact for Learning, in which Sobol sought, famously, to give "top-down support for bottom up" reform. In its September 2015 obituary of Sobol, the *New York Times* described the compact as "a broad manifesto aimed at transferring policy making from sluggish bureaucracies to educators and parents, and at creating grade-specific curriculum standards that local school districts could implement on their own."[134]

Deeply concerned about the steady drumbeat for standardized testing and recognizing an ally in Sobol, Meier and Cook were involved in an effort to both develop performance-based assessments and have them be recognized as part of a new assessment regime that New York State was developing.

To that end, a group of coalition school leaders met several times in the book-lined conference room at Julia Richman in the mid-1990s. Central

Park East Secondary School had been the first of the progressive-coalition schools to use performance-based assessments. Now, schools that represented both Sobel's Compact for Learning and Ted Sizer's Coalition of Essential Schools set out to formalize the practices already in place at about thirty high schools, creating the New York Performance Standards Consortium. They did so both to take a stand against the new testing policies and to lay out a rigorous system for performance standards.

"My argument was that we need to create a system—some way of assessing what we're doing," says Cook. She insisted that the consortium could not merely say "no to testing." Indeed, the consortium had no quibble with the state standards. It arranged to review the course offerings of every school in the consortium, including its reading assignments and performance tasks, to ensure that they were aligned with the state's learning standards. In fact, the consortium argued that its pedagogical approach *exceeded* those standards.[135] Thus, the consortium schools explicitly acknowledged that autonomy must be linked to accountability.

The consortium schools rolled out what they asserted was a far better alternative to testing, "an assessment system that included student performance, professional development, curriculum innovation, rubrics for assessment, and a documented success rate for college acceptance and perseverance." Students in consortium schools would complete "performance tasks" in literature, science, math, and social studies, as well as in such noncore subjects as art, music, and even community-service projects. Oversight of the system would be provided by two dozen national experts—an external board known as the Performance Assessment Review Board, which included a who's who of nationally recognized experts, including Meier, Stanford University's Linda Darling-Hammond, and Larry Rosenstock, the founder of the acclaimed High Tech High charter school in San Diego. The board would periodically review the schools' curriculum, assessment, and instruction.

The consortium also would meet annually to review the quality and rigor of student projects and to conduct professional development. (Consortium schools each require somewhat different performance tasks.)

Under Sobol, the so-called Curriculum and Assessment Council issued a report (the Compact for Learning) to the Regents, recommending performance assessments as a path to improving educational standards and as an alternative to standardized tests. Even as the state was getting ready to require that all students pass Regents exams as a prerequisite for graduation, Meier, in her role as director of the Coalition Campus School Project and principal of Central Park East Secondary School, and Stephen Phillips, as superintendent of the alternative high schools, petitioned Sobol for a waiver from state-mandated standardized testing on behalf of all the high schools in the performance-standards consortium.[136]

It was a watershed moment for the progressive coalition and for the small-schools movement in New York City. Even as Sobol was getting ready to back the testing waiver, the state, the city, Meier, and the Annenberg Foundation were nearing agreement on a potentially far-reaching plan aimed at essentially freeing up a tenth of the city's schools from bureaucratic oversight and putting the progressive coalition at the center of the education bureaucracy's strategy for school improvement.

At a White House ceremony in December 1993, Ambassador Walter Annenberg pledged $500 million over five years to help improve the nation's most troubled public school systems. As part of what became known as the Annenberg challenge grants—then the largest single gift ever made to American public schooling—Annenberg invited Meier to apply for one of the grants. The "challenge" was spearheaded by Ted Sizer and Vartan Gregorian, then-president of Brown University and a longtime adviser to Annenberg, who encouraged Meier to put together a politically diverse "coalition of intermediaries" that would serve as a support network for the schools. Meier would bring together four disparate organizations to collaborate on a proposal.[137]

Their plan was to create four interconnected networks of small schools. This network structure would build on the idea broadly shared among the progressive coalition—it was integral to Sizer's coalition, the Center for Collaborative Education; Alvarado and Phillips's alternative high schools; and Nadelstern's International Schools—that small autonomous schools work best if they are provided with support that links them to other small schools, sources of knowledge and professional practice, and funding.

The four organizations Meier brought together were the Center for Collaborative Education; New Visions for Public Schools; the Center for Educational Innovation, then a unit of the conservative Manhattan Institute that was run by Sy Fliegel, Alvarado's former deputy; and ACORN (Association of Community Organizations for Reform Now), a group of community-based organizations.[138]

Together they formed the New York City Networks for School Renewal (NYCNSR), which won a five-year, $25 million, two-to-one matching Annenberg challenge grant. The four coalition partners couldn't have been more different. Indeed, the goal was not to impose one-size-fits all progressivism on all the schools, but to create a network, an *infrastructure,* to support about 150 diverse schools with about 50,000 students, larger than the average urban school district. The project would encompass 5 percent of the city's students and 10 percent of its schools. It was a number that would prove that networks of small, autonomously run public schools could dramatically improve education for low-income children.[139]

Most importantly, both Ramon Cortines, the New York City chancellor who had succeeded Joe Fernandez in 1993, and Tom Sobol had signed on to the plan. For a brief time, it seemed "that all the powers-that-be had signed on to such a serious and visionary effort to innovate on a sufficient scale to really influence policy." Meier was beside herself with "disbelief and joy."[140]

Like the schools Debbie Meier had founded, the idea was both to push decision making and accountability to the level closest to the students and to allow the network to maintain a degree of autonomy from the districts and the bureaucracy of the Department of Education. Years later, Nadelstern would explain that the idea behind this "Learning Zone" was to allow creative ideas and expertise to flourish within its schools, and also to treat them as incubators for seeding new schools. Also, giving the most successful schools a degree of autonomy, he argued, would allow the bureaucracy to focus its energies on schools that needed it most.[141]

Conventional wisdom held that large schools were more economical than small ones, but the progressive coalition had long argued that their schools were cost-effective because virtually all the adults in small schools were teaching and a larger percentage of students were graduating on time. There was little money spent on middle management or ancillary services, such as security. A 1998 New York University study of the new small high schools in New York would confirm that, contrary to expectations, small schools were as cost-effective per graduate as large ones were, in large part because they produced more graduates than large high schools. "Small schools in New York City do cost somewhat more per pupil than larger schools, but when cost *per graduate* is used as the cost/output ratio, a set of small high schools cost among the least per graduate of all New York City high schools."[142]

But the Learning Zone's promise to reshape New York City bureaucracy was in trouble almost from the start, the result of shifting New York politics, a falling-out among the strong-willed leaders of the four network partners, and a feud with the new schools chancellor.

Just weeks after Sobol had agreed to a testing waiver for the performance-standards consortium, which was to take effect at the beginning of the 1995–1996 school year, and in the midst of planning for the Learning Zone, Sobol found himself at loggerheads with New York's new Republican governor George E. Pataki. In February 1995, Sobol abruptly announced his resignation.[143]

Sobol had agreed in principle to a waiver, but it had not yet been drafted or signed. "What the hell are we going to do?" Meier asked Phillips.

"I called Tom, who said 'you won't be able to get it through the bureaucracy,'" once he left, recalls Phillips. So Phillips set to work on the language of the waiver, in which he laid out the coalition's ideas.[144]

Faxes flew between Albany and Phillips's office. The day before Sobol stepped down, in late April 1995, Meier and Phillips got on a train to Albany, and Sobol signed the waiver, even though they had not completed the usual six-month review process. For good measure, Sobol also dictated a note to the legal department affirming his approval of the waiver.[145]

Back in New York City, the Annenberg project was in full swing. But here, too, trouble was brewing. A new Republican mayor, Rudy Giuliani, replaced Cortines, who had followed Fernandez as New York City chancellor. Cortines's successor, Rudolph "Rudy" Crew, was, at best, ambivalent to the "Learning Zone."

In one of his first references to the Annenberg-financed network structure, Crew voiced his reservations about "boutique" schools. Crew also was coming under increasing pressure to impose standards and to produce test results. Whatever the reason, to the leaders of the small-school movement, Crew seemed to "undercut a premise of New York small-school development up to that point—namely the focus on difference, insurgency, autonomy, and creative noncompliance."[146]

Crew, who is now president of CUNY's Medgar Evers College, does not entirely dispute that characterization—though he says it presents an incomplete picture of his views at the time and the pressures he faced as a schools chancellor who had to produce system-wide results quickly, as well as the difficulties of working with some of the progressives—Debbie Meier in particular. "I always liked Eric's basic core model," says Crew, referring to the idea of a network structure, "and the assumptions that undergirded it," of having like-minded schools working together, "less in isolation. I bought it. That was spot on," he adds.

"Where we differed is the pace at which that would happen," says Crew. "What I didn't agree with—that we can just forgo the idea of instructional supervision. The system I was running did not necessarily know how to disaggregate" networks of high-performing schools from the rest of the system.[147]

Crew notes that he saw a chief priority of his job as bringing along the "one-third" of schools that were not performing. To do that, Crew would create the "Chancellor's district," for the city's ailing schools, one in which those poorly performing schools would receive extra resources, much like the de Blasio administration's Renewal Schools. It's noteworthy that, a decade later, Crew described that approach as "dead wrong."[148]

Early in Crew's tenure, tensions were already building among the strong-willed leaders of the four network partners, especially among Beth Lief, who was then the head of New Visions, CEI's Fliegel, and Meier. Fearing that Crew threatened the small-school autonomy that would be key to the Learning Zone, Meier did something that, in retrospect, she "regretted." Meier had recently been named a senior fellow at the Annenberg Institute of School Reform at Brown University and was spending more time in Providence, Rhode Island. She went to Vartan Gregorian and suggested that he, in Annenberg's name, threaten Crew that Annenberg would withdraw its grant if he, Crew, did not make good on the original Learning Zone plan.

Gregorian refused, but the damage was done. The network partners saw Meier's actions as what Fliegel calls a "coup d'état." With that, three of the four network partners decided to fire Doug White, the top administrator of the Annenberg grant in New York City, who was seen as a Meier ally; Meier was furious.[149]

At the same time, the network partners were fighting Crew on another front, as well. Time Warner had ponied up $5 million as a match to the Annenberg grant. Crew insisted that $2 million of the Time Warner donation be allocated to the education department's coffers, resulting in a battle that would sow more discord among the network partners. In the end, Crew and the network came to a compromise. But, says Fliegel, "That was the beginning of some real difficulty."[150]

Then, in 1997, Phillips, the head of New York City's alternative high schools, abruptly resigned. Phillips's supporters said, at the time, that he had been forced out by Crew, who disapproved of giving schools autonomy; his resignation also would mark a new push to increase the size of the city's small schools. Throughout New York, small schools were pressured to add more students—and they did so at the Monroe campus and even at Central Park East Secondary; Julia Richman, by contrast, resisted. The testing waivers also ended, and Central Park East Secondary, for one, did not fight to renew it.[151]

In the aftermath of her unsuccessful "coup," Meier packed her bags and moved to Boston to start Mission Hill School as part of that city's Pilot School project, another effort at creating an independent network of semi-autonomous schools. The Learning Zone, as a system of collaborative networks, now appeared to be effectively dead. Sy Fliegel, however, argued that "the district was not likely to mess with success . . . and that a formal Learning Zone, as opposed to a virtual one, was not necessary."[152]

He was at least partly right. During the next five years, the Learning Zone partners went on to develop new schools that were by many measures—including test scores and graduation and suspension rates—more successful than their traditional counterparts. The schools also enrolled more poor students and students of color than did either the comparison schools or the city's schools as a whole—though fewer English language learners and special-education kids, according to Norm Fruchter.[153]

Early in Bloomberg's tenure, which began in 2002, the Carnegie Corporation (Gregorian was now its president), the Open Society Institute, and the Gates Foundation put up over $51 million to launch new small high schools in New York City; the grant would nearly double the $31 million the three foundations had already invested in New Visions to take over failing high schools and turn them into "condominiums" with dozens of what the funders were calling small New Century High School occupants. The Gates Foundation press release paid homage to New York City's small-schools movement, pointing out that it served "more than 50,000 low-income and minority students," and to Julia Richman in particular, which it called "one of the most successful high school turnaround stories in the country."[154]

Like the earlier progressive-coalition schools, this new generation of small schools also emphasized partnerships with community and civic organizations, collaboration among school educators, and nontraditional scheduling arrangements. In fall 2004, these New Century schools—most of them in the Bronx—counted seventy-five schools serving close to thirteen thousand students. At the time, Eric Nadelstern served as deputy superintendent for New and Small Bronx High Schools.[155]

Nadelstern as well as New Visions schools and Fliegel's CEI—the partners in the old Learning Zone—would continue to take a lead role in the proliferation of autonomous small schools and school networks under the Bloomberg administration, though the effort was no longer animated by the democratic vision of Meier, the progressive coalition, and the goals of the original Annenberg-funded network (see chapter 2).[156]

Meanwhile, the change in educational leadership in Albany would spark a years-long David-versus-Goliath battle waged by Cook against the State of New York in which she sought to force the state to honor the testing waiver that Sobol had granted and that his successor, Richard Mills, was determined to revoke.[157]

A "FIASCO INDEX" FOR STANDARDIZED TESTING

Mills, a "class-A politician" who sensed the direction in which the policy winds were blowing, was ready to jettison the reforms that Sobel had enacted under the Compact for Learning, including the alternative assessments, in order to adopt a statewide approach to assessment. In 1996, Mills rolled out a new high-stakes graduation requirement that all public high school students had to pass five subject-matter Regents exams in order to graduate.[158]

The move was seen by many New Yorkers as a socially progressive policy. New York had been giving standardized tests longer than any other state; high school entrance exams dated back to 1865 and its exit exams to 1878. And the Regents exams themselves were older than both the College Board and the Educational Testing Service.[159]

But, in recent years, what had been a two-track testing regime that had long allowed students to earn either a less-demanding "local diploma" or a more prestigious "Regents diploma," which indicated they were ready for college, had been roiled by questions of educational equity. Many students, especially in poor urban areas, took the less prestigious local option, which entailed less rigorous testing benchmarks.[160]

Requiring all students to take the Regents exams, and to earn a Regents diploma, was seen as a victory for poor inner-city communities and garnered support from many civil rights leaders who saw uniform testing—simplistically, according to Cook—as a question of equity.[161]

At about the same time, there was growing criticism of the quality of the Regents exams. A Curriculum and Assessment Council, which had been convened under Sobol but did not complete its work until the first year of the Mills administration, concluded that the existing state standards and assessments—the Regents exams—did not "encourage higher order thinking and performance skills needed for life and work in the 21st Century" because they relied too heavily on multiple-choice tests that "fail to adequately measure…a student's ability to, for example, write a paper beyond a few paragraphs, plan and conduct a scientific study, undertake a social science research project, find or synthesize information to answer an analytic question or solve problems in real world contexts." The SUNY Board of Trustees passed a resolution calling for the Regents to move toward a performance-based assessment system in which students would have to show samples of their work.[162]

Whatever the merits of his policy, Mills remained undeterred. He even tried to strong arm New York's elite private schools into taking the Regents exams. Of course, the private schools resisted. "Mills decided not to push it; he's going to take on Merryl Tisch?" asks Ann Cook acidly, referring to the then newly appointed member of the Board of Regents, a member of the family that owns Loews Corp. who would soon become chancellor of the Board of Regents. "Where do you think the Regents send their own kids?"[163]

To help decide the question of the standardized-testing waiver his predecessor had granted and that the consortium now wanted to extend, Mills appointed a Blue Ribbon panel. After a year of deliberations, in 2001 the panel finally decided in favor of the consortium, recommending that Mills continue the waivers for three years and conduct a study of the performance standards' validity and reliability. Mills, however, rejected his own panel's recommendations.

Cook, a slight woman with piercing blue eyes and a steely bearing, swung into action, dusting off the arsenal of protest tactics she had perfected during her years as a student and education activist. The terms of the waiver—terms that Phillips had crafted—specified that the state would conduct a five-year review process; without that review, the waiver would remain in effect, according to the terms of the agreement. New York State, Cook concluded, had violated that provision of the waiver.[164]

Cook approached Steve Jacobs at Weil, Gotshal, and Manges, a white-shoe New York City law firm, about suing the education department. Weil, Gotshal agreed to take the case on a pro bono basis. Thus, the twenty-eight schools then part of the consortium sued the commissioner and the state's Department of Education, arguing that in refusing to conduct the mandated study, they had acted in an "arbitrary and capricious" manner.[165]

Weil, Gotshal's legal brief cited the consortium's "impressive" record of high school graduation and college attendance. The brief's statistics pointed to the fact that the high success rate enjoyed by the Julia Richman complex was extant across the vast majority of consortium schools.

> While the drop-out rate in New York City public high schools overall is 19.3% (and often more than 50% in the neighborhoods from which NYPSC students typically come), NYPSC schools in New York City have an average drop-out rate of just 9.9%. While 62.6% of New York City public high school students go on to college overall, NYPSC students in New York City go on to college immediately upon graduation at a rate of 72.5%, and ultimately at a rate of 91%: Significantly, the NYPSC schools have achieved these results with students who come disproportionately from disadvantaged and historically under-performing groups.[166]

The consortium schools were so successful, the lawsuit pointed out, they had recently won a multimillion-dollar grant from the Gates Foundation.

The legal brief also included affidavits from a host of educators, including Tom Sobol, who explained why he had granted the waiver in the first place: "I knew their teachers and administrators were among the most successful educators in the state and that their pedagogical methods and system of assessment did not fit the traditional mold that had failed with many students in the communities served by those schools. . . . These schools were part of the solution to achieving higher standards, not part of the problem. They were involved in the kind of reform that I hoped would lift other schools statewide to higher levels of achievement."[167]

Mills, on the other hand, argued that "portfolios are impossible to standardize and costly to administer."[168]

The consortium lost the lawsuit, but Cook had already taken the protest to the state legislature. On May 7, 2001, one thousand parents and teachers marched to the steps of the state capitol. The thirty or so schools in the consortium eventually won their waiver.

In so doing, the consortium helped escalate a pitched battle between the education commissioner, the Board of Regents, and soon New York City's new mayor Michael Bloomberg, who advocated for tighter "quantitative standards," on the one hand, and parents and state legislators, on the other, who were advocating for alternative assessments.[169]

That battle would be echoed by the opt-out movement, which nearly a decade later galvanized parents throughout New York State.

In 2011, Michael Winerip, the longtime education writer for the *New York Times,* summed up what a decade of high-stakes testing had wrought. He recounted how, in 2003, New York had proudly become one of the first states to have its testing regime approved by the federal government under No Child Left Behind legislation; the Princeton Review rated the testing system number one in the country. New York's alacrity back then presaged its haste several years later, when it became the first state to jump, disastrously, into "common-core testing," before Common Core materials were available for teachers and students and before the official tests were ready.[170]

By the spring of 2003, the testing problems were so severe that New York was forced to ditch its algebra results. At the same time, the state's Council of School Superintendents found the physics scores so unreliable that, for the first time in its 130-year history, it sent a letter to colleges urging them to disregard the test result.

The Princeton Review also had a change of heart: "We're going to have to come up with a fiasco index for a state like New York that messes up a lot of people's lives."[171]

A special panel convened to assess the math fiasco determined that the tests had been done "on the cheap" and were full of "poorly worded" and "confusing" exam questions. The director of state testing resigned.[172]

Meanwhile, scores rose year after year. And, in 2005, New York City reported "amazing" gains, especially on the fourth-grade ELA test, results trumpeted by Mayor Bloomberg in his reelection campaign.

That fall, the National Assessment of Educational Progress, the nation's report card, which is considered to be more rigorous than the state tests, showed a drop in New York City reading scores. But the state insisted that its scores had not been inflated.

In fact, Mills challenged the validity of the NAEP scores.

Then, in 2008, children again had a banner year for scores on the New York State tests. As recently as 2009, the year Mills's fourteen-year tenure as New York's education commissioner ended, Chancellor Joel Klein said of the latest test scores: "This is a big victory for the city . . . we should bask" in the results.

Unfortunately, during all those years of rising state test scores, the performance of New York kids on the SATs had declined. Not until 2010 did Merryl Tisch, by then longtime chancellor of the Board of Regents, admit that the New York test scores had been inflated.[173]

BIG THINGS FOR SMALL SCHOOLS

This is the situation in the public schools of America: The farther you travel from the classroom the greater your financial and professional rewards. Get the license, teach for two or three years. Take courses in administration, supervision, guidance, and with your new certificates you can move to an office with air-conditioning, private toilets, long lunches, secretaries. You won't have to struggle with large groups of pain-in-the-arse kids. Hide out in your office, and you won't even have to see the little buggers.

—*Teacher Man*, Frank McCourt[174]

Even as Cook and the consortium were waging their opening battle for waivers from the state's standardized tests, Tom Vander Ark, executive director of education at the Gates Foundation, was testifying before Congress. Tall, handsome, and goateed, Vander Ark was the Gates Foundation's first director of education, a role in which he would disburse $1.6 billion, mostly to small high schools. Vander Ark was the former superintendent of a large school district in Washington State and was one of a new generation of education leaders considered qualified to run not just a school but an entire district with no prior K–12 classroom experience. Vander Ark became superintendent a year before Paul Vallas, another non-educator, became CEO of the Chicago school system. Vander Ark had come to education leadership via the business world, where he had worked as a consultant for Cap Gemini and as a vice president for seven years at the Pace Membership Warehouse unit of K-Mart.[175]

In recent years, Vander Ark has become an education technology evangelist and a charter-school entrepreneur—though a for-profit charter chain he founded faltered. He also walked away from three nonprofit charter schools for which he failed to raise sufficient funding—but not before one of them had secured space in an existing public school and had begun accepting student applications.[176]

But in March 2001, Vander Ark was in Washington, D.C., explaining to Congress why small schools are such a good idea, why they offer more bang for the buck than big, dysfunctional high schools, and why the Gates Foundation was backing a small-high-school strategy. To illustrate his point, Vander Ark pointed to the remarkable success of the consortium schools, especially the "Julia Richman story."[177]

> Today that center, it's now called the Julia Richman Education Complex, that complex now has four small focused high schools, a K-8 school, a school for autistic children and a day care center. So there's about 1,600 students on that campus. All four of those high schools have graduation rates between 90 and 95 percent and college attendance rates of the same. All of the students in that school share the amenities of a large school, gymnasiums, auditorium, performing arts center, and a library.[178]

For Vander Ark, Julia Richman was ground zero for the small-school strategy that would, for a time, be a key focus of both the Gates Foundation and, ironically—given the new mayor's pro-testing stance—the Bloomberg administration.

Vander Ark had spent a year trolling the halls of Julia Richman. Based at least partly on what he had seen there, Vander Ark reassured the committee, the Gates Foundation had found its blueprint for education reform: "We've developed a two-pronged approach of starting new small high schools and trying to help transform big bad schools into a multiplex of good small schools."

Vander Ark had seen the hodgepodge of schools, the big kids and the little kids, the shared facilities, including a beautifully appointed library that had been renovated with donor funds. No doubt he also saw the riot of artwork that covers almost every wall at Urban Academy—not just drawings, but giant three-dimensional papier-mâché sculptures, photographs, and murals. He was so impressed that when Ann Cook put together the consortium, and when the consortium hammered out the requirements for its common assessments, Vander Ark ponied up over $4.2 million in Gates funding.[179] Thus, it is notable that when Vander Ark offered Cook funding to open more small schools, she turned him down flat. "He never got it," says Cook impatiently. "I used to say to Vander Ark: 'Small is a necessary, but not sufficient'" requirement for quality. "I must have said it to him twenty-five times."

"It's not just about being small," says Cook, explaining where she believes the Gates Foundation and the Bloomberg administration went wrong with their small-school strategy. "They created these great big complexes. They were completely top down. They didn't care about bringing people together to plan."[180]

In other words, Vander Ark and, by extension, the Gates Foundation didn't see the collaboration, the teamwork, the democracy, the *trust* that provided the civic glue that held Julia Richman together and made the complex, and the schools and teachers and students within it, work.

In an interview fifteen years after he left the Gates Foundation, Vander Ark mulls the issue of teacher voice and how important it had been to Julia Richman's success. "It's challenging to create adherence to a set of design features much less do so across a national network for schools and to do it simultaneously with creating an environment that welcomes teacher voice; it's challenging and unusual," says Vander Ark.[181]

Later, he references Eva Moskowitz's Success Academy as an example of a network with "real design coherence" but not much teacher voice.

"Most of the 2,500 schools in managed networks—some may be great places to work, but many of them are going to be low on the teacher voice spectrum. The point is it's difficult to do these things simultaneously—high teacher voice and high fidelity to design attributes. I think they're both important, but it's challenging to do both really well."[182]

Design attributes. What Vander Ark did not seem to recognize is that the role of teachers—their role in planning curriculum, in mentoring students, in sharing decision making in almost every aspect of the management of schools like Urban Academy—*is the key design attribute* of the consortium schools.

Joel Klein, Bloomberg's chancellor, also visited Julia Richman and was impressed with what he saw. But, like Vander Ark, he didn't really get it either.

At some point early in Klein's tenure, Cook made a pitch to the new chancellor for scaling the sort of teacher training that she had perfected at Urban Academy and the Julia Richman Complex, as well as at the Inquiry Demonstration Project, while simultaneously seeding new small schools. "We proposed a plan for starting small schools that involve a teacher-training program," she explains. The idea was to bring in "say ten teachers of color on an apprenticeship line" over the course of two years. (High-quality teachers of color, especially, are considered a vital asset in inner-city schools, where they can serve as important role models for students.) The apprentice teachers would work closely with mentor teachers. Then, one of the mentors would take the newly trained teachers and start a new small school.

"Klein said it was a good idea and sent over Amy McIntosh," recalls Cook.[183]

McIntosh was then Klein's deputy chief of staff, one of an army of "Kleinbergs," the disparaging nickname for the Ivy League–trained MBAs—hers was from Harvard—who worked at Tweed. (One of Bloomberg's first acts as mayor was to move the education department from its relatively remote location at 110 Livingston Street in Brooklyn to the elegant, newly renovated old Courthouse building that had been built by, and named for, the notorious "Boss" Tweed and was located right behind City Hall.) McIntosh had plenty of corporate experience. She had worked as a consultant (at Bain) and in a series of mostly marketing-related jobs at Verizon, American Express, and the Zagat Survey.[184]

But McIntosh also was clearly interested in education reform. Although she had never worked in a school and had no training as an educator, she had spent eight years on the board of Teach for America and was the organization's first board chair.[185] McIntosh whipped out her calculator and did a cost-benefit analysis of Cook's proposal to scale small schools with a rigorous teacher-training program that would nurture existing schools while simultaneously developing the teachers and ecosystems for new schools. She concluded that the plan was too expensive because it involved hiring ten apprentice teachers.[186]

Cook is scathing about that judgment. Yes, they would hire ten teachers. "But I said, 'They're all going to end up in schools,'" explains Cook. "'You are running the teaching fellow's program, where every two to three years the turnover is more than 50 percent. So every few years you are having to start over.'"

Cook was referring to the New York City Teaching Fellows, an alternative certification program launched in 2000 to attract mid-career professionals and retirees to teaching. "We're saying we'll keep the ten people; we have a track record that works," says Cook, referring both to the Inquiry

Demonstration Project and to the training and mentoring that is routine among the progressive-coalition schools. "We know this training works. We're not throwing people into ridiculous situations . . . like TFA."

And, she adds, "it's probably less expensive than teaching fellows.

"She wasn't interested."[187]

Herb Mack sees the decision differently. The chancellor was looking for rapid systemic change, says Mack. What Cook and Mack proposed would be much more incremental, seeding two or three new schools every year. "It would have taken us twenty-five years to finish," says Mack.[188]

Whatever Klein and McIntosh's reason for turning down the project, she went on to work for the New York State education department and later as one of the top lieutenants in the Obama administration's education department. Most recently, she joined the City University of New York as associate vice chancellor.[189]

In the following years, the local, state, and federal governments would increasingly bank on policies that relied on improvement by standardized testing and privatization, and the repudiation of generative grassroots efforts to grow small schools.

As for the Gates Foundation, there were plenty of networks, among them New Visions, that were happy to accept its funding. Indeed, New Visions' longtime president Robert Hughes, who oversaw the New Century High Schools initiative, at the start of the Bloomberg administration, as well as a more recent push to open New Visions charter schools, would join the Gates Foundation, in 2016, as its K–12 director.[190]

The Bloomberg administration embraced the full panoply of education-reform remedies. It worshipped at the altar of standardized tests and all manner of quantitative analyses. The Bloomberg administration also had a penchant for reorganizations that seemed to create more disruption than continuous improvement among its 1.1 million students and 1,800 schools.[191]

Small schools proliferated in New York during the Bloomberg years. Some failed; others were highly successful. Klein's education department harbored a belief in strong school leadership combined with a willingness to get out of the way when things were working well. Thus, the administration created plenty of cracks in which the most entrepreneurial schools and school leaders were able to flourish. Then, in the final years of Klein's chancellorship, one of the myriad reorganizations created a network structure that was inspired by, and revived, the promise of the Learning Zone.

2

TESTING POWER

When Is Disruption Just . . . Disruptive?

Jack Welch, the former CEO of GE, paced the floor of a large, windowless conference room in Brooklyn in fall 2003. Alternately leaning into a table or striding across the makeshift stage, the straight-talking executive, once known as Neutron Jack for his penchant for slashing both businesses and personnel who were not among GE's top ranks, alternated between haranguing and cajoling his audience of sixty or so middle managers.

"Your job is harder than running a company," Welch told them. " 'Cause running a company, you have all the bullets in your gun. Well, you have sort of a water pistol, I guess." He paused. "And it's out of water."

The room erupted in laughter.

"But you've got to find a way to put water in that pistol anyway," Welch continued. "And eventually, put bullets in your gun." [1]

The would-be weapons experts in the room were no ordinary group of middle managers. They were New York City public school principals attending one of the first NYC Leadership Academy classes, a selective leadership training program for high-potential principals that had been established at the start of Mayor Michael Bloomberg's administration.

The Leadership Academy, launched in January 2003, was a cornerstone of the new Bloomberg administration's education-reform strategy for public schools, one focused on breaking up both the central bureaucracy and New York City's large, factory-style high schools. The new administration was determined to replace many large "failing" schools with an armada of smaller entrepreneurial schools. The Leadership Academy's mission was to recruit and train six hundred new entrepreneurial principals by the end of Bloomberg's first term, in 2006, to help run the many new mostly small schools that the new administration hoped to establish.

Like many of the Bloomberg-era reforms, there was much that was controversial about the Leadership Academy. For one thing, the academy boasted the ideal of a public–private partnership and the promise of helping to run both schools and the education bureaucracy more like businesses, a common theme throughout the administration of the new businessman mayor. To help sell the idea to educators, the administration promised to bring together the best of the business sector and educational expertise.

Indeed, the Leadership Academy traced its managerial and intellectual roots back to both the corporate and the education worlds. One key model was the Aspiring Leaders Program, which had been launched twenty years earlier in Tony Alvarado's District Two and had identified and trained District Two educators to become principals and assistant principals. The program was credited with helping to raise the district's citywide ranking in math and reading scores from tenth to second in less than a decade. It was subsequently adopted by other districts.[2]

The Leadership Academy also sought to model itself on GE's vaunted Leadership Development Center in Crotonville, New York, later renamed the John F. Welch Leadership Center. In addition to recruiting Welch as a board member and instructor, the academy enlisted Noel Tichy, who had once served as GE's manager of management education and was one of the primary developers of the Crotonville leadership center. At the time, Tichy also served as the director of the Global Leadership program at the University of Michigan Graduate School of Business.

Culture clash and mistrust, however, characterized the early years of the Leadership Academy, a harbinger of the challenges that the Bloomberg administration would face in reshaping the city's education-reform agenda. If the Leadership Academy had two parents—one drawn from the education world and one from the business world—its business pedigree clearly achieved ascendance early on. Sandra Stein, the former director of the Aspiring Leaders Program at Baruch College, which worked closely with Alvarado's District Two, would serve as the academy's academic dean. (Alvarado, who was then the superintendent of schools for San Diego, also served on the Leadership Academy board.) But it was Robert E. Knowling who would become the Leadership Academy's first CEO. Knowling, a tall African American who had served most recently as the CEO of Covad, a failed telecommunications company, had no education experience at all.[3]

Tensions soon flared, partly because Knowling brought former Covad employees with him to the Leadership Academy and partly because he favored admitting non-educators, including businesspeople and lawyers, to the academy's principal fast track. A number of early graduates also weren't up to the task, ruffling the feathers of teachers especially, many of whom were far more experienced than the new principals; some graduates were demoted or resigned. While a 2009 New York University study found that Leadership Academy principals produced some test-score gains, schools run by Leadership Academy principals had far higher teacher turnover and often received lower grades on city progress reports.[4]

Knowling resigned after just two years and was replaced by Sandra Stein. Henceforth, Leadership Academy training would be conducted primarily by educators, not executives, although the curriculum continued to focus on hands-on practical challenges faced by principals, including, importantly, helping principals navigate the complex budgeting process, as well as instruction in how best to use qualitative and quantitative data.[5]

The Bloomberg administration's focus on prioritizing leadership training for principals was lauded by many education experts, including the pioneers of New York's small-schools movement, who understood the critical connection between leadership and school quality.[6] But the rocky launch of the Leadership Academy—with its corporate CEO and its Jack Welch lectures—signaled a key tension that would characterize the Bloomberg administration's education strategy throughout the businessman mayor's twelve-year administration. In appointing Alvarado to its board and selecting Stein as its *second* CEO, the administration recognized the accomplishments of the District Two leadership-training efforts and the highly successful legacy of the city's small-schools movement. But by appointing as its first CEO a business executive—one with a less-than-sterling track record, no less—the Bloomberg administration signaled its devaluation of even the best educators.

The administration seemed to be saying that, in the Bloomberg education department, mediocre ("or worse") business expertise would trump the best educational know-how.[7] It also discounted the recent history of the city's robust small-schools movement.

Coming just a few years after New York's small-schools renaissance, one built on the foundational value of *trusting educators,* the education department's fundamental *mistrust* of the profession would characterize many of its most divisive policies. It helped to further destabilize a system that was regularly rocked by the serial reorganizations of the Bloomberg years—a strategy that would never allow the education department or the schools within it to assimilate lessons learned or best practices. (Though it's worth noting that if ever there was a bureaucracy that needed shaking up, it was New York City's infamous education department.)

The chief architect of this culture of disruption, if not of outright mistrust, was Bloomberg's choice to head the education department—the combative Joel Klein. No appointment could have more clearly signaled Bloomberg's determination to shake up the education bureaucracy than the appointment of Klein, who had made a name for himself in the Clinton administration's Department of Justice by serving as the lead prosecutor in the government's (unsuccessful) bid to break up Microsoft, and later as chief executive of Bertelsmann Inc., the U.S. arm of the German publishing giant. Klein would become one of the city's longest-serving chancellors, with a unique opportunity to redefine the city's approach to education.

The Bloomberg administration may not have trusted educators, but it focused its principal ire on the bureaucracy, long the bane of progressive educators and business reformers alike. The businessman mayor began by wresting control of the education department from thirty-two community school districts and by replacing the old board of education with a thirteen-member Panel for Educational Policy, a majority of whom were appointed by the mayor.[8]

The two overarching strategies of the administration's education-reform efforts, dubbed Children First, were to break the power of the central bureaucracy and to bet on new small schools as the principal vehicles for improving education; behind the new schools was a grand bargain—one that would have been familiar to the members of the progressive coalition: they would receive increased autonomy, with more power devolved to the principals, most crucially over school budgets, in exchange for greater accountability.

Klein began, during Bloomberg's first term, with an ambitious reorganization, one that broke the city into ten nongeographic regions with six "support centers." The regions were to include both high-needs districts and those with "instructional capacity" that could, presumably, be disseminated among the needier districts. Thus, what had been Tony Alvarado's highly successful District Two, which encompassed much of Manhattan south of 96th Street, was linked to several poorer districts, including those encompassing much of the South Bronx.[9]

But, by Bloomberg's second term, both the regions and the mandated curriculum were jettisoned by Klein, who insisted that his new move represented merely an "evolution" of his strategy. It was, in fact, a radical dismantling of the bureaucracy that was intended, more than ever before, to concentrate control in the hands of principals. Years later, education observers speculated that Klein's serial reorganizations were part of a "Humpty Dumpty strategy" designed to smash the bureaucracy such that it could never be put back together again. If so, Klein miscalculated, for the bureaucracy proved far more resilient than he ever imagined.[10]

By 2006, Klein seemed to be reviving the progressive coalition's New York City Networks for School Renewal, also known as the Learning Zone, which the Annenberg challenge had funded a decade earlier. The first iteration of the new Bloomberg plan hinted at its antecedents and was called the Autonomy Zone. By the time the effort was in full flower, it was called the Empowerment Zone and was led by Eric Nadelstern, one of the original progressive-coalition principals who had been associated with two of the earliest networks—the international schools and New Visions.

The Empowerment Zone began with 331 schools and included many of the original progressive-coalition schools, but soon the network structure would encompass the entire education department. Nadelstern would become Klein's chief deputy and chief schools officer, providing a direct link back to Meier & Co. (see chapter 1). Notes Joseph McDonald, the author of *American School Reform*:

> Although Nadelstern tended publicly to join other officials in describing the Bloomberg–Klein administration as discontinuous in its policymaking—that is, as an initiator of completely novel ideas—he operated privately as a connector. . . . Indeed, Klein's chief accountability officer, James Liebman, told a reporter that Nadelstern "has a vast historical perspective," one focused, he added, on insurgency. "He was long an insurgent voice for kids and for schools, saying, 'We really know how to move kids forward, just give us the responsibility and get out of the way and let us do that.'"[11]

NEW TECH, OLD LESSONS, AND EVERYTHING IN BETWEEN

It was a sultry Sunday afternoon in New York during the dog days of August 2009 when a group of battle-weary, though still idealistic, twenty-somethings gathered for the fifth or sixth time that summer in the ground-floor kitchen of Jackie Pryce-Harvey's brownstone on West 148th Street in Harlem. Pryce-Harvey, a youthful-looking Jamaican immigrant who wore her hair neatly pulled back in a ponytail, was several decades older than her young guests. She had hawked cosmetics after first coming to the United States. She had worked to get a PhD in geography while raising a daughter as a single parent. She had then parlayed that degree into a career in middle-school special education, most of it spent working in a school in the South Bronx. Along the way, she had moonlighted as a private gourmet chef for such elite clients as socialite Brooke Astor and at beachfront estates in the Hamptons on Long Island.[12]

Now, just a few years shy of retirement, Pryce-Harvey was serving up a Sunday brunch of spicy baked salmon, pasta, and spinach for an educational skunk works. Together with her best friend, Chrystina Russell, a blond twenty-eight-year-old from Muskegon, Michigan, Pryce-Harvey was laying the groundwork for a new public middle school in East Harlem that was scheduled to open in the fall.[13]

Pryce-Harvey and Russell were an unlikely buddy team—and not just because of the differences in their ages and backgrounds. Pryce-Harvey, who never missed a day at the gym and brought her healthy lunches to school, in part out of long-cultivated frugality and in part because it was the way she would keep her figure slim well into her sixties, was methodical and disciplined. Deeply practical, she shared the view, common among educated African Americans, that for young, poor, inner-city blacks to succeed, they needed to pass the same hurdles that white kids faced—including standardized tests. A little test prep, she was sure, never hurt anyone.

Russell, by contrast, was charismatic, passionate, and kinetic. Amid alternating periods of binge eating and exotic diets in which her weight yo-yoed ten, twenty, thirty pounds, Russell did hot yoga, rode her bike to work, and ran marathons—several of them. And, when it came to education, there was little about traditional education that she wanted for her kids; poor inner-city minority kids should have access to the best technology because once they learned how to surf the Web and become thoughtful consumers of online information they wouldn't have to worry about not knowing the standard texts written by old white men. Standardized tests, she was sure, were unfair to minority kids and a waste of time. Her kids should interact with professionals on Wall Street, in government, and in the art world and have hands-on learning experiences. They should learn the difference between the English they spoke in East Harlem and the "professional English" of the city's elites, and learn when to use them. And they should have opportunities—lots of them—to develop their leadership skills.

Pryce-Harvey and Russell had met as New York City Teaching Fellows and hit it off immediately. For a time, Russell even moved into Pryce-Harvey's brownstone, which the older teacher maintained as a sort of teacher's dormitory, renting out rooms to young women new to the profession—that is, before she turned it into a successful bed and breakfast. The two women were part of a generation of educators who had developed their careers in the wake of the small-school movement and were eager to participate in the Bloomberg administration's plan to open hundreds of new schools. Pryce-Harvey was willing to help midwife the project and to serve as the unofficial assistant principal—at least until she completed the principal's certification she would soon start working on. But, already in her mid-fifties, Pryce-Harvey was sure she was not prepared to run the show. Instead, she encouraged Russell to take the lead at the school they had decided to call Global Technology Preparatory—one that would provide a laptop for every child.

With just four years of teaching experience, Russell had enrolled in the Principals Leadership Academy in 2007. Before she had completed the yearlong program, Russell and Pryce-Harvey began planning their school.

And so it was that a half dozen young teachers gathered around Pryce-Harvey's kitchen table that summer afternoon in 2009. MacBooks precariously balanced on their knees and spreadsheets scattered amid their plates, the teachers tucked into their brunch and plotted strategy for the new school. The group included Jhonary Bridgemohan; half-Mexican, half-Guyanese, Bridge, as she is known to her colleagues, had once dreamed of becoming a mortician. Now she would be teaching English at Global Tech. David Baiz, who feared he would be unfairly forced out of the South Bronx school where he was then teaching, would be the lead math teacher and unofficial tech guru for the technology-oriented school. Pryce-Harvey had mentored both Baiz and Bridgemohan at P.S./M.S. 4 in the South Bronx, which all three described as utterly dysfunctional.[14]

Becky Rotelli was also at the brunch, although she wouldn't be hired until the following year. And there was Omar, a tall, broad-shouldered African American with a shaved head who was still working on his bachelor's degree. An old friend of Pryce-Harvey's, Omar had wrestled with his own demons and had worked with disadvantaged boys and girls in programs like the Boys Club. Certain that the black and brown boys in their school would need good male role models, Russell was determined to maneuver around Department of Education and union rules, which should have made it difficult to hire someone without a bachelor's degree, and bring Omar in as a counselor.[15]

Like the earlier generation of New York's small-school entrepreneurs, one of Russell's greatest gifts was the art of creative noncompliance.

Huddled in Pryce-Harvey's kitchen that afternoon, the Global Tech team plotted the school's mission and start-up challenges, which were formidable. Global Tech would be a one-to-one laptop school; much of the school's technology funding would come via donations to the Fund for Public Schools, which had been turned into a fund-raising juggernaut during the Bloomberg administration, building on the deep-pocketed connections of both the mayor and Caroline Kennedy, the fund's CEO.

The Global Tech team wrestled with a host of questions: would there be enough money to pay for software and maintenance and training for teachers like Pryce-Harvey who had only recently gotten an email account and were lost when it came to technology? Should students be allowed to take their laptops home, or would they be kept at school? And where? And should the school abide by the Bloomberg administration's strict, controversial, and oft-violated no-cell-phone policy? (In the end, Global Tech deferred to parents, who feared that carrying expensive laptops might make their children the targets of local criminals. The school also defied the Bloomberg administration by allowing kids to bring their phones to school.)[16]

Global Tech's plans were in many ways audacious. There was Russell's youth and relative inexperience. Russell and Pryce-Harvey also were planning to circumvent the education department's hiring process. Global Tech would be moving into the second-floor space of a former charter school that had been part of the Success Academy Charter Schools chain, on East 120th Street, which meant that most rooms had smartboards and other equipment that traditional public schools lacked. (A longtime public K–8 school, P.S. 7, occupied the rest of the building.) But, while Success Academy's CEO, Eva Moskowitz, had agreed to leave the smartboards behind, she refused to allow Russell and Pryce-Harvey's team access to the space before the start of the school year. Recruiting families was already an enormous challenge because Russell had gotten a green light for her school *after* the official spring enrollment period was over, and recruiting without an opportunity to show families the school would make it all the more difficult. So Russell and Pryce-Harvey posted flyers around Harlem and visited the local McDonald's and Dunkin' Donuts to recruit families; they were still shaking the bushes for students in late August, just days before the school was scheduled to open.[17]

Global Tech also would have to comply with stricter hiring rules. A key purpose of the Sunday brunches had been to develop a hiring strategy for Global Tech—one that would withstand the official hiring process, which gave both representatives of the union and education department a say in who was to be hired at the school. The teachers sitting around Pryce-Harvey's kitchen table discussed strategy, including the questions that Russell would ask each prospective candidate, as well as how they, individually, would answer her questions and present their own credentials. Thus, Russell would sit through the hiring meetings, grilling candidates she had already decided to hire, acting as though she were seeing them for the first time. While the union and education-department representatives questioned some of Russell's choices—including Pryce-Harvey—in the end she got everyone she wanted. Like the alternative schools of the 1970s and 1980s, Russell and her colleagues were planning to maneuver the system to get the teachers she and her start-up team had selected. Hiring, like most other major decisions at the school, would be collaboratively determined and would include teachers and, eventually, even kids, who turned out to be an enormous asset when it came to hiring. "We prepped the students; we set up scenarios," recalls Pryce-Harvey. "They knew what to ask."[18]

"If I came to school late every day, what would you do to me?" one child might ask.[19]

In that scenario, Global Tech was looking for a candidate who knew to ask kids the right questions: "Why do you come late? Do you have to drop off your baby brother? Do you wake up late? Does your mom go to work before you wake up? Does she know you're getting to school late?"[20]

Depending on the answers, the teacher would know whether to discipline the child or have a conversation with the parent.

The kids also vied for the chance to act out, "losing it" to see how the candidates would react.

Equally important, the kids got to vote on each candidate. "If they say no, we have to come up with a really compelling reason why we'll overrule the kids," says Pryce-Harvey. "They have a sixth sense. They'll tell you, 'We're OK with her, but other kids will walk all over her.'"[21]

Pryce-Harvey recalls at least one case in which the school overruled the kids to hire a smart former Peace Corp volunteer with great lesson plans. She turned out not to be a good fit for the school.

The Sunday brunch was indicative of a key understanding that would have been familiar to members of the quiet revolution and Global Tech's New York City predecessors in the progressive coalition: the school would be a collaborative venture in which teachers would be vital members of the team with an important voice in virtually all decision making. In the years to come, Russell would be scrupulous about finding money—so-called per-session payments—to compensate for work that went beyond the teacher's official contractual obligations; when there wasn't money available, she would find ways to reward teachers by giving them extra time off—a welcome benefit for a mostly young staff that relished travel. But there was no question that teaching at Global Tech would not begin at 8:45 a.m. when the bell rang, nor end at 3:30 p.m. when the official Department of Education day was over. While the millennials gathered at Pryce-Harvey's table never talked about Meier or Sizer and knew little about the struggles of the progressive coalition, they too were on a mission to improve education for the mostly black and Latino kids in East Harlem. Deeply skeptical about charter schools, which had come to educate 25 percent of the kids in Harlem, creating formidable challenges for neighboring public schools like Global Tech, they were committed to the ragtag bunch of students that Russell and Pryce-Harvey had been able to recruit to their new universal Title One school—a reference to a provision of the Elementary and Secondary Education Act, which provides financial assistance to schools with high percentages of children from low-income families—in the few short weeks before classes were to begin in September.

Bloomberg and Klein saw the question of teacher quality largely in binary terms—good teachers were the ones you wanted to hire, while bad teachers could be identified and eliminated. But the Global Tech team knew it was not so simple. David Baiz, for example, had found himself in the crosshairs of M.S. 4 administrators in the Bronx; he knew that, with time, they would find a way to force him out. But where his bosses saw a problem, Pryce-Harvey had seen a gifted, if somewhat green, young teacher who, with the proper nurturing and encouragement, could become an outstanding educator.

To Russell and Pryce-Harvey, the key wasn't so much finding "great" teachers as it was about building a team of like-minded educators who agreed on their mission; who could work and grow together; who could inspire the young, often-troubled students in their charge, as well as their fractured families; and, yes, who were—or could become—good teachers. In this, they fully shared the democratic principles and attitudes of the progressive coalition.

Equally important, while Russell was indeed young, she had extraordinary savvy for working the education system. Within the course of less than five years, she had steered hundreds of thousands of dollars in private funding from organizations like GE and Cisco to Global Tech and cultivated relationships with executives from Cisco, Apple, and CA Technologies, a software company. She had forged relationships with several outside organizations, including Citizen Schools, a Boston-based nonprofit that partners with public schools. Borrowing from charter schools, which often keep kids in school until 5 or 6 p.m., instead of the 3 or 4 p.m. dismissal more typical of public schools, Citizen Schools would create an extended-day program that Global Tech kids were required to attend until the late afternoon, and that provided rich educational opportunities, internships, and exposure to outside experts. And Russell had developed a knack for publicity that won the school, and one of its students, a cameo appearance at the White House.

Although Russell, in particular, harbored a number of educational ideas that were in congruence with the progressive coalition, Global Tech was no middle-school replica of Central Park East or Urban Academy. Where Debbie Meier and her followers had been rebellious "lefty hippies," Russell and

Pryce-Harvey saw themselves as part of a new cadre of twenty-first-century social entrepreneurs. While Meier & Co. emphasized hands-on learning, at Global Tech, what Tom Vander Ark would call the school's "design attribute" was unabashedly technological. Global Tech students would submit to standardized tests and attended a months-long Saturday Academy devoted to test prep. But when the testing period was over in April, during the final two months of the spring semester, most of the Global Tech curriculum would morph into a progressive focus on intensive, challenge-based projects. The projects included ones on the school-to-prison pipeline; a fashion unit in which students designed and sewed their own clothes; a course on wellness in which students studied the basics of nutrition and the benefits of exercise and developed their own wellness plans; and an ambitious fund-raising unit in which students planned every aspect of a Global Tech fund-raiser, from negotiating with a local restaurant and planning budgets to writing invitations and fund-raising letters. When Global Tech eventually hired a guidance counselor, it chose a woman who believed in the soft power of restorative justice, which aims to rehabilitate offenders via reconciliation with the community and/or victims; at the same time, the school explicitly borrowed from successful public and charter schools by creating the extended-day program as well as the modified paycheck discipline practices. (The latter is most associated with charter schools—though it was developed by Rafe Esquith, a public school teacher—and is most commonly used today as a discipline-cum-accounting system for allocating rewards or punishments.)

By the time Russell and Pryce-Harvey were ready to launch their school, the Bloomberg administration had been in office for nearly two terms and the city schools had experienced a dizzying number of reorganizations and policy changes.

In the coming years, Global Tech would come to be hailed as one of the more successful small schools launched during the Bloomberg years. Russell and Pryce-Harvey made some mistakes with some new hires whom they coaxed out of the school. One of Global Tech's counselors, for example, was eventually let go after a series of personal and professional lapses. Nor did the school have the curricular vision or the disciplined professional development practices of the most experienced members of the progressive coalition. But Global Tech would become home to a remarkably cohesive and motivated team of educators, including some who had been written off elsewhere as failures. (One staffer who became a valued member of the Global Tech team had languished for two years in the so-called Absent

Teacher Reserve, the notorious "rubber room.") More than anything else, Global Tech would demonstrate that a collaborative, improvement-oriented team of teachers working in an environment that fostered trust among both the staff and the students could make a big difference for poor minority kids via a range of both soft and hard measures.

Global Tech thrived on the promise of the Bloomberg reforms, on the benefits of granting principals increased autonomy over both their staffs and their budgets. But, in many ways, Global Tech was an outlier, the successful exponent of a scattershot strategy for launching small schools. The strategy's biggest Achilles' heel: it was unclear that it had either the infrastructure or the political capital to sustain the experiment or to help it grow once Bloomberg was out of office. Locked into a business-oriented mindset that consistently valued corporate experience over educational expertise, the Bloomberg administration failed to leverage the strengths of the progressive coalition and its educators, with whom, incongruously, it shared so much in common. The Bloomberg administration fostered neither the trust nor the relationships with the deep bench of respected educators who might have prolonged the life of the reforms.

THE PROMISE, AND PERILS, OF EDUCATION TECHNOLOGY

Somewhat perversely, Global Tech exemplified both the Bloomberg administration's roots in New York City's small-school movement and its refusal to recognize that intellectual debt. Implicitly acknowledging a core tenet of the progressive coalition—that small schools function best when they are part of a like-minded network of support—Global Tech was launched, in the fall of 2009, as a charter member of the so-called Innovation Zone, or iZone. The iZone aimed to address the disconnect between students' wired lives and the traditional chalk-and-blackboard classroom that, according to some education-technology experts, makes kids today less receptive to school. It also aimed to connect like-minded schools with each other as well as with technology partners who could help them innovate.[22]

But the iZone also was seen as wholly new and disruptive. As such, it failed to build on the legacy of the city's seasoned small schools.

The iZone began in the 2009–2010 school year with ten pilot schools. A few of the schools, including Global Tech, showed great promise. But within a few years, the majority of the pilot schools had left the iZone.

With those "failures," the education department wrote the pilot year out of its history books and began dating the launch of the iZone to the following 2010–2011 school year, when it expanded to eighty-one schools. By the end of the Bloomberg administration, the iZone initiative encompassed 250 schools, close to 15 percent of what grew to be more than 1,700 schools.[23]

The iZone—indeed, the entire Bloomberg reform apparatus—was, as one longtime insider put it, like the Hudson River, "constantly flowing; always changing." Dip your toe in at different points, and it would never be the same river. Nor would anyone ever capture its movements or fully understand its currents. Replication was out of the question.[24]

If the iZone was a river, its major source was Cisco Systems, a giant electronic networking company based in San Jose, California, and one of several key corporate partners that worked with Klein's education department. The iZone drew inspiration directly from a 2008 Cisco white paper, "Equipping Every Learner for the 21st Century," which argued that a changing and global workforce puts a premium on diverse skills and knowledge, including cross-cultural insight, multilingualism, problem solving, decision making, and creative and critical thinking. Company and district leaders explicitly spoke of each other as "thought partners."

The relationship between Cisco and the education department was forged in 2008 when the tech giant helped launch the iSchool, a small new selective high school in Soho at Sixth Avenue, just north of Broome Street, that emphasized blended learning—an approach that uses both in-person instruction by teachers and computer-assisted learning. During its first two years of operation, the school received at least $2 million in cash and in-kind grants, most of it from Cisco and Mortimer Zuckerman, owner of *U.S. News & World Report* and the *Daily News*.[25]

Much about this hundred-student school, with its relatively small suite of rooms on the fifth floor of an old Chelsea school building, is reminiscent of the progressive coalition's Urban Academy (see chapter 1). There's the interracial mix of students milling about in the hallways outside classrooms and around tables in a welcoming common room. The school also developed a team-taught "problem-based" curriculum with an emphasis on hands-on learning and using technology to reach beyond New York City. The iSchool's challenge-based modules—nine-week projects—cross disciplines and promote collaboration among students, who work in teams as well as with outsiders. For example, for the National September 11 Memorial and Museum at Ground Zero, students collaborated with museum officials and, via videoconference, interviewed young people worldwide about their views of the terrorist attacks. The course, called "Voices and Memory," was designed to develop traditional reading and writing skills; to incorporate some history, literature, and psychology; as well as to foster "twenty-first-century" abilities such as group-based problem solving and analysis.[26]

Cisco provided both technical advice and funding. Just a year after launching the school and touting the iSchool's standout results, including both attendance and Regents pass rates of over 90 percent, Cisco worked with the education department to "replicate" the iSchool model with what it was then calling the NYC Innovation Zone.[27]

Cisco continued to fund the iZone via the New York Fund for Public Schools and provided a range of support, including leadership development via "vision-setting workshops," educational consultants, and classroom technology. Teachers came to the Cisco offices near Penn Station in Manhattan for several all-day training sessions on a variety of classroom technologies—including teleconferencing with outside experts, using PowerPoints, and shooting video. Gene Longo, a manager with Cisco's Networking Academy, one of the company's corporate-responsibility programs, who oversaw Cisco's nonprofit initiatives with the education department, became a regular and trusted visitor at both Global Tech and the iSchool.

Cisco also sought to learn from the schools, sending teams of engineers into their classrooms to see how teachers and students were using digital technology. In the spring of 2010, a team of engineers spent the morning at the iSchool and then hopped a cab up to Global Tech, where they peppered teachers with questions during the lunch hour.[28]

To be sure, there was a commercial motive—one that ultimately raised questions about the close ties between the company and the education department's procurement practices. Cisco was developing a full-scale technology portal for commercial sale to other school systems that included a number of features designed to give students, parents, and educators better access to coursework and collaborative learning opportunities. As part of its arrangement with the education department, beginning in the fall of 2010 Cisco planned to give iZone schools free access to a much-anticipated prototype portal it was developing for commercial use. Eventually, Cisco was expected to be a leading candidate for developing an ambitious expanded portal—or "virtual learning environment"—for an education department bid.[29]

In August 2010, teachers voluntarily cut short their summer vacations to attend a Cisco training session. But in lieu of the high-tech practical sessions that they had gotten used to when attending at Cisco offices, they arrived to what was described by many as uninspiring old-school presentations given by education department officials. One iZone insider wondered aloud, "How many changes can the iZone sustain before it loses its credibility?"

The anticipated portal was replaced by a much more limited suite of off-the-shelf software. The reasons for the shift were never explained. According to iZone insiders, when work on the portal fell behind schedule during the summer of 2010, the education department decided to piece together an in-house version and took over the professional training that Cisco had been conducting. But iZone principals and teachers, who were counting on working with Cisco, were disappointed. A few insiders who had gotten a glimpse of the portal thought it was promising.[30]

What combination of political, organizational, or procurement issues derailed the Cisco portal may never be known. Had Cisco's close ties to the education department suggested a conflict of interest? Was the portal really behind schedule? At the time, Cisco spokeswoman Robyn Jenkins-Blum responded to questions about the episode with an email, insisting that "Cisco continues to support the New York City DOE," including "investment" in the iZone. Meanwhile, Arthur VanderVeen, chief of innovation research and development at the education department, denied the iZone project had hit any stumbling blocks at all.[31]

Not long after the portal episode, Cisco's Longo was transferred to a new job and was never replaced. At about the same time, Julian Cohen, the education department's executive director of school innovation, who had been the face of the iZone initiative for its first two years, a respected presence at both the iSchool and Global Tech, and a welcome buffer from department politics, was moved to a different job.[32]

Suddenly, schools like Global Tech, which were deeply invested in the iZone partnership, found themselves without an anchor.

From the beginning, the iZone had been touted as a cutting-edge twenty-first-century education network. It was "completely new." It was "innovative." It was "futuristic." Schools like iSchool would use technology "to rethink high school for the 21st Century," indeed, to "rethink every assumption" about public education. And they would do so in large part by "really engaging with the big ideas in our society," explained Alisa Berger, co-founder of iSchool, in a Cisco-sponsored video about the school.[33]

The iZone engaged in freewheeling technological experimentation. There was the Cisco portal that was intended to transform the education department itself. There were ambitious distance-learning experiments like iSchool's virtual geometry class and Global Tech's foreign-language software, which aimed to let a single teacher help students learn a wide range of languages, including German and Mandarin. Joel Klein even dreamed of beaming Richard Feynman, the Nobel laureate, into New York City classrooms via video conferencing to teach physics.

There was, perhaps most ambitiously of all, the School of One experiment to transform math education, hailed breathlessly by *Time* magazine as one of the fifty best inventions of 2009. The School of One, which was piloted at three schools in New York City, featured a computer algorithm that served as a digital sorting hat (think Hogwarts) that produced, each day, a personalized "playlist" for every student for both what they would be learning and by what "modality"—live teacher, virtual teacher, or perhaps some other technology. The algorithm also sorted the flesh-and-blood teachers, creating their schedules and assigning them students every day. It was nothing less than the education department's most audacious attempt to "teacher proof" education.[34]

One veteran teacher at I.S. 228 in the Gravesend section of Brooklyn, where School of One was being piloted, explained why the experiment was "a win win win" for everybody. "It's much better for the teachers," he said. "The computer does everything. It generates the lessons, the tests, and it grades the tests. Plus, most of the time the computer is giving the instruction. From the teacher's point of view there's no negative to it. Kids like it 'cause it's fancy. And from the administration's point of view, it's great. They get to save on salaries."

Of course, as a veteran teacher, he was not likely to lose his job.[35]

School of One was planning to expand to fifty schools in New York City within three years. That never happened and two of the original pilot schools pulled out of the experiment. It continues to operate in I.S. 228 and two new New York City schools. Meanwhile, School of One was rebranded Teach to One and expanded to twelve other states.[36]

Many of the most ambitious technology efforts, like the Cisco portal, didn't pan out. Global Tech eventually abandoned its experiments with the online language portal. Nobel laureates didn't become virtual teachers. And it was just two years after its veneration by *Time* magazine that two of the original three School of One schools pulled out of the program. Says Eric Nadelstern, summing up the shortcomings of Klein's love affair with technology: "Joel misses the essence of teacher–student interactions. Virtual communities don't raise children, people do."[37]

Some of the iZone schools, including Global Tech and the iSchool, understood intuitively that technology had to be used in the service of teachers and students. In fact, the iZone included experimentation with school designs and so-called seat-time waivers that were not all necessarily technology oriented. For example, West Side Collaborative, which had been founded during the heyday of the Learning Zone and the Annenberg challenge and was an early one-to-one laptop school, also pioneered block scheduling, interdisciplinary classes, and so-called personal learning modules. The latter mirrored the progressive coalition's performance-based standards, tailored to the literacy needs of middle-school students.[38]

Kids love technology, but it was often the small-bore efforts, like getting kids to videotape each other's oral presentations and creating PowerPoints, that were often the most useful. Similarly, the nontechnological innovations, including the real-life projects at the root of iSchool's and West Side's curriculums, as well as the challenge-based curriculum that becomes the focus at Global Tech during the final two months of the spring semester, *after* the annual standardized-testing season ends in April, made the biggest difference.

While Meier & Co. might have recoiled from the iZone's vision of technology-enabled learning and the ascendency of business thinking among many of its schools, it turns out that the most lasting innovations of the iZone—the collaboration, the interdisciplinary project teams taught in extended time blocks, the efforts to reach beyond the walls of the classroom—weren't actually that innovative at all. They were reminiscent of the progressive coalition's long-held commitment to finding better ways to engage both students and teachers and to building trust among teachers and administrators, the schools, their students, and the larger community. Thus, the Bloomberg administration's failure to tap into that history until it was almost too late proved to be one of its costliest failures.

In September 2011, Josniel Martinez, a Global Tech seventh grader, stood at a lectern at the White House in Washington, D.C., getting ready to introduce U.S. Education Secretary Arne Duncan at the launch of Digital Promise, a national center founded to spur development of breakthrough education technologies. Facing more than a hundred dignitaries, the eleven-year-old Dominican émigré explained how, during the sixth grade, his first year at Global Tech, he had been failing just about every class he took, until the school put together "a whole team to help" him. The team, he explained, included teachers, who aided him with his "nightmarish" organization skills and checked his backpack every day for the pencils, assignment sheets, and other items he needed to succeed in class; Computers for Youth, one of several Global Tech "partners" that provided a home computer for each child and, in Josniel's case, arranged for extra software; and his mother, who insisted he work on the software programs three times a week and cut back on TV. "Now look at me. In ten years, Secretary Duncan," he concluded, "I'm going to college . . . and maybe one day, you'll be working for me."[39]

Tellingly, the official blog of the U.S. Department of Education emphasized the role of digital technology, not the work of teachers, in helping Martinez succeed.[40]

Martinez's opening remarks were written with the help of one of the president's speechwriters. But toward the end of his talk, Martinez improvised. Where the speechwriter had cut out a long string of acknowledgments—to Martinez's mom, to his teachers, to his friends, to Computers for Youth—Martinez reinserted them.[41]

"They've cut out all my thank-yous!" he complained to Russell when he saw the final remarks a few days before his White House appearance. "What do you think Barack would do?" Russell asked him.

"I think he would say his thank-yous if he wanted to," Martinez responded.

"I think you're right," Russell replied.

"The interesting thing is, if you look at the original speech, he deviates pretty far," she remarked later, recalling the speech.[42]

So, with the encouragement of his principal, Martinez overruled the presidential speechwriter and reinserted his thank-yous, ad-libbing his concluding statements at the White House. At Global Tech, as among the schools of the progressive coalition, children are taught to think for themselves and to question the decisions of even the highest authorities. For kids, especially poor minority kids, a key part of their education was to develop a moral compass, a sense of empowerment, and the ability to stand up for their beliefs.

Martinez's star turn at the White House was indicative of Russell's political savvy. But it was also an indicator of how the school's approach has helped both kids and adults excel who had, or would likely have, failed elsewhere.

THE CHARTER BOOM AND THE TEST SCORE ARMS RACE

A corollary to new public schools like Global Tech is the proliferation of New York City's charter sector. The Bloomberg administration opened close to 150 new charter schools over the course of the mayor's three terms, up from the seventeen in operation when he took office. The majority are strict, no-excuses institutions. And, in a sharp departure from the concept of community-led charter schools first conceived by Albert Shanker, the legendary leader of the teachers union, most are led by local or national chains. (Indeed, while Debbie Meier had seen "choice" as a way to stem white flight from public schools, create opportunities for new pedagogical ideas, and increase the odds of desegregation, she also warned that charters might "become a means of transferring public dollars to private schools.")[43]

For scores of parents, the charter schools were a boon. Monique Bryan, for example, is the model of an informed and involved charter-school parent. A resident of West Harlem, which has become a magnet for charter-management organizations, Bryan tried her share of schools and settled on KIPP Infinity, perhaps the most highly rated KIPP school in New York City.

Bryan works as a crossing guard just five minutes from the school. The cheerful home in the Riverside Park Community apartments that she shares with her four children and their father is decorated with spotless modern chrome-and-white furniture. It is located in a tower that looms over the playground KIPP shares with three other schools in the Tolberg Educational Complex on West 133rd Street. "Me and Mr. Negron have developed a good relationship; Ms. Holley knows me too because I'm very involved," says Bryan, referring to KIPP Infinity's founding principal and his first successor. "They call me and I'm there. I do pop-up visits for my son to make sure he's on the right track.[44]

"Last year he had a horrible year; they called me almost every day, can you imagine?" she said, in 2012, of her oldest child, Daizon, and, since she worked nearby, she'd run right over. "He was in trouble every day, seemed like. He was just rebellious. He had about four in-school suspensions. But this year he's having a good year."[45]

Bryan said she planned to enroll each of her children in a KIPP school. The charter schools have definitely changed the family's outlook; for example, each of the Bryan children gets a bedtime story every night, an idea the couple picked up from Success Academy, the first charter school Daizon attended.[46]

Bryan tried two other schools before she finally settled on KIPP. The Success Academy school had "rubbed [her] the wrong way" when, among other things, it refused to allow Daizon, who has asthma, to take his asthma pump to the playground. Bryan worried that leaving the pump in his second-floor classroom was an unnecessary risk. When Bryan confronted school administrators, they told her they were educated professionals and knew how to administer the pump when needed.[47]

She thought the school was dismissive of her concerns. "The majority of parents are low income, they turned their noses up at us," Bryan says. She pulled Daizon out and sent him to a local public school, P.S. 161, which she said was "a really good school" but didn't "challenge" him enough. So, by the fourth grade, Bryan had enrolled Daizon at KIPP Infinity.[48]

Bloomberg's focus on charters has had two significant strategic impacts.

First, it helped to both shape the national narrative of charter-school success and further cement a standardized test–score definition of school quality. It also highlighted a question emerging in many communities with a preponderance of charter schools: what is the tipping point at which the charter sector gets so large that, by skimming off the most engaged parents, it turns nearby public schools into dumping schools for the most troubled kids? And what is the cost to those children and to society of essentially writing off the bottom 20 to 30 percent of poor children?

Harlem, in particular, has become the center of an unintentional education experiment—one that has been replicated in neighborhoods and cities around the country. During the Bloomberg years, when close to a quarter of students in the area were enrolled in charter schools, segregation increased, as did sizable across-the-board demographic disparities among the students who attended each type of school. An analysis of Bloomberg-era education department data revealed that public open-enrollment elementary and middle schools have double—and several have triple—the proportion of special-needs kids of nearby charter schools. The children in New York's traditional public schools are much poorer than their counterparts in charter schools. And public schools have far higher numbers of English-language learners.[49]

This pattern mirrors national trends. "Today, charters are actually more economically and racially segregated than traditional public schools," write Richard D. Kahlenberg and Halley Potter in *A Smarter Charter.* A 2012 report from the U.S. Government Accounting Office also found that charter schools have far fewer special-needs students—8 percent—versus public schools, which have 11 percent.[50]

To many New York members of the progressive coalition, the Bloomberg administration had "abdicate[d] all responsibility for educating high poverty kids by passing that over to charter schools," even though many of its members had flourished, even started new schools, during the Bloomberg years.[51]

In backing charter schools, Bloomberg and other advocates pointed to one clear benefit: charters, it was widely accepted, would increase standardized test scores. However, years of studies showed little difference between the test-score performance of students in charter schools and those in public schools. In 2015, new research by Stanford University's Center for Research on Education Outcomes (CREDO) seemed to prove that students who attended urban charter schools were outperforming public school students on tests. Among the high-scoring districts were New Orleans and New York City. The flaws in CREDO's data, it turned out, were numerous, arcane, and impactful.[52]

Yet in a number of states, including Ohio, public schools outperformed charters on the NAEP, known as the nation's report card. A 2013 analysis of NAEP scores undertaken at Arizona State University found that the difference between publics and charters nationwide was "really no different than the flip of a coin," with public schools outperforming charter schools on the NAEP test in half the states, and charter schools outperforming publics in the other half.[53]

Meanwhile, in New York City, the battle over charter schools served to obscure the very real gains of the progressive coalition, which rejected the primacy of standardized tests and measured achievement across a much broader range of indicators, including complex and often creatively developed real-world research projects, high school persistence and graduation, and college enrollment. Despite the success of many new Bloomberg-era small schools and the ability of the older progressive schools to thrive during the Bloomberg years, the drumbeat for charters and privatization helped to define "success" narrowly and reductively.

The administration had virtually written earlier school reforms out of New York's education-reform narrative—in particular those of the progressive coalition. At the same time, schools were increasingly being whipsawed by a growing focus on standardized tests' being used to measure both student and teacher performance, on the one hand, and, on the other, constantly changing tests and curricula that year after year sought to mitigate the mistakes of earlier generations of half-baked assessments, steadily eroding confidence in them all.

This cramped, test-based definition of schooling has been exemplified by New York City's most successful, and controversial, home-grown charter-management organization (CMO), Success Academy Charter Schools. The local CMO had grown in size and influence based on its ability to deliver sky-high test scores. Yet the network is only graduating its first class of seniors in the spring of 2018; and that first graduating class will have only seventeen students, down from a first-grade cohort of seventy-three. Thus, Success Academy's storied reputation has grown despite a complete lack of evidence for the most important indicators of a school's (or network's) success—graduation rates and success in college. What's worse, the tiny graduating class—and high attrition rate—illustrates why there can be no "apples-to-apples" comparison between open-admission public schools, which must take all students, and Success Academy, which has long been associated with "creaming"—for example, by pushing out all but the best test takers—and not "backfilling" past the fourth grade.[54]

Indeed, Success Academy has been dogged by its Dickensian reputation—including a penchant for systematically screening out the least desirable students and their families. In 2016, thirty-two parents sued the CMO for discriminating against special-needs children. Accusations of "creaming" gained traction when one Success Academy principal admitted to keeping a "got to go" list of students he wanted to cut from the rolls. No sooner had Eva Moskowitz, Success's combative founder, insisted that the list was an anomaly when a secretly recorded video showed the harsh discipline—including verbal abuse and humiliation—meted out to a first grader by a "model" Success teacher. The CMO also has battled government oversight—with some success—and has pressed charter personnel to resist questioning by outsiders, including government officials.[55]

Some of New York City's staunchest charter supporters began to sour on Moskowitz.[56] "I'm no fan of Eva Moskowitz," said Sy Fliegel. "I don't like the way they get rid of kids. That is a charge that has been made too often now, and I think it's true."[57]

Neither Success Academy's questionable education policies nor the bad publicity has deterred the businessmen and hedge-fund financiers who pour millions into the CMO every year. By contrast, one of the city's first charters, a Latino-run school called Amber, considered itself lucky when it raised a record $45,000 at its fifteenth anniversary party in 2015.[58]

Success Academy has maintained almost Kremlin-like secrecy, admitting few visitors. When it does organize tours, they are short, controlled visits mostly for fellow charter-school educators and potential funders. During one recent visit, a longtime New York educator said that she was "really impressed" with what she saw.[59]

The school had "extraordinarily strong systems and structures," said the educator, and, most surprisingly, "few worksheets" and a "strong student voice." Classrooms were "well provisioned, teachers seemed experienced, and the texts assigned to students were relatively sophisticated." However, the Success visitor also noted a high degree of regimentation—not a single uniform was out of order, and there were none of the "fidgets" common among small children, especially those with special needs.[60]

In part because of the secrecy and the distrust that have enveloped the CMO, Success's annual test scores telegraph menacingly, like sonar from a nuclear submarine. In 2015, for example, 68 percent of Success Academy test takers scored proficient in ELA, compared with 30 percent for the city overall; in math, the Success scores were "astonishing," with 93 percent of Success Academy students scoring proficient, compared with 35 percent citywide. As with many CMOs and districts under pressure to produce high test scores, Success Academy has faced cheating allegations, including from an internal study that the CMO subsequently rejected.[61]

Amplified by its own public relations apparatus and its legions of business supporters, Success has helped spur a test-score arms race that has redefined and narrowed the definition of what constitutes a good education among both public schools and charters.

"Oh, my gosh, all charters are under the gun when it comes to the scores," says Vasthi Acosta, the executive director at Amber, which recently opened its second charter school in the Bronx. Acosta notes that charter schools are reviewed and their contracts renewed every five years largely based on their test-score performance.[62]

At Amber, the pressure of test scores has meant more focus on academics at an ever earlier age. The school prides itself on teaching music and art, but those "specials" have been reduced to just one lesson per week. The focus on test scores helps to explain changes in kindergarten.

"That they get gym, recess, and art and music helps, but I have to tell you, there's very little play in kindergarten," says Acosta. "Kindergarteners get nap time in the beginning of the year, but in January that disappears."[63]

The classrooms at Amber have water tables and blocks, but it's "not what it used to be," explains Acosta, because the "demands of the common core are very high. Our kids have to use every minute" to prepare for the tests.[64]

Studies and common sense suggest that standardized tests have no place in kindergarten and that test scores have little ability to measure the most important intellectual abilities, including so-called fluid intelligence skills, which require the use of "logical thinking and problem solving in novel situations, rather than recalling previously learned facts and skills."[65]

Yet high test scores and political clout have made Success Academy the advance guard for those who wish to dismantle traditional public schools and their unions and replace them with a competitive marketplace of publicly funded, independently run, and lightly regulated institutions. So when Bill de Blasio, Bloomberg's successor, tried to keep Success Academy from moving into three public school buildings at the start of his term (Success Academy has a reputation for grabbing prime schoolhouse real estate and not collaborating with neighboring public schools) the CMO closed its schools and marched to Albany with an army of supporters. Governor Andrew Cuomo, whose major funders include hedge fund billionaires who are the biggest backers of the state's charter schools, and the New York State Legislature struck a deal ensuring that New York City charter schools would have access to space, either in already crowded public school buildings or in rented spaces largely paid for by the city, in a deal that gave charter schools "some of the most sweeping protections in the nation."[66]

By 2015, the New York business community was seeking to draft Moskowitz as a mayoral candidate to oppose de Blasio at the end of his first term. But, according to charter insiders, ed-reformers dreaded the prospect of a mayoral race featuring candidate Moskowitz, fearing it would only attract more bad charter publicity. Moskowitz, who had at one time served on the New York City Council, decided not to challenge de Blasio.[67]

THE UNLIKELY SUCCESS OF GLOBAL TECH

Surrounded by Harlem charter schools, Global Tech illustrates the special challenges faced by public schools and the stark difference between the student populations served by Harlem public schools versus charter schools. African American boys are often overidentified as special needs if they are seen as having behavioral problems, even if they don't have learning disabilities. If special-needs kids like Josniel Martinez are segregated when they get to high school, they are unlikely to graduate. Since its inception, Global Tech has been committed to both serving kids with special needs and mainstreaming them in general-education classes by providing a variety of educational and social supports.[68]

When Global Tech opened in 2009, about 30 percent of its students had so-called Individualized Education Programs, or I.E.Ps. Five years later, its special-needs population had topped 40 percent. At least part of that increase came from special-needs kids who transferred to Global Tech from nearby charters. Global Tech's Russell recalls charter school "refugees" showing up at her school after October 31, when the Department of Education makes key funding decisions for traditional public schools based on head counts. This means that it can be difficult for schools to hire additional teachers or support personnel when new students show up (though some funding is updated for special-education students who transfer by December 31).[69]

Unlike the no-excuses schools—known for their harsh discipline—that dominate the local charter landscape, Global Tech relied on a range of supports and disciplinary approaches both to keep kids engaged and to help them succeed in mainstream classes. For one thing, the school prided itself on integrating kids via so-called inclusion classes, taught by one general-education and one special-education teacher. While a small number of students—usually only about six—would be taught in self-contained classes in the sixth grade, they were mainstreamed by the seventh grade. Shael Polakow-Suransky, the Bloomberg administration's chief academic officer who is now president of Bank Street College of Education, has called "self-contained" classes, which segregate special-needs kids from the general-education population, "an academic death sentence."[70]

Research has shown that kids in inclusion classes are much more likely to graduate than those in segregated classrooms, without adversely affecting general-education kids. Some city educators also argue that it is precisely those kids with behavioral problems who are least likely to succeed in the no-excuses culture of charter schools.

During its first seven years, Global Tech tried a smorgasbord of disciplinary practices to keep its more "difficult" kids on the straight and narrow. By its second year, Global Tech had instituted a charter-like paycheck system. But instead of a largely punitive approach that often leads to detentions and suspensions at no-excuses charter schools, the Global Tech approach leaned toward rewarding children who rack up balances in their savings and checking accounts—ranging from extra computer time in the afternoons and uniform-free days to earning the right to participate in class trips and play on the school's basketball team.

Unlike at charter schools, at Global Tech faculty had considerable discretion in allocating bonus points or demerits. At the same time, detentions were generally served during lunch to ensure that kids weren't pulled away from their classes. Russell, who maintained an open-door policy during her entire tenure at the school, would spend hours talking to students about their behavior.

The school also took an active role in trying to ensure that its graduates would go to high schools that were a good fit. Eighth graders, instead of attending Citizens School's extended-day program, which was mandatory in grades six and seven, instead would participate in "Eighth Grade Academy," which involved researching high schools and writing application essays. The school even printed up business cards for each graduate and coached them on how, at the annual fall school fair, to introduce themselves to the faculty representing their top-choice schools.

Recognizing that many poor parents are ill-equipped—because of either language difficulties, job conflicts, the need to tend to small children at home, or other personal problems—to play an active role in the placement process, Global Tech encouraged children to double up with the parents who could go and dispatched teachers, who got per-session payments, to attend the fair. During its first high school fair, only six Global Tech parents out of a graduating class of sixty showed up, yet almost all Global Tech eighth graders attended.[71]

That year, most Global Tech kids got into the school of their choice, including several who were admitted to highly rated Manhattan Hunter Science High and the iSchool.[72]

The typical Global Tech graduate would, however, face seemingly insurmountable obstacles, even as they continued to find refuge and support in their old middle school. In his senior year of high school, Uri's family was featured in the *New York Times* when his father shot his mother and then himself in a grisly murder–suicide. Jaser lost his mother and grandmother in 2014, in a gas explosion in Spanish Harlem that destroyed two buildings; he remained in school but became withdrawn. Franklin, a troubled child who, nevertheless, went to Manhattan Hunter Science after graduating from Global Tech, got involved with a gang and was arrested for selling crack; in a letter he wrote to the judge while he was incarcerated at Riker's, at age seventeen, he pleaded for the opportunity to finish his education.[73]

Kaira Batiz, a student in Global Tech's first graduating class who went on to the iSchool, overcame one challenge after another as she carved out a path to college. The support networks she found at school, especially at Global Tech, helped her flourish. An undocumented immigrant and the child of a single mother who was so mentally unstable she was unable to care for her children, Kaira had no fixed home during much of high school. She lived at times with her aunt, who fostered her younger siblings, but she also spent long stretches with a former Global Tech teacher, as well as at the home of Sue Steinberg, who "mentored" several Global Tech students.[74]

To hear Kaira tell it, school, especially at Global Tech, was a refuge and a beacon. "It may be that I'm struggling with a problem in English class or math, but it's nothing like whatever struggle I deal with at home," says Kaira, who is slim and graceful, with an infectious smile that suffuses her gently rounded features.

"My education has always been a therapeutic experience," she adds. "That place where I can escape."[75]

Kaira remembers the encouragement she always got from her English teacher, Ms. Bridgemohan. Then there was the soft music played during study periods by another teacher, Ms. Kemp, who urged her to learn her times tables because it would make the state tests so much easier. Most of all, she recalls Mr. Baiz and the extra math classes he taught before school started and during lunch to kids who were interested. And Kaira was *very* interested. "He was the kind of teacher" where if you didn't understand "he would sit right next to you and explain it, and encourage you," recalls Kaira, adding that the school's creative use of educational technology helped her understand math concepts.[76]

At Global Tech, Kaira excelled academically. She scored 4s, on a scale of 1 to 4, on the New York State standardized tests for math, her favorite subject. In high school, she would score a solid 87 on the Regents math ("Almost a 90!" she laments).[77]

She also discovered poetry at Global Tech, and she has become a poster child for the power of humanities to serve as both an emotional and an intellectual anchor. Throughout high school, Kaira continued to write poetry and to read for pleasure. Two of her favorite recent books are *The Kite Runner* and *The Immortal Life of Henrietta Lacks.* The latter has made a particular impression on her. "I love the fact that she's still alive through her cells," says Kaira. "They've even been to space."[78]

Global Tech also exposed her to the possibility of college. At Citizens School, Kaira was introduced to the Opportunity Network (Opp Net), an organization that seeks to "level the playing field" for poor city kids, and she was accepted into its selective Opp Net prep program, which mentors students throughout high school and helps them apply to college.[79]

Without question, Kaira owes much of her success so far to her own resilience and determination. But for Kaira and many of her classmates, Global Tech remained a refuge long after middle school. A reunion of Global Tech's first class of sixty or so students drew close to half of its alumni for an informal afternoon of pizza and soda in spring 2015; months later, several of the same students would be found wandering into Global Tech during the late afternoons to get advice on college applications or help on their high school homework from their erstwhile middle school teachers.

Kaira, who had dreamed of going to college in California, would have to rein in her dreams; her undocumented status severely limited her options. But, by the summer of 2016, she was getting ready to enroll at John Jay College of Criminal Justice, part of the City University of New York.[80]

Perhaps no one exemplified the benefits of a leadership approach that aimed to give everyone both the benefit of the doubt and the support they needed more than David Baiz himself, whose teaching career began inauspiciously at P.S./M.S. 04 in the Bronx. Then twenty-three years old, Baiz was assigned to teach both seventh- and eighth-grade math—an overwhelming assignment for a first-year teacher because it required getting to know two different cohorts of students and to develop two entirely different lesson plans. To make matters worse, weeks into the start of his job, Baiz's sixteen-year-old sister was in a catastrophic car accident. He made several trips back home to Ohio and was frequently absent that year, for which, Baiz concedes, he may have deserved to get a "U" rating. But instead of mentoring Baiz, the assistant principal who would soon be promoted to principal at P.S./M.S. 04 made it clear that his days at the school were numbered.[81]

What happened next is what made the difference not only in keeping Baiz in the teaching profession and helping him excel, but also in building a school that has fostered a culture of collaborative improvement. When it became clear that Baiz "didn't stand a chance" at M.S. 04, Pryce-Harvey, who had served as his mentor there, encouraged Baiz to move to Global Tech.[82]

Once he joined Global Tech, Baiz began to distinguish himself not only as a first-rate teacher, but also as a respected school leader. In addition to his teaching duties and his unofficial role as tech guru, Baiz was selected by his colleagues to serve as their union representative. Baiz also led the math training for math staff at Global Tech, which consistently outperformed most of its "peer" middle schools.[83]

Baiz also won grants for the school, as well as a prestigious Math for America fellowship that came with a $15,000-per-year stipend. And he was selected as one of six New York City teachers to be part of the Digital Teacher Corps, a Ford Foundation–funded collaboration among educators, technologists, and designers to develop interactive digital learning tools. Visitors from around the country flocked to his classroom to see Baiz's innovative approach to mixing online tools and old-fashioned instruction.[84]

Reflecting on the difference between his experiences at the two very different schools, Baiz says of Global Tech that it was "more open to experimentation" and willing to bring in new ideas. He said at the time: "I don't have to worry about watching my back. I don't have to worry about documenting every little thing. I feel less stress on the job. I don't have a pit in my stomach every morning. It's a collaborative relationship."[85]

Russell, who asked all her faculty to plan out their career trajectories, encouraged Baiz to get his principal's license. And, when Russell decided to resign from Global Tech in 2014, she tapped Baiz as her successor.

THE ART OF NETWORKING

From its inception, Global Tech craved a connection and seized every opportunity to be a part of organizations that would help it improve and "push" the school's thinking. To improve, to evolve, you need that, Russell says. Cisco pushed her thinking. The iZone's Julian Cohen pushed her thinking, as did some of the iZone specialists hired at Tweed and the long partnership with Citizens Schools. A relatively short-lived "partnership" with Apple Computer also pushed her thinking. But as those connections fell away, what would take their place?

Another opportunity presented itself toward the end of Bloomberg's term with the administration's final reorganization—the establishment of the network structure so reminiscent of the progressive coalition's alternative high schools division and the Annenberg-funded Learning Zone (see chapter 1).

Through three mayoral terms and at least as many reorganizations, Bloomberg's education department found itself pulled toward the creation of autonomous school networks. The network structure grew out of the experiment it called the Autonomy Zone, which initially included twenty-nine schools and grew to over three hundred, close to one-fifth of the schools in the city, collectively a network the size of the nation's fifth-largest school district, just behind Dade County, Florida. In 2010, in what was perhaps the most far-reaching shift yet, networks of cross-functional teams of thirteen dedicated experts would provide "personalized" logistical and operational support—everything from advice on budgets to special-education regulations to professional development resources—system-wide, to an average of twenty-five schools each.

"We didn't need to be told by the powers-that-be what the right thing to do is for kids," recalls Julie Zuckerman, who was one of the original Autonomy Zone principals and, briefly, a successor to Debbie Meier at Central Park East. Although Zuckerman, an ardent progressive, was deeply ambivalent about the Bloomberg-era reforms, it was under Bloomberg that she was able to launch Castle Bridge School in Washington Heights, which preferences Spanish-language speakers and sets aside 10 percent of its seats for kids who have one incarcerated parent as a way to promote economic and racial diversity.[86]

To Bloomberg's supporters, principals like Zuckerman and schools like Castle Bridge demonstrated the system's support for strong schools, whatever their pedagogical bent. "I know that Klein considered there were two hundred exceptional schools in the system," says Sy Fliegel of the Center for Educational Innovation, which ran one of the city's largest networks. "He would empower them to the ultimate."[87]

The genius of the network structure was that it turned the traditional reporting relationship on its head; schools could choose their networks, using their own funds to pay for network services. "You could choose a support organization on Tuesday. If on the following Monday you weren't satisfied, you could change," says Fliegel. Now, in order to survive, networks would have to treat schools and principals as their customers.

"Reversing nearly a hundred years of hierarchical management in New York, the principals were given authority to retain, dismiss, and even give cash bonuses to their network support team members." In addition, the networks were urged to "follow up relentlessly when the system doesn't respond or performs unsatisfactorily, and 'filter' or 'block' other requests that may burden principals." As for the regional bureaucracies that had just been effectively put out of business, they were urged to "re-invent themselves" as fee-for-service providers.[88]

Urban Academy's Ann Cook, who disagrees with many, if not most, Bloomberg administration policies, said the network structure—if not each individual network—had enormous potential. "The superintendents are compliance driven," says Cook; they are paid to find fault. "The networks were not. That's very, very important."[89]

The most important player in this shift was Eric Nadelstern, the founding principal of the International School at LaGuardia College, alumnus of the alternative high schools, and an early member of the progressive coalition. A native New Yorker, Nadelstern grew up in the Bronx and attended public school and City College before beginning his teaching career. The most obvious benefit of the network structure was that "you could break through the old patterns of patronage and corruption," argues Nadelstern, noting that local politicians had, for years, used schools as a job bank for loyal constituents. "The ultimate goal is to streamline operations and build capacity within schools so school-based staff can focus their time on instruction and accelerate student achievement."[90]

Then, too, by stripping away the bureaucracy, Nadelstern estimated that the network structure saved the education department $565,000 per school. In his book *Ten Lessons from New York City Schools*, Nadelstern estimates that school superintendents who managed twenty schools under the old district structure, employing 120 nonteaching district staff, "skimmed" an estimated $650,000 per school in management fees. By contrast, the networks, which work with twenty-five to thirty schools each and employ only about fifteen nonteaching personnel, cost about $85,000 per school. The balance of that savings, in the main, went back into school budgets, according to Nadelstern.[91]

By giving principals power of the purse and allowing them to choose their networks—and switch if they weren't happy—network leaders were expected to serve more as coaches than bosses. "Schools find this arrangement of working with other schools and building professional relationships much more useful than the old superintendencies," said Nancy Mann, the founding principal of Fannie Lou Hamer Freedom High School in the

Bronx, a veteran of the progressive coalition. Mann also says she was able to rely on network staff for technical help and advice, especially as budgeting has become "more complex"; but, ultimately and importantly, she got to decide how to allocate the budget.[92]

With the new network structure, principals signed "performance agreements," which essentially bought them exemptions from a slew of education-department requirements that governed everything from curriculum and professional development mandates to mandatory attendance at education-department meetings. The Bloomberg administration was gambling that once the bureaucracy had been dismantled Humpty Dumpty–like, it would be nearly impossible to put back together again.[93]

At Global Tech, Russell had seized on the principal's newfound autonomy and protected the school, to a degree, by dint of sheer willpower and political savvy—even, for a while, after she left. She exerted control over the school budget with gusto: instead of buying new furniture, she borrowed and purchased used furniture wherever she could, plowing the savings into technology and per-session payments for her teachers. Creative budgeting also helped Global Tech hold on to two seasoned advisers. Russell recognized that she had far less experience as a principal than many of the other iZone stars, such as the iSchool's Alisa Berger or West Side Collaborative's respected Jeanne Rotunda, who remained a devotee of Debbie Meier and her methods. To help, Russell brought in Nick Siewert, an education consultant with Teaching Matters, a nonprofit that describes its mission as "developing and retaining great teachers," who served as a key architect of the school's professional-development practices; and Ann Wiener, a Leadership Academy coach who herself had founded a respected progressive-coalition school, Crossroads, on Manhattan's Upper West Side and who would serve as a sounding board for Russell and her eventual successor.

But Russell also ran up against the limits of creative budgeting. At first, Bloomberg's education department had allowed schools to roll money they had saved from one year's budget into the following year; eventually, though the education department ended that practice, and principals found that they needed to spend any excess at the end of each school year or be forced to return the funds to the education department.

Chancellor Joel Klein had encouraged principals to be entrepreneurial, but end runs around the bureaucracy also proved problematic. For example, behind the curtain at Global Tech, one of the school's most valuable assets was its even-tempered, soft-spoken school "secretary." Fluent in both Spanish and the education department's arcane 1980s-era computer system, the secretary served as an important liaison to parents and as Global Tech's de facto compliance officer. Russell says the secretary, a fifteen-year education-department veteran, had memorized seventy-odd computer codes for everything from attendance records to immunizations, saving her hours each day, allowing her to be a "big-picture thinker, instead of a paper pusher."[94]

When the secretary moved to Connecticut and her commuting expenses skyrocketed, Russell persuaded her not to quit by allowing her to take off Fridays and work extended days the rest of the week. Russell also corralled private donors to pony up the secretary's $300 monthly commuting expenses. The expenditure would become part of a months-long education-department investigation of Russell, covering more than two dozen allegations—most of which stemmed from accusations by a disgruntled former employee. Russell would be investigated by the education department's special commissioner of investigations, which handled the most egregious cases of misconduct. The special investigators were "big," "intimidating," trench-coat-clad former police detectives who showed up at the school a dozen times during the course of more than a year.[95]

Every allegation but one was eventually dismissed. The investigators found against Russell in the case involving the secretary's commuting expenses. But, according to Russell, the investigators had gotten one crucial detail wrong—they claimed she had used public, not private, funds to pay the secretary's commuting expenses.

In any event, by the time the investigation was concluded, Russell had left the school. Had she stayed, she probably would have had to repay the funds herself, says Pryce-Harvey.[96]

The investigation would prove to be "deeply disillusioning" for Russell. "She got worn out by the investigations and the bureaucratic bullshit," says Siewert acidly. "Chrystina Russell's story is tragic. People like that need to be in the system—twenty-eight [years old], student-centered, entrepreneurial, would do anything for the kids. . . . She martyred herself on the cross of rules and regulations."[97]

The investigation may have provided a final nudge, but Russell vehemently disagrees that she let the investigation push her out. "I don't give up that easily," she says, adding that she was ready to leave New York.

Without a doubt, Global Tech's entrepreneurial outlook and its focus on technology and "twenty-first-century skills" were at odds with the long-held assumptions and traditions of the education-department bureaucracy.

How principals like Russell were evaluated provides one of the clearest examples of the disconnect between the lofty aspirations of many Bloomberg-era reforms, such as the iZone, and the reality in schoolhouse trenches. On the one hand, Arthur VanderVeen, Tweed's innovation guru, beat out a steady rat-a-tat-tat for radical change, pushing quickly for the iZone to grow to an eye-popping four hundred schools and encouraging online and "mastery-based" learning, all the while intoning: "I'm not sure schools realize what we're asking for, how much change we're looking for."[98]

On the other hand, school principals were in the maw of old-school superintendents and their annual evaluations. Klein had sharply diminished the role and influence of the superintendents, even more so with the creation of the networks, but they retained one power that could make or break a principal: the dreaded principal performance reviews.

Russell learned this early on. "Already I've found that accountability measures are really hard to navigate," bemoaned Russell at the start of Global Tech's first full year of operation. Schools and principals, she found, were measured via "traditional" school-based rubrics. There was nothing about technology initiatives, "no credit" for the iZone initiatives. "They just evaluate the traditional school stuff."[99]

Although Global Tech was thriving, especially compared to the troubled schools in the rest of the district, Russell got a rude surprise at the start of the school's second year, when the superintendent sent back Russell's school goals as "unacceptable." They had included such unorthodox iZone aims as raising $250,000 for the school and setting up an extended-day program via a partnership with Citizens Schools.[100]

Eventually, Russell won over her superintendent. On the 2013–2014 so-called Quality Review, which serves as an evaluation of the school as a whole, Global Tech earned a solid "proficient"—not the "highly developed" of some other iZone schools, but still acceptable. Global Tech had "exceeded targets" for school environment and student progress. And for curriculum, Global Tech had earned its one-and-only "well developed" rating. The superintendent had praised Russell and her staff for crafting "engaging competency-based curricula" that aligned with state standards.[101]

By the end of the Bloomberg administration, the iZone had gone through multiple rebrandings, eventually becoming known as iZone360. Money also had become tighter.

Russell gauged correctly, early on, that the constant changes at the iZone and the education department, the lack of solid "infrastructure," the inconsistent accountability measures, the ever-changing mandates at both the state and local levels would to some degree stymie Global Tech's growth.

As soon as she had the chance, Russell decided to join a network of high-performing middle and high schools. Known as the Bridges for Learning, the network included a few other iZone schools, including the iSchool and West Side Collaborative. The like-minded network served as an important bulwark, especially during Russell's scuffles with her superintendent.

JUMPING THE GUN ON THE COMMON CORE

Even as Global Tech and other innovative small schools were facing the tectonic shifts of the networks and the iZone changes, threats arrived on two entirely different fronts—New York State's decision to *simultaneously* adopt the Common Core State Standards *and* new standardized tests that were in theory, but not in practice, aligned to the Common Core. The decision to adopt the Common Core was driven by the Obama administration's zero-sum Race to the Top initiative. In the wake of the 2008 financial crisis, with states and municipalities reeling from budget cuts, the federal government dangled a bucket of extra education funding for the states that agreed to a bundle of carrot-and-stick incentives. Behind Race to the Top was a well-worn set of assumptions: that competition, in the form of charter schools, and the Common Core would lift all pedagogical boats; that punitive teacher evaluations—extra funding in exchange for teacher evaluations linked to test scores—would motivate lazy and recalcitrant teachers to *finally* do their jobs; and that all you needed was a good teacher in every classroom and the detrimental effects of poverty, neglect, and social dysfunction could be significantly, if not entirely, mitigated.

This is not an all-excuses argument, dear reader. In chapter 1, we saw how the progressive coalition accomplished remarkable feats of improvement with a less-is-more, highly collaborative, student-focused strategy. In chapters 3 and 5, we will see how teamwork and collaboration did much the same in down-at-the-heels Brockton, Massachusetts, and a much more economically diverse Leander, Texas.

However, New York State's alacrity in adopting both the Common Core and faux–Common Core tests stands out for its sheer hubris and wrong-headedness. In the years since, it has widely been seen as one of the state's "biggest education fiascoes"—words from one of the state's own press releases.[102] This was no small feat. And, yet, John King, then education commissioner for New York State, was rewarded with a promotion; in 2016, he was appointed U.S. secretary of education to succeed Arne Duncan.

Beginning in 2008, the New York State Department of Education spent hundreds of thousands of dollars, perhaps millions, revamping the English Language Arts requirements. (I know because I was, for reasons that never became entirely clear, invited to be part of that effort.) The ELA team debated how to balance literature and nonfiction, how to accommodate the needs of immigrant kids struggling to learn English, and how to account for the radically different cultural experiences of the students who would be taking the tests—kids in remote rural areas, in suburbs, in New York City. Jackie Pryce-Harvey, one of the few African Americans on the committee, offered regular reminders of the differing experiences of inner-city minority kids and how those should be reflected in scaffolding and pedagogy.

In her classroom, Pryce-Harvey frequently reminded her students of the importance of code switching, especially on state reading tests; for example, to inner-city kids, a garage is a multilevel public structure for cars. It's not a private space that doubles as Dad's tool shed or a laboratory for a Silicon Valley whiz kid.

In 2010, the work of the committee was abruptly jettisoned when New York State decided to adopt the Common Core State Standards in a bid for Race to the Top funds.

Saul B. Cohen, a member of the Board of Regents who had chaired the Regents Standards Review Initiative, in an email to panel members dated May 4, 2010, explained the reasons for his resignation:

> I have done so because the Board and SED [State Education Department] leadership have signed on to the National Common Standards, overriding the New York State Legislative Mandate that called for the Regents to revise the current outdated standards. The agreement to adopt the National ELA Standards has been made in spite of the fact that the standards and performance indicators we submitted to the Board are widely acknowledged to be more rigorous, clearer, more focused and more comprehensive than the National Common Standards drafts.
>
> Given the dire fiscal situation that affects SED, the prospects for receiving Race-to-the-Top monies have led the leadership to override our proposed State standards. This, despite the fact that the short-term injection of federal money is not necessarily the solution to basic problems. . . . I have urged the Regents not to bow to the lure of Washington's financial incentives without a thorough discussion of the long-term consequences. This review has not yet been done.[103]

Adoption of the Common Core standards followed an about-face on education by the New York State Legislature. The Empire State had lost badly in its first Race to the Top bid in March 2010, sacrificing its greatest share of points because of its failure to increase the number of charter schools and to adopt test-based teacher evaluations. The legislature got the message and quickly voted to double the number of charter schools. And on May 11, just a few days after Cohen announced his resignation from the standards review panel, New York also adopted a controversial teacher-evaluation system that would tie 40 percent of teacher evaluations to student test data.[104]

In August, New York was finally rewarded. In its second Race to the Top competition, the federal government awarded New York $700 million in funding. In the RTTT scoring rubric, New York State came in second only to Massachusetts.[105]

What educators soon came to realize, though, is that neither the curriculum nor the teacher-training materials were anywhere near ready; thus, both students and teachers—for their evaluations hinged on the results—would be subjected to the new half-baked tests based on, well, nothing at all. New York State had joined the Partnership for Assessment of Readiness for College and Careers (PARCC), one of two consortia that were developing Common Core assessments (the Smarter Balanced Assessment Consortium was the other); PARCC planned to roll out its first assessment in the 2014–2015 school year. Yet the New York tests, which were developed by Pearson, the publisher and educational-testing giant, were first administered to students in April 2013, making New York one of the few states that rushed to roll out a purportedly Common Core–based test before PARCC itself had completed the work on its assessment. Schools, kids, and educators, in short, were being set up for failure.

Another problem was that under its $32 million contract with Pearson, New York was barred from making the tests public, a lack of transparency that fostered public distrust. At the same time, the gag order, which warned educators not to duplicate or disseminate any part of the tests, ensured that the tests would have no pedagogical value whatsoever, and that educators would have no role in improving the tests.[106]

An open letter to parents signed by 557 principals from across New York State outlined their concerns about the test. Elizabeth Phillips, the principal of P.S. 321 in Park Slope, Brooklyn, and one of the signatories of the letter, followed up with this critique of the tests in an April 2014 *New York Times* op-ed. It read in part:

> I want to be clear: We were not protesting testing; we were not protesting the Common Core standards. We were protesting the fact that we had just witnessed children being asked to answer questions that had little bearing on their reading ability and yet had huge stakes

> for students, teachers, principals and schools. (Among other things, test scores help determine teacher and principal evaluations, and in New York City they also have an impact on middle and high school admissions to some schools.) We were protesting the fact that it is our word against the state's, since we cannot reveal the content of the passages or the questions that were asked.[107]

Given the rushed rollout, it came as no surprise that the tests themselves were highly flawed. There were complaints about the length of the tests—the middle school passages were about seventy-two pages long and included fourteen reading passages, the vast majority of which were one to two pages in length; eight short-answer questions that called for writing about one long paragraph each; as well as two essay questions. Nonfiction texts dominated at the expense of literature and poetry. And there were numerous problems with individual questions, including what became known as the great "pineapple and hare" fiasco after a short story by the same name, which even its author, Daniel Pinkwater, conceded was "random and pointless," along with the "confusing questions that went with it."[108]

Students panicked and test scores plunged statewide compared with the test results in 2012. In their letter to John B. King, New York's education commissioner, veteran principals mounted a grassroots campaign in opposition to the "unfair" tests and warned of "an extreme toll on our teachers, families and most importantly, our students." The principals further wrote:

> Not one among us takes issue with the state's and city's efforts to bring more rigor and coherence to teaching and learning. In general, although we take exception to aspects of the Common Core Learning Standards, we have welcomed the opportunity to re-energize curriculum with greater emphasis on the kinds of critical, flexible thinking that our students must develop to meet the demands of their current and future lives. Unfortunately, in both their technical and task design, these tests do not align with the Common Core. The ELA test was narrowly focused, requiring students to analyze specific lines, words and structures of mostly informational text and their significance. In contrast, the Common Core emphasizes reading across different texts, both fiction and nonfiction, in order to determine and differentiate between central themes—an authentic adult practice. Answering granular questions about unrelated topics

> is not. Because schools have not had a lot of time to unpack Common Core, we fear that too many educators will use these high stakes tests to guide their curricula, rather than the more meaningful Common Core Standards themselves. And because the tests are missing Common Core's essential values, we fear that students will experience curriculum that misses the point as well.[109]

It was one of many skirmishes in what would lead to a widespread opt-out movement that would soon see one in five families in New York State refuse to allow their children to take standardized tests.

Then, after a months-long deadlock between the city and the teachers union, the state rolled out a complex evaluation system for New York City that pegged 20 percent of each teacher's rating to student improvement on standardized assessments, a reduction from the initial 40 percent to which New York State had agreed.[110]

Ironically, the deal meant *even more* standardized tests. Because the state's standardized assessments in elementary and middle schools focused on math and English Language Arts, the city decided to develop new assessments known as the Measurements of Student Learning (MOSL) for gauging the performance of teachers who specialize in what were thus far untested subjects, such as art and music. Although the MOSL was to be administered in the spring, in fall of 2013 many children were subjected to yet another test, which was meant to create baseline scores for the MOSL; the sole purpose of both rounds of tests was to measure teacher performance.

So, in addition to six days of "Common Core" testing, conducted over the course of two weeks, New York kids were forced to complete two rounds of MOSL tests—a baseline in the fall and the actual test in the spring. There were also field tests for next year's "Common Core" tests.[111]

Kindergarteners—children as young as five—were subjected to hours of standardized testing. Julie Zuckerman, of Castle Bridge elementary in the Washington Heights neighborhood in Manhattan, called the multiple-choice, fill-in-the-bubble MOSL tests for kindergarteners "obscene." After Zuckerman explained the new mandate, the school's parents voted to opt out of the assessment.[112]

The tests for older kids weren't much better. The sixth-grade social-studies assessment, for example, was based in part on a problematic color map of the Nile delta that was emailed to schools but was hard to read if printed out in black and white—which many schools did to save printing costs.[113]

There was also literally a massive increase in paperwork. Nick Siewert of Teaching Matters calculated that a school with 1,200 students would "churn" out 12,000 pages for the social-studies test alone, "with no compensation for the paper, for the time."[114]

Then, too, there was the question of how the assessments were being scored. Designated teachers at each school were marking the fall tests. Yet many of them had not been trained in norming, a procedure intended to ensure that two evaluators will give the same score for the same answer. That raised fears that the data would end up being unreliable.

In response, more than one hundred New York City principals sent a letter to Mayor-elect Bill de Blasio, who was about to succeed Mayor Bloomberg, asking, among other things, that he completely "revamp" the evaluation system and that he reduce standardized tests to the "minimum" federal requirement.[115]

Bloomberg had earned his share of criticism, especially for his ardent support of standardized testing. Ironically, now even some of the mayor's staunchest critics worried that the new mandates would undermine what was widely seen as the best part of the Bloomberg education initiatives—giving principals increased power over budgets and teaching methods in exchange for more accountability.

Here's how Castle Bridge's Zuckerman frames her highly conflicted feelings about the Bloomberg years: "I hated the Bloomberg administration, the ridiculous focus on testing, the way that test scores were used to rate schools. Everything was so draconian; the disrespect for everything but the almighty test score.

"Yet within that we were able to carve out space," Zuckerman adds. "They gave us space. There was an effort to scale what worked."[116]

Indeed, the city's arcane school-grading formula, which was heavily weighted toward measuring test-score improvement, favored relatively low-performing schools that succeed in improving over schools that were already doing well and for whom even incremental improvement was harder to achieve. During the Bloomberg years, it was not unusual for the school grades of the highest-rated schools in the city to yo-yo.[117]

Shortly before Bloomberg's term was to end, and as New York State was ratcheting up test-based accountability, another tsunami hit the city's schools when, in November 2010, Joel Klein stepped down as chancellor to join Rupert Murdoch's News Corp., where he would head the company's education-technology division.

During a decade as chancellor, Klein had been widely criticized by rank-and-file educators for hiring armies of young lawyers and MBAs in Tweed—the "Kleinbergs"—because they "lacked appreciation for experience" and for their "TFA attitude." Yet, in a move that may have proved to be one of his greatest failures as mayor, Bloomberg chose to pass up not just the Kleinbergs, but also the experienced progressive educators who had become Klein's top lieutenants, and chose Cathleen Black, a Hearst Corp. publishing executive with no education experience, to be the new chancellor. So doing, Bloomberg lost the last chance he had to cement his legacy and to win the backing of the progressive coalition.

Black resigned after just three months on the job. Bloomberg then backed down and selected a veteran education-department bureaucrat, Dennis Walcott, to serve as caretaker-in-chief until the end of the mayor's term.[118] Between Klein's departure and Walcott's appointment, the administration's education entrepreneurs headed for the exits. John White left to oversee New Orleans's controversial shift to being an all-charter city (see chapter 5) and, eventually, to serve as superintendent of schools for Louisiana. Santiago Taveras, who had started his teaching career at the Central Park East schools and served as deputy chancellor under Klein, also left—though he would return for a brief stint in the de Blasio administration. Perhaps most significantly for New York City, Nadelstern left in January 2011.[119]

With Nadelstern's departure, entropy soon set in, and the networks became ever more focused on compliance and moved away from helping principals solve problems. "The irony is that the vehicle used to decentralize the system proved equally effective when the folks at the top decided to recentralize," said Nadelstern from his new post as visiting professor of practice at Columbia University's Teachers College.[120]

Soon everyone from the principals' union to Merryl Tisch, chancellor of the New York State Board of Regents, to Mayor-elect Bill de Blasio targeted the networks for elimination. Tisch charged that the networks have "basically failed children" who are English language learners and have special needs. De Blasio, when he was running for mayor, said, "I am dubious about whether this current network structure can be kept."[121]

In response to the growing chorus of criticism, 120 principals—many of them progressive-coalition veterans—issued a plea in support of the network structure, which it sent to Mayor-elect de Blasio, the UFT, the principals' union, Schools Chancellor Dennis Walcott, and Shael Polakow-Suransky, newly ensconced as senior deputy chancellor. The letter argued that the networks offered schools the following supports, which were not "necessarily" provided through other more traditional structures at the Department of Education:

1. The gathering of schools of similar visions or purpose: the internationals, special ed reform focused, collaboratively structured, and schools committed to alternative assessment. This enables these schools to work more closely together and support each other towards better meeting their missions.
2. Shifting the supervisory structure into an advisory and support structure. It makes all the difference in the world that the network leader and team members are not the principals' rating officer. Our networks have been responsive to us and in many cases network principals have had a say in the selection of network staff.
3. Networks support professional development that better meets the needs of the teachers, administrators, and other support staff in our schools and that allows for cross-pollination across our schools.
4. Because of racial and economic segregation by neighborhood in New York City, geographic districts are often segregated as well. Self-selected networks offer the option of racially and economically diverse schools working together and benefitting greatly from this collaboration.[122]

In January 2015, *Chalkbeat* declared the networks "dead." The performance-standards consortium and international high schools were allowed to stay together under a superintendent, Kathy Rehfield-Pelles, who had served as a network leader under Bloomberg, offering a glimmer of hope that the old Learning Zone might yet survive. A few other networks with strong connections to the de Blasio administration also survived.[123]

The iZone, meanwhile, was fading fast. In December 2012, the city had lost a $40 million Race to the Top grant that was aimed at rewarding schools that promote "personalized learning," including those in the iZone. For the first time, Global Tech was about to start a new school year—2013–2014—without any new funding for technology. Russell decided to take a job with Kepler Kigali, a nonprofit university that pioneered a blended-learning program and offered Rwandan students U.S. college degrees, and moved to Africa.

Indeed, many of the principals who had pioneered the iZone schools, including the iSchool and West Side Collaborative Middle School, had left not only their schools, but the education department as well.

Russell, however, was sure she had left Global Tech in good hands. The 2013–2014 school year would begin with David Baiz at the helm, assisted by Jackie Pryce-Harvey, who was now the official assistant principal. Most of the teachers who had launched Global Tech were also still at the school. Morale was high, the transition seamless.

A PENDULUM SWING AND THE DEATH OF GLOBAL TECH

But Mayor de Blasio's new schools chancellor, Carmen Farina, was planning major changes. Among other things, Farina was wondering whether small schools made sense at all. Convinced that they were more costly, she began exploring the possibility of merging small schools.

In East Harlem, the chancellor's merger plans first filtered down to Global Tech in the spring of 2015. Alexandra Estrella, a new superintendent, had floated the idea of merging Global Tech with P.S. 7, the K–8 school in the same building; rumor had it that Sameer Talati, P.S. 7's principal, had been lobbying to be named the new head of the merged school. Seven years after she had founded Global Tech, Russell flew in from Rwanda on one of her frequent visits to New York City and told Baiz he would have to fight for the school because Global Tech was a much better school than P.S. 7.[124]

Though no warrior, Baiz stepped forward to defend Global Tech. In June 2015, sources close to Global Tech thought a merger, with Baiz in charge of the combined schools, would be announced any moment. A year later, the merger still had not taken place, but Talati had moved to a job at Tweed and was replaced by Pryce-Harvey as P.S. 7's acting principal.[125]

Then, the following summer, Estrella rejected Baiz's tenure application; under education-department rules, there was a good chance that he would lose his principalship. The following school year, the superintendent turned down the tenure applications of every teacher Baiz had recommended, including one who was a Math for America master teacher for science who also held a special-education certification—two specialties in short supply. Some thought the superintendent was gunning for the old Bloomberg-era principals. Others thought Baiz hadn't "kowtowed" sufficiently.[126]

In early April 2017, just before spring break and the start of standardized testing, Global Tech teachers sat stunned and teary-eyed at the weekly staff meeting, where Baiz announced that he would not be returning after the weeklong break. Baiz's offer to stay through the school year to help with the transition had been rejected by the superintendent. Meanwhile, at P.S. 7, Estrella also had pushed out Pryce-Harvey.[127]

The day he announced his departure, Baiz told his staff: "One thing I've been really proud of—I feel like we've created something special in East Harlem. Not every school is like this, in New York City, in East Harlem, in tough neighborhoods. You should be very proud."[128]

"This is a successful school; and yet, this is the kind of talent the DOE doesn't want to retain?" said Chrystina Russell, the former principal, referring wryly to Baiz's ouster. "Is there no cause for pause?"[129]

Within weeks, close to half of Global Tech's teachers had gotten job offers elsewhere. Hamilton Grange Middle School, a West Harlem school, scooped up three former Global Tech teachers.[130]

As for Baiz, he had been accepted into Harvard University's Doctor of Education Leadership program, the most prestigious and selective program for educators in the country.

"He's good enough for Harvard, but not for East Harlem," quipped one Global Tech teacher.[131]

Educators who knew the Global Tech story saw Baiz's ouster as not just the end of Global Tech, but also a sign that its progressive values were now endangered throughout the city.

Veterans of the progressive coalition and the small-schools movement always knew that small schools were fragile. Debbie Meier's legacy in New York is particularly poignant. Her Central Park East schools survive. Some have thrived. Others, such as Central Park East Secondary, which left the New York Performance Standards Consortium and reintroduced standardized tests, have strayed far from their roots.

At the same time, many of Meier's disciples had established schools across the city, including Fannie Lou Hamer in the Bronx, Castle Bridge in Washington Heights, and West Side Collaborative on the Upper West Side of Manhattan.

But in de Blasio's education department, the pendulum had swung decisively toward bureaucratic control and compliance and away from Bloomberg-style disruption or the small-school renaissance of the progressive era. The superintendents and apparatchiks that the Kleinbergs had sought to sideline were once again in power. Many, like Estrella in District Four, were Farina's friends. And, like Estrella, few were particularly accomplished; Estrella's chief claim to fame, prior to becoming superintendent, was to serve as the founding principal of Esperanza, a school with mediocre-to-poor academics, sky-high teacher turnover, dismal morale, and at least one cheating investigation during her tenure as principal. (The cheating was never proven.[132])

Notes one highly respected veteran educator: Farina brought back the superintendents who had been deemed "wasteful and incompetent" by the Bloomberg administration. But unlike the pre-Bloomberg years of powerful superintendents with large, powerful district bureaucracies, Farina's superintendents were given only skeleton staffs; thus, while they controlled principals like Baiz and Pryce-Harvey, they had no real control over the schools themselves.[133]

In the middle of the 2017–2018 school year, Global Tech effectively ceased to exist. Without consulting the community, Estrella merged Global Tech's students and classes with those of P.S. 7. The Global Tech signs were taken down after Thanksgiving 2017. Teachers reported chaos and confusion, including fights and classroom disruptions. Although over 150 alumni, parents, community members, and former teachers flocked to public hearings that were held in the new year, the Panel for Education Policy, which makes the final determination on proposed school closings, approved the merger in part because, as one panel member noted, the school had already been "decimated."[134]

Also in 2017, Farina ended the Leadership Academy's principal-training program, the cornerstone of Mayor Bloomberg's efforts to train more entrepreneurial leaders for new schools, and with it the most potent symbol of the Bloomberg years.[135]

3

STATE OF REFORM

The Not-So-Quiet Revolution in Massachusetts

Jami McDuffy was a bookish, freckle-faced thirteen-year-old with a penchant for pink clothing when she agreed to become the face of the fight for education reform in Massachusetts. In 1990, McDuffy became the lead plaintiff in a class-action lawsuit that had wended its way through the Massachusetts courts for more than a decade. Originally known as *Webby v. Dukakis*—the latter for Michael Dukakis, who was governor when the suit was first filed—the lead plaintiff, Roburn Webby, aged out of the lawsuit when she graduated from Brockton High long before the suit was resolved.

McDuffy was an ideal student to take Webby's place. Hardworking and sporty, McDuffy loved school and played soccer. Her father, Scott McDuffy, was a firefighter with the Brockton Fire Department and also served on the Brockton School Committee.[1]

Taking into account earlier court decisions, as well as research showing that kids in poor communities often need far more resources than more affluent students require to achieve the same educational outcomes, the plaintiffs—representing twenty Massachusetts school districts—sued for *adequate* school funding, asserting that the education clause of the state constitution compels the state government to ensure that public school students have the opportunity to receive an adequate education. (The plaintiffs deliberately chose not to sue for *equal* funding, which by itself might not have met the greater needs of low-income students.)[2]

It was soon after McDuffy joined the class action that the governor's Committee on Distressed School Systems and School Reform issued a scathing report on the state of education in the Commonwealth. Determined not to raise taxes, Governor William Weld no doubt was hoping for a more measured report, one that would "contain the financial impact" associated with the education proposals then being debated in the state legislature. Instead, Martin Kaplan, the report's principal author and a former law partner of the governor, and the only education outsider on the committee, minced no words. Having toured the struggling districts, he concluded that Brockton and other school districts across the state faced a "state of emergency due to grossly inadequate financial support."[3]

Kaplan warned that without significant reform, "more towns will be coming to us desperate next year, and the year after."[4]

Importantly, one of the four committee members was Piedad Robertson, then secretary of education. Although she resigned after the report was issued, the report itself had made it "virtually untenable" for the Department of Education to contend that it was providing students in the plaintiff school districts with an adequate education.

Instead, the state fell back on a much less convincing argument: that the language of the education clause in the state constitution was merely "aspirational" and "did not impose any enforceable duty on the Commonwealth."[5]

Once known as Shoe City, Brockton had been, long ago, a proud center of manufacturing and technological innovation. But Brockton's economy had been hit hard in the 1970s and 1980s by global competition, which would wipe out the local shoe manufacturers. Still, in 1970 the town inaugurated one of the nation's most state-of-the-art high schools. Brockton High boasted a planetarium, pool, ice rink, auditorium, and a 10,000-seat stadium. Brockton High regularly sent its jazz band to Europe, its football team to the state Super Bowl, and its students to Ivy League schools. Until the 1980s, Brockton schools regularly outperformed their counterparts in other urban areas. "This is not a rich city, but it's a city with a rich tradition of caring about education and getting involved," said Manthala George, Brockton's superintendent throughout most of the 1980s. "Schools are a point of light for this city, a real source of pride."[6]

On the edge of the football field, at the entrance to Brockton High, stands a statue of Brockton's favorite son, Rocky Marciano, a.k.a. the Brockton Blockbuster, in fighter pose. It was the scrappy pugilist who gave the town its new, and now increasingly ironic, moniker, the City of Champions.

Within a few short years, Brockton High, the Commonwealth's largest high school, also became its poorest. To the global restructuring that had gutted the local shoe-manufacturing industry, Brockton could now add the devastating impact of recession and the tax cap. A series of funding cuts slashed over $5 million from the school budget in 1991 and led to mass layoffs of nearly two hundred educators. Class sizes ballooned—forty-five kids squeezed into one class was not unusual—and the remaining teachers were forced to take on classes outside their subject-area expertise. Art, music, language, and most physical education and computer classes were dropped. Gifted programs were gutted.

Families who could afford it drove their children to schools in neighboring towns. Then too, as good manufacturing jobs disappeared, the children of the city's Italian and Irish immigrants moved to more affluent nearby towns and were replaced by newcomers from Haiti and Cape Verde, whose English-language deficiencies were compounded by interrupted schooling and often various types of trauma—all conditions that require extra services.

In short, by the early 1990s Brockton High had become the poster child for all that ailed education in Massachusetts—indeed, in the United States. Yet, in Massachusetts, the realization also dawned that blame could not be laid solely at the schoolhouse door.

The extraordinary story of Massachusetts's education reforms was, in large part, an unintended consequence of an antitax tsunami—one of many that has swept the nation in recent decades, gutting school budgets—and its impact on one struggling down-at-the-heels town. In Massachusetts, the storm hit in the early 1980s with a ballot initiative that imposed a "rigid" cap on local property taxes. The law, known as Proposition 2½ because it limited local property tax increases to just 2.5 percent, starved school districts and led to growing educational disparities between rich and poor communities. One result of the cap was that low-income communities paid "higher property tax rates for their schools, while spending less per pupil."[7]

During the early years of the initiative, state revenues mitigated the cap by supplementing education budgets in the poorest districts. But when the Massachusetts economy, and its tax receipts, collapsed in the late 1980s, education budgets took a hit on two fronts: state aid to municipalities shrank, and cities and towns gave schools a smaller share of the dwindling funds they were getting from the state. While many towns asked voters to "override" the tax cap for a given year, most such efforts failed.[8]

In the Commonwealth's poorest towns, the results were painful. In Ware, a mill town near Springfield, the local elementary school fell into such disrepair that the children were relocated by grade—some to schools in a nearby town, others to space carved out of a local courthouse, where children ate lunch in a makeshift basement cafeteria next to the lockup, where manacled prisoners waited to see the judge.[9]

For the town of Brockton, in particular, the budget squeeze would prove devastating. Governor Weld's Committee on Distressed School Systems and School Reform had investigated four of the most beleaguered cities in the state. Noting that Brockton had the highest tax rate, it concluded that "the state, not the city, had walked away from its duty to adequately fund public education."[10]

The committee's report concluded: "Brockton . . . seems to be an example where the commonwealth has not provided funding sufficient to satisfy its obligations vis-a-vis the shared responsibility for public education."[11]

Brockton's plight became a rallying cry for education reformers and an important catalyst for the Massachusetts Education Reform Act of 1993, a groundbreaking piece of legislation—one that would help establish a rare national model of collaborative and sustained education reform. The law was the result of three key interrelated factors.

First, and most importantly, the reform legislation was fueled by strong broad-based leadership and support—in the state legislature, the governor's office, the judiciary, the business community, the teachers unions, and among educators—and the development of a clear vision of what education reform should look like.

Second, the reforms established clear goals and a system for achieving them. The system in Massachusetts would be based on two important pillars. The first was what Tom Birmingham, the president of the state senate and the reform legislation's leading exponent, called "the grand bargain"—increased spending in exchange for increased accountability. The second was a collaborative, transparent, and iterative approach to developing both a new curriculum and a standardized test that became a graduation requirement.

Third, almost everything about the Massachusetts reforms grew out of a deliberate, often messy, and deeply democratic process that included key local constituents—parents, business leaders, and educators at all levels from policy experts to classroom teachers to teachers union staff—throughout the state. The reforms were not rushed, nor were they imposed from above.

Interestingly for a reform blueprint that would make Massachusetts public schools the highest performing in the nation, *charter schools were virtually irrelevant.* The 1993 legislation imposed a cap of just twenty-five charter schools statewide; during the next two decades, that cap was gradually lifted to 120 schools. Ten years after the legislation passed, Massachusetts still had only fifty-seven charter schools. Education reform in Massachusetts was largely the result of improving *traditional public schools.*[12]

The new legislation germinated at least partly in Brockton, and it would reverberate there as nowhere else in Massachusetts; before a decade had passed, Brockton—with its shuttered Main Street, its cottage industry of homeless hotels, and its swelling ranks of poor immigrants—would undertake one of the most remarkable turnarounds in American education.

In short, Brockton became for two decades—beginning in the 1980s and on up through the Great Recession—a litmus test for the not-so-quiet revolution that was the Massachusetts education reforms. In Brockton, specifically at Brockton High, the largest and once most dysfunctional high school in the state, education reform at the local level was both spurred by and mirrored the successes seen at the state level. It was also in Brockton that the key traits of the revolution were fully visible. They included a commitment to a school-wide continuous-improvement strategy; the development of a highly iterative literacy strategy that was hammered out democratically by the school community writ large—from teachers to local business leaders; and a school leader who was trusted and who, in turn, fostered trust among staff, parents, and the local community.

Colonial Massachusetts was one of the first places on earth to make the education of children a public responsibility. In 1642, Massachusetts became the first colony to pass a law requiring that children be taught to read and write. Five years later, the Commonwealth required that every town establish a public school—though it would be nearly two more centuries before all children were required to attend.[13]

John Adams had been a schoolteacher for a short time before becoming a lawyer and, importantly, before serving as chief justice of the Massachusetts Supreme Judicial Court and eventually as president of the United States. In his *Thoughts on Government* essay of 1776, Adams wrote: "Laws for the liberal education of youth, especially of the lower class of people, are so extremely wise and useful, that to a humane and generous mind, no expence for this purpose would be thought extravagant." And by "liberal education" he meant explicitly "not merely vocational" education.[14]

Four years later, Adams became the chief author of the Massachusetts constitution, in which he enshrined the education clause, arguing that it was the state's duty to "cherish" education—the word "cherish" having a more robust meaning in those days than it does today:[15]

> Wisdom, and knowledge, as well as virtue, diffused generally among the body of the people, being necessary for the preservation of their rights and liberties; and as these depend on spreading the opportunities and advantages of education in the various parts of the country, and among the different orders of the people, it shall be the duty of legislatures and magistrates, in all future periods of this commonwealth, to cherish the interests of literature and the sciences, and all seminaries of them; especially the university at Cambridge, public schools and grammar schools in the towns.[16]

Historically, Massachusetts has boasted education levels higher than the national average. Massachusetts also has one of the lowest poverty rates in the nation. Only a half dozen states had lower poverty rates than Massachusetts overall, according to the 1990 census. Among African Americans in particular, Massachusetts does better than three-quarters of the states.

The Massachusetts Constitution had, of course, served as a model for the federal Constitution. Chief Justice Paul Liacos, on the occasion of the three hundredth anniversary of the Commonwealth's Supreme Judicial Court, paid homage to the important role state courts and constitutions play in safeguarding individual rights. It was hard to imagine a judge who would be more disposed to rule in favor of McDuffy than Chief Justice Liacos. "If the Massachusetts Constitution established a right to an adequate education, he would protect that right without regard to the potentially difficult political consequences that might ensue," noted Vivek Rao, then an editor for the *California Law Review*.

"For a jurist of Chief Justice Liacos's leanings, Adams's powerful words all but decided *McDuffy*." The court quoted John Adams's language from the Massachusetts Constitution, noting that the Commonwealth of Massachusetts "has a duty to provide an education for all its children, rich and poor, in every city and town of the Commonwealth at the public school level."[17]

Moreover, the court argued that the responsibility lay with the state government, not local municipalities, and that the state had failed in its constitutional duties.[18]

The court's decision actually proved far more influential *after* the passage of the education-reform act than in the lead-up to it. The court case, which would be decided almost exactly one week after the education act's passage, may have served as a catalyst for the reforms. But its most important effect, argues Paul Reville, another Weld appointee on the Committee on Distressed Schools who would go on to become state education secretary under Governor Deval Patrick, was in holding "the Commonwealth's feet to the fire anytime anyone wanted to back down" from funding the legislation, knowing it might throw the case back into the courts.[19]

While the courts and the governor's committee had laid important groundwork for education reform, the business community turned out to be a pivotal—if somewhat surprising—driver in the reform effort. Surprising because Proposition 2½ had been championed by the business community.

Aware that many blamed the business community for the tax cap and concerned about the toll it had taken on public education, in 1990 several business leaders came together under the leadership of Jack Rennie, the founder of Pacer Systems, a builder of military software and hardware, to form the Massachusetts Business Alliance for Education. MBAE raised private funds for a thorough analysis of Massachusetts education and reached out to a broad constituency to develop its proposals.[20]

Rennie's approach was unorthodox and would put him at odds with many business reformers; Rennie, for example, insisted on bringing the union to the table and making it a partner in education reform. Kathy Kelley, then president of the Massachusetts Federation of Teachers, called Rennie her "hero." And unlike the business leaders who had recently established the Pioneer Institute, a conservative think tank that sought to apply "market principles to public policy," Rennie opposed charter schools and "school choice." In Massachusetts, "choice" meant giving parents the option to select schools outside their district, which often led white parents to abandon schools with large numbers of minority kids.[21] While Rennie had attended a Catholic high school, he and his wife, Carol, sent all five of their children to public schools in Bedford, Massachusetts.[22]

Rennie asked Paul Reville to spearhead the MBAE's effort—a key reason Reville was later chosen by Weld to serve on the Committee on Distressed Schools. In 1991, just as *McDuffy* was wending its way through the courts and just a few months before Weld's committee released its own condemnation of education in Massachusetts, MBAE issued "Every Child a Winner! A Proposal for a Legislative Action Plan for Systemic Reform of Massachusetts' Public Primary and Secondary Education System."

The MBAE report embodied the "grand bargain"—a lot more education funding in exchange for accountability—that came to characterize the 1993 legislation. It called for "equity across all school districts." And in its specifics, the report outlined what would become the key characteristics of the reform law, including:

- accountability via statewide standards;
- operational reforms to improve teacher quality and school management; and
- a "foundation" budget that called for an "ideal" in which "all communities in the state be able to provide funding for their students with the same school tax rate."

This foundation—or baseline—budget was complex and included everything from teacher and administrative salaries to funding for books and computers, as well as allocations for maintenance and teacher training. The budget also allocated special funds for programs for "disadvantaged" youth in recognition of the fact that among the eleven poorest communities, which made up a quarter of public school enrollment, "none . . . come within $2,000 per student of funding we think they need."[23]

Under the plan, every district would have to spend at least as much as its "foundation budget." At the same time, no district would be required to levy a school tax rate greater than one percent of its property value. "If monies generated by these local property taxes were insufficient to meet the foundation budget, state aid funds would make up the difference."[24]

Under the existing system for financing schools, the state did redistribute funds progressively, but the extra monies received by poor districts didn't make up for the disparities in tax revenue between rich and poor districts. Consequently, poor communities taxed their residents at higher property levels, yet per-pupil spending in Massachusetts still "varied from as low as $3,382 in Douglas to $10,000 in Lincoln."[25]

Ultimately, the MBAE's foundation funding level was set at $5,000 per student for "typical" districts and $6,000 in districts with high numbers of low-income students. Poor cities, like Lawrence and Brockton, would get large cash infusions, while wealthy communities like Andover and Wellesley got "relative spare change."[26]

Equally important, rather than issuing the report from some ivory tower or oak-paneled corporate—or philanthropic—boardroom, Reville had crafted the report carefully and *collaboratively,* bringing in a wide range of stakeholders, including state legislators, the leaders of the teachers union, the president of the Massachusetts Parent-Teacher-Student Association, superintendents, principals, school committee members, and the dean of the Harvard Graduate School of Education, as well as experts in vocational and bilingual education. "Reville's career in education had taken him through the roles of volunteer, teacher, principal, administrator, and policymaker, and he believed that meaningful reform of something as complex as a statewide public education system required the input—and support—of a wide range of interested parties."[27]

By positioning the MBAE as an "ally" of educators and as "reform done with the [education] field, not to the field," for a time the business community set itself apart—and insulated the state's efforts—from the divisive top-down impulses of business reformers elsewhere.[28]

Buoyed by the brisk winds of judicial activism, business backing, and public support, lawmakers and the Commonwealth's education bureaucracy knew that change was necessary and that the time was ripe for a new education law. The next act in the reform drama would play out in the state legislature.

TEAM OF RIVALS

The new law would be crafted by a team of rivals, all of whom had a deep appreciation for history and the role of education in a democracy, as well as for the intricacies of back-room deal making. The authors of the bill were two Democrats: Tom Birmingham, an up-by-the-bootstraps state senator from South Boston, and Mark Roosevelt, a great-grandson of Theodore Roosevelt who served as Birmingham's counterpart on the Massachusetts House of Representatives education committee. The bill was signed into law by a Republican governor, William Weld, who, like Mark Roosevelt, was a patrician. Once accused of being a *Mayflower* elitist, Weld responded, "Actually, they weren't on the *Mayflower*. They sent the servants over first to get the cottage ready."[29]

Not even the fact that Roosevelt and Weld loathed each other, though they were related by marriage, impeded the grand bargain.[30]

All three politicians were the products of elite Ivy League institutions. All three had graduated from Harvard Law School.

A few years after the education-reform law's passage, Governor Weld, Tom Finneran, then the speaker of the house, and a "somber looking" Birmingham emerged onto the statehouse steps. Before a gaggle of reporters, Birmingham declaimed: "I am fearful that we are adopting a struthian approach to the reductions coming out of the federal government."

Weld and Finneran grinned. The reporters assembled on the statehouse steps scratched their heads.

Struthian is a variation on *struthious*, meaning ostrich-like.

What the reporters didn't know was that that carefully chosen word was part of an intellectual game among the three politicians: Every Monday, one of the three would proffer an arcane word. Within the next twenty-four hours, the others would have to drop the word into a speech or interview. *Struthian* had been Weld's choice; Birmingham quickly rose to the challenge.[31]

Unlike his two patrician collaborators, Birmingham had deep working-class roots. He grew up in a triple-decker in Chelsea, the hardscrabble Southie town that had also been the home of the real-life Horatio Alger. Birmingham was named for his uncle, a local gangster who had been shot to death in a rooming house in 1969. The Birmingham family also was close to the Bulger clan—William "Billy" Bulger would become president of the Massachusetts State Senate, while his brother, James "Whitey" Bulger, was a legendary gangster—a relationship that would prove important during the fight over education reform.[32]

Despite his Ivy League pedigree, Birmingham never left Chelsea behind, though it should be noted he was *not* among his many colleagues in the state legislature who would one day be indicted. He married his high-school sweetheart, Selma Botman, and raised his family in Chelsea. And, importantly for this story, he also remained close to Billy Bulger. "It was as if Al Capone's brother was president of the state senate in Illinois," says Roosevelt. "Serendipitously, his young star was Tom."[33]

With his mentor's backing, Birmingham succeeded Bulger as president of the state senate, just six years after first being elected. He used his position to become the chief guardian and protector of the school reforms. Until he left the state legislature almost a decade later, Birmingham was widely credited with "single-handedly" securing the extra funding needed to support poor school districts—without which the Massachusetts reforms would almost certainly have been a failure—and championing additional funds for remediation to help kids pass the rigorous state test that would become a key component of the reforms.[34]

Roosevelt had been elected to the Massachusetts House of Representatives in 1987, but he would leave the house just two years after the law was passed to run a quixotic race against Weld for the governorship. Having lost by a landslide, Roosevelt left Massachusetts to become superintendent of schools in Pittsburgh.[35]

Bulger, Weld, and Charles Flaherty, the house majority leader, "agreed" that education reform was something they wanted done. In effect, they said: "Let's do it together."[36]

But there were big disagreements—many centered on the money needed to fund the legislation. Not only Weld, but also fiscally conservative Democrats in the Massachusetts house, balked at the law's high price tag. At one point, the speaker even kept the draft legislation from going through the powerful Ways and Means Committee to prevent any changes.[37]

Negotiations finally broke down in the spring of 1992. Weld declared that he could not go along with the "financial assumptions" of the proposed bill and said he would craft his own.[38]

Charter schools proved to be another sticking point. Weld and Birmingham favored them, and the Senate bill would have included no charter cap and supported controversial "choice" legislation.[39] Local business leaders mounted a campaign for school choice and charter schools, forming an insurgency against Rennie.[40]

Weld submitted his own education bill in June 1992. Although the bill provided $3.2 billion extra for public education, it also sought to abolish teacher tenure and seniority.

Incredibly, the bill did not die then and there. That summer there was a lot of back and forth. The legislators eventually acquiesced to Weld's refusal to raise taxes as a way to fund the legislation, but teacher-tenure protections remained in place. Charter school creation would be capped at twenty-five, and school choice would be limited. At the same time, the final bill reflected broad cross-partisan agreement that Massachusetts could not set high expectations without giving schools and students the capacity, in both time and money, to reach those goals.[41]

The Education Reform Act of 1993 would be signed into law just days after Judge Liacos ruled in the *McDuffy* case that Massachusetts had failed in its constitutional obligation to provide poor children with an adequate education. The funding formula sought to eliminate that yawning gap between rich and poor districts. The new "foundation" funding formula would channel $350 million in additional dollars each year to poor districts. (An additional $100 million went toward remediation.[42]) By 2000, every town would be able to afford $5,500 to $6,000 per student, as much as double what some of the poorest towns were then spending on education.[43]

It helped that the legislation passed at the start of a booming economy. As a result of the new reform law and the strong economic growth of the 1990s, real net state aid grew at an annual rate of 6 percent in the decade leading up to 2002, with much of that growth earmarked for education. But when the economy slowed again in 2002, aid fell sharply and has yet to recover to the spending levels seen in 1999 (after adjusting for inflation.)[44]

"I don't think anyone appreciated how progressive the funding formula was" at the time, says Birmingham, noting that once the redistributive nature of the formula became clear, there was considerable "push back" from wealthy towns. By 2004, the formula was changed to ensure that wealthy districts were entitled to 20 percent of the foundation budget. While Birmingham considers the change "reactionary and retrograde," Massachusetts's school-funding formula remained, for years, among the most progressive in the country.[45]

If the law's funding formula was progressive, its "curriculum frameworks" were built on a deeply traditional commitment to teaching core knowledge, including history and classical literature. The ELA frameworks included an appendix with recommended texts, a major departure from many other states. The history frameworks invoked a Jeffersonian vision of "general education" and the importance of "educating a democracy." (Noting that "liberal and humane values are neither revealed truths nor natural habits," the curriculum called for an in-depth look at U.S. history, its institutions, and its values, as well as those of alternative systems.)

The history frameworks didn't propose to teach political "truths" or policy prescriptions, noting that "good democrats can and do differ." Rather, it argued: "The kind of critical thinking we wish to encourage must rest on a solid base of factual knowledge. The central ideas, events, people, and works that have shaped our world, for good and ill, are not at all obsolete. Instead, the quicker the pace of change, the more critical it will be for us to remember them and understand them well . . . without this knowledge, citizens remain helpless to make the wise judgments hoped for by Jefferson."[46]

That vision was conservative, but it was not unilaterally established. Beginning in 1993, the state convened thousands of educators—from the classroom to universities—as well as ordinary citizens to help develop both the state's curriculum frameworks and a high-stakes state test that would ensure students met the new education standards. They met in ten "well-publicized regional open-house forums" that directly solicited comments on the curricula. The state board of education also hosted a two-day televised forum at the statehouse that featured a who's who of distinguished legislators, educators, and business people to discuss the standards. Finally, the state distributed brochures and a twenty-two-minute videotape entitled *Voices of Reform* throughout Commonwealth school districts.

"We developed traveling groups of educators to go around the state and find out what should be included in the curriculum frameworks," recalls Sandra Stotsky, who then served as senior associate commissioner of the state's Department of Elementary and Secondary Education. By the time the accountability piece of the reforms kicked in in 2001—the standardized tests that would determine whether kids received a high school diploma—there was widespread acceptance of the process.[47]

The result of a five-year colloquy—the social-studies curriculum alone went through at least seven contentious drafts—the standards were based in large measure on a rigorous core-knowledge foundation that was not without controversy. The Massachusetts curriculum had ultimately been hammered home by an acerbic, confrontational education "czar," John Silber, the chancellor of Boston University, who had run for governor against Weld (whom Silber had once called "an orange-headed WASP"). Weld had returned the compliment by appointing Silber to be the head the Massachusetts Board of Education in 1996, the same year Silber began serving as chancellor of Boston University; Silber continued to serve in both positions. Critics complained that Silber, in the end, had imposed a white-man's view of history and literature on the curriculum, giving short shrift to readings by women and minorities. Conceded James Peyser, a board member and head of the Pioneer Institute who, years later, would succeed Silber as chair: "There may be some truth to the fact that the framework concentrates too much on Western European history and not enough on Asian, African, not enough on social history, if you will, and that that gives a certain color to the entire document. But there's a point that's inescapable: To understand where we come from, we have to understand that our political values are well grounded in Western history. We'd be ill-advised to avoid it."[48]

To give the reforms teeth, Massachusetts also developed a highly rigorous accountability system based on a new high-stakes test, the Massachusetts Comprehensive Assessment System (or MCAS). Importantly, the MCAS was a graduation requirement and, unlike many modern-day education reforms, placed some of the onus on students; with a few exceptions, high school students would have to pass the tenth-grade-level MCAS in order to earn a high school diploma. Massachusetts also instituted a requirement that teachers pass a basic skills and subject-matter test.[49]

In sharp contrast to the recent Common Core–aligned tests, MCAS was iterative and transparent—a process that not only helped to improve the tests over time but also to legitimize them. The vast majority of test questions were released each year to educators, parents, and students. As a result, when during the early years the MCAS requirements came under fire in many low-performing districts, such as Brockton, for being too rigorous, the publication of student work examples "proved enormously helpful" because they showed "just how *minimal*" the passing requirements were.[50]

TO READ OR NOT TO READ—IT'S THE ONLY QUESTION

Sue Quagg graduated from Brockton High in 1971, two years after the opening of the state-of-the art high school and twenty years before Jami McDuffy joined the lawsuit against the State of Massachusetts. Perky and blond, hair styled in a Gidget-like flip, Sue smiles broadly out of the pages of the Brockton High School yearbook's graduating-class photo. As Sue remembers it, her high school years were about as idyllic as the 1960s sitcom of the Malibu surfer chick who had a penchant for zany escapades and a doting but wise father. Years before Title IX, Sue played four sports. On weekends and after school, she worked at the local Swedish bakery on Main Street or swept hair at her aunt's downtown beauty salon. Summers, she organized activities for kids at a nearby playground, where she fell in love with a boy named Bill, who was a few years ahead of her at Brockton High and supervisor of the summer program.

But school always held a special fascination for Sue. She excelled academically; history was by far her favorite subject. The best days of all were those when her classes at Brockton High were canceled, and her father, Eddie Quagg, would take her to a school in a neighboring town. There, Sue would get to watch her dad, the best teacher in the world, at work.

There was never any doubt that Sue, too, would become a teacher. What she did not anticipate is that her career would never take her beyond the two-to-three-square-mile radius in which she lived with her parents and four siblings in a neat white clapboard house near the high school.

Sue and several of her classmates would attend nearby colleges and return to teach at Brockton High. Sue married Bill Szachowicz, her high school sweetheart, who also taught at Brockton. They moved into an apartment not far from her parents' home.

But the ground beneath Brockton and the Szachowiczes was shifting. Sue's forebears—the Quagliozzis, as they were once called, who hailed from Casino, Italy—had come to Brockton as part of a wave of immigrants seeking well-paying manufacturing jobs—as had Bill's. Brockton, just twenty miles from Boston, had once shod the feet of one in five Americans, including Union soldiers during the Civil War. In its heyday, the town's industrial vibrancy had attracted a polyglot mix of European immigrants—Irish and Italians mostly, but also immigrants from Eastern Europe and Armenia. Its unions were so muscular, it was said, that at one time they had scared away General Motors.[51]

As the European immigrants prospered they moved on to more affluent suburbs. Once solidly white, working class, and a beacon of immigrant aspirations, Brockton became largely black, poor, and a symbol of urban decay, a trend that was hastened by the town's industrial decline. As the shoe industry shifted overseas to cheaper manufacturers, Brockton's factories closed, taking with them the town's manufacturing jobs.

Brockton became a twenty-one-square-mile island of poverty—amid the vast spread of affluent, mostly white suburbs surrounding Boston. "Geographically, it's easy to avoid Brockton," says Chris Cooney, the head of the local chamber of commerce.[52]

Easy to circumvent, easy to forget.

As Brockton declined, so did its high school. The proud alma mater of Rocky "The Brockton Blockbuster" Marciano and Marvelous Marvin Hagler (years before he added "Marvelous" to his legal name), Brockton High came to care more about its sports teams than its academics.

By 1993, when Massachusetts passed its groundbreaking education-reform legislation, Brockton High was in deep crisis. It had suffered millions of dollars in budget cuts, mass teacher layoffs, ballooning class size, and the widespread neglect of its once state-of-the-art buildings and equipment. At the same time, the student body had also been transformed; it was poorer, browner, and less prepared for high school. The new education reform law would gradually restore some of that funding, but uplifting morale and expectations would require more than money.

The legislation's new accountability system, which made passing the new high-stakes MCAS test a graduation requirement, would prove a major hurdle for Brockton students. Its failure rate in English Language Arts was 44 percent in 1998; its failure rate in math was 75 percent. A year later and just two years shy of when the new rules for earning a high school diploma would go into effect, the failure rate in ELA remained stubbornly high and had actually gotten worse in math, reaching 77 percent. Then, on December 8, 1999, Brockton High found itself publicly shamed on the front page of the *Boston Globe* as one of the worst schools in Massachusetts.[53]

"We faced the very real possibility that the majority of our students would not earn a high school diploma," recalls Sue Szachowicz, who was then head of the school's social studies department. Now affectionately known by almost everyone in town as Dr. Szach, she was convinced that the problem at Brockton was one of culture—not lack of capability. Brockton's teachers, most of whom were white and many of whom hailed from the mostly blue-collar Brockton of her girlhood days, believed it was every student's "right to fail."

And fail they did. Brockton was so accustomed to low expectations that one administrator joked at the time that since only students who could pass the MCAS would graduate, they could move the graduation ceremony from the football stadium to the school's Little Theater.

Leadership had not been a strong suit at Brockton for a while. But for Dr. Szach and several of her colleagues, such public failure—the very real possibility that a majority of their students might not graduate high school and that, once again, the school might find itself shamed on the front page of the newspapers—was not an option. They set about trying to figure out what to do. It was, at least partly, a mark of desperation that a small group of teachers persuaded the principal to let them try a new idea.

Eugene Marrow, Brockton High's principal at the time, had been a gym teacher and a football coach. Marrow recognized that he was "not a curriculum guy," says Dr. Szach, but "he believed in improvement." Like most Brockton students, Marrow was African American. He had grown up in Brockton, had high expectations of kids, and believed in the idea that Brockton High could improve what it was doing. Besides, the school was doing so poorly, they had "nothing to lose," quips Dr. Szach.[54]

The Brockton teachers behind the restructuring were led by Dr. Szach and Paul Larino, then the head of Brockton High's English department. The teachers set out to form a school-wide, multidisciplinary literacy strategy that focused on developing a standard writing curriculum for all classes and retraining all the teachers in the school to teach that curriculum. It was a wholly homegrown effort, but one that would come to include everyone from teachers to the local business community.[55]

Within a little over a decade, Brockton would go from one of the lowest performing schools in the state to one of the highest and, in 2009, it would be featured in a Harvard University report on exemplary schools that have narrowed the minority achievement gap.[56] Today, 85 percent of Brockton students score advanced or proficient on the MCAS, the state's standardized tests, and 64 percent score advanced or proficient in math. Close to 90 percent of Brockton students go to college and, in the two years leading up to 2016, a third of the school's graduates won the state's Adams tuition scholarships to attend college.[57]

Two decades after the literacy strategy was launched, Brockton was still focused on the same process-obsessed approach to literacy. At a time when school systems are under growing pressure to institute ever-changing remedies to improve their performance, Brockton has focused single-mindedly on improving its literacy strategy.

Yet, says Dr. Szach, who was appointed associate principal for curriculum and instruction in 2000 and became principal three years later: "This was no fast pirouette." Although Brockton's scores began to improve within the first year of the literacy initiative, she adds, it was always about "doing it systematically and doing it the same way" year after year.

It was also about getting everyone at Brockton High to "row in the same direction."

Of course, persuading over three hundred veteran teachers in a school that had grown used to failure to try something new wasn't easy. It helped that Marrow, who backed the experiment, was "not an outsider," says Dr. Szach.

The first big challenge was to find a critical mass of teachers who would join what came to be known as the "restructuring committee." Dr. Szach and Larino begged and cajoled and finally recruited about twenty teachers whom they considered school leaders and who represented most of the disciplines at Brockton. Over the course of several months, the restructuring committee developed what would be a four-part definition of literacy as well as a detailed calendar for implementing the literacy strategy in every discipline from English and social studies to math and science. Not even P.E. was exempt.

Significantly, almost every facet of the strategy was homegrown. Just about the only thing for which the literacy committee turned to outside help was in developing a system for evaluating how the strategy was being implemented.

Importantly, the literacy strategy also was designed to be highly collaborative.

Yet the rollout was neither quick nor easy. Although the first MCAS had been given in 1998—the occasion for Brockton's public shaming in the *Boston Globe*—the test wouldn't "count" toward graduation until 2001. From the start, the Massachusetts education reformers agreed to a deliberative ramp-up of the tests. "I didn't think it was fair to students to deny them a high school diploma, which is an awesome responsibility, if they didn't have every opportunity to bring themselves up to speed," says Birmingham. "The deliberate approach was intentional and justified."[58]

Brockton had three years in which to get its students prepared. Meanwhile, Brockton students kept taking the MCAS. And because the test was open, each year Brockton's restructuring committee pored over the questions and the students' answers trying to analyze their specific areas of weakness. That's when Brockton made its first big mistake—but one that would be highly instructive.

"We noticed a large number of questions about Shakespeare on the ELA test," recalls Dr. Szach. There were a lot of plays and sonnets.

The English teachers mobilized, planning a "grand Shakespearean learning experience" for the months of March and April. For two months, Brockton students acted out plays and analyzed sonnets. Imagine the teachers' dismay when Brockton students opened their test booklets that spring and found not one question about the Bard.[59]

For the third year in a row, Brockton's MCAS scores barely budged. The ELA failure rate decreased by only three points to 41 percent, and the math failure rate remained stubbornly high at 64 percent.[60]

The restructuring committee reconvened that summer, but instead of trying to psych out what questions would be on the test, this time the committee asked a different question: "What skills and knowledge did our students need to know and demonstrate to be successful?"

"We noticed that students had to read many difficult, complex passages and write responses to those reading passages," recalls Dr. Szach. "We also noticed that they had to solve many complex problems with multiple parts."[61]

A school-wide item analysis showed that students were performing poorly on the written portions of the test, which accounted for more than half the test. Many students were leaving the writing portions blank, not even attempting to answer those questions. Even the math questions required students to explain their thinking. The restructuring committee concluded that Brockton "students were not prepared for the complex problem solving and critical thinking that was required of them."[62]

To solve both the critical-thinking and the writing challenges, the restructuring committee agreed they had to focus on literacy. But what exactly did that mean?

First, Brockton High had to come up with a definition of literacy. Did it mean kids could read a newspaper or a textbook? Did it mean reading at grade level or that they could solve word problems?[63]

There were almost as many definitions of literacy as there were members of the restructuring committee. "We decided we needed to broaden the conversation," recalls Dr. Szach. "We realized we weren't preparing kids for Brockton High, but for life after school."[64]

So Dr. Szach and her colleagues invited parents to attend the restructuring committee meetings. They also invited Chris Cooney, the newly appointed head of Brockton's Metro South Chamber of Commerce.

GETTING BUY-IN AT BROCKTON HIGH

Boyishly handsome, with dark hair and blue eyes, Cooney had just taken the job at the Chamber of Commerce when Dr. Szach invited him to meet with the Brockton High restructuring committee in 1998. Asked what the business community thought the school should focus on—the skills that kids needed more than anything else—Cooney's response may have surprised them: "I said, if they can truly write, it means they can read and truly comprehend and we can train them. We know that as high school graduates, they won't have all the skills they need for a job. But if they read and write, employers have found they are much more likely to be successful.

"My belief and that of the business community was that reading and writing are more important than anything else. I can give you a book and teach you math if you can read and write and think," says Cooney, his voice trailing off. "We talked about critical thinking too."[65]

Cooney's view reflected that of John Silber, the controversial education "czar" who had once declared that reading "was everything."[66]

That conversation with Cooney reaffirmed that "we were onto something with our focus on writing," says Dr. Szach. "If Chris had said 'we need more thinking around math' we might have gone that route."

But as they hashed through their ideas, the teachers came to agree that literacy meant "much more than reading and writing; it included critical thinking and problem solving."[67] To develop specific literacy skills, the restructuring committee split into subcommittees that worked on articulating the skills and competencies students needed to have in four areas—reading, writing, speaking, and critical thinking.

Here is how Dr. Szach describes the effort: "The subcommittees drafted their lists of skills and then reconvened with the committee to share their suggestions. Members reviewed, argued, and revised. Discussions were spirited, excited, and always focused on what was best for the students. The group's goal was to develop a list that was comprehensive but also simply stated."[68]

The literacy strategy would have to pass what Dr. Szach called the 7-Eleven test. "If you show someone at the 7-Eleven these are the important skills that we think every graduate at Brockton needs to master, clearly and concisely," everyone should be able to understand exactly what is being described.[69]

The literacy objectives would also have to meet two other key criteria: they would be applicable to all students—from those with special needs to the gifted and talented—and they had to be interdisciplinary so that they could be taught in every class and subject.[70]

The next challenge was to engage the faculty in the discussion. The restructuring committee built an iterative process whereby it kept going back to the faculty with drafts of the literacy objectives and the skills it expected students to learn. "We kept asking the faculty three questions," recalls Dr. Szach. "One, did we include everything that you think is necessary, and is anything missing? Two, did we state it clearly? Three, what would you change/add?"[71]

The restructuring committee came up with a chart of specific literacy skills that had to be posted in every classroom, and they made sure that the skills were applicable in all content areas. The committee also developed a ten-step process for writing an "open response"—an assignment that requires students to read a text and to write an essay responding to a question about the text. The benefit of the "open response" assignment was that it crossed "all disciplinary lines." No class or teacher would be exempt—not math, not science or gym.[72] The literacy strategy would be refined over time. In recent years, for example, it has focused on honing students' ability to read graphs and charts.[73]

"One of the things that played out in Brockton was an acknowledgment that teachers should have minimum comprehension of English themselves, of reading and writing, and a responsibility to encourage proper reading and writing—regardless of whether they are a math or a gym teacher," explains Cooney.[74]

To implement the strategy, Brockton created a strict schedule of literacy assignments that every department was required to follow. The schedule was designed to ensure that over the course of the academic year, the same skills would be repeated over and over in a variety of different disciplines so that students would get the same consistent message about the Brockton writing process in every subject. When they were done hammering out the literacy charts and showed them to Cooney, he said: "If you could get kids to master these skills, they'd be ready for everything."[75]

Adult learning would be key to the success of Brockton's literacy strategy. "I was a history teacher and I used primary source readings all the time, but I didn't know how to teach reading," recalls Dr. Szach. "What we were onto is if we're going to ask people to do things differently, we have to show them how."[76]

The restructuring committee recognized that a school-wide literacy initiative would very likely run into "tremendous resistance." Consequently, the committee "spent many hours planning how to involve the faculty. Dr. Szach and her colleagues also recognized that for the literacy initiative to take hold, "[e]nsuring that the faculty had a strong voice in the development and implementation was critical."[77]

The restructuring committee would also have to work within the strict rules of the teachers union contract, which allowed for just two teacher meetings per month of one hour each. The meetings had always been a chore, a time when teachers were reluctantly corralled to listen to announcements that could just as easily have been put into a memo. The restructuring committee got permission from the principal to use the meetings to hash out the literacy strategy and to conduct teacher training. This meant that the training sessions could last no more than an hour. The union was known to file a grievance when the meetings went over by a single minute. Even the one time that the restructuring committee tried to schedule some voluntary meetings, a grievance was filed.

So the restructuring committee developed a step-by-step training module that lasted just under an hour. Teachers would learn the module twice—first as part of an interdisciplinary group, and two weeks later they would take the same training module, but this time within their respective departments, where they could plan ways to integrate content.

Quality monitoring and evaluations—of the literacy strategy, not of individual teachers—were also key, and were the only part of the strategy for which Brockton brought in outside help. Dr. Szach notes that Brockton High's initiative was highly influenced by Jon Saphier's Research for Better Teaching program, which emphasizes "skillfully and relentlessly" monitoring quality, and, in about 2004, she hired Saphier's organization to train administrators on how to evaluate whether the literacy initiative was being properly implemented. Dr. Szach estimates that the school typically spent no more than $35,000 per year on the literacy initiative. (The restructuring committee had initially been funded by a town grant.)[78]

The observations were key to ensuring that teachers were using the process and teaching it on schedule. Equally important, the evaluations were designed to monitor and improve the process, *but not to punish teachers.* After all, for the first time, Brockton High was expecting science teachers, math teachers, even gym teachers to teach writing. "They were nervous about doing something they've never done before," says Dr. Szach.[79]

To make sure that the evaluations were not considered punitive, the school decoupled the literacy observations from teachers' formal job evaluations.

Still, in the early days, getting the teachers to buy in was not easy. "We had some very difficult closed-door conversations," recalls Dr. Szach. "Some left in a way that was not pleasant. But most were in the cautious middle, saying, 'I don't know whether I like it or not.'

"We were a failing school. I said: 'What else do you suggest?'"[80]

Dr. Szach recalls one teacher who covered the mandatory literacy charts in his classroom with posters. When he taught his literacy module, he did so with "sarcasm."

"It was not a good situation; he eventually retired," says Dr. Szach, who acknowledges that the restructuring committee cajoled and pressured teachers to follow the program.[81]

During the literacy brainstorming sessions, the most negative teachers were deliberately grouped together so they wouldn't undermine the majority of teachers, who were willing to give the strategy a try. Dr. Szach estimates that about a dozen teachers left as a direct result of the literacy initiative (about 4 percent of the entire faculty). It was Brockton's "good fortune," she says, that in 2004 the state offered an early-retirement incentive, which allowed the fence-sitters to "walk out the door." In all, some forty teachers, a little over 10 percent of Brockton High's workforce at the time, left, though Dr. Szach notes that not all the teachers who took early retirement were leaving because of the literacy initiative.[82]

Eventually, the majority of Brockton's teachers fell into line. But Dr. Szach makes it clear that the restructuring committee "didn't wait for buy-in," she says. If they had, "we would still be waiting. We got buy-in when we got results."[83]

Also key to the sturdy foundation of Brockton's strategy was the fact that it was an entirely homegrown affair. Marrow, the principal, was born and raised in Brockton, as was Dr. Szach. And the teachers who formed the restructuring committee were almost all longtime Brocktonians.

"Sue Szachowicz had the influence, the authority, the reputation to pull this off," explains Cooney. "If she was from another district or not born here, she'd have been suspect or dismissed."[84]

In short, Brockton High had a strong *local* leader who was able to sell the Brockton literacy strategy to the community—to the teachers, the parents, and, crucially, to the local business community. As the drumbeat of the education-reform movement and the allure of charter schools increased even in the Bay State, Dr. Szach's influence and those relationships would help protect Brockton High's strategy and its results, at least for a time.

WELL SUITED FOR SUCCESS

While Dr. Szach measured Brockton's decline in its dismal test scores, John Merian measured it in flagging tuxedo rentals. At one time, Tuxedos by Merian, located on Main Street in downtown Brockton, had outfitted 325 teenagers each year for Brockton High's junior prom. These days, he's lucky if he does 200. The senior prom business is still robust, but during the Great Recession, even that took a beating.[85]

Like Dr. Szach, Merian is a third-generation Brocktonian. The grandchild of Armenian refugees who fled Smyrna, Turkey, in 1915, Merian remains among the few business owners who still see their lives as being tied to the town, the high school, and the future of both. Implausibly, Merian has doubled down on this depressed community. Today, Merian's customers are Cape Verdean and Haitian immigrants, not Greeks and Italians. The tailor who nips the lapels and tucks the pants legs in Merian's brightly lit dressing room is also Cape Verdean.[86]

Merian's grandfather began working in a local shoe factory soon after arriving in Brockton. His mother, Alyce Reizian, finished college and, after an apprenticeship in Boston at Bonwit Teller, the luxury retailer, opened a millenary shop in Brockton with a $10,000 loan from her working-class parents. Reizian sold veils and headpieces to immigrant brides; when she married an out-of-towner, she persuaded her husband to join her in Brockton. With time, Reizian expanded, creating a bridal salon, Alyce Reizian's. John Merian, her oldest son, eventually opened his tuxedo shop next door.[87]

When she retired a few years ago, Reizian closed the bridal shop, one of the oldest in the state. Like the shoe industry, the U.S. bridal business was now facing tough foreign competition, especially from China, which began mass-producing gowns for a fraction of what they could be made for in the United States. Today, megastores like David's Bridal sell gowns for less than what Reizian used to pay wholesale.

The bridal store remains dark, the fifties-era lettering a fading reminder of a more vibrant past. But next door, Tuxedos by Merian is one of the only large businesses downtown with its lights still on. "I breathe Brockton, and Brockton breathes me," says Merian by way of explanation.[88]

Tuxedos by Merian has bucked the trend of almost inevitable decline, just like Brockton High—and, at least in part, because of Brockton High. It had always been a "challenge" to win over Brockton's ever-changing immigrant community. "Dressing up in a tuxedo isn't necessarily the cultural thing to do for a Cape Verdean or Haitian," explains Merian. "As they get into our society, they are learning that this is something we do. As they're crossing over, they're learning this is a custom here."[89]

High school prom parties, explains Merian, are one place new immigrants learn about assimilation. For his part, Merian has tied his fortunes ever closer to the town's immigrant community and its schools.

Dr. Szach remembers a rich assortment of retailers on Main Street, where you could buy everything from Capezio's dancewear to jewelry to furs as recently as the early 1970s. But most of the retailers—sixty-five to seventy businesses by Alyce Reizian's count—eventually fled to Michael's Plaza, a nearby shopping mall. When Romm & Company, the "Tiffany's to the working classes," abandoned its home at 162 Main Street in 1993, the *New York Times* ran a story signaling the decline of Brockton's Main Street.[90]

Of course, without their foothold on Main Street and in the community, the refugee retailers were unable to support the much higher rents at the mall and soon closed. (Romm's was an exception.)

For the tuxedo store, the decision to stay in Brockton has been challenging. Merian recently opened a fire-restoration business that helps salvage clothing damaged in fires. He has diversified and now sells suits as well. And he uses the Internet like a teleflorist, he says, to expand sales statewide, taking measurements of tuxedo customers online and then visiting schools to deliver the suits and do last-minute adjustments.[91]

A compact man with thinning black hair and a carefully trimmed door-knocker goatee, Merian sits at the kitchen table of his brightly refurbished Victorian home. One of the nicest houses in Brockton, it is comfortable, but no mansion. Merian's four kids—ages eleven to nineteen—and numerous nieces and nephews roam in and out of the kitchen as Maral, Merian's oldest daughter, gets ready for her senior prom. It's cold and foggy outside and threatening rain, but some twenty teenagers, all seniors at Brockton High, pose on the front lawn for their pre-prom photos. The girls are wearing jewel-colored gowns; the boys are dressed in Merian's tuxedos. Reizian, in a glittery black pantsuit, large squarish glasses, and a coiffed helmet of gray hair, watches her granddaughter and their friends from a window overlooking the front porch.

Merian came of high school age just as Brockton High was experiencing a period of record growth and overcrowding. It was just before the new building opened, so the old Brockton High ran double shifts—bleary-eyed teenagers dragging in at 7:30 a.m., with the rest arriving shortly after noon. Dr. Szach did the double shift too during tenth grade and hated it; the new high school opened when she was a junior. Until then, many families who could afford to sent their kids to private school. Reizian worried that her Johnny, "a small kid," wouldn't make the sports teams at Brockton High; determined that he should "not be deprived," she enrolled her son as a day student at Tabor Academy, a boarding school in nearby Marion.[92]

Merian's own children, by contrast, would attend Brockton High.

Each winter, Merian dons a red cap trimmed in white fur and runs the annual Holiday Day parade down Main Street as the self-appointed chief elf, a post-Thanksgiving event that he calls "the ultimate community gathering" in a downtown with little left to boast about except that it once had the first department-store Santa. Edgar's, originator of the department-store Santa and Brockton's last major retailer, had closed by the 1980s.[93]

One year, Merian made Dr. Szach the grand marshal of the parade. But it wasn't until about 2011, when Merian took his son Levon to Brockton High orientation and heard Dr. Szach speak, that he had an epiphany. "This woman is like my counterpart," he recalls thinking. "She was very clear about what she wanted. Everyone in that high school knew exactly what she stood for; that's the best thing about a leader."

Merian's connection to Brockton High deepened under Dr. Szach's stewardship and came to symbolize her highly local, heterodox approach to turning around the school.

"She believed in me based on what I'm doing in the community," says Merian. "I wasn't going in there peddling tuxedos."[94]

Dr. Szach concedes: "I know fully well, if John's in the school, of course his business will benefit. The kids will say: 'Oh that's the Elf guy who sells tuxedos. I'll go to his store.'"

"I always saw [the] business connection as a win-win," says Dr. Szach. "Obviously, you have to walk the line," she adds. But in a town like Brockton, one of the poorest in Massachusetts, where the median family income in the poorest neighborhoods straddling Main Street was just $16,000 per year in 2010, she knew that local business people were a vital resource—as role models, as occasional sources of funding, and, perhaps most importantly, as beacons of hope. Men like Merian, in their steadfast commitment to Main Street, seemed to be saying: I could leave, but I'm not, because I believe in you.[95]

And Dr. Szach was determined to tap Merian as a resource.

"At the time, one of our literacy skills was speaking, presenting yourself," she says. A "partnership" with a guy like Merian, a parent and a local civic leader, would be helpful.

"We didn't have a plan," says Dr. Szach of her conversations with Merian. "We were just talking." But the one thing she knew was that Brockton kids didn't "know how to present themselves. I used to tell the kids: 'There are many things you can change about yourself'; but I tell them you can't change someone's first impression of you. It remains with them forever."

That message would be much more powerful coming from a respected member of the business community who says: "I'm not going to hire you if you come in looking like that."

So Dr. Szach invited Merian to the school on dress-for-success day, and Merian arrived looking ragged, his scruffy garb the ideal foil for a lecture on the importance of first impressions.[96]

Merian also organizes history tours of downtown Brockton for local kids. Stops along the tour include the now defunct shoe factories and Thomas Edison's first central power station, the "first perfect and entirely safe and practical" underground system for manufacturing and distributing electricity. Erected in the heart of downtown Brockton, where it could "safely and inexpensively" power homes, offices, and shoe factories, the Brockton experiment proved that electricity could be reliably generated for places miles away from a central power station.[97]

"People tend to want to belong to things if they have a stake or a kindred feeling," explains Merian. How else, he asks, are kids from such a diverse community—one that today speaks fifty different languages—to "find common ground?"

How else to "bring pride back to the community?" asks Merian. "I figured that if we developed the premise we all live in the city of Brockton, share the same history, we can move forward and develop a pride that will take us to wanting to develop an ownership stake."

The owners of Brockton family businesses used to send their kids to local Brockton schools, says Merian. Many of those businesses are now gone. But Merian laments something else: these days "there's not the same level of connection" between wealthy people and schools like Brockton High, he says, identifying what he sees as a key loss for public education.[98]

In 2012, after more than a decade leading Brockton High, Dr. Szach was ready to retire. She understood that the transition to a new principal would pose new challenges to the school's culture and its decade-long record of steady improvement. On its latest state assessments, 96 percent of Brockton students passed English Language Arts.

"Brockton's success has come from an administrative team that has worked together, and I would like to see that consistency of leadership continue," said Dr. Szach at the time.[99]

Succession planning poses the ultimate challenge for both large and small organizations. Major corporations, such as Hewlett Packard, which had six CEOs during the course of a decade, aren't very good at it. And just a few months before Dr. Szach announced her retirement, in New York City, Mayor Michael Bloomberg jeopardized his own education legacy when he botched the succession of his long-serving schools chancellor Joel Klein (see chapter 2).

Dr. Szach, by contrast, had planned carefully. She had spent years grooming Sharon Wolder, who started at Brockton as a student teacher in 1994 and eventually became associate principal and Dr. Szach's right hand.

Wolder grew up in Iowa, not Brockton. She is African American, one of the few at a school where most students now were black and brown. Of course, Wolder would have to go through the school committee and the superintendent. But Dr. Szach had positioned her well, and in the end Wolder was chosen unanimously over three other candidates.[100]

The leadership transition at Brockton, though, would be fraught with peril. By 2010, a very different narrative of reform had begun to make inroads in Brockton, in Massachusetts, and, indeed, throughout the country.

THE COMMON CORE TRUMPS THE BAY STATE REFORMS

At the end of the movie *The Big Short*, the narrator tells us that after the financial crisis, the wealthy got bailed out while economic woes were blamed on "immigrants, the poor, and, for the first time, teachers."

Schools, teachers, and students would pay for the financial crisis, and nowhere was there more to lose than in Massachusetts. In state after state, governors and education departments strapped for money would compete desperately for billions of dollars in Race to the Top funds. The catch was that to get the money, states would have to sign on to its education-reform remedies, including developing punitive teacher evaluations, agreeing to follow the Common Core State Standards, and expanding charter schools.

In retrospect, the unraveling of Massachusetts's education reforms goes back, at least, to 2008 and the financial crisis, which devastated local and state economies. By the time Silber resigned as chair of the board of education in 1999 he had sowed division in the education community, according to Paul Reville, the former head of MBAE. His replacement, Jim Peyser, the executive director of the Pioneer Institute, was far more diplomatic than Silber—he had graduated from Tufts University's Fletcher School of Diplomacy, after all—and would become a fierce adversary of teachers and a vigorous advocate for charters, and was "credited with helping to move what was a fringe educational experiment" in Massachusetts "toward the mainstream."[101]

By 2003, there were growing tensions over the push for charters and the expansion of Boston's pilot schools, semi-autonomous public schools akin to the New York City Learning Zone schools (see chapter 2), as well as conflicts among the district, education reformers, and an increasingly restive union.

Then, just months before the financial crisis, a group of private organizations—the National Governors Association, the Council of Chief State School Officers, and Achieve Inc.—issued a call for new K–12 education standards, setting in motion the development of the Common Core State Standards. The effort and its subsequent promotion would be funded with a $233 million investment by the Gates Foundation. By controlling the purse strings and the megaphone, the Gates Foundation engineered what has been called "one of the swiftest and most remarkable shifts in education policy in U.S. history."[102]

Gates's funding allowed states to work together on the Common Core such that they "avoided the usual collision between states' rights and national interests that had undercut every previous effort, dating from the Eisenhower administration." Here is how the *Washington Post* explained what followed:

> The Gates Foundation spread money across the political spectrum, to entities including the big teachers unions, the American Federation of Teachers and the National Education Association, and business organizations such as the U.S. Chamber of Commerce—groups that have clashed in the past but became vocal backers of the standards.
>
> Money flowed to policy groups on the right and left, funding research by scholars of varying political persuasions who promoted

> the idea of common standards. Liberals at the Center for American Progress and conservatives affiliated with the American Legislative Exchange Council who routinely disagree on nearly every issue accepted Gates money and found common ground on the Common Core.
>
> One 2009 study, conducted by the conservative Thomas B. Fordham Institute with a $959,116 Gates grant, described the proposed standards as being "very, very strong" and "clearly superior" to many existing state standards.[103]

In Massachusetts, as elsewhere, the Gates Foundation also funded local groups, among them the MBAE, which became a leading proponent of the Common Core and Common Core–aligned testing regimes. The MBAE, we should recall, was the business group that two decades earlier had proven a leading catalyst for the Massachusetts education reforms.

The Common Core may well have marked an improvement for many states. And Paul Reville, the former head of MBAE, argued that the implementation of the Common Core was a matter of national, not just state, interest: "We're citizens of the nation. People in Mississippi are part of this country too, and if we're going to develop this country, and thrive as a democracy, it makes sense for them to develop too. There is an element of national citizenship involved in thinking about the Common Core."[104]

Whatever the rationale, money was a key factor. States became ever more dependent on federal education revenue, "as state and local budget cuts precipitated by the onset of the Great Recession coincided with a large infusion of federal stimulus funds."[105] That cash infusion included Race to the Top funding. In 2010, when the U.S. Education Department held its first Race to the Top competition, the Bay State's bid came in at a miserable thirteenth place. The reason seemed obvious—the Commonwealth had not yet adopted the Common Core. "There's a lot of disappointment and anger in Massachusetts that our outstanding track record in education reform was not recognized," said Reville, then the state's education secretary.[106]

Like other states, including New York, Massachusetts came around quickly. It no doubt helped that then-Governor Deval Patrick was a friend of President Barack Obama's. After agreeing to adopt the Common Core, Massachusetts won $250 million in a second RTTT competition. That "win" marked the beginning of a series of changes to the state's highly regarded, two-decade-old education system, changes that would put the reforms in Brockton at risk.[107]

Ironically, the debate over the Common Core pitted local free-market reformers—MBAE and the Pioneer Institute, in particular—against each other. The Pioneer Institute sided with a number of respected local education experts who insisted, convincingly, that it was not clear the standards represented an improvement for Massachusetts over its own painstakingly and collaboratively developed curriculum. "Gov. Patrick and education commissioner Mitchell Chester, by adopting weaker federal standards, killed off the commonwealth's proven, poetry-rich state English standards for $250 million in federal money," wrote Jamie Gass, director of the Center for School Reform at the Pioneer Institute.[108]

What is clear is that the Common Core was pushed forward with remarkable haste and virtually no meaningful input from local educators or from the public writ large. How could there be when forty-five states and the District of Columbia had signed on in just two years?

Equally important, for a national standard to be politically palatable in low-performing states, the standards couldn't be set at the highest level. Tom Birmingham, who is now also affiliated with the Pioneer Institute, explained:

> What concerns me is a political issue. Forty-five states plus D.C. have signed onto Common Core, including some of our poorest-performing states—Mississippi and Alabama. If they were taking the MCAS they would have staggeringly high failure rates—like Brockton had. As a political matter, if you have what amounts to a national standard, it has to be a standard that is reachable by all the students, it has to be within the realistic reach of all the states . . .
>
> This is a problem we faced in education reform in Massachusetts; we had high-performing districts and low-performing districts. But we had an intellectually honest answer to that. We said: We're going to pour much more money into the poor districts to lift them up. Nobody is saying: Let's bring Mississippi and Alabama up to Massachusetts's levels of school spending! I think the pressure will be not a race to the top, but a race to the middle regarding the standards. Those standards, by definition, will be lower than what we are insisting on in Massachusetts today.[109]

Some of the strongest criticism of the Common Core came from Sandra Stotsky, a fiery, diminutive education expert with a list of credentials as long the Charles River. As senior associate commissioner of the state's Department of Elementary and Secondary Education, Stotsky had helped develop the Massachusetts education standards. She had worked on Achieve's American Diploma Project, a Gates Foundation–funded effort to develop high school exit-test standards for English in 2004. She had been appointed by then–Secretary of Education Margaret Spellings to the National Mathematics Advisory Panel and served from 2006 to 2008. She was also appointed to the Common Core's "validation committee."[110]

Stotsky condemned the Common Core for the "mediocre quality" of its English Language Arts and reading standards and for the lack of transparency in the way it was both developed and promoted as a de facto national standard. She was also concerned, and offended, that the majority of those who developed the standards were test developers, not educators.[111]

Testifying before the Texas State Legislature in 2011, Stotsky said:

> After the Common Core Initiative was launched in early 2009, the National Governors Association and the Council of Chief State School Officers never explained to the public what the qualifications were for membership on the standards-writing committees or how it would justify the specific standards they created. Most important, it never explained why Common Core's high school exit standards were equal to college admission requirements without qualification, even though this country's wide ranging post-secondary institutions use a variety of criteria for admission.[112]

Stotsky and several members of the Common Core "validation committee"—what she calls a "rubber-stamp committee"—submitted detailed critiques between October 2009 and May 2010, hoping to remedy what they viewed as its many deficiencies. Eventually, Stotsky and four other members of the validation committee declined to sign off on the final version of the Common Core.[113]

Stotsky would crisscross the country speaking about the problems with the Common Core. But the subject she kept coming back to, again and again, was that contrary to the well-funded public-relations rhetoric of the Gates Foundation and the National Governors Association, the Common Core was deeply undemocratic. At a crowded forum in Bridgeport, West Virginia, Stotsky talked about how much she had "always loved the idea behind open town-hall meetings" and "being able to participate in the affairs of one's own community that you live in and pay taxes for."

The development of the Common Core, by contrast, was "in violation of almost everything [she] had ever learned about civic procedures."

Because the standards were developed by private organizations, you couldn't even conduct a Freedom of Information Act request, Stotsky explained. "There was no way anyone could ever get information from any of these organizations about why anyone was appointed to the committees, what their charge was, what they were paid," she said.[114]

By 2016, the Gates Foundation had admitted as much. In an open letter that spanned the breadth of its operations in everything from global health to education, CEO Sue Desmond-Hellmann touched on the Achilles' heel of the foundation's education strategy: "We missed an early opportunity to sufficiently engage educators—particularly teachers—but also parents and communities so that the benefits of the standards could take flight from the beginning." (Though I suspect Desmond-Hellmann was more interested in *selling* educators on the standards than in engaging in a vigorous discussion of its contents and implementation.)[115]

In any event, damage was already being done in Massachusetts. By early 2015, another education-reform campaign was under way, this time to jettison the MCAS test in favor of a new, speculative, Common Core–aligned assessment. Massachusetts Common Core proponents advocated adopting the so-called PARCC test, one of two new tests that were being developed by government-funded consortia as part of the Common Core effort.

That February, the MBAE endorsed the PARCC test over MCAS, saying it held "*the promise*" of being a better indicator of "college- and career-readiness."

"The current MCAS high school tests do not identify students who are college- and career-ready, and they do not contain the right content to measure college- and career-readiness," concluded the MBAE study.

Stotsky countered: "Almost all the students at the Advanced level and about 80 percent of the students at the Proficient level [on the MCAS] who had enrolled in four-year public colleges and universities in the Bay State in 2005 needed no remediation in mathematics or reading. They were college-ready as well as high-school-diploma ready."[116]

Meanwhile, researchers at the Pioneer Institute argued that many of PARCC's backers, and the flurry of anti-MCAS research, were riddled with conflicts of interest. The PARCC proponents, they said, had all received funding—lots of it—from the Gates Foundation.

In an April 2015 op-ed, Charles Chieppo and Jamie Gass detail the tangled web of relationships that tie the critics of the Massachusetts reforms to the Gates Foundation, the PARCC tests, and the Common Core. The op-ed is particularly scathing about the role of the MBAE:

> The Mass. Business Alliance study's credibility was further compromised by the fact that its author is an adviser to PARCC. An earlier report from the Alliance—written by the senior education adviser to

> the giant testing company Pearson, which is near the top of a long list of entities that stand to gain from the switch to Common Core—was so bereft of intellectual integrity that it lifted an entire purported "case study" from *The Boston Globe* without attribution.[117]

However, the winner of the "conflict-of-interest derby," according to Chieppo and Gass, was Teach Plus, a Boston-based education-reform organization, which published a report, "Massachusetts Teachers Examine PARCC," recommending that the commonwealth "ditch" MCAS for PARCC. Teach Plus received over $17 million from the Gates Foundation, including stipends for each of the twenty-three fellows who worked on the report.[118]

The Pioneer Institute said that while it has neither solicited nor received funding from the Gates Foundation, it has been approached by it. "The more noise we made the more they seemed interested in 'working with' us," said Gass.[119]

In 2015, for the first time, Massachusetts elementary and middle schools had the choice of taking the PARCC test or the MCAS. In the fall of 2015, the state's Board of Elementary and Secondary Education voted to develop a hybrid version of the MCAS test that would incorporate some elements of PARCC, the first major overhaul of Massachusetts's standardized test in over two decades. The decision left educators and students in limbo for a year and a half as the new hybrid test was being developed.[120]

Ironically, even the Common Core's staunchest advocates couched their support in conditional terms. "[I]t is not possible to know how much" of the "promise" of the PARCC tests "will be fulfilled," conceded the MBAE report. Reville, meanwhile, said: "*Our hope* is that they're a more sophisticated generation of tests, they'll be aligned with the Common Core and will generate information more quickly and in a more useful fashion than we've been able to do in the past" (emphasis added).[121]

THE CHARTER WARS COME TO MASSACHUSETTS

In her first year on the job as Brockton's new principal, Sharon Wolder faced a host of new challenges. She would need to complete the school's periodic accreditation process, phase in a new district-wide teacher-evaluation system (the price for Massachusetts's Race to the Top funding), and prepare for the arrival of the new Common Core–aligned tests that would likely replace the MCAS.

At the same time, Wolder was committed to maintaining Brockton High's literacy strategy. She selected Bob Perkins, a longtime Brockton math teacher and contemporary of Dr. Szach, to serve as associate principal, and she continued the work of the restructuring committee.

Yet there were forces at work that could undermine Brockton's focus. During her first fall semester, in 2013, Wolder and her team spent months implementing the new RTTT-driven state-mandated teacher evaluations, which were meant to make teachers more accountable. At the time, a study by the Government Accounting Office found numerous problems with how teacher evaluations were working on the ground and cited the challenge states were facing in "prioritizing evaluation reform amid multiple educational initiatives."[122]

One consequence for Brockton was the reluctant back-burnering of the literacy strategy. It wasn't until the Saturday before Thanksgiving that the restructuring committee finally had an opportunity to return to its work on literacy. "Every faculty meeting, with one exception, we focused on preparing for the teacher evaluations," explained Wolder with more than a hint of exasperation.[123]

At the same time, Brockton and Wolder faced the growing threat of charter schools. Over the years, Brockton had fought off several efforts to establish a charter high school. Now, the attacks were coming fast and furious, fueled by a nationwide network of education reformers who would spend millions of dollars to promote the spread of charter schools, as well as by local education reformers led by Governor Charlie Baker. And the push to establish a charter high school in Brockton came despite strong, broad-based opposition to charters in Brockton itself.

Local opposition was driven, in part, by satisfaction with the quality of Brockton High, and in part by concern that a charter school would siphon off funds from Brockton High even as it cherry-picked the least hard-to-teach students.

Take the 2012 proposal by SABIS to establish a charter in Brockton. Despite Brockton's huge non-English-speaking community—35 percent of Brockton High students are English-language learners—SABIS, a for-profit company that operates several charters elsewhere in Massachusetts (as well as in twenty foreign countries), budgeted for only one bilingual teacher. "If you want to reflect the city and say you're working hard on behalf of the city, you have to reflect the city," says Dr. Szach.[124]

Close to three hundred people packed a hearing on the SABIS proposal in late 2012. Lidia DeBarros, a Brockton senior who had recently emigrated from Cape Verde and who had known no English when she enrolled at Brockton High, was among scores of students, parents, teachers, and union leaders who came out to oppose the SABIS proposal. Fighting back tears, DeBarros described how, within just eighteen months of starting school at Brockton High, a "multilayered" set of programs to support students who were not proficient in English had enabled her to become fluent in English. "It taught me so much in so little time and these teachers still help me every day," DeBarros said.[125]

This is how Daniela Belice, another recent Brockton graduate who left Haiti right after the 2010 earthquake, describes her experience at Brockton High: "The bilingual program was very good." Belice started Brockton in a beginner's English-language learner class in the ninth grade, in a sequence that usually lasts three years. But with the help of her teachers, many of whom spent "one-on-one time" with her, Belice completed the sequence within a year and a half. Even as she was getting up to speed in English, Belice was taking "Haitian" math and science courses, which were taught by Brockton teachers who spoke Haitian Creole. Belice enrolled at Quincy College after graduating from Brockton and plans to become an immigration attorney.[126]

Indeed, SABIS's record on English-language learners was not encouraging to Brockton families. While touting the relatively high test scores of its flagship school in Springfield, a local Massachusetts blogger, Jennifer Berkshire, a.k.a. *Edushyster*, suggested that immigrant students like DeBarros and Belice would not fare well at SABIS, noting its "record on educating English Language Learners cannot compare to Brockton's. While 25 percent of students in Springfield are English Language Learners, a mere 4 percent of students" at SABIS are learning English.[127]

In 2015, another charter proposal was derailed, at least in part, by the proposed school's failure to address Brockton's large population of English-language learners. In a scathing fourteen-page analysis of New Heights Charter School's application to the state board, local officials, including School Superintendent Kathleen Smith and Mayor Bill Carpenter, urged the state to reject the application, noting that the proposal "lacks services and supports for English language learners and students with disabilities."[128]

Behind the protests was also a sweeping defense of Brockton and its strategy. Wrote Berkshire: "Brockton High outperformed 90% of the high schools in Massachusetts last year—an astonishing feat given that the school has 4,100 students. But most notable is the school's stellar success with so-called target groups, including special education, low-income and minority students. . . . Brockton High has made Annual Yearly Progress in all student categories on the MCAS without sacrificing specials such as music, sports and art. That's virtually unheard of for an urban high school, especially one in a community as diverse as Brockton."[129]

Within a year, Brockton High was under attack again as New Heights renewed its charter application.

Once again, the opposition was widespread. Opponents of New Heights's application included the local newspaper, *The Enterprise*, which says it is generally "supportive" of charter schools. It included the mayor of Brockton, city council members, state representatives, members of the local school committee, and parents—lots of them.

The New Heights Charter School would not serve Brockton's diverse educational needs, charged Tom Minichiello, vice chair of the Brockton School Committee:

> Let's look at what students the charter school wants: not our 30-plus percent English language learner population or our approximately 14 percent special education population. No, charter advocates want students from our grades 6–12 student population that testing shows are making progress. The data shows that the longer students remain within the Brockton school system, the more successful the test results.[130]

Equally important, the new charter threatened Brockton High's steady trajectory and its ability to serve the neediest students, who are unlikely to attend New Heights. After the charter school's first year of operation, the Brockton school district would expect to lose $10 million in funding, about 6 percent of its annual school budget; by contrast, in 1991, at the peak of the local school crisis, Brockton lost $5 million in funding. Tight budgets already have led to a net loss of funding at Brockton during the preceding two years. In the 2014–2015 school year, Brockton High had to cut four consumer-science teachers, who taught electives in nutrition, cooking, and personal finance. The school also has lost teachers via attrition.[131]

The result, says Wolder, may be larger class sizes, which for many subjects already average around thirty-five students per class.[132]

New Heights's new application, which would be approved in February 2016, seemed to address some of the flaws of its earlier proposal. For its first year, when the school anticipated a student population of 315 kids, it planned to hire three "English Language Learner teachers" and one lead ELL teacher who would also double as a "world language teacher," as well as three special-education teachers. But it's doubtful that New Heights would have dual-certified Creole or Spanish speakers who could also teach science and math to immigrant kids like Daniela Belice. It's noteworthy that for such a small school, the first year's budget included three deans as well as a head of school.[133]

Unlike the first application, which focused exclusively on Brockton, the new application tried to sell itself as a "regional charter" that would be open to students in two other towns, Taunton and Randolph, as well as Brockton. Taunton is seventeen miles from Brockton, while Randolph is six miles away. Unlike Brockton, both towns are on the list of schools in the state's lowest 10 percent in achievement, so their inclusion in the charter school's "region" was perhaps intended to answer critics who argued that Brockton didn't need charter schools.[134]

But the regional designation was just a fig leaf for a school that squarely targeted Brockton students. New Heights expected to take only about 10 percent of kids from Taunton or Randolph, according to its own prospectus.[135]

Nor did New Heights's boasts of offering college courses distinguish it from Brockton High, which offers both college courses and an International Baccalaureate, as well as an array of vocational options.

A key reason for local opposition to the charter was that New Heights offered nothing new. While Brockton High maintains a rich array of electives, arts, and sports, the New Heights budget included not a single teacher for arts or music in its first five years of operation, and just one physical education teacher in a school that expected to grow to 420 students in its second year.[136]

"There is size; the one thing Brockton High can never be is small," says Wolder.[137]

There were families of color who supported the new charter school, families for whom a small school was appealing. But there are others in Brockton who speculate that New Heights will be a much whiter school than Brockton High and that the one thing it offers is a haven for families who'd rather have their kids in a school without the poorest and neediest immigrant kids, a school that is also likely to be less black and brown.

Whatever the offerings, New Heights will be exempt from many rules that constrain public schools—indeed, that make them *public* schools. "If a kid shows up in March and is 19 years old, we say welcome and we own that kid," including their challenges and special needs, says Dr. Szach, who continues to keep tabs on her alma mater. "That's what public education is. If this charter really served kids who were English Language Learners, overage, under-credited, I'd have a hard time fighting against it."[138]

The opposition was vindicated, at least in the short term, by numerous problems that plagued New Heights's first year, including construction snafus that delayed the start of school and forced the charter to occupy temporary quarters in a neighboring town, as well as severe under enrollment. The school signed up 15 to 18 percent fewer students than it had anticipated.[139]

It's hard to escape the conclusion that, once again, politics was behind this latest reform effort. New Heights's victory in Brockton had almost nothing to do with local demand from the families and citizens of Brockton or its civic leaders, and certainly not from its educators.

Rather, it was driven by powerful state politicians and "edu-crats." There was Michael Sullivan, a Republican and former U.S. attorney who is chair of the New Heights board. Fellow Republican Charlie Baker, who had become the new governor of Massachusetts, in 2015 (and was a former leader of the Pioneer Institute), was pushing to expand the charter sector, as was MBAE.

The Enterprise, a local news organization, concluded in its editorial opposing the new charter school that for Brockton, a model of Massachusetts's proven education reforms, little good is likely to come from the exercise:

> New Heights is an example of what public school supporters predicted as the worst-case scenario. Its aim is to skim the best students off the top of local schools, leaving those schools with less money and students who need more tending. New Heights has a website, but it is in many ways a stealth proposal. The people behind it have been very low profile. Community forums to present the idea to people? If they happened, we're sorry, but we missed them. So take the best and brightest out of traditional public school systems and make sure those kids get into college. That's not what American education is about.[140]

Back at the local chamber of commerce, Chris Cooney and Dr. Szach are reflecting on charter schools, the Common Core, and unions and what all the changes might mean for Brockton. Dr. Szach is a skeptic. But Cooney, even though he has witnessed the Brockton transformation from the beginning, trusts the decisions made by the Commonwealth's leadership. "They wouldn't embrace something that was destructive or would bring us backwards," says Cooney. They wouldn't make a decision "without some data and research."[141]

Cooney was there from the beginning of the Brockton reforms, but he has forgotten a key piece of the puzzle. The turnaround, he's convinced, was due to a massive turnover of teachers in 2004 when forty teachers left their jobs at Brockton High thanks to the statewide early-retirement incentive.

Not true, replies Dr. Szach. The early retirements, the departures, took place *after* Brockton had seen the first significant improvements in its MCAS results. "We improved with the group we had," says Dr. Szach. "None of this firing the masses. When we got that big jump in improvement, it was essentially the same crew" of teachers who had worked at Brockton when it was a failing school.[142]

Dr. Szach notes that Brockton got its "big change" in results in 2001, 2002, and 2003, before the early retirements.

But Dr. Szach doesn't entirely disagree with Cooney. She laments an education bureaucracy that too often fosters mediocrity. But, she adds, "Unions are necessary because every principal is not a good leader; I worked for a principal who told me to change a grade for a kid who otherwise wouldn't be eligible to play in a football game."[143]

Yet, like many business people, Cooney is skeptical about the teachers union. He quotes Jack Welch's dictum that 20 percent of employees are probably "stealing from you, underperforming, costing you profit." That's probably true of teachers, too, he says.[144]

Massachusetts should have been the place where public education with a capital "P" would prevail. Before the American Revolution, John Adams had tied the robust public schools to the very survival of democracy. The passage of the 1993 education law represented one of the most successful and sustained efforts at education reform in the nation; it endured because it was forged *democratically* in the messy public arenas of local school boards, town halls, and the state legislature.

A robust element of public school improvement, "school choice" had always been part of the plan. Although the education reforms made room for relatively few charter schools, they did open the way for so-called pilot schools, which were akin to New York City's small autonomous public schools. Indeed, one of the first pilots, Mission Hill, was established by Debbie Meier (see chapter 1). Created in 1995, pilot schools are public schools that function under union contracts but are free of many union and school-district restrictions. They have much greater control over their budgets and school schedules, as well as over hiring and curriculum decisions, than traditional public schools have and are, effectively, in-district alternatives to independent charter schools.[145]

The steady drumbeat for an increase in charter schools was based partly on test-score data that *seemed* to give charters an edge over both pilots and publics. The pro-charter Boston Foundation commissioned a series of studies that showed Boston charters outperforming public and pilot schools. At the same time, the studies' sponsor concedes that "it is important to note that the analysis showed that charter school students are less likely to have special needs or to be designated as English Language Learners."[146] Student performance in non-urban charters is much more mixed; middle schoolers "may even be falling behind their counterparts in traditional public schools," the study found.[147] (Meanwhile, a much-publicized study by Stanford University's Center for Research on Education Outcomes [CREDO] was plagued with methodological problems; see footnote 52, chapter 2.)[148]

In any event, the charter school test-score successes turn out to be not very good indicators of college preparedness. For one thing, as recently as 2015, graduates of Boston public schools had a far higher college-graduation rate than did their charter counterparts, according to another study funded by, among others, the Boston Foundation. The study, which also notes higher test-score data for charter schools, sums up *public school* college achievement with almost breathless praise: "The 27 Boston Public high schools are making tremendous progress on college completion. Since the baseline class of 2000, the percentage of students who complete a college degree or other postsecondary credential within six years of high-school graduation has grown from 35% to 50%. Additionally, the number of students enrolling at public institutions in Massachusetts who require developmental education or remediation is also declining."[149]

A deeper dive into the numbers produces some even more startling surprises. The charter schools that produced college-graduation rates of 42 percent, eight points *below* their public school counterparts, have graduation classes dominated by girls. Somewhere along the way, the boys disappeared. In fact, among all these charter schools, only about fifteen boys took home a sheepskin, according to *Edushyster*. In a subsequent 2016 study, college graduation rates for public and charter school students were comparable, with 50 percent of public school students graduating and 51 percent of charter school students graduating. However, with 855 college graduates, the public school cohort had twenty times the number of students as the charters (forty-three students), suggesting a much wider variety of abilities and backgrounds.[150]

The bottom line, again, is that in Massachusetts, and especially in Boston, charter schools are a minuscule part of the story. The limits placed on charters in the 1993 law ensured that Massachusetts would not "empty the public schools of all high-achieving students," said Tom Birmingham before joining the Pioneer Institute. "The answer is not unlimited charter schools; I used to believe that," he added. "There are repercussions if you do it too broadly."[151]

Indeed, given their small number and the rigorous process for approving charters in Massachusetts, the real questions are: Why are college-completion rates so low? And what happened to the boys?

During his speech at the 2012 Democratic Convention, Governor Deval Patrick praised a miraculous turnaround—that of Boston's Orchard Gardens Pilot School, which under its latest principal, Andrew Bott, had been doing just fine (though Bott would resign in 2013, just four years into his tenure).

Governor Patrick's choice of Orchard Gardens as a model of education reform was striking for several reasons. First, at the time, Orchard Gardens had been under new leadership for only about two years; after seven years of failure, the governor's shout-out seemed premature.

Second, Orchard Gardens's principal had borrowed a popular corporate strategy by firing 80 percent of the school's teachers, thus reinforcing the principal education-reform meme that teachers are the problem. (In the business world, firing rank-and-file employees is often a way for a new CEO to boost share price, at least in the short term.) In six years, Orchard Gardens's teachers had had a new principal almost every year. Teaching with whiplash can't be easy. Of note: after its house cleaning, Orchard Gardens also invested in teacher development and in arts programming.

Third, Orchard Gardens would become a prime example of how education reformers can turn a flash-in-the-pan into a national model of success. That same year, the White House invited Orchard Gardens second graders to recite Martin Luther King Jr.'s "I Have a Dream" speech to President Obama.[152]

Back in 2012, if Governor Patrick had wanted to highlight an example of reform, Brockton High, with its four-thousand-plus students, surely would have been a much more appropriate choice. For years, Patrick had been visiting, and had declared himself a huge fan of, Brockton High, the Commonwealth's most remarkable and *enduring* example of real reform. But Brockton had not followed a fire-the-teachers, quick-change education-reform narrative. Quite the contrary, the school demonstrated that real reform is a years-long, steady-as-she-goes, teacher-driven effort.

In Massachusetts, nearly twenty-five years after passing the most comprehensive, locally driven, and enduring education reform effort in the nation, top-down change permeates the atmosphere—and much of it seems directed at undermining public schools instead of supporting them.

By 2011, in recognition of growing acrimony and "distrust" around education reform, Boston established the so-called Boston Compact, which was intended to promote both a "portfolio" approach to schooling among public schools, charters, and parochial schools as well as "cross-sector collaboration."

But education-reform skeptics and many Bostonians believed the Boston Compact was actually a plan to support charters at the expense of public schools. Indeed, in spring of 2016, the legislature was poised to increase the state's charter cap and introduce a Compact-backed unified electronic enrollment system à la New Orleans that would automatically distribute school applications among both charters and public schools; in the current system, parents apply to charters and publics separately. During the fall of 2015, in seven public meetings across the Boston area, parents assailed the unified enrollment plan as "a Trojan horse for charter school expansion." [153]

Fueling such suspicions, a public-records request by Mary Lewis-Pierce, a blogger known as Public School Mama, revealed that behind the Boston Compact and Enroll Boston, the electronic enrollment system, were a familiar group of education-reform philanthropists—the Gates and Walton foundations.[154]

Another Compact document said it expected more funding from Gates for Enroll Boston and referenced a "tri-sector facilities plan." [155] Local public school parents feared that the plan—one that would encompass public schools, charter schools, and parochial schools—would likely transfer public school space to charter schools.

The Gates-funded Common Core already had displaced the Massachusetts curriculum and the MCAS. It had influenced the push for test-based teacher evaluations. And now, at a time of shrinking budgets, money from nationwide philanthropists was getting ready to push a major charter school expansion.

During the 2016 election, Massachusetts became an education-reform battleground. With the most expensive ballot campaign in state history, pro- and anti-charter forces spent over $33 million to influence the outcome of the initiative known as Question 2, which proposed to lift the state's charter cap by twelve schools per year in perpetuity. (The last effort, in 2010, provided for "exemptions" from the 120-charter cap in low-performing districts.) While two hundred school committees came out against Question 2, and Boston mayor Marty Walsh warned that it would "radically destabilize school governance" and municipal funding, two in three businesses favored the measure, and dark money—funds that are given to nonprofits by corporations, individuals, or unions, and intended to influence elections, but that are not required to disclose their donors—flooded in to support it. Despite ponying up $20.5 million in support of Question 2—double the amount spent by the anti-charter forces—the ballot initiative was roundly defeated. Sixty-two percent of Bay Staters voted against the initiative, thus forestalling what would almost certainly have been the death knell for Massachusetts's successful public school system.[156]

Almost a year after the election, the Massachusetts Office of Campaign and Political Finance imposed a $426,466 fine on a New York–based organization, Families for Excellent Schools-Advocacy, for violating campaign-finance laws. The group had backed Question 2 to the tune of $15.6 million. What was remarkable was not just the fine, but the fact that the public got a rare look at how dark money worked to hide both the names of contributors and their contribution levels and, of course, the fact that, despite so much money, Question 2 lost handily. At the top of the list of dark-money contributors were two top lieutenants to Governor Charlie Baker: Both Mark Nunnelly, the executive director of the Massachusetts Office of Information Technology, and Paul Sagan, chair of the Massachusetts Board of Elementary and Secondary Education, had contributed hundreds of thousands of dollars in previously undisclosed funds.[157]

Moreover, twenty-five years after the historic Massachusetts education reform law of 1993, Brockton was getting ready to file a new school-equity lawsuit, arguing that the state is once again shortchanging students in poor urban districts. In particular, the Brockton superintendent argued, most recently, that the state was failing to maintain "adequate" foundation budgets for school districts, leading to huge inequities between rich and poor districts. "The Commonwealth is not doing enough for the neediest districts," Paul Reville, the former education secretary, told the *Boston Globe*. "How can the state hold them accountable for results if they are not providing adequate resources?"[158]

4

NO LONE STARS

How Trust and Collaboration in One Texas School District Have Created Lasting Reform

The Leander school district in central Texas is nearly the size of New Orleans. In 2015, at a time when many districts around the country were suffering from an acute teacher shortage, 2,572 teachers applied for 408 openings in Leander—a six-to-one applicant-per-job ratio—including some teachers who were lured back from retirement.[1]

"Cedar chopper," considered a pejorative, is the way longtime residents of Leander describe themselves. Until recently, the area around the town was settled by ranchers, cotton farmers, and cedar choppers. The latter got their name from the forests of low-slung, gnarly trees that are commonly known as cedars but are actually ashe juniper. Native Americans used the trees primarily for firewood. European settlers built homes and fences with them, and when, in the late nineteenth century, the railroads came through, they built railroad ties from the sturdy and plentiful wood.

It was the cedar choppers—independent contractors, sometimes lone men, sometimes entire migrant families—who cut the wood and were paid by the cedar log. When the wood ran out, they moved to follow the timber.

These are the families who made up the community that would become the Leander school district. Here and there the area is still dotted with trailer homes, but they are increasingly crowded out by high-end subdivisions.[2]

In the district's early days, there were no highways linking nearby Austin and Leander. The district was so far flung that teachers used to ride the school bus so they'd "understand how far kids had to travel."

Nor were there grocery stores or restaurants. No Wendy's. No McDonald's or any other fast-food chain. At staff meetings, if you didn't bring lunch, you didn't eat.

This was the district that Monta Akin, a petite auburn-brunette, joined in 1976. Something of a self-described hippie, Akin had quit her first teaching job to run off to Central America with a boyfriend. Wandering the villages of Mexico and Guatemala, she would drop into rural schools and, despite almost nonexistent Spanish, ask local teachers if she could sit in on their classes. Akin eventually left the boyfriend and returned to Texas. Somewhat at sea, she dropped in on a former professor at the University of Texas at Austin who recommended her for a job in Leander.[3]

At the time, Akin was twenty-eight years old, and Leander was on so-called advised status, a step that could, if left unattended, result in the loss of the school's accreditation.

Leander owed its dubious status not to any egregious failures, but simply to the fact that one of the half dozen or so men who occupied the superintendent's office in about as many years had neglected to fill out the necessary paperwork.[4]

After a year or two on the job, Akin grew restless again. She remembers that time as a period of "lots of turnover and no consistency." In short, Leander was "not a place to be proud of."[5]

Finally, Akin told the latest occupant of the superintendent's office, a man named Fred Hopson, that she was planning to resign, that she didn't see the district as one "interested in improving," and so it was not right for her.

"You're running away from a hard situation," Hopson told Akin, challenging her to stay.

Akin had tendered her resignation without actually having a new job lined up. So, with the Guatemalan episode not far behind her, Akin decided to give Leander a little more time.

By the early 1980s, Leander had won its accreditation. The district was improving.

The little boy went first day of school
He got some crayons and started to draw
He put colors all over the paper
For colors was what he saw
And the teacher said. What you doin' young man
I'm paintin' flowers he said
She said . . . It's not the time for art young man
And anyway flowers are green and red
There's a time for everything young man
And a way it should be done
You've got to show concern for everyone else
For you're not the only one

And she said . . .
Flowers are red young man
Green leaves are green
There's no need to see flowers any other way
Than the way they always have been seen

But the little boy said . . .
There are so many colors in the rainbow
So many colors in the morning sun
So many colors in the flower and I see every one

Well the teacher said . . . You're sassy
There's ways that things should be
And you'll paint flowers the way they are
So repeat after me . . .

And she said . . .
Flowers are red young man
Green leaves are green
There's no need to see flowers any other way
Than the way they always have been seen

Time went by like it always does
And they moved to another town
And the little boy went to another school
And this is what he found
The teacher there was smilin'
She said . . . Painting should be fun
And there are so many colors in a flower
So let's use every one

But that little boy painted flowers
In neat rows of green and red
And when the teacher asked him why
This is what he said . . . and he said

Flowers are red, green leaves are green
There's no need to see flowers any other way
Than the way they always have been seen.
—"Flowers Are Red," by Harry Chapin

It is midmorning on a hot August day in 2015 in Leander ISD, and it is the start of Culture Day, an all-day event that every new employee to the district—from teachers to custodians—must attend. Some three hundred newcomers are gathered around tables, covered in bright primary-colored tablecloths, in a room the size of two basketball courts.

Culture Day is led by Superintendent Bret Champion and several key administrators. Toward the end of the morning session, the boyish-looking Champion—think Bill Gates with a Texas drawl and keen sense of humor—sets up a video. It is a child's illustration set to the Harry Chapin song "Flowers Are Red" (see lyrics in box).

Leander has been playing those lyrics to teachers since the 1980s, Champion explains, even though it's a little bit of a "downer" because it represents a "powerful" message of what the district does *not* want Leander teachers to do. As the clip winds to a close, Champion continues the lesson, recounting the most searing memory of his otherwise bucolic boyhood, growing up in the tiny town of Goldthwaite, Texas, population 2,000.

Back then, Champion explained, students at his elementary school had to get each test signed by a parent. Young Bret was not very organized, and just never got around to handing in a signed copy of one of those tests. "I got a 95 on that particular test," he says with mock defensiveness. "I wasn't trying to hide anything. I just wasn't responsive."

But rules are rules. There were threats. The principal got involved.

Terrified, the boy snuck out of class to call his mother, who was teaching at the local high school. "I'm weeping on the phone to my mother, 'They're gonna swat me!'" Champion recounts with gusto.

"Where are you calling from?" his mother demanded to know, just as the principal walked into his office, catching young Bret at his desk using the phone.

The principal, sympathetic to his plight, walked the weeping boy back to the classroom and asked his teacher if it was true that she had threatened to "swat him" if he didn't turn over the test.

"Of course not," the teacher replied.

Champion, a former drama teacher, pauses for effect; his audience laughs, recognizing a lie when they hear one.

At some point, someone, perhaps the principal, suggested young Bret go through his desk where, lo and behold, they found the test wadded up at the back. His mother had, in fact, signed it.

"But isn't it interesting how we can remember these things like it was yesterday," Champion said to the newcomers to his district, pacing among the rows of brightly clad tables. The reason he continues to show the video, he explains, is to remind teachers of the "power of influence that we have. To remember how much power we have in our roles as the lead educator in the classroom."[6]

The other lesson in that anecdote that Champion and his colleagues reiterate throughout the course of Culture Day is a mantra the Leander educators have been intoning since the district's first Culture Day back sometime in the 1980s: instilling fear helps nobody.

Before lunch, Champion drives home another subversive message. "You are required to teach a lot of content," he says. "The TEKs are chock-full of content. Ridiculously full," he adds, referring disdainfully to the Texas state standards. "I'm not going to get on my soapbox now."

But, he reminds them: "We're charged with so much more than just academics" or, he implies, producing test scores. "We must remind ourselves, academics is just one sixth of that graduate profile."[7]

Champion is referencing one of the myriad "guiding documents" that Leander has developed over the course of decades to describe, and to institutionalize, the district's educational values and systems, as well as its continuous-improvement philosophy. The graduate profile, for example, was developed years ago to describe the key attributes the district expects to instill in its students; it begins with academics, but says much more about the character—honesty, integrity, promise keeping—and the life skills—problem-solving skills, physical wellness, and service to community—of the students it seeks to educate.

A key purpose of Culture Day is to begin to familiarize all newcomers with those guiding documents and with an entirely new language to use around education improvement.

"We remind ourselves that we are always pulling the thread through" all those processes, Champion intones.

Before the teachers head out to lunch, Champion leaves them with a parting thought: thirty-five years from now, he asks, "what stories do we want our students to be saying about us?"

And this: "Picture that kindergarten kid with his backpack," says Champion, still pacing. "That may have been you. With that excited expression on his face."

Now, picture that child thirteen years later. "What would it look like if our kids exit with the same excitement as our kindergarteners have and without the economics determining our success?"[8]

An excited buzz emanates from the crowd as the teachers file out to lunch.

"Someone said to me when they heard I was coming to Leander—you're going to heaven," exclaims Rhonda Bliss, a tall, blond woman. "I told her I'd know by the end of orientation week. But I know now. This is what education should be."[9]

A board-certified teacher who left the classroom to follow her husband, an Army general, around the country and to homeschool her seven children, Bliss settled in Texas after her divorce, determined to return to teaching. When she heard about the opening at Leander, she jumped at the chance.

Gloria Vela, fifty-one, another seasoned educator new to Leander, also embraced the message she just heard. Vela, a former principal, had left teaching, "disheartened."

"Not what I thought it would be—the testing culture," she said, her voice trailing off.

But, says Vela, this morning she is feeling that old inspiration again. She is "awed" by Champion's address to the teachers and by Leander's values. That the superintendent should take the time and be so immersed in the educational mission of the district speaks volumes, she says. Like many educators, she assumes that the superintendent's job is more political than educational. But, at Leander, everything from the classroom instruction to school construction to the superintendent's interactions with the school board is informed by the district's singular education philosophy.[10]

Culture Day is held in one of the district's oldest buildings in a gymnasium-sized room where two walls are lined with a timeline of Leander's extraordinary journey. As with so much else at Leander, key ideas only make it onto the timeline two or three years after a group of district educators agree that the ideas are having a lasting impact. Thus, even though Leander's continuous-improvement journey began in the 1980s, the timeline starts in 1990. It includes the graduate profile, which years before "grit" became the latest education buzzword encompassed that and more. There is also the map of Leander "viewed as a system" connecting students, staff, parents, community, businesses, and the board. There is the Leander "learning model," a wheel-and-spoke diagram in which "focus on student learning" is at the center, and everything else—curriculum, assessments, the graduate profile, the district's ten ethical principles—radiates outward. And, most important, there is the photo of W. Edwards Deming, the quality guru whose ideas more than anything else have informed Leander's approach to education for over thirty years.

Deming is not an entirely new name to education. Japanese lesson study, popular in Japan for decades and more recently in some U.S. education circles, is based on Deming's ideas about continuous improvement. But

Leander is probably the largest district in the country to build an entire education system—from curriculum to management to school construction—based on the quality-improvement ideas of Deming's teachings. Much about the "Leander Way" is uniquely Texas. Almost all the educators in the district hail from the Lone Star State.

Yet the district's approach is utterly Japanese in one important respect: Leander has maintained a singular focus on continuous improvement—more so than perhaps any of the dozens of U.S. institutions, including major corporations, that have relied on his ideas. At a time when education reformers nationwide are looking for quick-change solutions, often driven by business leaders and multimillion-dollar consultants—Newark's $200 million failed plan for creating a new national education model in just five years comes to mind—Leander's approach has been defiantly deliberate, studious, systematic, and local.

Indeed, almost everything the district does is designed to create a shared vision that "appears more akin to quilt work with the most repeated patterns consisting of collaboration, teamwork."[11] These include the community-building events and ceremonies, of which Culture Day is one of more than a half dozen; the interlinked guiding documents; and a multitude of training opportunities, almost all of which are led by local educators.

Although Deming was also a Westerner, his ideas have grown their strongest roots in Japan, where they inform both business and education. There, Deming's ideas about systems and quality improvement were introduced after World War II, when they helped rebuild a devastated nation, including corporate giants like Toyota. Later, when the United States was being bested by those Japanese companies, several major companies turned to Deming for help. But no American institution stuck with his ideas about systems thinking, collaboration, and continuous improvement as consistently as the Japanese companies did—except, perhaps, the Leander school district.

While Leander is a non-union district in a red state, its collaborative, continuous-improvement approach shares much in common with similar blue-state experiments with strong unions. Consider the small-school, teacher-leader movement pioneered by Debbie Meier in New York City—one that continued to some degree under Mayor Bloomberg—as well as the educator-led reforms that followed the 1993 Education Reform Act in Massachusetts.

The story of Leander's remarkable transformation is something of a chicken-and-egg story. The area's enormous growth—the shopping malls and suburban subdivisions that have crowded out what were once wide expanses of ranch land and cedar forest—is partly the result of the boom in the Austin-area economy. The growth of this particular region, however, owes much to the school district itself, which has managed a remarkable feat: exponential growth in size while fostering one of the most successful examples of school improvement in the country.

Leander enrolled about 40,000 students in 2015, almost as many children as the charter schools in New Orleans and a nearly twenty-fold increase since the early 1980s. In the process, Leander has bucked virtually every education-reform trend.

A two-hundred-square-mile district northwest of Austin, straddling Williamson and Travis counties, the Leander area is far more conservative than is the Texas state capital. Yet Leander serves as another key counterpoint to the modern education-reform movement, with its focus on charter schools, test-based accountability, and privatization.

Eschewing revolution and miracles, Leander has spent over thirty years with a laser-like focus on continuous improvement. Instead of teacher bashing, Leander strives to empower its educators. Collaboration and constant communication—among grade-level teachers, across academic disciplines, and across schools—is a bedrock value practiced throughout the district. So it's not a surprise that all the teachers interviewed in a years-long research project at Texas A&M University said they were involved in one or more team-planning efforts within a grade or department, and/or a vertical team that cuts across the district in some way, and/or across a program or content area. "Sharing or working in teams was viewed as enjoyable and beneficial by every teacher interviewed. In many instances, the teachers associated 'sharing of vision' with the 'sharing of strategies' used to achieve the vision," according to Joe Robinson, a former Texas district superintendent who wrote his PhD dissertation about Leander.[12]

Meanwhile, the administration understood that for collaboration to succeed, Leander would have to build and sustain relationships across the district. That in turn would involve asking the right questions, "not being afraid of the answers, developing processes, and continually redesigning processes so that communication can happen."[13]

In sharp contrast to the top-down accountability-obsessed culture that dominates American education, the Leander ethic is based on an underlying conviction that education improvement must be a group effort, often the result of vigorous debate. Only by soliciting diverse opinions can the district acquire the information it needs to develop and refine its processes and pursue continuous improvement.[14]

While data and measurement tools suffuse the district, they are used by teachers, principals, and students in the service of improvement, not punishment. They are also considered an adjunct to, not a substitute for, professional judgment. At a time when accountability has been used as a cudgel to threaten teachers, the single cultural guidepost that, more than anything else, has sustained the district's improvement efforts is the group of linked values of trust, collaboration, and teamwork. In this spirit, Leander has firmly resisted tying test scores to teacher evaluations.

Leander also has eschewed formal organization charts because they are seen as too restrictive and "inviting treks down the 'trail of blame.'" Instead, Champion cultivates "fuzzy" lines of authority among his administrators as a way to encourage collaboration and teamwork.[15]

Moreover, the district's commitment to continuous and sustainable improvement is intertwined with its goals for kids. That interconnection is at the heart of the district's "four challenges," which were articulated in 2005 and joined the myriad interlocking "guiding documents":

1. Eliminate the link between economic disadvantage and low achievement, while improving overall student performance.
2. Ensure that all students read at or above grade level.
3. Increase the percentage of students enrolling in and successfully completing our most challenging courses.
4. Accomplish the above while maintaining our district's culture of respect, trust, continuous improvement, and learning.

The 1980s coincided with a new statewide focus on accountability. Texas introduced its first standardized state tests in 1980, a criterion-referenced test for grades three, five, and nine that was intended to be used as a diagnostic tool for schools.[16]

Four years later, the state added a teacher rating-and-ranking system that offered bonuses of as much as $6,000 to the highest-performing teachers, but that also encouraged districts to fire or demote teachers who didn't do well on the twice-yearly appraisals. The so-called career-ladder system was deeply unpopular and came to be seen as "demoralizing."[17]

"The system created a negative atmosphere of competition, rather than collaboration, among educators. Finally, some questioned the training, qualifications, and impartiality of some of the school administrators who conducted the performance appraisals," according to a report by the Texas House of Representatives.[18]

For a time, Leander also bet that carrots-and-stick incentive schemes would improve performance. Local newspapers published full-page spreads on school test scores, highlighting the schools with the best and worst grades. Akin decided it would be a good idea to identify the teachers whose test scores were in the lowest 10 percent and ask them how principals could "better support them."

Of course, for the teachers who were singled out, "it didn't come across as support," recalls Akin, wryly.

It just fomented fear.

Akin was beginning to think it would take "something really different" to take Leander to the next level.

Akin's epiphany took place almost at the exact moment when Texas—indeed, the nation—was going in precisely the opposite direction. In 1993, the Texas State Legislature approved a new market-based accountability framework that would become the cornerstone of George W. Bush's No Child Left Behind. The new law "required schools to disaggregate standardized testing data for the first time—breaking down how well minority, poor, and disabled students were performing as individual groups—and began ranking campuses based on their test scores and graduation rates."[19]

A *Texas Monthly* article on the Texas testing regime summed it up this way:

> The shaming effect of public rankings had administrators scrambling to improve performance. As the exams became more and more difficult and the stakes grew higher and higher, the school year in Texas became more and more centered on testing. It wasn't just the test days themselves. Schools also employed so-called benchmark tests, to see how students were progressing throughout the school year. In the weeks leading up to the actual tests, they pulled kids from "nonessential" classes like art and gym to do endless drills and work sheets, a dreaded routine that came to be known as "drill and kill."[20]

A NEW LANGUAGE OF QUALITY

Late one Saturday night in January 1991, unable to sleep, Akin tuned in to her local PBS station and stumbled upon *Quality . . . Or Else!*, a PBS series on the problems of globalization and American ingenuity in the workplace, school, and government. The documentary was a sequel to *If Japan Can, Why Can't We?*, which a decade earlier had inspired the Ford Motor Company and other automakers to bring Deming to Detroit.

Akin caught just the last ten minutes of the show about an unlikely example of school renewal in Sitka, Alaska. "Rather than help me sleep, the message presented in the video excited me so that I could hardly wait for the bookstores to open the next morning," recalls Akin.[21]

By then, Leander had begun to add one to two schools every year, creating academic, financial, and logistical pressures that, with time, would severely test the district.

Akin wears a small, diamond-encrusted Texas longhorn medallion around her neck. Soon after joining Leander, Akin met and married Jim Roberson, and the couple bought a forty-four-acre ranch—one of the few remaining bulwarks against fast-encroaching development—in a foreclosure sale. The couple's evenings were often taken up with ballroom dancing; Akin and Roberson became fierce competitors, winning gold medals in everything from the cha-cha to the West Coast swing in statewide championships.

But Akin, who speaks with a soft Texas twang, is also deeply intellectual; that Sunday January morning after watching the PBS show, she picked up every book on Deming she could find and started reading.

By then, Hopson had retired. He had been succeeded, in 1987, by Tom Glenn, a tall, somewhat reserved Texan. The next Monday, Akin arrived to a regularly scheduled meeting to find that Glenn was running late; Akin, pacing impatiently outside his office, picked up a magazine on a nearby coffee table. When it fell open to a page with a sidebar advertisement for a seminar run by David Langford, the Sitka, Alaska, teacher she had heard about on PBS that Saturday night, she took it as a sign.[22]

As soon as Glenn was ready to see her, Akin launched breathlessly into her pitch: "I said, 'We need to send people here,'" referring to the seminar. "'I think there's something going on.'" She then told Glenn about what was, at that point, not much more than a gut feeling.[23]

Glenn gave her a green light, and Akin corralled eight colleagues, including a few teachers, a principal, and some administrators—"people who I knew would shoot straight with me," says Akin—for the two-day seminar in Dallas.[24]

The Leander delegation came away "wowed," says Akin. Next, she secured funding to take forty-one Leander educators to Langford's next four-day seminar in Dallas.[25]

Langford spoke an entirely new language. Education, he argued, is built on a faulty premise. "Behaviorism is rampant throughout the system," he would say. "We manipulate people with rewards and punishments and trophies. It's all built on extrinsic motivators, and not intrinsic motivation."[26]

While Langford's ideas had the ring of social psychology, they were based on the complex edifice of Deming's work. Perhaps the twentieth century's most underappreciated management thinker, Deming was a larger-than-life westerner, the child of a Wyoming pioneer family. He held a PhD in physics from Yale but had spent much of his career as a statistician. During World War II, Deming had been recruited by the administration of General Douglas MacArthur to visit Japan, where his ideas would be widely embraced and become part of the foundation for the quality-management systems that became synonymous with Japan's leading companies.[27]

The scions of the Toyoda family worked with Deming to develop the Toyota Production System. The emperor of Japan conferred the so-called Deming Prize, beginning in 1951, on companies that exemplified leadership in systems-oriented quality improvement, fueling a national obsession. Statistical theory was taught as part of the basic Japanese school curriculum. And while Japanese lesson study predated Deming in Japan, it got a boost from the popularity of his work; lesson study "is now viewed as a specific example of the ongoing Japanese devotion to the Plan-Do-Check-Act (PDCA) decision making process pioneered by W. Edwards Deming."[28]

Thanks in large measure to the quality movement, Japanese industry rose from the ashes of World War II stronger than ever, with Japanese companies challenging the Detroit automakers head on. By the time NBC aired *If Japan Can Why Can't We*, the prequel to the documentary that had captivated Akin, the U.S. auto industry was desperate to learn the secret of the "Japanese miracle" and found, to its surprise, that the keeper of that secret worked in virtual obscurity, out of a basement office, in a modest home in Washington, D.C.

The real miracle was that the Motor City executives were willing to listen to Deming at all. Already in his eighties, Deming descended on Detroit like a wrathful redeemer. "Why can't America compete?" Deming would thunder in his rumbling baritone to a roomful of senior auto executives. "The aaanswer iiis—MANAGEMENT!"[29]

Handed the microphone at a gathering of senior executives at a Society of Automotive Engineers function, Deming gave Jim McDonald, then president of GM, the dressing down of his career, publicly accusing him of responsibility for "85 percent of GM's quality problems."[30]

Indeed, Deming always saved his wrath for senior executives because it was senior management alone, he believed, who had the power to change the system. To do so, executives would have to learn to take criticism and see the error of their ways.

Indeed, if it hadn't been for Don Petersen, then CEO of the Ford Motor

Company, Deming might not have made an impact at all. Petersen alone among Detroit's CEOs embraced Deming's ideas and encouraged all his managers, from the established Lincoln division to the new low-cost Taurus/Sable unit, which incorporated Deming's ideas from the earliest conceptual stage, to embrace his ideas. Meanwhile, product managers at GM practically put their careers at risk when they smuggled Deming into their meetings—but smuggle him in they did.[31]

Deming's breakthrough was in combining an understanding of how science—in particular, statistical theory—can be used to achieve meaningful systems improvement with what had heretofore been seen as touchy-feely, unscientific approaches to empowerment. He used statistical theory to demonstrate how employees, properly trained, can serve as a key resource for identifying organizational problems, solutions, and opportunities for improvement. Importantly, he believed that employees can only meet this challenge if they work in an atmosphere that is collaborative and free of fear.

At a time when American industry was becoming ever more siloed and focused on the bottom line, Deming advocated a collaborative, systems-focused, process-obsessed approach to management. While he was often derided as a mere statistician, Deming made a crucial breakthrough by linking the scientific explanation for how systems work (in particular, how to understand and manage the statistical variation that erodes the quality of all processes) and the humanistic—an intuitive feel for the organization as a social system.

Both strains—the scientific and humanistic—could be traced to a single deceptively simple, and profoundly elegant, understanding of how all processes work. Every process is subject to some level of variation that is likely to diminish quality. Process variation is the enemy of quality, yet it is as ubiquitous as gravity.

What makes variation a particular nuisance is that it comes in two distinct guises: "special causes" of variation, which are the result of special circumstances or a temporary glitch in the system, are opportunistic and, by definition, *unpredictable*; thus, they can wreak havoc with a process and give management no basis on which to predict the quality level of an organization's products or services. They can, however, be identified and eliminated by workers who have been trained to analyze the process.

On a recent New York State English test, students were required to answer questions based on a color map. Most schools, however, lacked color copiers and gave their students the test in black and white, which made the distinctions on the map difficult to read. As a result, many students couldn't answer the map-based questions correctly. Teachers would have been best equipped to both identify and solve the problem—perhaps by finding a nearby copy shop or arranging a temporary copier rental—assuming they had been given the authority to do so.

"Common causes" of variation, by contrast, are more difficult to isolate because they are inherent in the system. As such, they are, by definition, *predictable*. While common causes can never be fully eliminated, they allow the process to function at a predictable level of variation. Thus, an organization that has only common causes to contend with will produce a level of product quality that is predetermined by the capabilities of its systems.

For example, a school that doesn't invest in new textbooks, choosing to recycle outdated ones, is likely to diminish student performance. This decline will be predictable. While teachers might be able to identify the problem, only senior management (the principal or the district) has the power to change the purchasing policy. Because they are systemic, common-cause variations hold the greatest opportunity for long-term improvement.

The key to reducing variation and improving quality, Deming believed, was to train employees who work with the system every day and who know it best to distinguish between special- and common-cause variations and to empower them to develop creative improvements. Ordinary employees—not senior management or hired experts—are in the best position to see the cause-and-effect relationships in each process. Management's challenge is to tap into that knowledge on a consistent basis and to make that knowledge actionable. To do so, management must shake up the hierarchy (if not eliminate it entirely), drive fear out of the workplace, provide relevant training, and foster the intrinsic motivation of its employees.

Statistical theory also led directly to Deming's most controversial ideas, in particular his opposition to individual pay incentives (see introduction).

Of course, Deming's focus on the role of leadership and organizational culture may appear to present special challenges for schools working under strict union contracts. But the strides made at companies like Ford during the years when Deming was advising Petersen demonstrate that unionization in and of itself does not prevent quality-improvement practices from being applied, especially not if union workers—the UAW, in Ford's case—are made part of the solution.

Just as it had taken a crisis to galvanize the quality movement in the auto industry, so too was it a crisis, on a much smaller scale, that inspired David

Langford's research into Deming's methods. Langford had recently taken a job in Sitka, Alaska, at Mt. Edgecumbe High School, a small boarding school of about 175 students and about a dozen teachers.

Located on Baranof Island, Mt. Edgecumbe had been founded in 1947 and was operated by the Bureau of Indian Affairs as a school for Native Americans. Mt. Edgecumbe had a terrible reputation, with some native pupils having been forcibly pulled away from their homes. The school also suffered from poor management and huge cost overruns.[32]

The school was briefly closed in 1983, but reopened two years later as an "alternative experimental" state-run boarding school that drew students from the Haida and Tsimpshian tribes, as well as Tlingit natives who predominated in the Sitka area. About a quarter of Mt. Edgecumbe's students were children living in poverty. About 40 percent—mostly kids whose families worked in the fishing industry—qualified for migrant education services. Close to half had struggled at their previous schools.[33]

Concern for the education and employment opportunities of native youth shaped the state's decision to focus Mt. Edgecumbe's curriculum on technology applications, "real-life entrepreneurship," as well as on Pacific Region studies, which was designed to teach students about Alaska's economy and its connections to Asia and Russia. That course of study came to include a focus on marine science and the salmon-fishing industry, as well as instruction in Chinese and Japanese. One of the objectives, recalls Langford, was "to turn these students into entrepreneurs who would go back to their villages and make a difference."[34]

Mt. Edgecumbe's small size—it more than doubled to about four hundred students by the 1990s—along with its status as an experimental school with a strong focus on business and entrepreneurship and its relatively ample budget make the school an outlier in many ways. However, as a laboratory for the continuous-improvement ideas that Langford brought to the school district, it served as a valuable example.

Larrae Rocheleau, the superintendent at the time, had recruited Langford as the school's computer and entrepreneurship teacher.[35]

But the improvement effort didn't get off to a good start. Mt. Edgecumbe opened with "the same school management theory" it had always used except it was going to do things "better," meaning it would be stricter and have more rules and regulations. "Our idea of quality was to get rid of the bad students," says Langford with a touch of irony and thirty years of hindsight. Mt. Edgecumbe ranked its teachers and taught the staff to rank students. After the first year, Mt. Edgecumbe lost 42 percent of its students and 33 percent of the original staff—some of the latter to ulcers and heart attacks.

"And this was the high-powered staff we had hired out of two thousand applicants," says Langford. "The best of the best."[36]

The school's efforts didn't really bear fruit until Langford attended one of Deming's four-day quality-management conferences in Phoenix in 1986. On his return, Langford began to introduce the ideas he had learned from Deming in his computer class. Chief among them was to put his students—his customers—at the center of everything he did, including the process for improving his computer classes. "Will you help me improve?" he asked the students. "I need insight and I need your help."[37]

Before long, Mt. Edgecumbe's administration was won over by Deming's ideas and Langford's efforts in his classroom. His students began giving presentations on quality management and the positive influence it had had on their classwork and personal lives. There were trips to Harvard and Stanford, to London and Japan. Langford remembers a trip to Phillips Petroleum in Texas. The students gave a thirty-minute multimedia presentation on quality improvement, after which they were expecting to listen to a company presentation. Instead, the vice president for quality cut short the company presentation and said: "You guys know more than we ever will," and invited Langford's students to debate policy on bonuses and performance appraisals, process tools, and intrinsic motivation with company managers.[38]

Mt. Edgecumbe's accomplishments by more standard academic measures also were considerable. The students showed modest—though steady—gains on standardized tests over the seven years that Deming's principles had been applied at the school, according to a study by Kathleen Cotton. Students also showed a "trend toward broader understanding and more sophisticated expression of learning material."[39]

Meanwhile, Mt. Edgecumbe enjoyed high attendance, low dropout rates, and an increase in applications. Eighty-six percent of its graduates went to technical school or—the majority—to college. On a 1993 survey, graduates ranked the quality of the courses they had taken between 4.1 and 4.7 on a 5-point scale. And almost all graduates said "the quality of education they received was better than what they would have received in their home communities."[40]

Three-quarters said Mt. Edgecumbe did a "good or very good job" preparing them for college.[41]

DRIVING OUT FEAR

It's after lunch at Leander's Culture Day, the lights dim, and Champion shows another video.

Lucy and Ethel are on an assembly line. The chocolates move down the line, emerging from a room at the right of the screen, not visible to the viewer; their job is to pluck each chocolate off the line, wrap it, and return it to the line, which moves inexorably toward another unseen room on the left—the packing room.

A stern supervisor hovers over them. "If one piece of candy gets past you and into the packing room unwrapped, you're fired!" she warns.

The chocolates begin to emerge from the kitchen. At first, the two pals seem to be doing well. Says Lucy: "This is easy, we can handle this OK."

But then the assembly line speeds up. "Ethel, I think we're fighting a losing game," says Lucy, her voice rising in panic.

To a roaring laugh track, the assembly line gradually speeds up and the two friends start shoving chocolates they can't wrap fast enough into their mouths, down the front of their uniforms, and under their caps.

The Lucy and Ethel video clip has been shown at Culture Day for years. Eating chocolates, one administrator explains, has become a Leander metaphor for fear and the systemic havoc it unleashes.

Langford had explained Deming's teachings and his ideas about continuous improvement. Langford had also taught Glenn, Akin, and their colleagues a raft of statistical tools that would help the district promote collaboration, troubleshoot problems, and identify opportunities for improvement. Or "probletunities," as Langford calls them.

Later, Leander would adopt "failing forward"—the idea that "it is OK not to know" but decidedly "not OK not to ask"—as one of myriad mantras that would define the Leander Way. Failing Forward along with Eating Chocolates and Probletunities were all part of a new language that was designed to help newcomers acclimate to the district culture.

Langford insisted on a relentless focus on the customer, which he no longer simply defined as students. Customers were anyone on the receiving end of a process; thus, students were customers of teachers; teachers, students, and parents were the customers of both administrators and custodians (whose work—cleaning and maintenance—influences the environment in which learning happens).[42]

The biggest shift, however, was Langford's insistence that, for change to work in the long run and to be meaningful, the Leander culture would have to relentlessly drive out fear and build trust with the staff.

It was this focus on trust that most intrigued Akin and Glenn. Years later, Akin thought about why Deming had emphasized "driving out fear" instead of "building trust." She came to realize, Akin says, "how much fear is sucked into any organization. Fear just creeps into the system unless you are aggressively trying to drive it out." Worse, she says, if you have a fearful system, you don't know because people won't talk about it.[43]

"And the high-stakes testing just magnifies that."[44]

Akin began to ask her staff what they considered the biggest source of fear in the district. "The same answer came back time and time again," recalls Akin. The problem was the teacher-evaluation system with its ratings and rankings.[45]

At around this time, a battle over school funding was brewing in the Texas courts. In a series of decisions, the courts found that Texas school funding based on local property taxes was unconstitutional because it left schools in the poorest districts with scant resources, amounting to "a denial of equal opportunity."[46]

In response to that lawsuit, Governor Ann Richards signed into law a new funding scheme popularly known as the Robin Hood Law. She was also determined to devolve control of education to local districts, and appointed Lionel (Skip) Meno as the next Texas education commissioner. Richards could not have made a more unorthodox choice. Not only was Meno a New Yorker, he was also said to be the first person nominated to a statewide position in Texas who was not a Texan.

Meno had grown up in upstate New York, where his father had been a longtime school superintendent who had worked in a number of small upstate districts. Meno himself had been a superintendent in Syracuse, New York, where he had earned a reputation for fearlessness by integrating the Syracuse schools. His mentor, Sid Johnson, called Meno "the greatest change artist I've ever known." Meno returned the compliment, once calling Johnson, his predecessor as Syracuse superintendent, "the smartest guy" he knew.[47] (Meno and Steve Phillips of New York City's alternative schools division both worked for, and were influenced by, Johnson and Tom Sobol [see chapter 1.])

Under Johnson, Meno had launched a storefront school in Syracuse, a "dropout retrieval project"; it was the 1960s, and Meno was still in his twenties. Later, he "shepherded" the local schools through a "very difficult and hostile integration" by holding more than two hundred community meetings. In years to come, the "open door" and "open dialogue" would become his signature style. When Meno succeeded Johnson as Syracuse superintendent in 1979, he was just thirty-two, the youngest superintendent in the state.[48]

During his ten years leading the Syracuse schools, Meno introduced a slew of policies aimed at improving education for poor and minority kids. To cut down truancy—a quarter of the district's first-grade students were missing school 20 percent of the time—Meno instituted an aggressive computer-assisted attendance policy that would eventually be adopted statewide; truant children were tracked down, and parents who didn't get their kids to school were charged with "educational neglect." Meno also introduced the state's first mandatory kindergarten program and brought social services into the schools.[49]

At the time of his Texas appointment, Richards said prophetically: "[W]e are not going to have any more of these writ-in-cement policies. We are going to give local communities local control."[50]

Meno, tall and mustachioed, began traveling the state on what today might be called a listening tour. Everywhere he went, he repeated some version of this refrain: if there is anything the state is doing to "get in the way" of your improvement, let me know, and we'll help you get rid of it.

He even mailed a letter to every school superintendent in Texas, guaranteeing waivers from state mandates (excluding civil rights matters).[51]

Akin decided to take the new commissioner at his word. She applied for a waiver from the state's onerous teacher-evaluation system. The state agreed on the condition that Leander develop an alternative evaluation system. Akin convened a team of teachers and central staff, which set out to "unbundle" the teacher-evaluation system. Henceforth, one part focused solely on hiring and firing decisions; the other comprised a separate teacher portfolio system aimed at ongoing learning and self-improvement. Since teachers were rarely fired, the first part of the system was fairly rote.[52]

The new approach allowed the district to focus on meaningful teacher-driven improvement. It also allowed Leander to "get out of the numerical rating game," says Akin, adding that "the old system was geared heavily to rating and ranking" teachers. Perhaps most importantly, she added, "We never had to incorporate test scores" into the evaluations.[53]

When Meno left, many of the waivers ended. But Leander's waivers kept getting extended.[54]

By unbundling the evaluation system so that hiring and firing decisions would be handled separately, the district was able to reshape the core "evaluation" process so that it became part of Leander's improvement strategy. "We'd sit down with teachers in small groups and have them present their portfolios," recalled Glenn. Akin describes this evaluation process as a "genius hour," "a celebration" during which teachers present a portfolio of goals, what they did to achieve them, and what remained to be done, along with a new set of goals for the following year.[55]

The evaluation system was a key building block for Akin's larger strategy. Akin focused rigorously on hiring and promotion, putting people who she believed were receptive to the continuous-improvement philosophy into key leadership positions, and hiring those she believed would be sympathetic to it. By fostering trust and collegiality, Akin transformed her recruits into a loyal and cohesive team of educators who stayed in the district and would prove essential during Leander's years of exponential growth in sustaining—and evolving—the district's continuous-improvement culture. In 2006, the average principal tenure at Leander was over a dozen years—i.e., those who were already principals or became principals in the early 1990s had remained at Leander.[56]

That longevity is also reflected in the teaching force. In the 2014–2015 school year, just 2 percent of the district's teachers, 45 teachers out of 2,524, left the district.[57]

Years after hammering out its evaluation system, the State of Texas offered school districts extra money to offer teachers merit pay. Leander turned down the money.[58]

Not surprisingly, employee longevity at Leander could be traced all the way back to the superintendent's office, where the long-spinning revolving door had finally ground to a halt, allowing a consistent, cohesive leadership strategy—a cornerstone of Deming's management philosophy—to take root. At a time when the average Texas superintendent served for 4.2 years, Tom Glenn, who became superintendent in 1987, remained in office for twenty years. When he finally retired, he was succeeded by Champion, who had served in multiple positions in Leander, including teacher, principal, and finally assistant superintendent. Significantly, three of the eight school board members who would have voted on that succession plan were at Leander when the continuous-improvement plan was first put in place. As of 2015, Akin had served as the district's chief curriculum and culture strategist for over thirty years.[59]

That collaboration and consistency paid off. In recent years, Leander has achieved some of the highest test scores in Texas, ranking eleventh out of sixty districts in the state. While one in five students was eligible for free or reduced-price lunch, in the 2016–2017 school year, the district had a 98 percent four-year high school graduation rate and a 2 percent dropout rate. [60]

Akin used her network of longtime educators to help seed ideas throughout the district, trusting loyal lieutenants to try new innovations, many of which, in recent years, have centered on cultivating the inner-kindergartener, with all his enthusiasm for learning, in all students.

Akin likens the process to cultivating St. Augustine grass, a hearty sapphire-green sod that is favored in hot climates and one that, over time, will crowd out most weeds and other grasses.

"There are two different ways to grow St. Augustine grass," explains Akin. "If you have the money, you can buy pallets of it and cover your lawn. And voilà! But if you don't have the money, you can buy plugs—a little piece of grass with roots attached. You plant the plugs, leaving substantial space in between.

"Given the right environment—with light and water—over a year or two, you can develop a full lawn."[61]

Akin lives on a ranch, but she saves her gardening for the office, preferring to plant plugs with the help of principals she has nurtured for years. There is nothing coercive or predictable about the process, a bottom-up approach that sometimes morphs far beyond what Akin had initially conceived. But because they were devised at the grassroots, by principals working with teachers and later, after young shoots have taken root, with nurturing from the district, the ideas proved to be remarkably hardy.

The district identified seven student-learning behaviors that it believed were key to ensuring that "students have ownership in their learning," according to Champion.[62]

Of course, declaring that students would be at the center of learning was one thing. Making it happen would require seeding a lot of St. Augustine's grass. To do so, Akin turned to her veteran principals.

"Most leaders don't have much control—but a great deal of influence," explains Akin. "I was looking to see where can I make an impact and use my influence to guide the system forward."[63]

At the time, Sharon Hejl was the principal of Ada Mae Faubion Elementary School. Hejl had joined Leander in 1985; like Akin, she had spent most of her career in the district and had become one of the most ardent converts to the continuous-improvement philosophy.

Hejl had participated in the first seminar Langford agreed to hold at Leander—in the high school cafeteria. "It was an amazing big-picture idea—this continuous improvement," she recalls—though like many of her colleagues, she "figured this will come and go." Hejl didn't think much more about the seminar until two years later when Eric Haug took over as principal of Blockhouse Creek Elementary, where Hejl was then teaching second grade. Hejl calls Haug the "epitome of continuous improvement—always asking questions and the 'why' of things."

Haug had a questioning strategy that pulled you in "to the point where you were so involved with what you were doing and why you're doing it."[64]

The "five whys"—a process of asking *why* five times—is a technique used to "detect the root cause or meaning of a particular problem or situation." The repetition helps a group come to agreement around the root cause of a given challenge. It is often an integral part of the PDCA process.[65]

One of the first improvement projects Hejl became involved with was to develop a more systematic way of identifying kindergarteners who had learning problems and conveying that information to both parents and teachers in ongoing grades. "Kindergarten teachers normally know who might have a problem and what's just a maturity issue for an average learner," explains Hejl. But, when she got them in second grade, their parents often claimed they had never heard about the problem.

"It was frustrating to have to start over every year, identifying problems with each new class," said Hejl, explaining that there wasn't a process for communicating, from grade to grade, about a child without speaking directly to the kindergarten or first-grade teacher. "You spent half a year just trying to figure out a kid."[66]

Response to Intervention (RTI) was ushered in during the early aughts by No Child Left Behind and the 2004 reauthorization of the Individuals with Disabilities Education Act. The RTI approach tests children's reading skills at an early age to identify kids who may be struggling. Teachers then use a variety of interventions to improve their reading and to monitor their progress. If the interventions are successful, the child leaves the process. If not, the child could be referred for a full special-education evaluation.[67]

But years before RTI became standard practice in Texas, Hejl and her team created a process using Deming's Plan-Do-Check-Act cycle for documenting information about kids, including the interventions that worked and those that didn't. Before schools had computers to track data, Hejl and her colleagues developed a standard folder of each kindergartener's reading abilities as well as, if a child struggled, the strategies that had been used to address the problem.[68]

That process—working with teachers, using a Plan-Do-Check-Act process to come up with a standard folder for each kindergarten child—won Hejl over. Not only did it solve what had been a persistent source of frustration for her and other teachers, it was soon picked up by Leander's central office and disseminated districtwide. She also had seen how the opportunity to participate "in a meaningful" way in an important improvement project had galvanized the teachers.[69]

When Akin decided that she wanted to develop a new, more child-centered school—a concept that would be reflected in both the physical design of the school and its pedagogy—she thought Hejl might be just the one to lead the effort. Akin would rely on Hejl, one of dozens of principals she had nurtured over the years, to realize and shape that vision.

Leander couldn't build schools fast enough. In 2014, the overcrowded district housed classrooms in thirty-nine trailers; without new construction, it would have had many more students in trailers. Trailers were hardly ideal, especially for elementary schools. For one thing, they had no bathroom facilities, and so kids would need to get in and out of the main school building on their own, which presented security problems. The extra kids in trailers would also tax a school's infrastructure—from bathrooms to lab space. And in bad weather, kids and teachers would get soaked moving to and from a trailer and the main school building.

So build they did. In keeping with the district's continuous-improvement strategy, Leander developed a collaborative approach to school design, including everyone from teachers to maintenance personnel in the design process, and came up with a final design based on the school's pedagogical vision—for example, building classrooms around a central pod that could serve as a communal space for science, art, and group projects, instead of linear hallways. According to a 2014 survey of new school construction by the Texas comptroller, the cost of Leander schools consistently came in "well below average." The report also noted that its "well-designed standards" included science labs that were shared among classrooms, which minimized "transit time" and saved on square footage.[70]

School construction represented a key triumph of the Leander system. It tied form to function. It also demonstrated how continuous improvement and collaboration—among architects, contractors, and educators—could influence everything from school design to student learning to school culture.

Yet Leander's construction boom—despite its careful design and cost-efficiency—didn't come cheap. The district had $1.7 billion of debt in 2014, more than would normally be allowed under state law.[71] And Leander's heavy reliance on bonds raised hackles among fiscal conservatives, including local Tea Party insurgents who have railed against the district's construction strategy and relatively high debt. The high-stakes debates about how to meet Leander's exponential growth—whether by adding relatively inexpensive trailers to already overcrowded schools or with new school construction that had to be paid for with bonds—would, over the years, pose one of the gravest challenges to the district and its culture.

In the increasingly polarized world of Texas politics, the Leander board has had its share of controversy and in-fighting. Yet the combination of strong superintendents and a handful of strong, long-term board members has made the Leander board, in the main, an ally of its continuous-improvement strategy.

Don "Donnie" Hisle, the district's longest-serving board member, has been Leander's fiercest supporter. Hisle is, in some ways, an unlikely school board champion. He grew up in Lexington, Kentucky, in the 1950s, part of a working-class family where education had never been much of a priority. After graduating high school, Hisle followed his dad to a local IBM plant and got a job on the IBM Selectric typewriter assembly line. In 1967, Hisle was twenty years old and earning $70 per week when he jumped at the chance to move to Austin, Texas, in exchange for a 10 percent raise.[72]

Those were the days when a smart guy with a good work ethic could go places at a company like IBM, even without a college degree. By the time he retired, Hisle was managing five hundred people in the company's computer- and server-assembly operations.

Early on, Tom Glenn, Champion's predecessor as superintendent, had identified winning over the board and getting its members to understand the continuous-improvement strategy as perhaps the "biggest challenge" he faced. In that struggle, Hisle turned out to be an important ally.[73]

A few years before Hisle retired and joined the Leander board, IBM's Rochester, Minnesota, operation had won the Malcolm Baldrige National Quality Award, which had been modeled on Japan's Deming Prize. As an IBMer, Hisle was well versed in the mantra of process-driven, customer-focused quality improvement. He immediately understood what Glenn and the district were trying to do and, over the years, as new directors were elected to the board, he sought to explain the philosophy to the newcomers.

But in 2015, Hisle's seat was challenged by a Tea Party candidate whose campaign focused on cutting the district's debt and reining in school construction. Hisle's opponent was backed by the Cedar Park City Council, which is part of the Leander district, and other local politicians. Hisle managed to hold on to his seat by just fifty-six votes.[74]

Although the Tea Party insurgents have never come close to taking over the board, they remain a vocal minority, galvanized by their opposition to both new school construction as well as curricular changes that smack of the Common Core. At the time, insiders viewed Hisle's reelection as confirmation of the district's strength. But Hisle isn't sanguine. After close to two decades on the board, Hisle has seen his role become helping new board members understand the school district's culture. "Generally, this board is really good," says Hisle.[75]

But he warns: "The wrong board could destroy the district."

Interestingly, despite his commitment to the Leander strategy, despite his fear of Tea Party "outsiders," Hisle says local control is the only answer. If the board elected to stop building new buildings and to put kids in more portables, "the community would be up in arms."[76]

The careful attention not just to data, but to the systems that produce the data and how the data are interpreted. The careful hiring and placement of trusted veterans at each grade level. The collaborative work of a leadership team. These were all characteristic of the Leander district. But Akin wanted to take the district to the next level.

Akin posed a question that has occupied educators everywhere: what would it look like if kids were really put in charge of their own learning? As Hejl frames it: "A teacher could be tap-dancing on the table, and kids might still be disengaged."

The challenge was to figure out how to get kids to "own" their own learning. What Akin was doing, as a district leader, was planting a St. Augustine's plug in the most fertile patch of her garden. Akin was gambling that at Parkside Elementary, with Hejl in charge and surrounded by a team of like-minded teachers, the school would come up with an answer to what she was looking for. She was giving them a conceptual goal, a destination. But how they got there—and whether they settled in the valley or in nearby hills—would be up to them.

"I came to her with the idea and a list of possible traits, but it morphed into a slightly different product than what I would have created by myself," says Akin, adding: "But it's a much more robust and accepted outcome" precisely because the teachers planned it on their own.

At the end of the process, says Akin, "they are so proud, and rightfully so."[77]

Both Akin and Hejl relied on their influence as leaders and the trust they had developed with their subordinates.

GETTING KIDS TO TAKE OWNERSHIP OF THEIR LEARNING

In the past, I provided questions to my kids, and they had to research them. This year, I decided to let them come up with the questions; we'd model what is a good question. My kids just took off.

After the students had completed their research, the class looked back and reflected on what they had learned. I got the ball rolling by explaining how, in the old days, I used to give the questions, but thought this might be a better way.

To which one little boy responded: "What do you mean you used to give the questions? Isn't that silly! How did you know what we wanted to learn?"
—Jasmin Razminsk, third-grade teacher, Parkside Elementary[78]

To start the process for a student-centered culture, Hejl enlisted her leadership team. Always inclined to be inclusive, she also encouraged others to join the team. "What I don't like about team leaders or leadership teams," says Hejl, as an aside, "is it identifies one person [as being] over seven others."

Then, she stepped back and let the teachers take the lead. Using quality-improvement and consensus-building tools, the teachers brainstormed and came up with a concept they called the Parkside Scholar. A line drawing of an androgynous child—the "scholar dude," as he came to be called—was gradually invested with a set of twelve scholarly characteristics. Using a consensogram, a survey that provides a snapshot of a group's perceptions and understanding of a task, over two dozen teachers came up with twelve Parkside scholar traits. By far the most agreement—twenty-six teachers—was on "Parkside Scholars Make Connections," followed by "Parkside Scholars Wonder and Question" and "Parkside Scholars Thrive in Learning Communities."[79]

Beginning in 2010, Parkside focused on one of the twelve traits each month in classroom activities, on the school website, and in an assembly. The month focused on reflection brought a tsunami of mirrored objects to school. "We talked about the importance of reflection," says Hejl. "That's one of your highest learning tools either privately, written, or shared verbally. We tried to start building reflection into regular practice."[80]

To drive home the idea of "making connections," kids made link chains to show connections between ideas in the books they were reading and what they saw in the outside world.

When they focused on "giving back," another of the scholarly traits, Hejl brought in stacks of heart-shaped Post-it notes for students to mark places in books where characters were giving back.

Kids also were encouraged to bring the traits to life. Thus, giving back might mean helping a classmate who spilled her juice or offering to help parents at home. Hejl says she began hearing from parents about kids who started offering to do the dishes. For the concept to be meaningful, says Hejl, the traits would "need to transfer to your everyday life."[81]

Five years later, a child-sized model of the scholar dude made of wood and colorful beads and buttons greets you inside the door and remains an intimate part of life and the curriculum at Parkside. In one classroom, a teacher has used the scholar dude to crowdsource the classroom expectations with her kindergarten students. The traits of a good friend include smile, have nice manners, think nice thoughts, think about saying sorry, make eye contact, high-five, shake hands, hugs, no put-downs, and love.

> *School culture is ultimately controlled by students—no matter how much influence adults have (or think they have). Students must be the drivers of change, not just the passengers along for the ride. Which raises the question: How can adult educational leaders help actualize this change under the leadership of students?*
>
> —Sarah Ambrus and Christine Simpson, *Riding Shotgun*[82]

Even as a student-centered approach was taking root in the curriculum at Parkside Elementary and other district schools, eight miles away at Leander High School, a small group of educators wondered if a similar strategy might not help tackle a bullying epidemic among older kids. While Leander insists that the problem was no worse than at any other high school, it had morphed to the web. "There was a lot of cyber-bullying," recalls Terry Ballard, a Leander graduate and school leader who went on to the University of Texas at San Antonio. "It was verbal, not really physical . . . we didn't have any physical bullying. But it was really, really bad psychological and verbal bullying." Ballard remembers it even being "life-threatening" in some cases. The underclassmen, he said, were the "most vulnerable."[83]

For Christine Simpson, who was then the assistant principal at Leander High, the need to find a solution crystalized in the spring of 2010 when conflict erupted in the lead-up to the National Day of Silence, a student-led effort to raise awareness and acceptance of the LGBTQ community.[84]

Having begun her career as a Leander English teacher, Simpson was part of a large cadre of longtime Leander educators, one that included her husband—coincidentally named Chris Simpson. The Simpsons have four children—all of them in school at Leander—so the concerns about bullying were both personal and professional.[85]

That year, the tension at Leander High had "morphed into a point of contention between belief factions" at the school, in particular between students who wanted to participate and honor the day and those—primarily the religious students—who believed that any recognition of LGBTQ rights was a violation of their own rights.[86]

Historically, Leander has been a predominantly white and religious community. There are churches—Baptist, Methodist, and Presbyterian—on almost every street. As it has grown, however, the district has become more "blended," explains Greg Graham, who is now the assistant principal. (Christine Simpson has since become principal of Rouse, another Leander high school.) That has raised challenges at Leander High, where the in-crowd is dominated by kids who identify as Christian. Explains Ballard: "Like in every Texas school, football was the biggest thing at Leander High. And almost everyone on the team was Christian." Almost everyone, he says, is part of the Fellowship of Christian Athletes, an organization that says it aims to "use the powerful medium of athletics to impact the world for Jesus Christ." [87]

Football, says Ballard, was "extremely Christian." Almost everyone on the team was part of FCA.

Leander High includes among its many clubs an FCA "huddle," which is led by one of the school's athletic coaches. The "huddle" describes itself as "giving athletes a positive peer group to nurture Christian growth and service. With Christ as the center of these 'HUDDLES' and using the Bible as the authority, students are inspired to grow spiritually and use their influence to challenge others to know Christ." [88]

There were a few students "with very strong opinions" about marking the National Day of Silence, explains Simpson, but their effort was opposed by the school's much more dominant religious faction.[89]

Initially, Simpson called together a group of club leaders and student athletes in a "focus group" setting to talk through "students' general take of the school, their experiences, and any ideas for how to improve." Of the school's thirty or so clubs, nine student representatives showed up to the meeting, which, predictably, began with a focus on relatively low-level issues: the price of parking permits, allowing seniors to eat lunch off campus, "mean" teachers.[90]

Simpson, however, kept prodding. In true Leander fashion, Simpson used the continuous-improvement tools—especially the "five whys"; for example: Why did different groups dislike each other? Did the students feel powerless? If so, why?

Or, for that matter, why do administrators limit student input to just a "laundry list" of "surface-level issues"? [91]

Finally, the "b-word" surfaced, and the students began to talk about the culture of cliques and the fact that kids from different backgrounds never mixed.

Simpson's "whys" soon morphed into a "how" question: how would Leander deal with the problem to explore "what would bring greater unity to the community?"

The students' reply was "the administration needs to take care of that.

The principal needs to do more," recalls Simpson. "That's a start. But how will it change bullying on campus? How do we change the issue?"[92]

Implicit in Simpson's question was the acknowledgment that the administration was not an effective lever for changing student behavior. In fact, Simpson's effort was driven by two key convictions. First, schools need to create a safe and secure learning environment—one free of fear—in order for students to achieve their full potential. Second, as Simpson puts it, "The greatest untapped resource in school improvement is student-led change."[93]

Using the dispute over the Day of Silence as a starting point, Simpson's aim was to demonstrate that the Christian students and the LGBTQ students both had "similar core beliefs about helping others."[94]

Eventually, the student leaders agreed to form a coalition of clubs to promote kindness and understanding instead of bullying. What became known as C-Squared would be open to all students. And Simpson recruited Sarah Ambrus, Leander High's new ELA teacher, to serve as a facilitator. Ambrus, twenty-four at the time, still doesn't look much older than many students at Leander High. Her face is framed by long, loose blond curls that give her a look vaguely reminiscent of a youthful Sarah Jessica Parker, but with more gravitas and without the heels.[95]

Ambrus worked with the student leaders to develop an action plan. She introduced them to the Anti-defamation League's "No Place for Hate" initiative, which she says gave C-Squared "some structure."

The students already had decided that the club should have no officers. "They decided they didn't want hierarchy, as that would defeat the purpose," says Ambrus. "They talk about how leaders emerge naturally depending on what it is they are doing and their individual strengths. That's worked really well all these years," she adds, though the question of voting on officers comes up periodically.[96]

Having identified bullying as the problem, the students decided on a plan. The leaders of schoolwide clubs came together to work on bullying *prevention*. Ambrus and Simpson later wrote about the effort in a short book, *Riding Shotgun:* "Allowing students to define the issue created a sense of commonality. Students . . . put differences aside for the greater good. All students agreed to commit to the change and spread the message to their individual clubs and organizations. The 'Plan' was in place."[97]

Ambrus and Simpson also introduced the C-Squared students to process-improvement tools, in particular the iterative Plan-Do-Check-Act cycle popularized by Deming. This was key because without a clear road map for "doing" something about the problem, "checking" their assumptions and results, and "acting" on what they'd learned, teenagers would get swept up in the "brain hurricane" of the planning cycle.

Ambrus also taught the students how to use action plans or "Who/What/By When" structures.

Eventually, C-Squared took on a number of strategies both for changing the school culture and for creating a safe space for students to air social concerns. Leander High also began holding twice-yearly forums focused on everything from "be humane," with the emphasis being on "human," to creating "random acts of kindness."[98]

The most important part of the effort, however, was much less formal. The club met on Thursdays, and members were encouraged to "bring a buddy." Terry Ballard recalls that this was how he got his friends involved. "We started out with maybe twenty people at the meetings. But because everyone brought a friend—it exponentially grew to hundreds of people."[99]

The meetings were often held in Ambrus's classroom and functioned as a peer-led "support group." Ballard says the administration was "doing what it could" to combat bullying. But what was really needed was support among students. It was much harder, he said, for students to admit bullying to the administration than to a friend or close teacher. "That was what was really beneficial" about the club, he adds. "It allowed people to tell their stories to someone they could relate to."[100]

The group followed strict protocols. When students came with specific complaints, their stories were held in confidence—unless the complaints raised legal issues, in which case students were told the problem would be conveyed to Simpson. The most active members were upperclassmen and leaders of other clubs, which made it safer for younger students to unburden themselves. Ballard himself served as president of both his senior class and the school's International Baccalaureate program.[101]

There was almost always an adult present at the meetings—usually Ambrus, who would sit quietly at the back of the room. "People forgot that she was a teacher. She was sympathetic enough that they could comfortably talk to her," says Ballard.

"They didn't want to be the bully police," Ambrus says of C-Squared. Rather, the purpose of the club was to "be pro-active and to promote a culture of kindness and tolerance and inclusivity."

The weekly C-Squared meetings also began serving as an alternative disciplinary process. When students engaged in bullying, Simpson pulled them into C-Squared meetings as part of their consequence. All but one of those kids ended up joining the club and leading an action plan.[102]

That's how Emily Roberts became involved with C-Squared. Roberts recalls being bullied when she was younger. By high school, she had become a self-confessed Facebook bully. Simpson approached her one day and suggested she attend a C-Squared meeting. Roberts was reluctant at first, but soon became a spokesperson for the group. "Once I joined, I loved feeling important and making a change," says Roberts.[103]

Perhaps the most unexpected bonus of the club was that it attracted a high number of low-income kids, especially Latinos. "Our school is not diverse," recalls Ballard. "But C-Squared is very diverse. There are rich, poor, every cultural group. It really drew kids out of isolation."[104]

It helped, according to Akin, that unlike football or dance or band there was no financial cost associated with joining the club.[105]

Over a third of the kids at Leander High are black or Latino. So Ballard's comment may point to the relative invisibility of many minority kids within the social life of the high school.[106]

C-Squared caught on throughout Leander. From just nine students in 2010, the initiative has spread to thirty-three (out of thirty-eight) district schools, and remains strong.[107] C-Squared has attracted some attention outside the district, but has spawned few followers outside Leander. Greg Graham, then assistant principal at Leander High, guesses that entrusting a student-led effort with an anti-bullying mandate might be daunting for other districts. "It's got to be kid generated and has to grow from them; and it's going to look different than here," says Graham, echoing a familiar Leander refrain—that for improvement projects to work, they have to be generated by the key stakeholders, and thus can't serve as cookie-cutter replicas of something that worked elsewhere. "If they use the tools and give students ownership, then it will be successful," Graham says. "If adults run it, I'm not so sure."[108]

One uncharacteristically dank, chilly day in February 2015, roughly two thousand teachers streamed into Leander High School for another decades-old district ritual—the continuous-improvement conference that is held the first weekend of each February. Everyone is expected to attend, but no one takes attendance. It is a measure of the district's culture that almost everybody shows up. By 8 a.m. each day of the conference, two enormous parking lots are full.

Over two to three days, depending on the school-year schedule, the teachers select from hundreds of forty-five-minute presentations, most conducted by colleagues. These include sessions like Physical Sciences Share-a-thon and Love and Logic: Handling Arguing and Avoiding Power Struggles. The majority of sessions—and easily the most popular—are about improbable-sounding subjects, such as Making Data Collection Fun, Easy, and Meaningful!!! Or, How Can Continuous-Improvement Tools Help Students Track Their Progress and Increase Student Learning. Then, there's the ubiquitous David Langford's How Can Brain Theory and Continuous Improvement Boost Student Learning, which will be offered several times during the course of the conference.[109]

This year, one popular session was on developing questioning strategies for students. Led by Greg Graham and Sarah Ambrus, and a half dozen Leander High School juniors and seniors, it was designed to help teachers get students to ask better questions. As Graham explained: "When teachers ask questions, students are usually sitting there thinking 'When is lunch? Why is my girlfriend mad at me? What am I going to do tonight?' "[110]

But when students ask questions, that unleashes curiosity and intrinsic motivation.

After a brief introduction by Graham and Ambrus, the high school students led the conference participants through a series of prompts intended to elicit different levels of questions—relatively simple yes-or-no "closed questions," as well as "open questions." The latter allow for "more contemplation and broader thinking," explained Jasmine Peralez, a senior at Leander High who has been facilitating the questioning sessions at the continuous-improvement conference since her freshman year.[111]

Later that year, Monta Akin is relaxing at her ranch, her shorts and tank top still wet from a late-afternoon dip in the pool, a rare moment of relaxation—one that usually involves a floaty that keeps her hands free to cradle a glass of wine. It is mid-August 2015; Akin and her colleagues had just finished Culture Day, including an hour poring over plus-delta reviews on what the new teachers had liked—and not liked—about Culture Day and discussing possible changes for next year, including more time for lunch.

A soft breeze stirs the air below the oak and pecan trees that shade the single-level house Akin shares with her husband, Jim. A hummingbird nips at the glass jar containing the last drops of sugar water that is suspended from a shepherd's hook. A small fountain gurgles nearby.

And then there are the pink flamingos—one in the yard, another near the pool—colorful sentries from an earlier teacher orientation when several of the administrators dressed in pink boas or as pink flamingos to drive home the point that beautiful flamingos, like students, need a carefully balanced ecosystem to thrive. The flamingos were such a hit they have joined "eating chocolate" and "flowers are red" as touchstones of Leander's ever-evolving efforts to drive home the importance of developing an ever-improving and sustainable education system.

It's been thirty years since Akin launched Leander's continuous-improvement journey, yet she knows there is still much left to do.

Recently, Leander administrators took a hard look at the district's continuous-improvement strategy and determined that it needed, well, more improvement. "What we were doing was mostly building capacity without establishing expectations or providing much feedback or monitoring the progress," said Akin. "Those were two holes in our system."[112]

With its continuing growth, Leander will need to be clearer about where responsibility for institutionalizing the continuous improvement lies, says Akin. What exactly is the role of principals? Of assistant principals? Of the central administration? "Do we expect principals to send teams to the continuous-improvement institute every year? Or not?" asks Akin, not at all rhetorically.[113]

Akin has always been clear that continuous improvement cannot be a mandate. It has to infuse the district culture by fostering a grassroots buy-in. That commitment to buy-in is embraced because it makes sense, because it gives teachers agency. But that gets harder both with growth and with success. "We've shied away from dictating to people," says Akin. But "there's a balance you have to strike."[114]

As dusk settles over the ranch, Akin's energy begins to flag. She feels the familiar fever beginning to overtake her. Ever since cancer surgery, she has been subject to frequent bouts of debilitating cellulitis.

Tomorrow will be round two of Culture Day. For the first time in the district's history, the number of new teachers has been so large—a product of both district growth and retirements—that Akin and Champion decided to run two sessions back-to-back. And tonight, Akin is feeling so ill she's sure she will have to miss that session.

"Everything has been planned" well ahead, says Akin. "I'd like to be there. But I don't have to be. Everyone can proceed without me."[115]

That, in fact, will be Leander's greatest test. At the end of the fall semester 2015, after nearly forty years in the district, Akin retired. Unexpectedly, Bret Champion was recruited to another, larger Texas district, and he too left. Several other veterans of Leander's continuous-improvement strategy, including Hejl and Haug, retired at about the same time.

After a contentious board fight, Melinda Golden, another top lieutenant to Champion and Akin, lost a bid for the superintendency. The Leander board, which now included three new members, selected an outsider—Dan Troxell.[116]

Then, the Texas State Legislature passed a new teacher and principal performance-evaluation system that requires teachers be rated on a seventeen-point rubric by the end of the 2017–2018 school year. Leander is now rewriting its appraisal system to comply with the law—though it has resisted one key requirement, that teachers receive a final, single numerical rating. "When you start labeling and putting scores and ranking people, that's not how you have people grow," says Haug, who was still at Leander when the new appraisal system was being developed.[117]

Rank-and-file educators at Leander are worried and have been burning up the newly retired Akin's phone lines. Notes one teacher: almost all the administrators "who were strong advocates have retired or moved on; now [it's] almost like our central office staff is trying to understand the district's vision." She remembers one of the first talks given by Troxell: "We're not losing it," he said of the continuous-improvement system. "It's not the system. It's the people."

"That's interesting, because the Leander Way has always been the *Leander System*," says the teacher. "It raises the question [of] whether he understands."[118]

Akin is cautiously optimistic. It gives her hope that Troxell chose to show the Leander Way video at a recent convocation. That he has invited her, Eric Haug, and even Tom Glenn to the district.

Then, she suddenly remembers one of Deming's frequent questions: "How could they know? How could they possibly know?"[119]

By that, he meant that to embrace continuous improvement you need to have an *operational definition* of what it means—of the philosophy, of statistical theory, of systems thinking. "There are no shortcuts," was another of Deming's mantras.

To understand the Leander Way, its new senior management will have to study and learn.

5

THE HURRICANE AND THE CHARTERS

New Schools Unearth Old Ways in New Orleans

Long before Sci Academy, a charter school in New Orleans, had graduated its first senior class, the school was being heaped with accolades.

In September 2010, when Sci Academy was just two years old, its two hundred excited students—then all freshmen and sophomores—filed into Greater St. Stephen Baptist Church next door to the school. Together with local dignitaries, journalists, and a brass band, the students watched on jumbo screens as the leaders of six charter schools from around the country appeared on the *Oprah Winfrey Show*. At the end of the show, they watched as Oprah handed each charter-school leader—including Ben Marcovitz, Sci Academy's founder—a $1 million check.[1] Sci Academy is a flagship charter school and a model of the new data-driven, business-infused approach to education that has reached its apotheosis in New Orleans. After Hurricane Katrina in 2005, education reformers swept away what remained of the traditional public schools in what had been one of the nation's lowest-performing districts.[2]

Before the storm, the New Orleans public school system had suffered from white flight, neglect, mismanagement, and corruption, which left the schools in a state of disrepair. The hurricane almost literally wiped out the schools: only 16 of 128 buildings were left relatively unscathed. As of 2013, the student population was still under 45,000, compared with 65,000 students before the storm. Following the storm, some 7,500 unionized teachers and other school employees, most of them African American and making up a sizable swath of the city's middle class, were put on unpaid leave and eventually fired.[3]

Two years before the storm, the State of Louisiana had set up a so-called Recovery School District to take over individual failing schools. After Katrina, the district eventually took over about sixty local schools, most of which were *not* failing, according to Louisiana's own measures; more than 75 percent of New Orleans kids landed in schools controlled by the RSD. And most of the RSD schools were, like Sci Academy, strict-discipline, no-excuses charter schools.[4]

About twenty well-performing schools remained in the Orleans Parish

School Board, creating, in essence, a two-tier system. And nearly all the schools in both parts of the system have since been converted to charters, which promised choice and increased accountability.[5] The leaders of the New Orleans charter movement also wrapped themselves in the mantle of the civil rights movement.

"This transformation of the New Orleans educational system may turn out to be the most significant national development in education since desegregation," wrote Neerav Kingsland, then CEO of New Schools for New Orleans, the city's leading venture-philanthropy group incubating local charter schools, in 2012. "New Orleans students have access to educational opportunities that are far superior to any in recent memory."[6]

Meanwhile, Arne Duncan, then the secretary of education, asked: was Hurricane Katrina "the best thing that happened to the education system in New Orleans?"[7]

A decade after Hurricane Katrina, New Orleans students enrolled in charter schools were making progress on state tests. In 2014, 63 percent of children in local elementary and middle schools were proficient on state tests, up from 37 percent in 2005. Research by Tulane University's Education Research Alliance showed that the gains were largely because of the charter school reforms, according to Douglas N. Harris, the alliance's director. Graduation and college-entry rates also increased over pre-Katrina levels.[8]

But what had long been touted as a New Orleans miracle was not all that it seemed. Louisiana state standards remained among the lowest in the nation. The average composite ACT score for the Recovery School District went up "by a hair" to 16.6 in 2015, from 16.4 a year earlier, still well below the minimum score required for admission to either a two-year community college (without remediation) or a four-year public university in Louisiana. Indeed, the new research said little about student performance in high school—ERA's research focused entirely on elementary and middle school students—the time when the city's youth are most susceptible to the lure of drugs and the streets, and most likely to drop out.[9] Harris says ERA didn't include high school data primarily because "the tests switched from the graduation exam to end-of-course exams." Another problem, he says, was that the tests were "not taken at the same grade by all students," making comparisons difficult.[10]

Indeed, there is growing evidence that the reforms came at the expense of the city's most disadvantaged children, who often disappear from school entirely and thus are no longer included in the data. "We don't want to replicate a lot of the things that took place to get here," said Andre Perry, who was one of the few black charter school leaders in the city, when ERA presented its data at a conference pegged to the ten-year anniversary of the storm. "There were some pretty nefarious things done in the pursuit of academic gain," Mr. Perry acknowledged, including "suspensions, pushouts, skimming, counseling out, and not handling special needs kids well." [11]

New Orleans has emerged as the antithesis of a generative teacher- and parent-driven effort to experiment with new education ideas, as the charter movement was originally conceived by the legendary labor leader Albert Shanker. While a few independent, community-led charters have emerged in New Orleans, they have mostly done so against great odds and often in opposition to the existing charter establishment.

As Brian Beabout, a professor at the University of New Orleans who has written extensively about school reform after Hurricane Katrina, put it: "[C]an socially just ends be served by autocratic means? The answer, of course depends on our definition of socially just. If closing the racial achievement gap on state examinations is social justice, then perhaps. If our definition hinges on marginalized communities gaining some agency in the public institutions that serve them, probably not." [12]

For all its youthful, twenty-first-century philanthro-capitalist trappings, the first decade of the New Orleans charter revolution hearkens back to an early age of oligopoly, union-busting, and top-down hierarchy. For most of the city's poor African American parents, school choice has boiled down to a thin-gruel menu of test-prep and strict-discipline, no-excuses schools. For teachers, it has been an unsustainable slog of long hours and low pay, which has created sky-high teacher-turnover rates. For charter operators, especially the smaller, less-well-connected ones, there are the perils of a low-margin business—too many operators hoping to outperform the market for test scores, chasing a limited supply of philanthropic dollars. For children, there is the Darwinian game of musical chairs—with the weakest kids left out when the music stops and failing schools close, or when they are counseled out of schools that can't, or won't, deal with their problems. And all this among a population of children and families displaced—often for years—and traumatized by the devastating storm in a state that offers poor children virtually no mental-health supports.

Behind this new regime are a handful of wealthy, unelected, mostly out-of-town organizations and benefactors, and their acolytes, who control the shots and help set the city's education agenda. Many, no doubt, have been motivated by a genuine desire to rebuild the inundated school system and to avoid the considerable mistakes—and corruption—of the past. But they are also driven by a deep and blinding animus to unions, a distrust of grassroots organizing in poor communities, and an ideological belief in the power of markets and their ability to transform American education. It is hard to escape the fact that the business-minded leaders and funders of the New Orleans experiment also harbor a bias against the collaborative, generative, antihierarchical model of continuous improvement outlined by systems thinkers like W. Edwards Deming and that has informed successful business practices ever since, including the open-source software movement and the newly popular Japanese lesson study (chapter 4).

Nor do the New Orleans reformers seem willing to acknowledge the rich, decades-old history of collaborative improvement efforts in other districts, including the sort that led to Massachusetts's Education Reform Act, the progressive movement in New York City, or the ideas practiced by the Leander school district in Texas.

Notes Harold Meyerson, executive editor of *The American Prospect*:

> In their mix of good intentions and self-serving blindness, the billionaire education reformers have much in common with some of the upper-class progressives of a century ago, another time of great wealth and pervasive poverty. Some of those progressives, in the tradition of Jane Addams, genuinely sought to diminish the economy's structural inequities, but others focused more on the presumed moral deficiencies and lack of discipline of the poor. Whatever the merits of charters, the very rich who see them as the great equalizer are no closer to the mark than their Gilded Age predecessors who preached temperance as the answer to squalor.[13]

There is also a growing consensus in New Orleans that the reforms were done "*to* black people, not *with* black people." Thus, New Orleans also has helped inspire a growing backlash against charter schools by African American civil rights organizations and the very people the movement was intended to help.

Sci Academy, for years one of the highest-rated open-admissions schools in New Orleans—and, for much of the last decade, one of the few RSD high schools to earn a B on its state report card (as of this writing there were no A-rated open-admission schools in New Orleans)—offers one of the best vantage points from which to view how the New Orleans experiment unfolded, as well as its results.

Sci Academy, with its chain-link fence and campus of modular buildings, the result of a continuing post–Hurricane Katrina building shortage, didn't look much like a model school for its first decade after Katrina. The school has since moved into a new building and was renamed Abramson Sci Academy, a nod to a high school that once occupied that location. During several visits in 2012 and 2013, neatly uniformed freshmen in polo shirts and khakis walked along straight red lines that snaked through the school's breezeways. Placards bearing slogans, such as "No Short Cuts; No Excuses" and "Go Above and Beyond," hung overhead.[14]

Everything at Sci Academy is carefully choreographed to maintain discipline and a laser-like focus on its principal mission, which is to get every student into college. Each morning, at 8 a.m., the teachers, almost all white and in their twenties, gather for a rousing thigh-slapping, hand-clapping, rap-chanting staff revival meeting, the beginning of what will be, for most, a fourteen- to sixteen-hour workday. Students arrive a half hour later, and if asked "Why are you here?" and "What will it take?" are expected to respond "To learn," followed by a recitation of the school's six core values: "achievement, respect, responsibility, perseverance, teamwork, and enthusiasm."[15]

Both curriculum and behavior are meticulously scripted. As kids file into class, a teacher hands them a "do now," a survey that helps determine how much students retained from the previous day's class. An "exit ticket" filled out at the end of class establishes how much kids have absorbed. Exit ticket and attendance data, demerits for bad behavior, and "Sci bucks" for good behavior are keyed into the Sci software system by teachers every night to help monitor both student and teacher performance.[16]

Sci Academy's teachers are mostly inexperienced young, white out-of-towners who are willing, at least in the short run, to put in grueling hours. But at many schools, including Sci Academy, plenty of teachers last for less than two years. As of 2013, teachers with certifications from Teach for America numbered close to four hundred in New Orleans, five times the level of a few years earlier. Within the RSD, in 2011, 38 percent of teachers had less than three years of experience; 21 percent have spent just one year or less in the classroom, according to "The State of Public Education in New Orleans," a 2013 report by the Cowen Institute at Tulane University.[17]

To help novice teachers control their classrooms, charter schools train them in highly regimented routines. The city's charter school advocates argue that in the aftermath of the storm, when charter operators had to scale up quickly, they needed to start with basics: first order and security, then skill building. "Kids expect high school to be dangerous. They come to school with their backs up," explained Sci Academy's Marcovitz, a graduate of the elite Maret School in Washington, D.C., and Yale University. He says the routines, which were pioneered by San Francisco–based KIPP, the CMO with the most charter schools in New Orleans, are intended to keep students focused and feeling safe.[18]

During one English class visit in 2012, a teacher who had been at Sci for about a year held forth on the fine points of grammar, including the subtle difference between modal and auxiliary verbs. As a few heads drifted downward, she employed a popular charter school management routine to hold the class's attention. "SPARK check!" she called. The acronym stands for sit straight; pencil to paper (or place hands folded in front); ask and answer questions; respect; and keep tracking the speaker.

"Heads up, sit straight—fifteen seconds to go," she said, trying to get her students' attention.

"All scholars, please raise your homework in THREE, TWO, ONE. We need to set a goal around homework completion. I only see about one third complete homework."[19]

Sci Academy, like most post-Katrina charter schools, has strayed far from the progressive roots of the city's pre-hurricane charter schools. Anthony Recasner, a child psychologist, was a partner in founding the city's first charter school, New Orleans Charter Middle School, in 1998. The school's progressive curriculum included traditional academics as well as experiential projects and electives, such as bicycle repair and African dance, to foster a love of learning, as well as healthy "social and emotional growth." NOCM's motto was "No Work, No Benefits," and once kids had done their school work, they could choose from a menu of field trips, including visits to Audubon Zoo, the roller-skating rink, bowling alley, and sometimes even a movie. Students visited local businesses and participated in internships. Three-quarters of NOCM students were African American, and at least 86 percent were eligible for free- or reduced-price lunch.[20] Yet by the time they had completed middle school, over three-quarters of the graduating eighth graders were admitted into selective magnet schools, making NOCM the top-rated nonselective school in New Orleans.[21]

Years later, Recasner was visibly torn between his hopes for the New Orleans charter experiment and his disappointment in the distance that remains between today's no-excuses charter school culture and the movement's progressive roots. "Education should be a higher-order exploration," explained Recasner. The typical charter school in New Orleans today "is not sustainable for the adults, not fun for kids." Recasner's own experience as a poor child raised by a single parent mirrored that of most students in the charter schools. One of the few African American charter leaders in New Orleans, Recasner resigned from FirstLine, the CMO that succeeded New Orleans Charter Middle, soon after the storm.[22]

Indeed, for all its dysfunction, New Orleans had some innovative nonselective schools and programs before the storm. In addition to NOCM, there was the Free School, a "hippie" school in the Debbie Meier tradition. John McDonogh, a traditional high school, had, under the leadership of Raynard Sanders, founded the city's first high school DNA lab and launched an experiment known as the Creole cottages, which taught students about architecture, construction, and building trades; the students even helped build actual homes.[23]

And, in the years immediately before Hurricane Katrina, Frederick Douglass High School, which had suffered years of neglect and earned a dubious distinction as the worst school in the city, developed an innovative, nationally recognized writing and student-mentoring program.[24]

The new charter schools have little in common with those earlier experiments, and few of these earlier efforts fared well under the new charter system. Even FirstLine, which succeeded NOCM, strayed far from its pioneering roots. While Recasner's partner, Jay Altman, continues to run FirstLine, now one of the leading charter operators in New Orleans, the progressive roots of the charter movement have been overrun by the new realities of the marketplace and the no-excuses ideology.

TWO SEPARATE AND UNEQUAL CHARTER SYSTEMS

Driven by the binary goals of both government policy and philanthropic funding—which reward schools for test scores and for getting kids into college, any college, and penalizes those that don't—most nonselective charter high schools in New Orleans, like Sci Academy, describe themselves as "college prep."[25]

This may seem an admirable goal, but not one well-suited to the neediest kids in New Orleans who struggled the most in school. The number of eighth graders who passed the end-of-course tests at nonselective RSD schools in the 2010–2011 school year (five years after Katrina) was a miserable 60 percent for RSD charters. Passing rates were even worse—just 35 percent—at the few remaining last-chance direct-run public schools in the RSD. For youngsters who struggled to complete eighth grade, the push toward college would leave behind many of the most disadvantaged kids who already faced enormous hurdles because of poverty, parental abandonment, and one of the highest rates of gun violence in the nation. (In the 2015–2016 school year, by which time there were virtually no public schools left in the RSD, 46 percent of eighth graders in the RSD reached the "basic" level or higher on the ELA test, and 58 percent in math.[26]) In 2008, the RSD no longer made passing the end-of-course test an entry requirement for ninth grade—a recognition that doing so often led students to drop out before they had even reached high school—and offered remediation instead. But subterranean ACT scores well into the 2014–2015 school year suggest that most New Orleans students in nonselective RSD schools are in reality nowhere near ready for college.[27]

Part of the problem for the first six or seven years after Katrina was that families—many of them poor, displaced, and lacking transportation—had to run a grueling gauntlet just to apply to a charter school. What made the application process so complicated is that New Orleans, post-Katrina, has what is, essentially, two separate and unequal school systems: the smaller, high-performing, mostly selective schools, which were never taken over by the state and remained mostly under the purview of the Orleans Parish School Board (OPSB)—though many were converted to charters—and the roughly sixty schools within the RSD. In 2012, the RSD rolled out a central application system known as OneApp, though, for several years, most OPSB schools did not participate.[28]

This meant that, in the years before OneApp, the only kids who really had a chance in the charter system were those with savvy families. The luckiest were kids such as Eddie Barnes, a star student at Sci Academy whose mother was able to navigate the highly confusing application process that, especially in the early years of the RSD, stumped many parents.

Like most of his classmates, Eddie came to Sci Academy after a traumatic post-Katrina odyssey that began when he was eleven and fled the city with his parents and younger brothers, first for Texas and then eventually Georgia. When Eddie's mother, Anya Barnes, decided to return to New Orleans in 2008, her husband, the father of her two youngest sons, didn't join her. So the family returned to New Orleans fatherless, arriving three months after the start of Eddie's freshman year. That was during the chaotic first years of the RSD, when parents had to apply to every charter school individually, and every school had a different application, which led to widespread allegations that schools cherry-picked their students.[29]

Eddie and his mother made the rounds of the few RSD schools that still had openings and eventually found their way to Sci Academy, which had just enrolled its first class. (The two other schools Eddie tried have since been closed or taken over.) Barnes, who never completed college, was "inspired by Sci" and its college-prep mission. Eddie, in turn, was inspired by his mother and, three years later, wrote his college essay about the role she had played in his academic achievements.[30]

In school, Eddie was a class leader. At 160 pounds and 5 feet 8 inches tall, he became captain of the fledgling basketball and football teams. He won Mr. Sci Academy, an award given to the student who best exemplifies the school's cooperative values. He was voted prom king. And he excelled academically: in his junior year, Eddie's standardized test scores met the requirements for a scholarship to a Louisiana state school, as well as for a Sci Academy–organized college trip to the East Coast.[31]

By the time Eddie was ready to graduate in the spring of 2012, his class seemed to offer vindication not only for the school's no-excuses college-prep approach, but for the entire New Orleans charter model. Almost all the graduating seniors at Sci Academy—close to 95 percent—had been accepted to a college. Eddie and a half dozen of his classmates would be returning to the East Coast, where they had won scholarships, to attend schools such as Middlebury, Wesleyan, Amherst, and Bard.[32]

Yet the results were not all they seemed for either Sci Academy's college-bound kids or the ones who never made it to graduation.

NO PLAN B IN THE COLLEGE-FOR-ALL UNIVERSE

During the summer of 2010, Sci Academy founder Ben Marcovitz had recruited Allie Levey, an assistant dean of admissions at Wesleyan University in Middletown, Connecticut, to be Sci's college counselor and to make sure his graduates would go college. The idea, explained Levey, twenty-five at the time, was for him to become a kind of "double agent" and help students navigate the ins and outs of admissions at elite colleges.[33]

Like Marcovitz, Levey had attended a D.C.-area private school and an elite college—Sidwell Friends and Wesleyan. Marcovitz, said Levey, "wants this to be like a group of people who believe."[34]

Levey, boyish and intense, bought into the Sci Academy approach. At morning meetings, he could be seen leading fellow faculty members in the motivational chants and rallying students. But the task was daunting from the start. "I'll never forget the first time they showed me the spreadsheet of the kids' GPAs and ACT scores going into senior year," recalled Levey. "I was like, there's no way." The average ACT score was 17, well below the cutoff for a state scholarship, which was 20 in 2012, out of a possible 36. Levey says he was certain he had taken on an impossible task.[35]

But Levey and Marcovitz were determined. Levey organized college trips, mentored seniors, and worked the phones to his former college-admissions colleagues. Meanwhile, Sci Academy pulled out the stops when it came to standardized tests. In the spring, classes were regularly suspended for added test prep. Seniors who scored below 20 on their ACT spent three weeks being tutored by Alex Gershanik, the local "test-prep guru," at a cost, to Sci Academy, of $1,000 per student.[36]

By the time Sci Academy's first senior class was about to graduate, Levey's doubts were deepening—about both the school's college-for-all mission and the toll his work was having on his personal life. By the next spring, less than two years after joining Sci Academy, Levey decided to resign. "I believe every member of [the] school leadership team deeply in their hearts wants to make this sustainable," said Levey at the time, visibly saddened. "I also know that that's not possible right now."[37]

Indeed, behind Sci Academy's impressive college-acceptance rate were some troubling numbers. The school's first graduating class was 37 percent smaller than the same class had been in the ninth grade—even though some students came to the school after freshman year and filled seats left vacant by departing students. The attrition rate did improve; the class of 2013 was 28 percent smaller than it had been in the ninth grade. But Sci Academy's out-of-school suspension rate had been rising, reaching 49 percent in 2012, the second highest in the city and one reason kids transferred to other schools. Sci Academy says that when it tried to reduce suspensions by loosening some rules, it led to increased violence, including weapons on campus, which, in turn, led to a spike in suspensions.[38]

Even kids who make it to college face hurdles. While the majority of Sci Academy's graduates enrolled in four-year colleges in the fall of 2012, over 10 percent had either dropped out or transferred to junior colleges within six months of matriculating. To increase college persistence, Sci Academy created an advisory system for alumni; advisers help college-bound graduates with everything from financial aid to social integration to general crisis management. In 2016, 50 percent of Sci Academy graduates either were enrolled in college or had graduated from college, a rate that Sci Academy acknowledges is "nowhere near" its goal.[39]

Another fact that troubled Levey was student debt: the average Sci Academy student, if he or she completed college, would graduate with $22,000 to $27,000 in debt, according to Levey's 2012 calculations, even if the student were eligible for state or federal aid. Meanwhile, students who dropped out would leave with thousands of dollars in loans. Says Levey: "A kid who is barely passing, but qualifies for a four-year college, who really doesn't have any academic interests—why am I having them mark general studies on their college application? Or nursing or chemical engineering?"[40]

Take the case of a student named Trevon who, before enrolling at Sci Academy in his senior year, attended two other New Orleans charter high schools. The first, Warren Easton, declined to reenroll him in his sophomore year. The second, Sojourner Truth, was by most accounts a chaotic failure and closed after his junior year. Trevon fell behind a grade level and didn't learn to write a research paper until late in his senior year. As recently as spring of his senior year at Sci, Trevon wasn't sure college was for him; he was thinking of enlisting in the Army instead.[41]

But, encouraged by Sci Academy's college-prep culture and after months of test prep, including a stint with the test-prep guru, Trevon eked out an 18 on his ACT—not enough for a state scholarship. But, with a student loan, Trevon decided to enroll at Southern University at New Orleans. Even though the college had one of the nation's lowest graduation rates—as of 2017, a four-year graduation rate of 5 percent and a six-year rate of 16 percent[42]—Levey steered him and several classmates to SUNO because it was "cheap"; with work-study and living at home, he would have to take out no more than $1,000 or so per year in loans.[43]

A Sci Academy administrator helped him register and pick a major—entrepreneurship—but two weeks into the fall semester, Trevon, unsure how to navigate a problem with his student loans, had neither purchased his books nor accessed Blackboard, the online portal where professors posted class materials.[44]

There has been no plan B in the college-for-all charter universe, in part because both the state's accountability systems and philanthropists' expectations have been based on how successful the schools are in qualifying kids for college. Louisiana's school-grading system has rewarded those whose students graduate in four years and score well on college-entry tests such as the ACT and advanced-placement tests. It has penalized schools—by giving them lower grades—if students take longer to graduate or perform poorly on the college-placement tests.

Schools typically are reviewed every five years, but can be closed down after three if they do not meet the charter's goals. In the 2010–2011 school year alone, ten New Orleans schools were closed or taken over, according to Research on Reforms, a local research and advocacy organization. The process left hundreds of kids in ninth to twelfth grades scrambling to find space at a new school.[45]

Paradoxically, as New Orleans encouraged existing charters to take over the last of the schools the RSD directly ran, the charter system was finally forced to confront the flaws in its one-size-fits-all college-prep model. Some of the city's charter schools began experimenting with alternatives, like vocational programs and so-called alternative schools designed specifically to help students who have struggled in, or dropped out of, school. In 2014,

John White, Louisiana's superintendent of education, in a notable departure from the state's college-for-all mantra, unveiled a proposal to revamp high school diplomas by creating a vocational track that would qualify graduates for technical careers. Although Louisiana already had a "career diploma," it was widely seen as a dead-end certification because it neither prepared students for college nor provided them with specialized training.[46]

But for these experiments to work, the incentives would have to change. Under the post-Katrina accountability regime, alternative schools would always score an "F" and—if the system functioned as it should—would eventually be closed, argued Elizabeth Ostberg, former head of human resources at FirstLine and founder of the NET, an alternative school, in 2012. Indeed, the NET, a last-chance school for overaged young adults, most of whom have had their schooling interrupted, got an "F" on its first 2012–2013 report card. Two years later, the NET was still scoring an "F"—though it had received a "top-gains" designation.[47]

"Why would you do this if you care about your school's accountability score?" asked Jay Altman, the CEO of FirstLine, who gave the NET space at one of his schools during its first year of operation. In 2014, he began to pilot a vocational program as part of a takeover of Joseph S. Clark, a historic but failing high school.[48]

Over the years, Louisiana has modified its rigid test-based school-performance measurements, most recently adding criteria to reflect "more robust" indicators relating to discipline, special education, health, and safety.[49]

However, private donors still want to see as many students as possible go to college—an understandable inclination, but one that isn't helpful for all kids. And heedful of their bottom line, charter schools are eager to oblige. At their peak, private donations could equal a sizable chunk of charter school budgets. In 2011, fully one-third of Sci Academy's $3.9 million budget came from private donations. (In a sign that philanthropic dollars are becoming scarcer, in 2013, private donations to Collegiate Academies, the new CMO formed by Sci's founders to encompass both its original school and two new charters, totaled less than $1 million, just 8.6 percent of its total budget.)[50]

Meanwhile, Ostberg was convinced that her school was initially denied funding by a major foundation because the school's mission did not emphasize college prep. It finally got the money, she says, in part by convincing the foundation that if New Orleans is to have a "successful education system," it has to "address" the kids who aren't going to college. "If we build great alternative schools, our college-prep schools will be better," she says.[51]

FAILING KIDS WITH SPECIAL NEEDS

The premise of the New Orleans charter school experiment has been that charters—most of which serve as independent so-called local education agencies (LEAs) responsible for everything from busing to serving every possible special need of its students—can educate all children. However, the experiences of kids like Lawrence Melrose, another Sci Academy student, do not support that claim. At eighteen, Lawrence's life was a testament to both the high levels of social dysfunction in New Orleans, including poverty and violence, and the inability of even the most well-intentioned charter schools to meet the needs of the most disadvantaged kids.

It is hard to know when Lawrence's life began to spin out of control. It may have been when his grandmother, who raised him, was diagnosed with cancer and he began shuttling back and forth between Georgia, where the family moved after Hurricane Katrina, and his great-uncle Shelton Joseph's house in New Orleans. It may have been during a basketball game, near his great-uncle's house, on a hot August day of his fourteenth year, when another kid shot him in the back, nearly killing him. Or it may have been during his dizzying spin through half a dozen struggling RSD schools in the two years before he enrolled at Sci Academy.[52]

During the weeks Lawrence spent at Children's Hospital recovering from his gunshot wound, a report on his neuropsychological state concluded that Lawrence "appears to have the skills necessary to be a productive member of society," but also that he should continue to receive "special-education services at the highest level possible."[53]

A year later, in 2010, Lawrence enrolled as a freshman at Sci Academy; he had spent two years—with multiple suspensions and expulsions—in the RSD. His first months at Sci Academy were rocky. When the school celebrated Marcovitz's appearance on the *Oprah Winfrey Show* at the church next door, Lawrence was not there; he was kept back in the school's office.[54]

In 2010, Lawrence became one of ten plaintiffs in a class-action lawsuit filed by the Southern Poverty Law Center against the Louisiana Department of Education, charging that the city's fragmented education system had resulted in "systemic failures to ensure that students with disabilities have equal access to educational services and are protected from discrimination."[55]

Of all the New Orleans schools he had attended, Sci Academy was the first that had actually tried to grapple with Lawrence's problems. But, as an independent LEA, Sci Academy apparently did not have the resources to meet all of Lawrence's needs. The school eventually concluded that he needed an intensive therapy program, but was unable to find one for him.

As part of a statewide privatization effort that had begun a few years earlier, Governor Bobby Jindal had closed the last of the public hospitals that offered residential programs for adolescents with mental disabilities.[56]

Lawrence spent less and less time at school. At seventeen, he was arrested for armed robbery; repeatedly found incompetent to stand trial, Lawrence spent a year and a half in jail. He finally pleaded guilty and agreed to a ten-year sentence, minus time already served.[57]

In August 2013, Lawrence sat behind a Plexiglas barrier at Orleans Parish Prison, his jaw slightly swollen after being broken in a jailhouse beating. Lawrence was wearing a bulky, sleeveless "suicide" smock that also covered a knife wound from another incident in the jail. Lawrence wasn't really a suicide risk, explained Chaseray Griffin, Lawrence's advocate from the Southern Poverty Law Center; placement on the suicide ward was his best chance of staying safe until he was moved to a state penitentiary.[58]

Although Lawrence had taken classes in Orleans Parish Prison, he had not graduated. Yet when the State of Louisiana calculated its dropout statistics, Lawrence and other incarcerated teens were not included.[59]

It is tempting to look at Lawrence as an exception. But his case points to problems not only with the quality of individual schools in New Orleans, but also with government oversight, the incentive structure of charter schools, and the legacy of Jim Crow.

For young African Americans, New Orleans has long been a treacherous landscape of violence, racism, and extreme poverty. In the aftermath of Hurricane Katrina, the young people who made their way back to the city were traumatized by the effects of the storm. Yet instead of providing services, the state under Governor Jindal cut budgets for mental health to the bone. In 2009, New Orleans Adolescent Hospital, which supplied a "limited number of in-patient beds" for children with severe mental health problems, closed; Jindal moved many of its beds and programs to St. Tammany, a wealthier community.[60] "There are still no residential juvenile mental health services in Louisiana," says Eden Heilman, managing attorney for the Louisiana office of the Southern Poverty Law Center. "It's incredible. Deinstitutionalization if coupled with community-based services is OK. But we didn't have that."[61]

In fact, there is an acute lack of any kind of crisis stabilization in New Orleans, and a tendency among law enforcement and charter schools to criminalize even relatively minor school-yard infractions. Thus, when an adolescent goes off the rails, he is likely to get arrested. In years past, data on student arrests in Louisiana have been hard to come by, especially among charter schools. But in 2015, for the first time, the New Orleans Police

Department issued a report showing that the number of schoolhouse arrests totaled 187 in New Orleans. Among these were some serious charges, including fourteen cases of weapons possession. There were also twenty-seven counts of marijuana possession and forty-seven cases of "disturbing the peace," which, in Louisiana, can include anything from verbal threats to engaging in fisticuffs.[62]

The majority of charges were for relatively minor offenses, according to the SPLC's Heilman. "What we've seen is as simple as banging on lockers," says Heilman. "Simple battery could be shoving. Those arrests are the most concerning; they should be dealt with in the disciplinary system" of individual schools.[63]

It is common knowledge in New Orleans that the kids who need mental health services the most are the ones who are most likely to get arrested. The problem is so severe that the SPLC is expected to file a new lawsuit against the state.[64]

The SPLC already has filed a complaint with the U.S. Education Department against nearby Jefferson Parish, charging that African American students are disproportionately arrested for minor rule violations across the school district, such as skipping school and being in the hall without a pass. The SPLC's complaint also alleges that students often experience physical abuse and racial slurs while being detained.[65]

Heilman explains that the reason there are so many arrests in Jefferson Parish is that the school system has contracted security to the sheriff's office, and the "sheriffs on campuses take it upon themselves to make arrests," she says. "What's worrisome in New Orleans is that most schools *don't* have the police department on campus." So when kids are arrested at New Orleans schools it's because administrators "deliberately call law enforcement."[66]

Arrests, suspensions, and expulsions, along with low test scores, all increase the likelihood that kids will drop out. In 2012, the Cowen Institute estimated that between 12,195 and 15,781 low-income youth aged sixteen to twenty-four, equal to as much as a quarter of the entire school-aged population of the city, were neither in school nor working.[67]

THE MCDONOUGH THREE AND THE LEGACY OF RACISM

Leona Tate's round, youthful face easily brightens into a smile; as a child she was so sunny that adults called her gigglebox.[68] But on a hot August afternoon in 2016, as she drove past the old boarded-up Sims School building in the Upper Ninth Ward, just off St. Claude and across the avenue from the small matchbox house on Tennessee Street that she inherited from her father, Tate's face visibly darkens. She slowly swivels her head, her eyes tracking the school, almost as though she expects a projectile to shoot out from behind the building or one of the trees that dot the disused school yard.

Sims is one of the many schools that were never resurrected after Hurricane Katrina. The large brick structure—boarded up, graffitied, its school yard overgrown with grass and weeds—looks menacing. "We had a tree in the yard—our comfort zone," recalls Tate, her eyes still riveted to the school yard, her voice fading to a whisper. "They'd play ball and throw the ball at us. It was horrific to attend Sims. It's a feeling I will never get over; I can hardly talk about it."

After a long pause, she adds: "I wouldn't wish that on anyone's child."[69]

It's been fifty years since Tate attended Sims, one of several schools that she and two other girls, Tessie Prevost and Gail Etienne, integrated in the wake of *Brown v. Board of Education*, the landmark school desegregation lawsuit. Together, they became known as the McDonogh Three, after McDonogh No. 19, the elementary school where they had been the first African American girls to enroll at age six. A fourth girl, Ruby Bridges, who integrated the William Frantz School, became the most famous.

Talk to the charter school advocates in New Orleans about the bad old days and they tend to focus on the considerable dysfunction and corruption of the OPSB in the years preceding Hurricane Katrina. But you don't hear much talk these days about the legacy of white supremacy that disenfranchised the city's majority-black residents and sought to keep them in ignorance. (As recently as the turn of the millennium, 50 percent of the city's entire population was functionally illiterate.)[70] Nor will you hear much about how the city's white citizens fought hard against integration well into the 1960s and then, when the gig was up, fled the schools. Or about how the business community abandoned the school system as soon as the student population became mostly minority and when minorities became heads of key departments in the central office. "In twenty-five to thirty years we couldn't get a millage passed," recalls Raynard Sanders, a well-respected former high school principal who has been a leading education advocate.[71] Writes Brian Beabout, associate professor of education at the University of New Orleans:

> Ever since the New Orleans desegregation battles of the 1960s . . . there has been a continuous loss of support for the public schools as white and middle class black students left for the suburbs, private schools, or the few magnet schools created to stem the tide of students from the increasingly black and increasingly poor district.[72]

At the same time, Beabout notes the "adversarial," "negative," and distrustful relationship between many in the African American community and their schools.[73]

Thus, the public schools were allowed to fall into serious decay. Says Sanders: "While other school districts were renovating and building new buildings, it was not until '99 that we air-conditioned the schools. Louisiana has a troublesome history of not supporting public schools even when they were segregated. They never really valued education."[74]

Patricia Perkins, who worked at Lusher, an elite public school, for years before Hurricane Katrina, agrees: "We were in a 1700s courthouse that had been converted 150 years ago into a school. It was ancient. It once served as a jail." Then, when it became home to Lusher's middle school, "always the roof leaked. It never got a paint job, never had AC until the parents bought individual window units."[75]

The lives of women like Tate, who recently became a great-grandmother and whose children attended the pre-Katrina schools and grandchildren are enrolled in the charters—as will likely her great-grandchildren—are a direct link between that period of deep racial hate and white flight and today's charter experiment. Tate herself encompasses the deep ambivalence, as well as the sense of resignation, that characterizes the feelings of so many black New Orleanians toward both the charter movement and the insults inflicted on their community over the years.

On the one hand, she is grateful for the discipline and structure that the charter schools provide for her grandchildren, kids for whom she is one of the few adult anchors in their lives. On the other hand, her grandchildren were shuffled from school to school, as were so many other local children, during the early ill-planned charter-formation period when kids were bused hither and yon and many early charter schools failed.

The phrase she used to describe her experience at Sims—"I wouldn't wish that on any child"—is also the one she uses to describe the predawn wake-up calls and hours-long commutes to which her grandchildren were subjected after being placed in charter schools far from their home.[76]

For young Leona, who was born in 1954, the years following *Brown v. Board of Education* were filled with anticipation and even excitement. The school board had determined the eligibility of black students wishing to attend an all-white school by submitting the children to a battery of psychological testing, as well as academic aptitude and character assessments. Only a handful of the 137 students who applied were approved for transfer in 1960—*four years* after a federal judge had ordered the New Orleans public schools to desegregate.[77]

Leona remembers her kindergarten teacher, Ms. Jackson, a young black teacher who started to give Leona extra attention and even invited her to a family party—a birthday celebration she remembers hazily.[78]

She remembers the crowds of people and the marshals who blocked off her street and walked her to school every day for over a year. To a young child, at times it almost felt like Mardi Gras.[79]

For the first few months of the year and a half that Tate, Prevost, and Etienne were at McDonogh 19, the three girls were in school alone. The white children were pulled out as soon as they arrived. After Christmas break, twenty-five more children arrived—and most were black. Their teacher, an older white woman named Ms. Meyers, was friendly and protective. "She was wonderful," recalls Tate. "She was like a mother. Growing up, realizing how racist everyone was, I thought maybe she wasn't from here. But they say she was."[80]

That soon changed, though, when in the middle of second grade the three girls were transferred to Sims. Tate's new teacher, a Ms. Dunn, wasn't friendly at all. "She coerced the kids to do things—they'd pass us and cover their noses as though we had an odor," recalls Tate. The girls dreaded going to the cafeteria, where children would spit in their food or knock their lunch trays to the ground. And then there was the bullying in the school yard.[81]

Tate eventually changed schools—Prevost and Etienne would stay at Sims—and graduated from Frances T. Nicholls High School, which she had also helped to integrate and which would later become Frederick Douglass High. By graduation, she had fallen in love and become pregnant.[82]

She also "had had enough" of school. Tate followed her husband, a military man, to Texas and eventually attended a business college in San Antonio. Over the years, she worked as a cashier in a lumber yard. She also worked eleven years for the phone company and, after returning to New Orleans, for her sister's home-health agency. But eventually, after her divorce, Tate began to stay home with her children and then her grandchildren.[83]

Tate has seen her childhood community disintegrate. Before the storm, there was a supermarket nearby. Tate remembers a roller-skating rink and an ice-cream parlor. Today, much of the neighborhood has gone the way of the boarded-up Sims school. There are a few sad-looking corner stores, but Tate has to drive ten minutes to a supermarket in Chaumet. The nearest coffee shop is miles away. Nor is there the feeling of neighborliness, as many longtime residents have left their homes on Tennessee Street.[84]

Always ambivalent about funding public education—for either black or white kids—the problems in New Orleans schools have been manifold. In addition to all the attendant evils of racism and segregation and the wasteful duplicate school system maintained for nearly a century—schools for black children were always the worst—there were ethnic and language rivalries among French- and English-speakers. Corruption, of course, suffused Louisiana politics at both the state and local levels. New Orleans has always ranked at the bottom of the nation in funding its schools, its elected officials cannibalizing the school coffers whenever a hurricane—man-made or the real McCoy—blew through the Crescent City. Part of the problem with New Orleans was that it served as the country's "first experiment with trying to impose its institutions, not only of education but also of language and democratic government, upon an essentially foreign society," argue Donald E. DeVore and Joseph Logsdon in *Crescent City Schools*. "It would be hard to find an urban public school system anywhere in the Western world which has faced a level of turmoil and travail comparable to that of New Orleans."[85]

Ironically, the New Orleans schools were imported from New England—including its teachers and its education philosophy, which was drawn straight from Horace Mann.[86]

The most obvious problems with the city's public schools—historically and in the years leading up to Hurricane Katrina—centered on racial inequality. But dysfunction—then and now—encompassed much more than the intractable challenges of prejudice, segregation, and white supremacy. Scarce funding, chronic neglect, as well as half-baked incentive schemes promulgated by a business community that, as far back as a century ago, antagonized a much-beleaguered, mostly female teaching force all contributed to the chaotic and poor learning environments of the schools.

The state of the city's schools before Katrina—and, to some extent, the alacrity with which the virtually all-black public schools were taken over after the storm by a mostly white establishment—is inseparable from New Orleans's history, and especially its role as "the only large city of the slave South in a majority black state. Racial oppression rested at the center of all of the city's institutions. Public authorities not only excluded all black New Orleanians—free or slave—from public education, but they deliberately tried to shackle them with ignorance."[87]

Before the Civil War, merely teaching a slave to read had been a serious crime, as it was in several southern territories. Even the city's sizable free-black population of 11,000 people was denied public education. Some of the latter attended private or parochial schools, the Catholic Church having set up its own segregated classrooms. Still, by the end of the Civil War, 61 percent of blacks were illiterate compared with only 6.5 percent of whites.[88]

In 1867, Robert Mills Lusher, a new state superintendent of education and a "rabid Confederate and outspoken racist," argued that all-white schools should be "properly preserved as a bastion of white supremacy." It is nothing short of ironic that today's debate about the city's two-tier education system often centers around Lusher's eponymously named school, which has long been considered one of the city's top selective schools—both when it was a public school and in its latest incarnation as a charter.[89]

Reconstruction compounded the school system's challenges. For a decade following the Civil War, and after the bloody New Orleans massacre in which white supremacists slaughtered fifty blacks who were participating in the Louisiana Constitutional Convention of 1866, a pitched battle for school integration was fought in New Orleans. By the end of Reconstruction, an estimated one-third of New Orleans schools were integrated, and "virtually every school had some black children." Eleven percent of the teachers were black. In fact, the integration effort worked so well that some white parents who had fled the system returned their children to the public schools because they considered them better and cheaper than private alternatives. The Compromise of 1877, which settled the disputed election that brought Rutherford B. Hayes to the White House in exchange for pulling federal troops out of southern states, including Louisiana, brought an end to the integration experiment in New Orleans.[90]

A new school board resegregated the schools and paved the way for the "steady deterioration" of public education in both the city and the state for years to come.

New Orleans schools did have two advantages—its teachers and its school buildings. In 1838, John McDonogh, "an eccentric, millionaire slaveholder," bequeathed half of his estate for the education of both white and free black New Orleans children. For years after McDonogh's death in 1850 and the resolution of litigation over his estate in 1858, many of the school buildings built or refurbished in New Orleans were financed by the McDonogh Fund. During more than thirty years leading up to 1893, no public funds financed any new school construction in New Orleans. As of 1894, close to half of all school buildings had been constructed and repaired with proceeds from the McDonogh Fund. That legacy is immortalized in the numbered McDonogh schools, including McDonogh 19, the elementary school that Tate, Prevost, and Etienne integrated, as well as McDonogh 35, which became the city's first black high school in 1917.[91]

In what was an all-too-familiar pattern, poor pay and conditions made teaching in New Orleans a woman-dominated profession—though in New Orleans the pay was even worse than elsewhere in the country. "Perhaps the most remarkable story during the difficult years of the late nineteenth century was the loyalty, competence, and initiative of the almost totally female teaching staff," argue DeVore and Logsdon. In 1850, 80 percent of the teachers were women. By 1886, the boys' high school was the only school in New Orleans that still employed male teachers; all other classrooms were run by women—including "subversive Yankee schoolmarms" who had come to New Orleans from the North during the Civil War. In most cases, the principals too were women.[92]

But the subordination of women educators, in the coming years, laid the foundation for a bitter, decades-long "feud"—one that would reverberate again following Hurricane Katrina.[93]

White women taught in integrated schools, and some volunteered to teach in black schools to meet the shortage of certified black teachers. As today, both black and white teachers struggled to meet the special needs of their poorest students. Women were responsible for bringing the first kindergartens to New Orleans and the first free night schools for girls. Since New Orleans schools also were segregated by gender, from 1886 to 1940, women teachers at the city's so-called normal school trained successive generations of New Orleans teachers.[94]

The city's male leadership was committed to segregating boys and girls long after the practice had ended elsewhere. Those two policies—segregation by race and by gender—inevitably contributed to the deterioration of all schools. Instead of one school that could serve all children in a neighborhood—black and white, boys and girls—four schools had to be built and staffed. In addition, the state legislature and city council regularly slashed school funding. Support for education, in general, was so weak that in 1877 one school board committee even proposed eliminating high school education entirely. Archibald Mitchell, the leader of the anti–high school group, called the funding of high school at the public expense "an abuse of our educational system."[95]

In short, education in New Orleans and Louisiana fell victim to tough economic times following the Civil War, to bigotry, to a culture that devalued education, and to endemic corruption. A former Republican school board member, the Rev. Joseph C. Hartell, summed up the situation this way:

> To such straits has Bourbon ignorance, stupidity and folly brought the late bountiful system of free schools established and maintained during the existence of a republican form of government.
>
> The minority, now in power by virtue of stuffed ballot boxes, and the physical enforcement of their rule in defiance of the laws

> of the land, have shown themselves to be incompetent to deal with any great measures of public welfare dictated by enlightened statesmanship. Repudiation of the state debt, destruction of the school system, and the exodus of thousands of her people from misrule are the manifest results of White League supremacy in Louisiana.[96]

By 1883, the schools were so underfunded that the school board closed the schools for an entire semester. During the fall, only students whose parents could pay tuition were permitted to attend. Still, the city council refused to appropriate money for the schools. With funding still bleak in 1884, the superintendent of New Orleans schools resigned and, in his last appearance before the school board, noted the "privations and embarrassments" of the city's schools.

Not until the 1890s was some financing restored to the schools, but the price was high. High school would include only three grades, operating on an eleven-year, not a twelve-year, basis. In 1898, a constitutional convention disenfranchised almost all black voters by imposing a literacy test and proof of property ownership as the price for voting. The new constitution did, however, dedicate the new mandatory poll tax for funding the public schools.[97]

While white public education benefited from an influx of new funds, under the new regime black children would be educated only through the fifth grade, an explicit effort to ensure that blacks remained in a servile position doing manual labor. Not even technical training would be permitted for black students. In reality, the black children were leaving school far earlier than the fifth grade, if they ever attended at all. In the 1907–1908 school year, for example, there were 329 black students enrolled in the first grade, according to the Russell Sage Foundation. The enrollment numbers decreased sharply each year, with only fifty-two black students enrolled in fifth grade.[98]

In 1909, nearly a century before Hurricane Katrina, the Russell Sage Foundation released a study noting that public schools were failing to educate the urban poor. New Orleans ranked at the bottom of the study's list of national "laggards." But New Orleans, unlike in northern cities, could not avoid responsibility by blaming the weak performance of its schools on an influx of new immigrants or on the presence of poor black students, because these students were relegated to inferior schools that ended at the fifth grade and were listed separately in the study.[99]

Most important, education in New Orleans just wasn't a local priority. During the early part of the previous century, school dropouts were a national problem. Children left school to work—either at home or in menial jobs—because of poor health or because they performed so poorly. In New Orleans at that time, school enrollment even among white children dropped off sharply after the fourth grade—though not as much as among black children. At the same time, close to 30 percent of school budgets supported children who repeated a grade, more than any other city except Memphis, Tennessee, and Camden, New Jersey; children who were held back one grade or more were a key driver behind the high dropout rates.[100]

A primary reason why children failed to move up a grade was that they didn't attend school. In the 1907–1908 school year, only 62 percent of students were present at least three-quarters of the school year. That year, just half of the students were promoted to the next grade level; the rest either dropped out or were held back.[101]

Thirty years later, a new survey of New Orleans schools found that only about a quarter of white boys and one-third of white girls got through elementary school without failing at least once. Of those who made it to high school, almost one-half of all girls never completed their schooling. The dropout rate for boys was very likely higher, though the survey never obtained "satisfactory" data. Of course, boys and girls in New Orleans still received one year less of schooling than public school students elsewhere in the country.[102]

Then, as now, students at the best New Orleans public schools received "as good an education as existed anywhere in America's public schools. In fact, the seniors of its five white academic high schools scored better on achievement tests . . . than most high school seniors in the rest of the U.S." But, overall, student achievement in New Orleans public schools ranked last among urban school districts.[103]

Despite the truancy epidemic, neither the state legislature nor the local establishment made universal schooling a priority. Local school reformers, led by women who still couldn't vote or sit on school boards, mounted a years-long campaign for compulsory attendance laws; a measure finally passed in 1910, but enforcement was weak.[104]

Nor was the local establishment willing to invest in its schools. During the early twentieth century, per-pupil spending in New Orleans remained 30 to 50 percent below that of northern cities.[105] Then, as in the post-Katrina years, education-reform efforts led by businessmen recommended an onerous reporting system for its underpaid, mostly female teaching force, "elaborate" new teacher evaluations, and a merit pay system.[106] At the start of World War I, the teachers finally formed a union, the Associate Teachers'

League, which became, in 1919, Local 26 of the central Trades and Labor Council of New Orleans, the first teachers union in the Deep South.[107]

World War I also led to a severe teacher shortage when women took advantage of the new job opportunities created when young men enlisted in the army, and they exited the classroom. Finally, in 1920, the school board agreed to significantly raise teacher salaries.[108]

That same year, Fannie Ellen Baumgartner was elected to the school board, becoming not only the first woman school-board member, but also the first woman elected to public office in Louisiana. Baumgartner had advocated for schools long before her election, pioneering a long tradition of local community activism for school reform. Among other things, she had fought (unsuccessfully) for equal pay for women teachers and for giving women educators the opportunity to serve in more senior positions on the central office staff. She was also among the few board members who were sympathetic to pleas from the black community for better schools.[109]

The victory was short-lived. When the soldiers came back from the front, the women were, once again, expendable. This time, though, it wasn't just women who took the hit. The Orleans Parish School Board—so named in 1916—lowered men's salaries to those of women, a "solution" that "ended unity among male and female teachers, shattered their union local, and also set off a bitter struggle between women teachers and the school board that lasted for almost twenty years."[110]

In 1923, the school board once again cut teacher salaries, and in 1926 Baumgartner was ousted from the school board. In subsequent years and throughout the Depression, teacher salaries were cut repeatedly. Huey Long, who had served as governor until 1932, before being elected to the U.S. Senate, had done little for the schools of New Orleans, which, for all their failings, received the most funding in the state. But a new generation of women activists, joined by the state Parent Teacher Association, formed an "assertive" education lobby in Baton Rouge to increase teacher pay as well as to eliminate the pay differential between men and women and the ban on married women in the classroom. Finally, in 1935, teachers formed a new labor union, Local 353 of the American Federation of Teachers.[111]

However wanting the white schools were, the schools for black students were far worse. In 1917, New Orleans finally opened its first high school for black students, the white establishment having "realized that if they were going to maintain a fully segregated society, the separate black community needed its own physicians, teachers, lawyers and clergymen."[112]

McDonogh 35 remained the only black high school until 1940. In the decades leading up to the construction of its second black high school, Booker T. Washington, black enrollment in the schools grew twice as fast as white enrollment. (Characteristically, Washington was built on the site of the Silver City Dump, which had once been called the "ulcer" of New Orleans.)[113]

All of this meant more crowding and fewer resources for black students. During the 1939–1940 school year, New Orleans spent more than three times as much per white pupil as on each black student. In some black schools, two children had to share a single desk. As recently as the years immediately preceding Hurricane Katrina, it was not unusual to have thirty-four students "crammed" into a ninth-ward elementary classroom, while wealthier public schools uptown had just twenty-four students per class, according to a charter school principal describing her pre-Katrina classes.[114] The average annual salary for white teachers was double what a black teacher earned. Class sizes were almost 50 percent bigger in black schools than in white schools, and the buildings were of far inferior quality.[115]

The African American community, through its civic, religious, and education organizations, had long sought to improve the sorry state of its schools, most of them "makeshift" structures in dire states of disrepair. Between the early 1940s and the 1960s, Alexander Pierre (A.P.) Tureaud, an attorney for the NAACP Legal Defense and Education Fund and a friend of the late U.S. Supreme Court justice Thurgood Marshall, filed a series of desegregation cases. He brought the first case demanding equal pay for African American teachers, resulting in a "minimum salary schedule" passed by the state legislature in 1948. At about the same time, the Ninth Ward Civic and Improvement League lobbied the school board for equal school facilities for blacks.[116]

In 1952, Tureaud filed a lawsuit to force the desegregation of New Orleans schools on behalf of Oliver Bush, an insurance salesman with the "all-black Louisiana Industrial Life Insurance Company," who agreed to have the case brought on behalf of his eight children.[117] The presiding judge, J. Skelly Wright, ordered the school board "to make arrangements for admission of children . . . on a racially non-discriminatory basis with all deliberate speed."[118] In Washington that same year, the Supreme Court had agreed to hear five similar cases, which would be consolidated into *Brown v. Board of Education of Topeka, Kansas*. The court's unanimous 1954 decision found that "in the field of public education the doctrine of 'separate but equal' has no place."[119]

White supremacy, however, dies hard in Louisiana. Within months of the Supreme Court decision, the Louisiana legislature passed several bills designed to thwart the will of the court and to maintain segregation.[120] Finally, in 1960, Judge Wright issued his own desegregation plan, which would pave the way for Leona Tate and the three other young girls to take their seats in what had been, heretofore, all-white schools.[121]

Judge Wright and his family would pay dearly for his decision. The family was ostracized. Wright himself, vilified as "J. Wrong," was subjected to a slew of attacks, including an effort to impeach him. A newspaper published a photograph of an effigy of Skelly on the steps of the Louisiana Capitol, with a swastika on one side and a hammer and sickle on the other.[122]

Yet, as of the 1964–1965 school year, "only 873 black students attended desegregated schools in what was now a majority black school system with over 100,000 students." The NAACP returned to the courts, and a federal judge ordered a "speeded-up process" that officially desegregated schools by the 1969–1970 school year."[123]

School enrollment plunged during the 1970s. At the same time, a century-long legacy of poverty, segregation, and explicit efforts to keep African Americans in ignorance had taken its toll. In 1978, only about a quarter of blacks in New Orleans finished high school compared to just over half of all whites.[124]

"CROOKED AS A CORKSCREW"

Louisiana is the state that A.J. Liebling once called "America's answer to Lebanon." In his renowned *New Yorker* series on Louisiana, Liebling wrote of Huey Long that he had "a deduct" system for his political fund by which he managed to pocket 10 percent of the salary of every state employee. "It sounds raw, but he had to take the money where he could; the other side had all the money of Standard Oil."[125]

As one local wag once explained, before Huey Long "the state was tight as a drum and crooked as a corkscrew." After Long, "it may still be crooked, but it's open to everybody."[126]

School districts were not immune. As long ago as 1895, an editorial in the *Daily Picayune* argued, somewhat optimistically, that "the presence of a respectable minority of ladies on the board would have redeemed it from the scandalously suggestive and really serious charges made against that body."[127]

Corruption suffused every part of Louisiana's public life and continues to do so. Those indicted in recent years include former governor Edwin G.

Edwards, the longest-serving governor in the state's history. Before being elected to his final term in 1992, his supporters produced bumper stickers exclaiming "vote for the crook; it's important." In that election, Edwards, who would receive a ten-year prison sentence for extortion in 2001, was running against David Duke, a former Klansman who would later be convicted and jailed for a mail-fraud scheme. The problem is so bad that Louisiana has been ranked the country's most corrupt state, according to a 2006 report by the U.S. Justice Department's Public Integrity Section.[128]

The Orleans Parish School Board marked a new low in the years immediately preceding Hurricane Katrina.

When the OPSB met in January 2004, little did the board members suspect that they were in the early phases of a Shakespearean drama that would, during the course of the next two years, feature an FBI probe, indictments, a palace coup, and, finally, an unprecedented move on the part of the state to wrest control of the schools away from the board.

At the time, Ellenese Brooks-Simms, the elegant, well-connected president of the board, was mounting an effort to oust Anthony Amato, the well-regarded schools superintendent who had been hired just a year earlier. When Amato arrived in New Orleans from Hartford, Connecticut, he enjoyed widespread support, having "mesmerized audiences with inspired speeches and grand promises, including a vow to bring the fastest test score improvement of any system in the state."[129]

That January night, as Brian Thevenot recounted in the *Times-Picayune*, when Brooks-Simms pulled her burgundy late-model Cadillac up to McDonogh 35 High School, where the board meeting was being held, she had "no idea" that she would soon be ousted as school board president.[130]

"And Brooks-Simms's board colleagues had no clue she had taken a $50,000 bribe that same day, the second in a series of three kickbacks totaling $140,000."[131]

Instead, "amid shouting and cursing," her onetime allies demanded that Brooks-Simms "stop meddling in system patronage and undermining" Amato. "Minutes later, just before voting to dethrone Brooks-Simms as president," Una Anderson, a fellow board member, "summed up the intrigue in a whispered aside: 'Welcome to the Roman Arena.'"[132]

That day marked the beginning of the end of the Orleans Parish School Board—that is, until its revival more than a decade later. The board proved so dysfunctional that, by the time Hurricane Katrina hit, the state takeover of the city's public schools would become "a fait accompli."[133]

In the years immediately preceding Hurricane Katrina, Brooks-Simms was the only school board member convicted of wrongdoing, and the first since 1992, when Dwight McKenna had been convicted of income-tax evasion—though his crime was unrelated to his school board duties. Brooks-Simms's indictment and eventual conviction were wrapped up in the takedown of the powerful Jefferson clan—Mose Jefferson, a notorious political boss; Mose's brother, William, who made history as Louisiana's first African American representative to Congress; and their sister, Betty, who was elected to the school board. All three would serve jail time on an array of charges ranging from bribery to racketeering.[134]

At the time, Brooks-Simms's graft seemed the least of the OPSB's problems. A year before Katrina, the U.S. Department of Education issued a draft audit report to the Louisiana Department of Education charging that the OPSB had improperly accounted for $69.6 million in Title 1 funds over a two-and-a-half-year period ending in 2003. Cecil Picard, then the schools superintendent for Louisiana, ordered an audit of the OPSB records; while the auditor located almost all of the funds, he noted "severe deficiencies" in the OPSB accounting systems. The U.S. Department of Education required the State of Louisiana to put the OPSB on "high risk" status, its accounting problems having put "all federal education funding for the state at risk."[135]

On February 15, 2005, Picard and the Louisiana state auditor attended an OPSB meeting and informed the board that it would hire an independent "turnaround" firm to "develop, implement and monitor" improvements in its accounting and financial-management policies. Picard chose the New York firm Alvarez and Marsal.

In April, following a "particularly rancorous school board meeting," Amato resigned after just two years on the job. He had been the seventh New Orleans superintendent in just ten years.[136]

A month later, on May 23, the OPSB narrowly voted to approve a "memorandum of understanding" with Alvarez and Marsal. That summer, the OPSB signed a two-year $16.8 million contract with the firm in an arrangement that effectively stripped OPSB of control over its schools. While the OPSB would pay for the firm, the Louisiana Department of Education would retain control of the city's public schools.[137]

It was not the first effort by the state to wrest control from what it viewed as a hopelessly dysfunctional school board. In 2003, Louisiana passed a constitutional amendment creating the so-called Recovery School District to take over schools that were deemed "academically unacceptable" for four consecutive years. "Academically unacceptable" meant any school that received a School Performance Score, which was largely based on test scores, below 60. Before Hurricane Katrina, five schools had received that designation.[138]

In November 2005, just after Hurricane Katrina, the Louisiana State Legislature passed Act 35, which transferred all schools deemed to be "academically in crisis" to the RSD. Importantly, Act 35 also *raised* the passing performance score to the state's *average* SPS score of 87.5. Anything below that was considered a school "in crisis"—but only in New Orleans; everywhere else in Louisiana, 60 was still considered a passing score.[139]

While a score of 60 was a "passing" score before the hurricane, it was deemed "failing" as of November 30, 2005, the effective date of the state takeover of the OPSB schools, wrote Judge Ethel Simms Julien in her ruling in favor of the teachers in their class-action suit for wrongful termination (her ruling would be upheld by an appellate court, but later overturned by Louisiana's Supreme Court). She also noted that the "passing score reverted to 60 in 2010."[140]

Thus, in one fell swoop, the state had created a giant, custom-built earthmover that scooped up an *additional* 102 schools, fully four-fifths of the schools in the OPSB, and dumped them in the RSD, an entity that had been created to "serve as a temporary custodian" over just a few schools at a time.[141]

Act 35 paved the way for charter-management organizations in both the RSD and OPSB—though, for the first few years after the storm, there were still several direct-run schools, most of them in the RSD. The takeover also abolished attendance zones—and neighborhood schools—in favor of a citywide system of "choice." It led to the firing of 7,500 school-district employees, and the effective end of collective bargaining, at least for the coming decade. Before the storm, the school board had been the city's largest employer.[142]

Many local residents cried foul. The takeover, which often invoked the rhetoric of community involvement, was done while much of the city's African American population—those who didn't have the wherewithal to return to the city immediately after the storm, those whose homes were so badly damaged they couldn't return, or whose neighborhoods remained sealed off by the National Guard—was absent.[143]

At the same time, the RSD reconstituted the educational inequality that had existed in New Orleans before Hurricane Katrina, an inequality that was, possibly, a "far more important problem than the issues of teacher quality" or community apathy, writes University of New Orleans's Beabout. The RSD became, quite simply, "the dumping ground" for the "transient, the poor, and the special needs students," a dumping ground unanimously condemned by the principals who ran the schools in this district of last resort.[144]

Lip service to community involvement was a key feature of the New Orleans school revolution, but rarely more than that. With the OPSB scandals still fresh, and with the influx of an army of Ivy League–trained technocrats and venture philanthropists, the last thing anyone wanted to do was hand any part of the system back to the kind of local people who might re-create the morass.

Yet, ironically, under a new state schools superintendent, John White—a former "Kleinberg" from New York City (see chapter 2)—the State of Louisiana suppressed key educational data needed to accurately assess the performance of the charter experiment. Year after year, the Louisiana legislative auditor found that the state's education department "no longer conducts on-site audits or reviews that help ensure the electronic data in its systems is accurate."[145] For at least two years, in 2013 and 2014, the Louisiana auditor found major problems when verifying the data on which the RSD based its graduation data—a key metric for SPS scores and thus school-performance ratings—as well as data for its much disputed dropout rate. In 2014, among a sample of 1,417 students, the auditor could not verify *a single one* of the fourteen students who were listed as having "transferred" to another school; in fact, the RSD had the worst record for transfer verification in the state.[146]

"At best, the findings point to the difficulty of obtaining proof that students have transferred into new education settings. Or they might show nothing more than sloppy bookkeeping," wrote Danielle Dreilinger for the *Times-Picayune.*[147]

Or, as Michael Deshotels, a veteran teacher and education blogger, suggested: the state was "cooking the books" to inflate the RSD's graduation rate, its performance scores, and the overall performance of the charter school experiment.[148]

When Deshotels sued the state for the data after multiple public-records requests were denied, Superintendent White countersued Deshotels and another blogger, James Finney. In October 2016, a Louisiana district court ordered the state to make a decade's worth of school data available.[149]

The data war illustrates a key problem with the New Orleans charter experiment. An education department that embraced a reform establishment that made "accountability" its mantra selectively doled out data to organizations it deemed friendly but was remarkably unforthcoming with the numbers needed to assess its own performance—not just SPS scores but also graduation and dropout statistics. In a side-by-side comparison of school data in Massachusetts or in Bloomberg's New York City—where Superintendent White had been a top lieutenant—Louisiana's numbers look stunningly opaque.

The key question is not whether something needed to be done about a school system that was overly bureaucratic and corrupt. Nor is it whether the new regime has managed to raise performance scores. The key questions are as follows: first, was blowing up the school system with *virtually no community input* the right—or even the best—decision? Second, in the wake of more than a century of white supremacy and discrimination, was a massive experiment with the school district's mostly black children—many of whom were severely scarred by the storm—conducted by the state's mostly white establishment with little input from the city's majority-black population morally or practically justified?

The answer to both of these questions is *no*. Successful and unsuccessful charter schools alike show that locking the community out of decision making damaged the legitimacy of the city's charter system. It also failed to protect the system from epic failures. Moreover, some of the most successful open-enrollment charters turned out to be a handful of community schools that succeeded *despite* the charter establishment, not because of it.

In the months after the storm, Walter Isaacson, a native of New Orleans and the president of the Aspen Institute, a nonpartisan think tank, was one of the leading public intellectuals and policymakers who waxed optimistic about the new elite-controlled education regime:

> The old Orleans Parish School Board ran one of the worst districts in the nation, and it has now effectively been abolished. A system of competing charter schools has sprung up, nurtured by the state and fostered in Washington by Education Secretary Margaret Spellings and Senators Mary Landrieu and Lamar Alexander. Eager local principals are getting to run their own schools, and education innovators who want to show what they can do, like the ones from the Knowledge Is Power Program, are rushing in to seize the opportunity.[150]

A year later, in his *Time* magazine cover story, "The Greatest Education Lab," Isaacson extolled the social entrepreneurs who, like loyal retainers to "Henry V at the Battle of Agincourt," flocked to New Orleans to transform its schools. "The reform movement is allowing neighborhoods to take matters into their own hands and run their own schools," wrote Isaacson, pointing to Broadmoor, the "racially and economically" mixed neighborhood in which he grew up (and where he attended private school). Isaacson describes how, with the help of about ninety students and faculty from the Kennedy School of Government at Harvard University, the Broadmoor

Neighborhood Association and the Broadmoor Development Corporation "helped the community take control of the neighborhood school" by bringing in Edison Schools, a for-profit charter organization (though Isaacson's article doesn't mention the for-profit part).[151]

Edison, it turns out, was the antithesis of what most New Orleanians think of as a community school. In fact, its stewardship of Andrew H. Wilson Charter School was worthy of the worst days of the OPSB.

Edison, the brainchild of Chris Whittle, had once been hailed as the hottest invention since the Internet; in 2000, Michael Moe, a Merrill Lynch equity analyst, predicted the company would be running 423 schools and generating $1.8 billion in revenue by 2005.[152] As Samuel Abrams, in his insightful book *Education and the Commercial Mindset*, observes, it wasn't just die-hard free marketeers who were persuaded by Whittle; Benno Schmidt resigned the presidency of Yale to run the company, and both Al Shanker and Linda Darling Hammond became affiliated, albeit briefly, with Whittle projects.[153] In 2002, the SEC found that Edison had exaggerated its revenues, booking money designated by districts for school expenses as company revenue; the SEC required Edison to revise its books and hire an audit manager. Edison schools also often produced poor academic results, and some Edison-run schools—in Maryland, Pennsylvania, and Kansas, for example—were associated with cheating and test tampering.[154]

Back in New Orleans, at the Andrew Wilson School, the state auditor pointed to five years of "troubled bookkeeping" by Edison, including charges that the company had inaccurately recorded some federal grant expenses, payroll expenses, and revenue; that it had poor internal financial controls; and that it had failed to provide financial documentation to the board. The school also ran a $410,824 deficit, which the board blamed on Edison; the company's relationship with the school ended in 2011.[155]

Edison's stewardship of Wilson and another local charter, the Intercultural Charter School, was hailed as recently as 2009 by Caroline Roemer Shirley, executive director of the Louisiana Association of Public Charter Schools, for being on "the right track." But, by 2015, Wilson would be taken over by another CMO.[156]

What happened at Intercultural is equally telling. The education department "strong-armed the charter board into partnering with Edison Schools." After Edison's removal, "Intercultural struggled to regain its financial footing" and was eventually closed.[157]

Edison's brief sojourn in New Orleans points to the experiment's hubris and its considerable flaws. Rather than including the community, the charter revolution was driven mostly by outsiders. In 2007, Paul Pastorek, then the state schools superintendent, appointed Paul Vallas, previously the controversial chief of both Chicago and Philadelphia schools, to run the RSD. Together, Vallas and New Schools for New Orleans played a key role in anointing charter school operators, often favoring out-of-state CMOs over community-led charter proposals. While caution might have dictated favoring experienced operators over local groups that had never run a school before, the record shows that even community groups with strong education credentials and experience were often blocked by the sentries guarding the city's new charter fortress.

Social entrepreneurs were key to reshaping the system. There was Wendy Kopp, Teach for America's "intensely focused leader," promising to bring hundreds of teachers to New Orleans. There was John Schnur, the "cheery and tenacious" founder of New Leaders for New Schools, who opened an office in New Orleans and resettled there with his family. The state board of education granted New Leaders authority to license and certify around forty new principals it was hoping to bring to New Orleans. Together, notes Isaacson, TFA and New Leaders would serve as a "brain magnet" for New Orleans.[158]

There was also Sarah Newell Usdin, who founded New Schools for New Orleans (and had earlier served as executive director of TFA in Greater New Orleans). A native of Louisville, Kentucky, Usdin created NSNO with the express purpose of bringing outside charter organizations and money to New Orleans to run Crescent City schools. Fittingly, when Usdin ran for the OPSB school board in 2012, she received more than $110,000 in contributions from wealthy out-of-town education-reform advocates—most of whom ponied up $2,500 to $5,000 each. These sizable contributions came from, among others, New York City's billionaire former mayor, Michael Bloomberg, and his former schools chancellor Joel Klein. Doris and John Fischer, California-based heirs to the Gap fortune; Reed Hastings, the founder of Netflix; and John Arnold, a Houston hedge-fund magnate, all contributed. Laurene Powell Jobs, the widow of Steve Jobs, sent two contributions, as did Boykin Curry, a New York–based hedge-fund manager. Katherine Bradley, a funder of charter schools in Washington, D.C., where she lives with her husband, David G. Bradley, the owner of *The Atlantic*, contributed twice as well.[159]

Having outspent her opponents, incumbent Brett Bonin and Karran Harper Royal, a respected local parent advocate, more than five-to-one, Usdin won handily. Harper Royal, the only African American in the race and "the only candidate in the district with first-hand experience as a public school parent"—her youngest son attends Lusher—raised about $12,000, roughly half from unions and the rest mostly in increments of $10 to $100.[160] Usdin's six-figure victory presaged education-reform battles across the country in which wealthy business tycoons fought on opposite sides of parent groups, teachers, and, yes, teachers unions.

New Schools for New Orleans was backed by the New Schools Venture Fund (NSVF), which is based in San Francisco and is designed to apply the principles of venture-capital investing to education. The New Schools Venture Fund was incubated at Isaacson's Aspen Institute, making him a key player—albeit indirectly—in the New Orleans charter strategy. (Isaacson also contributed $1,000 to Usdin's 2012 campaign.[161]) When, in 2006, NSVF decided to make New Orleans a focal point for educational entrepreneurism, some participants worried that they had taken on a "daunting" task, prompting Isaacson to quip that if they "were not willing to take on such a challenge, they should find an easier line of work, such as managing a hedge fund."[162]

To borrow another ancient military metaphor, the New Schools Venture Fund, and its New Schools for New Orleans offshoot, is the Trojan horse that funnels outside money, expertise, and influence to New Orleans.[163] In 2007, NSVF received $100 million from the Gates Foundation alone, which also supports Teach for America and KIPP, two of the city's key "outsider" reform organizations. NSNO boasts that it has supported the launch or expansion of thirty-one schools, more than *half* the schools in the RSD. The organization also administers the NOLA Charter Excellence Fund and promises to "invest in the creation of 15,000 new high quality school 'seats' in New Orleans." And it provides a one-stop shop for "leadership training" for everyone from principals and entire CMOs to teacher-training programs. NSNO visits schools and provides "high-bar feedback" on their performance and disseminates best practices. And it also coordinates "solutions to citywide challenges."[164]

THE GATEKEEPERS

Now, what's wrong with serving as the "harbor master" for fledgling New Orleans schools—with supporting leadership training and school reviews, and acting as a conduit for millions of dollars in funding—skeptical readers who discern a sinister ring to the term "Trojan horse," might well ask. The answer hinges on whether NSNO works like an open-source project, attracting diverse ideas, refining them, and letting the best ones bubble to the top—or if it operates as a cartel with a narrow menu of offerings that limits participation and the range of acceptable ideas.

Few would dispute that, during the past decade, NSNO has become the principal gatekeeper in New Orleans, bringing outside charter organizations and educators to the city and serving as a key conduit for tens of millions of dollars in both outside philanthropic and federal grants. The Walton Family Foundation, the Eli and Edythe Broad Foundation, and the Gates Foundation are among NSNO's chief philanthropic donors, both through direct donations and via donations to the New Schools Venture Fund.[165] As Sarah Reckhow notes in *Follow the Money*, those three philanthropies *quadrupled* their grant making for K–12 education nationwide to $400 million in 2005, over the 2000 level, and led a movement to "give more funding to districts with political and organizational features that appear to increase the likelihood of foundation influence."[166]

These three philanthropies also would help turn New Orleans, via NSNO, into the chief laboratory for promoting charter schools, competition, and test-based accountability. As Diane Ravitch charged:

> [The new foundations] wanted nothing less than to transform American Education. They would not leave local communities to design their own reforms and would not risk having their money wasted. Their boldness was unprecedented.[167]

Indeed, there is evidence that NSNO functions more like a cartel than an open-source project. Among the thirty-one schools it has incubated are those operated by KIPP, which now runs eleven schools in New Orleans—nearly 20 percent of the open-admissions schools. Indeed, the majority of schools in which NSNO has "invested" adhere to KIPP's no-excuses model.[168]

There are also questions about the research that comes out of New Orleans. The Cowen Institute for Public Education Initiatives was forced to retract a major study in 2014 that suggested New Orleans high schools were outperforming expectations.[169] In 2013, the university had sponsored another organization, the Educational Research Alliance, which published at least one study critical of the charter industry, "How Do School Leaders Respond to Competition," which found that one-third of New Orleans charter school principals engage in so-called creaming.[170]

Yet ERA's 2016 report, "Is There Choice in School Choice," is a remarkable document because it makes virtually no reference to the prevalence of schools that practice "no excuses" discipline practices.[171] The study's nine-page policy brief makes no mention at all of "no excuses" or "discipline."[172] The accompanying technical document makes the following disclaimer—the only place in the fifty-six-page document where either term is mentioned: "Because several New Orleans CMOs are known as 'no excuses' schools with strict discipline, we also attempted groupings with measures of strictness." The researchers consulted *The New Orleans Parents' Guide to Public Schools* and the LDOE's discipline data. Concluded ERA's Harris: "We spent a lot of time talking about the no-excuses stuff, but there was no way of measuring it other than going to the schools. It would have taken years to pull that off because it's very hard to get into the schools.

"Believe me if I thought we could have, I wanted to do that. Going into the study, that's what I thought was going to be the main point. I agree it's a big deal," he says about the prevalence of no-excuses policies.[173]

Ignoring no-excuses discipline practices at New Orleans charters is like covering the New England Patriots and ignoring Deflategate. Yet in the wake of a 2014 judicial-consent decree that tightened oversight of charters whose discipline practices, according to the SPLC lawsuit, subjected kids with special needs to "discrimination" and "excluded" them from school, the ERA study focused on such school characteristics as "college prep" and extracurricular and sports offerings, not no-excuses culture.[174]

Given the large number of no-excuses KIPP schools, and at least an equal number of schools that model themselves on KIPP, it is puzzling that ERA could not come up with a no-excuses index based on counting the number of CMOs that practice some combination of the following: *SLANTING*; silent walks along straight red or white lines; mandated silence at lunch and/or in the hallways; and suspensions for minor infractions, such as uniform violations.

Harris bristles at the suggestion that his research organization is anything but neutral in its assessment of the city's charters.[175] Yet ERA's job must be especially difficult given its co-location with NSNO and the Cowen Institute on the seventh floor of 1555 Poydras Street. Harris says Tulane controls the location of the research center.[176]

I experienced the difficulty of being perceived as critical firsthand. While most of the charter gatekeepers, including NSNO, granted me interviews during my first three visits to New Orleans, during my last trip, in 2016, following publication of two articles that questioned whether the most vulnerable New Orleans kids were being served well by the charter system, most charter organizations, including NSNO, ignored interview requests. And a senior OPSB executive, an hour after confirming an appointment with me, canceled our interview after a local pro-charter gadfly posted on twitter: "JUST SAY NO: @aagabor is coming to #NOLAed & wants interviews. Don't talk to her."[177]

It's also noteworthy that neither of the first two schools that have unionized voluntarily in New Orleans was featured on the list of schools in which NSNO has "invested" until recently.[178] (One of the schools, as we shall see later in this chapter, was repeatedly refused funding from NSNO and major philanthropies that was routinely given to most of the city's charter school start-ups.) Indeed, charter-incubation and school choice, à la NSNO, suggest nothing so much as Henry Ford's famous dictum that customers can pick any color car they want as long as it's black.

Meanwhile, until the 2017 appointment of Patrick Dobard, the former head of the RSD, as NSNO's CEO, senior staff was mostly white—poor optics in a majority-black school system—and close to half of its entire staff are Teach for America alums. In any other city, this would not be an issue, but in New Orleans, where TFA is viewed by much of the majority African American community as providing the "scabs" who replaced a largely black unionized teaching force, it is not a reassuring credential.[179]

Not surprisingly, many longtime New Orleanians—including African American New Orleanians—were less than thrilled by this invasion of what has been young, mostly white "talent" from afar (though, in recent years, organizations like TFA have made concerted efforts to include more African Americans among their recruits[180]). Ashana Bigard is an at-least fifth-generation New Orleanian who attended and dropped out of (before "dropping back in to") public schools in New Orleans. She is the mother of three children who are enrolled in local charter schools and has become a parent advocate and critic of the outsider influence on the charter establishment. "There is a stark difference in the demographics when you look at leadership, decision makers, consultants, and the stakeholders" and by stakeholders she means "the children and the people from the communities who are in our schools every day."[181]

Like African American education reformers and charter advocates Howard Fuller and Deborah McGriff, Bigard yearns for schools that reflect the influence of the local community and an end to a system in which "things happening to us, not with us, for us, not by us."[182]

To be sure, many, perhaps most, of the newcomers mean well. But, in Act 35, in the firing of the teachers, and in the decision not to reopen most of the schools in the Lower Ninth Ward, many locals saw the long shadow of white supremacy that had, for more than a century, disenfranchised the city's African American citizens, sought to keep them in ignorance, or relegated them to mean, overcrowded, and underresourced schools. Granted the authority to take over "failing schools," power over what remained of most New Orleans schools was delegated to the state's Board of Elementary and Secondary Education, seventy miles away in Baton Rouge and with just two board members from New Orleans. BESE, in turn, initially handed over most decision-making authority about new charters to Chicago-based National Association of Charter School Authorizers. Of the forty-four organizations, many of them community-led groups, that applied to BESE for charter authorization in 2006, only six were approved.[183]

The reformers used the crisis of Hurricane Katrina and the dysfunction of the OPSB in the years before the storm to define their raison d'être. Yet what made their actions suspect was not just the sudden influx of TFA and Ivy League out-of-towners. Rather, it was the willful, systematic, and prolonged effort to lock the local community out of key decisions or a meaningful role in the city's education future. "We do have a process where for some reason groups that are trying to come up organically are having trouble getting through," conceded Caroline Roemer Shirley, who heads the Louisiana Association of Public Charter Schools.[184]

Indeed, shortcutting the community was baked into the new charter system from the get-go. In 2005, Governor Blanco signed Executive Orders 58 and 79, suspending key provisions of charter school law, such as the need to consult with, and to obtain the votes of, affected faculty *and parents* before converting an existing public school into a charter school.[185]

In 2011, an article in the *Times-Picayune* reported: "With so many local groups getting turned down, some critics have worried aloud that the people running New Orleans schools won't reflect the city's African-American majority or culture."[186]

Writes Bob Peterson about NACSA's role in New Orleans charters in his book *Keeping the Promise*: "Allowing a group hundreds of miles away to choose which charter applications were approved in New Orleans may have been expedient, given the post-storm chaos. But it also disadvantaged community groups that wanted to open their own schools."[187]

A pause. A sigh. A knowing look. In interview after interview, New Orleans charter advocates had their way of letting you know that those community organizations just weren't ready for prime time. They mean well, those alumni groups and community activists who want to revive the quaint notion of neighborhood schools, but their plans would surely lead to more low-quality schools, if not corruption.

A NINTH WARD SCHOOL FIGHTS BACK

When banks threatened to foreclose on tens of thousands of home owners in the wake of Hurricane Katrina—the banks had given middle-class mortgage owners three months to make good on their payments, but only one month to poor holders of so-called subprime mortgages—ACORN, a national community organization, mounted a campaign to expose the banking industry's double standard. The ensuing publicity forced subprime lenders to the negotiating table and saved countless homes from foreclosure. In their insightful article "The Missing Katrina Story," Peter Dreier and John Atlas document the vital role played by grassroots organizations, such as ACORN and the Industrial Areas Foundation, in the post-Katrina rebuilding, and how these groups "comprised mainly of working class and poor people have been a critical factor in catalyzing the rebuilding of New Orleans' more vulnerable areas." Quite simply, to the extent that the city's poorest neighborhoods, including the Lower Ninth, made a comeback, "their recovery is due largely to the grassroots organizing groups that would not let the powerbrokers forget them."[188]

No doubt there were half-baked chartering schemes put forth by local community groups. But, as with the effort to save and rebuild homes after Katrina, a handful of community groups—championed by *both* black and white New Orleanians—worked against great odds, and often with fewer resources than the establishment-sanctioned charters, to establish schools.

Working with community groups to reopen schools may well have been messier. But New Orleans missed a historic chance to incorporate a more generative, community-based approach to chartering and school renewal. As some of the most successful open-admissions schools would demonstrate, community-backed charters could add some much-needed diversity not only to the offerings of charter schools, but also to their student bodies. They also would have helped to legitimize the new charter regime, especially among local African Americans.

Consider the struggles of Martin Luther King Jr. School of Science and Technology, an elementary school in the Lower Ninth Ward. Before Hurricane Katrina, MLK was a proud neighborhood beacon. Built in 1995, a bright yellow-brick building with red trim, MLK housed a branch of the local library as well as "a room designed to host all manner of meetings and activities for the neighborhood after school and on weekends."[189] Since 2001, MLK had enjoyed steadily increasing performance scores, exceeding its growth targets each year. By 2005, the school had garnered an SPS score of 85.9, 10.5 points higher than its 2004 score and well above the 60 SPS that had long been considered a passing score. Yet, in a post-Katrina world, MLK fell just shy of the *revised* (made exclusively for New Orleans) 86.5 cutoff for a failing school and was unceremoniously dumped into the RSD.[190]

After Hurricane Katrina, the city said it would take three to five years to reopen MLK. At one point, the city even decided to raze MLK's building, even though a Denver engineering firm had assessed the building in January 2006 and concluded that it was structurally sound. "That's when we realized they didn't want any of the schools in the Lower Ninth to open," Hilda Young, an administrator in the OPSB, told *The Nation's* Gary Rivlin.[191]

Doris Hicks, the school's indomitable principal, fought back, determined to save MLK by turning it into one of the rare community-led charter schools in the city and to make the school an example of renewal for the devastated Lower Ninth Ward.

Few will forget the images of "poor, predominantly African-American families huddled, dehydrated, and dying at the New Orleans Convention Center and Superdome waiting for much-delayed assistance from the government."[192] Or the thousands of "refugees" stuck on the side of Highway I10 at a squalid, muddy receiving center. Or the terrified seniors winched down from nursing home rooftops, or the hospital patients, left for days, who were finally evacuated via helicopters.[193]

Whether by ineptitude or design, in the wake of Hurricane Katrina both the federal government and the white Louisiana establishment seemed ready to write off the Lower Ninth Ward, which, while poor and 98 percent black, was one of the most cohesive communities in the city. The Lower Ninth was more "small village" than a neighborhood, "more Mississippi Delta than big-city jazz," writes Rivlin in *The Nation*. Yet "long after other flooded communities were reopened, the Lower Ninth's residents were barred from returning even to assess the damage." The Lower Ninth was the last neighborhood in the city to have its electricity restored, the last to have its water taps turned back on, and the last to get FEMA trailers, which began to arrive in June 2006, months after they had been delivered to other communities.[194]

Before the storm, there had been five schools in the Lower Ninth. For months after the hurricane, long after schools were being opened in other neighborhoods, not a single school was reopened in the Lower Ninth.

The ostensible reason for this neglect was the erroneous assumption—perpetuated by city and federal officials—that the neighborhood was low-lying and "too vulnerable to rebuild."[195]

Noted Dan Baum in his detailed account in the *New Yorker*:

> From the earliest days of the crisis, the Lower Ninth Ward seemed to be in a special category. No other neighborhood, for example, was cordoned off by troops. When outside help arrived in force, six days after the storm, the National Guard roadblocked the bridges leading into the Lower Nine. Of all those people who were toughing it out

in attics across the flooded city, only those of the Lower Nine were forbidden to return if they waded out for supplies. Though eighty per cent of New Orleans was inundated, the city's homeland security director, Terry Ebbert, appeared to single out the Lower Nine when he told a reporter that "nothing out there can be saved at all," and Mayor Clarence Ray Nagin, Jr., said, inaccurately, "I don't think it can ever be what it was, because it's the lowest-lying area." Ebbert and Nagin were exhausted, stunned by the vastness of the destruction, and lacking solid information. But nobody seriously proposed ditching Lakeview, an upscale white neighborhood that had borne the force of another breach, that of the Seventeenth Street Canal, and lay under even deeper water. Some bluntly welcomed an opportunity to abandon the Lower Ninth Ward. "I don't want those people from the Lower Ninth Ward back," Robby Robinson, the owner of French Quarter Candles, said. "I don't think any businessperson does. They didn't contribute anything to this city."[196]

Alphonso Jackson, the secretary of housing and urban development under President George W. Bush, added fuel to the flames. "It would be a mistake to rebuild the Ninth Ward," he said.[197]

In fact, much of the Lower Ninth is above sea level. Neighborhoods like Lakeview, an affluent white community, and New Orleans East, which is home to middle-class and affluent African Americans, were lower lying and suffered much greater flood damage. Yet long after these communities had reopened, armed guards still stood at the channel bridges that provided the only access to the Lower Ninth and blocked access by residents.[198]

As in the years before *Brown v. Board of Education*, the community in the Lower Ninth rallied to open schools. Hicks, who grew up in the neighborhood, reached out to Common Ground, a nonprofit community-advocacy group founded after the storm by Malik Rahim, a former Black Panther. Working with Common Ground, Hicks organized hundreds of volunteers from the Lower Ninth and from around the country to come together on March 17, 2006, to help rebuild MLK. But someone leaked the news to the authorities so, when Hicks and the Tyvek-clad Common Ground volunteers arrived at the building, they found the doors padlocked and police on horseback blocking their path. Hicks was told: "If you go into the school, you are going to be arrested."[199]

Hicks, however, had won the support of the local sheriff, and the standoff soon ended. "Locks are just meant to be sawed off," she said years later.[200]

Over that weekend, representatives from the school and Common

Ground met with Robin Jarvis, then the head of the RSD (Paul Vallas would take over a year later). In the end, Jarvis and the city council affirmed that the volunteers had the right to clean up the school "for immediate use and with the hope of reopening it sooner than the three to five years originally promised. The City Council eventually passed the resolution."[201]

Even as the school was being cleaned, MLK encountered fresh obstacles. MLK was to move into the old Charles Colton Middle School temporarily while its building was readied for occupancy. But when Hicks visited the school, she found it to be moldy and rat-infested. The building was in such a state of disrepair, it had been shuttered even before the storm. "No, not my babies. My children deserve to be in a school facility that gives them dignity and respects them as human beings," she declared.[202]

"Promises were made to clean the building."[203]

But delays prevented the school from opening on time. To protest the delays, MLK teachers and leaders from the Southern Christian Leadership Conference (SCLC) held classes on the steps of the Colton building and even served breakfast. Said Hicks at the time: "I wanted the world to see: We're ready to educate our children of color. But we seemed to be the only ones who cared about really doing that."[204]

Eventually, MLK opened in the Edgar P. Harney Elementary School on Willow Street in Uptown, not far from the watchful gaze of a statue of Martin Luther King Jr.[205]

On August 30, 2007, two years after Hurricane Katrina, the Original Pin-Stripe Brass Band and the Zulu Walking Warriors paraded into the MLK auditorium. A thousand parents and community members gathered to dance and celebrate, New Orleans–style, the reopening of their school. It had been two years since Hurricane Katrina, and MLK was the first school in the Lower Ninth to reopen.[206]

"It has been a Herculean effort to get this school open," Louella Givens of the Louisiana State Board of Elementary and Secondary Education (BESE) said at the time.[207]

But for New Orleans, in its nascent struggle over charter schools, the story of MLK's rebirth, as well as its David-versus-Goliath battle to reopen, represented much more. Said Lisa Fithian, one of the Common Ground organizers, at the time: "It really became a symbol of hope and got a lot of people active. It was hugely significant because this was the first mass direct action in New Orleans" after the storm.[208]

Nor was MLK the only community school that encountered resistance from the city's new charter establishment, or that—by dint of hard work, discipline, and community cohesion—succeeded in opening in spite of that establishment.

TO REVIVE A NEIGHBORHOOD, BUILD A SCHOOL

Jennifer Weishaupt, a transplanted New Yorker, sits at the long conference table in a historic building in the Marigny section of New Orleans above one of her cafés, which are collectively known as the Ruby Slipper. Weishaupt is wearing jeans and, appropriately, a black T-shirt embossed with a giant bejeweled ruby slipper. She laughs easily. But Weishaupt's mood turns serious as she describes a familiar tale of exodus and return. Unlike the city's poor and dispossessed, Weishaupt and her husband, Erich, moved to Houston to escape the storm; at the time, she was still an executive with Shell and kept an apartment there. When Weishaupt, pregnant with her first child, returned to New Orleans, she found her Mid City neighborhood had been devastated. At the time, Weishaupt was essentially working two jobs—the one at Shell and one at the start-up of the Ruby Slipper, a chain that now stretches as far as Pensacola, Florida. "I had an immediate interest in economic development," says Weishaupt. "I figured if we bring business back, there's more incentive for home owners."[209]

So Weishaupt began working to revive the Mid City Neighborhood Organization. But to bring back home owners, Mid City also needed schools. "One thing we were looking closely at was the return of schools and how school seats were going to be allocated in the school facilities master plan. We had a large number of elementary schools, in particular, because we had a very large school-age population."[210]

Before long, Weishaupt and the Mid City Neighborhood Organization set their sights on reopening the John Dibert Elementary School on Orleans Avenue.

Broderick Bagert, the scion of an old New Orleans family, was also a Mid City resident. Bagert had grown up in the Gentilly neighborhood and would go on to Oxford and the London School of Economics, but he was also a community organizer in the Saul Alinsky mode. His LSU master's thesis had focused on alternative public-housing projects, inspired by those in his hometown. At twenty-six, three years before Hurricane Katrina, Bagert made a name for himself locally with what was virtually a one-man battle against a real estate developer who wanted to use tax revenue from a planned Walmart to help finance a mixed-use development at the St. Thomas housing complex in New Orleans. Bagert would lose that fight, but his crusade helped him get job offers from "every nonprofit in the city."[211]

Bagert, with his pressed Oxford shirts and neatly trimmed black hair, has the look of a young man educated, as he says, "soup-to-nuts" in Catholic schools—at least until his graduate-school sojourn in England. Eventually, he would go work for the Industrial Areas Foundation, a community organization praised by Dreier and Atlas for its role in rebuilding post-Katrina.[212]

Before long, Bagert also would turn his organizing skills to saving another Mid City school, Morris F.X. Jeff Sr. Elementary School.

Soon after Bagert and his wife, Celeste Lofton, returned to the city after Hurricane Katrina, his sister, Jenny, phoned to tell him about a public meeting that was to be held about an abandoned school behind her house in the Faubourg St. John neighborhood, a sliver of land by the bayou, in the northeast corner of the Mid City planning district. The gathering would be one of several held that winter as a way to gather public input for a school-facilities master plan that would determine the educational fate of many neighborhoods—which buildings to reopen and renovate and which to tear down. Morris Jeff occupied an elegant hundred-year-old brick structure on North Rendon Street that was built on a berm and thus had not suffered much flood damage beyond a foot-or-so of water in the basement. "In typical New Orleans fashion, the school was tucked away in the middle of a residential neighborhood, a few blocks from both the palatial, high ground homes on Ursuline and Esplanade Avenues as well as a few blocks from some of the city's most violence-plagued streets."[213]

Built in 1904 with money from the McDonogh fund, the school opened under the name McDonogh 31, starting out as a co-educational, whites-only school. In 1995, its name was changed to honor Jeff, the revered and recently deceased educator who had led the city's recreation department. Since the 1960s and the start of white flight, the school had become almost entirely African American, with 98 percent of the students eligible for free- or reduced-price lunch. Yet Morris Jeff was never labeled as "persistently dangerous." Attendance rates were close to 95 percent, and class sizes were typically below twenty-five. On the norm-referenced Iowa Test of Basic Skills, Morris Jeff ranked at the twentieth percentile nationally, which placed it "slightly below average when compared with other public schools in New Orleans, but far from the bottom." Until Hurricane Katrina, it was an African American institution "serving low-income families that enjoyed high regard as a safe and caring place for children."[214]

Like MLK, Morris Jeff had been moved into the RSD after Hurricane Katrina.

The building, which had "a serendipitous roof-replacement" just before the hurricane, served as a refuge for nearby families during the storm. But, for a year and a half afterward, it stood empty. Then, in March 2007, a government-contracted cleanup crew showed up and began clearing "debris" from the building, including what seemed to many neighbors as "useful books and supplies."[215]

Writes Beabout in his account of the Morris Jeff origin story:

> The micro-narrative of Morris Jeff's neighbors parallels the broader macro-narrative in which the post-storm reforms were perceived as being done to a community rather than with a community. The Morris Jeff neighbors understandably defined the school as theirs. It was across the street from their houses, and there was a tremendous distrust of governmental authorities that emerged from Katrina and the catastrophic failures of the Army Corps of Engineers. There was a feeling that something as important as the neighborhood school could not be trusted to distant authorities.[216]

The meeting the Bagerts were to attend in January 2008 was held at the Crossman school, about a mile from Morris Jeff. When they arrived, they found that many attendees had questions about the Morris Jeff building. A group gathered at the end of the meeting to discuss their shared interest.[217]

The next public meeting was scheduled for the end of February, and the Bagerts decided to call a neighborhood planning meeting in advance at Jenny Bagert's house. At the time, "there wasn't some preestablished vision," recalls Bagert. "We were just trying to get a building fixed up. I was thinking apartments."[218]

But there were some residents who knew exactly what they wanted, and it wasn't an apartment building. One neighbor, Davina Allen, a physics teacher who had gotten her start at TFA, wanted Morris Jeff to be reopened as a school. Anne Daniell, the wife of a local pastor who had a school-aged daughter, also was determined to see Morris Jeff remain a school. The neighbors who gathered together that evening at Jenny Bagert's house would form the core of a community group that would lobby, over the course of the next two years, to have the Morris Jeff building reopened as a school.[219]

The group, which would call itself Neighbors for Morris F.X. Jeff School, made posters and flyers and invited their neighbors to local meetings. They also surveyed five hundred households in the neighborhood and confirmed that the vast majority of residents had children and wanted a school. "We had to make sure the neighborhood was as interested" in the project as was the core organizing group, recalled Bagert.[220]

They also arranged rides to the next RSD facilities meeting on February 28.[221]

Equally important, the committee that emerged was as diverse as the neighborhood itself and included "educators, preachers, teachers, black and white, old and young." In fact, the "membership cut across all the lines that ordinarily divide New Orleans."[222]

The group soon developed a singular goal—to create a racially and economically integrated community school, the kind of school that had, thus far, largely eluded New Orleans. With time, Morris Jeff also would seek to create a school that was as inclusive and collaborative as its organizing committee. But, in doing so, it was bucking the prevailing trend of New Orleans CMOs, dominated by out-of-towners and a top-down, no-excuses philosophy. And bucking that trend, as countless community groups had found, usually resulted in having your charter application turned down.

At the February meeting, which was held in another school building, the group got bad news. The RSD planning board announced that it intended to "repurpose" the Morris Jeff building and send the neighborhood children elsewhere. The leaders of the Morris Jeff contingent, which took up half the seats in the school cafeteria, rose to their feet and challenged the decision. By the end of the meeting, the planning board assured the group that no final decision had been made and that their request would be considered.[223]

The Morris Jeff committee, inspired by local determination and Bagert's organizing savvy, continued to seek meetings with elected officials and to attend civic meetings—lots of meetings. When BESE scheduled a public hearing on the School Facilities Master Plan in Baton Rouge, fifty members of the Morris Jeff group, wearing "Neighbors for Morris F.X. Jeff School" T-shirts, traveled to the state capital to make their case.[224]

But "it became clear, early on, that their minds were made up about this school and this area," recalls Bagert, referring to Paul Vallas, the RSD's controversial chief. "They weren't going to build schools in this place."[225]

Vallas rarely said "no."

"Vallas's style was to say 'yes' to your face," recalls Bagert, even if he often did the opposite. But at least with a provisional "yes," "we at least had a chance to get him to live up to his commitments."[226]

Weishaupt had gotten in touch with Bagert early on, primarily to discuss housing issues in the Mid City area. But by the summer of 2008, Bagert and Weishaupt were also speaking regularly about the school situation. At one point, both the Morris Jeff contingent and Weishaupt's larger Mid City group were told that there wasn't a large enough school-age population in the area, which had once boasted five elementary schools, to support the schools they wanted to reopen. The RSD planned to reopen only two of the area's five school buildings.[227]

Both Bagert and Weishaupt were stunned. The RSD was actually planning to close schools in Mid City. "We all scratched our heads and said, this makes no sense, why would they not reopen all these schools, in a neighborhood that's full of people with school-age children and planning to have school-age children," recalls Weishaupt.[228]

"From a neighborhood standpoint, we thought this was devastating," says Weishaupt. "What were they going to do with these school buildings? How were kids going to get educated? How were we going to attract people to move to the neighborhood if they couldn't get their kids educated there, and had to bus them all around?"

That last worry, about kids getting bused, reflected a growing concern in New Orleans, one also voiced by Leona Tate, that, in the atomized new charter system, there were no longer going to be "neighborhood schools."[229]

The Morris Jeff committee continued to lobby for its building and to save the Mid City schools and its park. They talked to Senator Mary Landrieu's office, to functionaries in Vallas's office, and to other elected officials.

When the School Facilities Master Plan was unveiled in August 2008, it was clear that the Morris Jeff committee had won a partial victory. The RSD plan included a "New Jeff site," but it would be located at Easton Park, one of the few green spaces in the neighborhood, which was home to a playground and served as the venue for local football and baseball games.[230]

Borrowing a page from MLK, Neighbors for Morris F.X. Jeff called a press conference at the Rendon Street school building on August 22, 2008, where they criticized the RSD plan and its tone deafness to community concerns. "This is an unfunded plan to take a neighborhood park and to close three neighborhood schools," Bagert said at the press conference.[231]

Morris Jeff also had gotten hold of a spreadsheet on projected population growth from someone who worked with Greg Rigamer, a statistician and chief executive of GCR, a New Orleans consulting firm that studied the storm's aftermath. The study "showed that the largest increase in projected student enrollment was in our zip code," recalls Bagert. "It showed, in essence, that the entire facilities planning process had been a charade. The RSD's decisions had had nothing to do with population projections vs. capacity."[232]

When it comes to the RSD and its decision making, conspiracy theories abound in New Orleans. But Bagert was convinced that the RSD had simply decided to build where there were large tracts of available land, which "ironically, were often the areas that had seen the heaviest depopulation from Katrina" and thus had the lowest enrollment needs.[233]

Although Mid City had the highest projected current and future enrollment in the city, according to Rigamer's projections, the original master plan draft not only rejected Morris Jeff's pleas to reopen the school, but proposed closing all five of its schools—two that were already open and three that were not, including Morris Jeff.[234]

On September 18, 2008, at McDonogh 35, the RSD held the first of two planned hearings on the School Facilities Master Plan, which would help determine which new schools would open, and where, and how $1.8 billion in federal funds would be spent.[235]

The Morris Jeff group was ready. It rolled out a projector and a PowerPoint presentation with a spreadsheet showing enrollment versus capacity. Projecting eight-feet high onto the meeting-room wall, Bagert showed, "with big, bold negative numbers," how the data on projected school capacity and population in the area would actually result in *a growing shortage* of available school seats. Using Rigamer's numbers and their own calculations of school capacity, Morris Jeff showed that, in 2008, there was already a shortage of 698 seats and that the shortage would nearly double to 1,307 needed seats in 2012, reaching a 1,531-seat shortfall by 2016.[236]

"We were alleging, with numbers and bar graphs, that the plan was an absurdity, that the planners had not conducted the seating capacity vs. enrollment need analysis that was supposed to have been the driver—the very purpose—of the entire master plan.

"Then we asked the RSD to put up their spreadsheet of projected enrollment vs. projected capacity up on the wall next to ours. We could then see where there were discrepancies between our analysis and their analysis and could talk through those discrepancies one by one."[237]

Bagert says that, at the time, he was sure that the RSD had done the analysis but had chosen, for some reason, not to share it. But no, there was no RSD spreadsheet. It didn't exist.

Says Bagert: "They had spit-balled the entire master plan. They had gotten it right in some places, wrong in others—and DISASTROUSLY wrong in our case, despite us packing out every public hearing, taking a bus trip to Baton Rouge to present before BESE, meeting several times with Vallas, etc., etc.

"I remember feeling happy and nauseous at the same time. Happy that we had them cold. Disgusted at the rest of it. (What in the hell were all those people running around doing for the last year? What a goddamn farce.)"[238]

Bagert's analysis very likely also saved John Dibert from being mothballed. But unlike Morris Jeff, Weishaupt's Mid City group would never get the go-ahead to open a community charter. Although, early on, Chicago-based NACSA gave "provisional approval" to the Mid City group to charter John Dibert, ultimately, in late fall of 2006, the charter request was denied.[239] Michael Homan, a professor at Xavier University who led the chartering effort for Mid City, asked for the rubrics used to deny the group's application, and "reading them over it seemed they didn't understand how a neighborhood group like MCNO"—the Mid City Neighborhood Organization—"which does so much, would govern a school."[240]

To reassure NACSA, Mid City set up a separate nonprofit for its charter school and partnered with an established local education organization. The group had just one month to revise its proposal. This time, having been denied access to John Dibert, the Mid City group applied to charter the Thurgood Marshall School. But, once again, the group's application was denied by NACSA. Writes Homan:

> We've heard through the grapevine that NACSA is only giving charters to groups who partner with national education companies that have political and financial ties to NACSA . . . only non-Louisiana education management companies get charters, and no neighborhood groups using Louisiana based management companies are trusted to run a school. It seems companies from Houston and Chicago know more about schools in Louisiana. And again, so many companies are profiting from Katrina.[241]

Rumors surfaced that the Thurgood Marshall building was to be turned over to Edison Schools, with a school set to open in fall of 2007. Other out-of-state for-profit institutions, including Mosaica, Leona Group, and SABIS, also were designated to manage New Orleans charters.[242] Michael and Susan Klonsky wrote, at the time, that New Orleans was becoming "a sort of Mecca of for-profit charter management organizations."[243]

The for-profit management companies, however, didn't last long in New Orleans.[244]

Finally, in 2009, Dibert would be turned over to FirstLine and renamed the John Dibert Community School (and, later, moved and renamed the Phillis Wheatley Community School). In its charter application, FirstLine referenced its "long-standing relationship with New Schools for New Orleans" and a litany of education experts affiliated with the no-excuses school of pedagogy in its charter application.[245]

Says Bagert, acidly: "That, I remember thinking at one point, will be our lasting contribution to school reform in New Orleans. Everything will be the same, but schools, henceforth, will have the word 'community' in their name."[246]

"It wasn't a very transparent process," adds Weishaupt. Having lost the effort to launch her own community school, Weishaupt signed on with Bagert's group, working to get Morris Jeff approved and launched. Speculates Weishaupt: "It's possible that once they said 'no' to ours, they didn't want to say 'no'" to another group of school advocates "in the same neighborhood and risk what that would look like."[247]

Morris Jeff, it turned out, would be the exception that proved the rule. Although Morris Jeff would never get its building on North Rendon Street, by 2008 Neighbors for Morris F.X. Jeff School, working with the Faubourg St. John neighborhood committee, would be well on its way to realizing its mission of opening a community school. Easton Park also would be preserved as a neighborhood park.

Equally important was what had happened, along the way, to the Morris Jeff committee itself. "Outrageously important things were happening here between us," recalls Bagert, who would become chairman of the new charter school's board. "Black people and white people are fighting a common foe. We are seeing who among us doesn't fold in the face of opposition and controversy. We are experiencing disappointment, resilience and joy, and humor. And relationships are forming that are grounds for trust, which at the end of the day are the grounds on which people send their kids to school."[248]

Trust.

In December 2008, the Morris Jeff group held another meeting at Bibleway Missionary Baptist Church, led by Bagert and Aesha Rasheed, a parent advocate who would become the publisher of the *New Orleans Parents Guide*. The attendees formed groups of five to seven participants each to hash out their definition of what constituted an "excellent neighborhood school" and gradually hammered out its core values.[249]

What they came up with was a different kind of charter school from the type that was becoming prevalent in New Orleans, coalescing around an ideal of a school that would provide open access to all children, that was community centered, and that would draw on the area's diverse population.

During the course of the school's fight for a building, the Morris Jeff activists had heard countless people, from Paul Vallas to the folks at RSD planning meetings, welcome "citizen input." Though Vallas's opening promise should have offered a hint to the groups that would receive priority under his leadership: "This will be the greatest opportunity for educational entrepreneurs, charter schools, competition and parental choice in America," Vallas had promised when he first got to town.[250]

Wrote Michael Homan of Xavier University, referring to both Paul Vallas and Paul Pastorek, the Louisiana schools superintendent: "When they took over our schools they promised transparency and community collaboration, and neither has happened thus far. Both Pauls promised they would work closely with the community. . . . Instead they told us what would happen to our neighborhood schools."[251]

At the end of the day, says Bagert, "The way in which we went about winning a school was by not accepting the swim lanes of the RSD."

"We would get what we have the power to get," said Bagert, paraphrasing Frederick Douglass.[252]

To have their voices heard, the Morris Jeff committee learned that it had to have "standing and power in some fashion." That standing came in large part from the steadfastness of the community and careful planning, as well as from the growing collaboration and trust among its diverse membership.

Morris Jeff also came to the realization that to build an excellent school, its teachers, too, would have to have some standing and power so their voices could be heard. And for that, they were determined to do what, in New Orleans, was unthinkable and sanction a teachers union. "Teacher collaboration and participation were outgrowths of the school's focus on student diversity," write Richard Kahlenberg and Halley Potter about Morris Jeff in *A Smarter Charter.* Diversity at Morris Jeff would apply not just to race, but to culture, opinions, and voice.[253]

In 2010, Morris Jeff submitted its application for a charter school under the RSD. Its mission and values statements set Morris Jeff apart from many of the city's other charters. For one thing, the mission statement put preparing students for democratic citizenship on a par with college and career readiness:

> Morris Jeff Community School will offer an education that is a source of freedom and possibility for children, permitting them to develop their talents fully, become contributing citizens in our democracy, and attain the foundation they need to excel at high schools, colleges, careers, and pursuits.[254]

Morris Jeff's lofty mission, so out of sync with the prevailing New Orleans test-prep culture, presented a raft of challenges. In January 2009, the school had formed a search committee for a principal. Before the process was over, the Morris Jeff board would review fifty applications.[255] In the end, the final decision boiled down to two candidates. One was black and one was white. The decision would, for the first time since the founding of Neighbors for the Morris F.X. Jeff School, threaten to cleave—along racial lines—what was then still a school steering committee.

The division was not at first obvious. "Most of us felt we had two good candidates," recalls one participant. "When we finally called the vote, we realized 'Holy shit, we just voted on racial lines'" with a one-vote majority for Patricia Perkins.[256]

Yet the group had built deep enough reservoirs of trust that they agreed to table their decision and *not* move forward with a closely divided vote. "To a person," the steering committee agreed that this was not how Morris Jeff would make its decision.[257]

It was then that Laura Krebs, a reading specialist who now serves as the school's "primary years coordinator" and who served as a member of the Morris Jeff steering committee, proposed that they conduct a Quaker-style meeting to resolve the group's disagreements about the principal search. A TFA alumna, Krebs had, like many of the Morris Jeff pioneers, joined the group out of concern for the direction in which New Orleans schools were going. Krebs, who would eventually enroll her two sons at the school, said she wanted to help build an institution to which she would send her own children—not a common practice in New Orleans among nonselective schools, then or now.[258]

Rather than proceeding to a quick vote, twenty or so members of various committees sat in a circle at one member's house on Dumaine Street and discussed what they had learned and how they felt about the candidates. "After about an hour, it became clear that there was much more support" for Patricia Perkins, one of the finalists, than anyone had previously thought. Several members were drawn to Perkins's previous experience at Lusher, the high-performing selective OPSB school where she had worked for years; her knowledge of curriculum and "an overwhelming number of positive references from colleagues" finally carried the day.[259]

During Mardi Gras that year, members of the Morris Jeff community—neighbors and prospective teachers—formed a procession, beating drums and handing out flyers for their school.[260] In August, after a three-year odyssey, Morris Jeff finally opened its doors at a temporary facility on Poydras Street. The school would later move to a brand-new building on S. Lopez Street. An open-admissions RSD school, Morris Jeff represented the culmination of one of the few grassroots school campaigns, thus one of the few that had earned the "community" designation in its moniker. It also bucked the prevailing post-Katrina no-excuses trend. Serving children in grades

K–8, Morris Jeff would offer an academically rigorous International Baccalaureate program. Most surprisingly, its student body on that opening day was about 60 percent black, 30 percent white, and 10 percent consisting of a mix of Asian, Hispanic, and other ethnic groups—"in short, a near-mirror of New Orleans."[261]

Morris Jeff's daughter, Jolene Jeff, would join the new school's board. And Andre Perry, who five years later would warn against replicating all the "nefarious" things that had been done by the city's charter schools in the name of academic gain, had nothing but praise for Morris Jeff. "The goal of any urban district in particular is to get people across lines of race, class, gender, sexuality and religion on the same page and to work in harmony for the betterment of all those schools," said Perry, who then served as associate dean of the University of New Orleans College of Education and Human Development and the chief executive officer of the UNO charter school network. Morris Jeff, Perry said, had gotten the school-development challenge "exactly right."[262]

Yet no sooner had the new school opened its doors when another crisis loomed—one again born in part from the school's commitment to what Bagert calls "democracy with a small 'd.'"

Three months into the school year, Perkins fired a teacher, Dana French Christian, for "excessive tardiness" and for exhibiting "abrasive behavior." Christian countered that she had been fired for complaining about colleagues' leaving children in a so-called seclusion room, a disciplinary procedure that is restricted by law. The school countered that it used a "time-out" room, which is not restricted by law. And Perkins defended the practice as "one of our most successful ways of working with children who have had a meltdown, or are disobeying a rule," noting that teachers either stay in the room with the student or remain just outside. Parents complained about the practice at school board meetings in February and March of 2011.[263]

What exacerbated the problem was Christian's close relationship with Davina Allen, a member of both the school board and the Morris Jeff founding committee, who charged that the board "never really investigated the seclusion issue, and that three parents withdrew children from the school as a consequence." Allen submitted her resignation to the board.[264]

In fact, it wasn't until the March board meeting of the school's first year of operation that Morris Jeff unveiled a draft of a grievance procedure for parents. As of February 2011, six months after the school opened, its student handbook also still lacked details on the school's expulsion guidelines and special-education policies and wasn't in line with the "legal guidebook" developed by NSNO.[265]

What must have especially stung the Morris Jeff founders was Allen's accusation that "transparency and accountability were clearly not the priority of Mr. Bagert and Ms. Rasheed." [266]

Five years later, Bagert is defiant about the seclusion-room controversy and sees it as part of the necessary "messiness" involved in democratic governance. "A defining reality of our first year ended up being around this toxic situation that could have been avoided if we had just vested dictatorial power in our principal," says Bagert. "The first year where you are constantly attentive to reputation, you've managed, beyond any reasonable expectation, to have a very broad and economically and racially diverse set of parents send their kids to this school, folks who wouldn't have their kids in a public school. It's a tenuous trust. . . . Ultimately, it was the commitment to those small 'd,' democratic ways of doing things that allowed us to build that trust in the first place. I'd argue it is better to have that horrible, horrible situation every year versus an institution run unilaterally from the top down." [267]

Most poignant of all was the response of Courtney Clark, the mother of one of the children who had been given a "time-out" alone in a room: "I did not remove my son from MJCS, because all the charter schools have these type of problems—being able to properly deal with kids with special needs of any kind. Because of my son's needs, a change would have made this situation more difficult and would have added a more traumatic outcome. I will not deny that I also took a backseat to the situation because of a fear that all parents have [that] shaking up things may cause things to be more difficult for my son and daughter who are still attending MJCS as well as making things more difficult for me being a single mother." [268]

For Clark, the one thing she knew was that the situation at another charter could have been far worse.

As for Morris Jeff, it continued to walk a fine line in New Orleans. "When there's diversity, there's going to be conflict," says Krebs. "It's important to hold two ideals at once . . . child centeredness with reasonable behavior expectations. Sometimes it goes well, sometimes . . ." Krebs's voice trails off.

The school also tries to balance "teacher autonomy and school consistency." Again, says Krebs, "Sometimes we're in balance, other times it doesn't work as well." [269]

Five years after the school opened, Morris Jeff and its teachers finalized a teachers' contract after a grueling yearlong negotiation, becoming only the second school in post-Katrina New Orleans to do so.

The contract seeks to protect teachers, which is rare in New Orleans. The agreement called for a new "fair and transparent" discipline process. It also *froze* teachers' salaries for three years. And it set the hours of a typical work day from 7:30 a.m.–3:45 p.m., with an unbroken ninety-minute period for teachers to plan.[270]

In addition, the agreement was designed, in many ways, to support input from both teachers and parents. A committee of teachers and administrators are to examine and improve teacher performance evaluations. "The agreement creates a Student Support Committee with power to set discipline and special education policy for the school. Decisions require a supermajority vote, and parents are on the panel."[271]

Said Matthew Tuttle, a fifth-grade teacher: "From what I'm told, there's no other committee like this in the country."[272]

Danielle Dreilinger of the *Times-Picayune* notes how out of the ordinary this agreement is: "Even at traditional public schools in Louisiana, teachers have little pull: school boards are not required to bargain with unions, and the Legislature removed most tenure protections in 2012. But charters are especially known for swift hiring and firing, and job insecurity."[273]

In June 2015, Perkins showed up for a meeting of the Morris Jeff board, with Jennifer Weishaupt serving as board secretary; Weishaupt had joined the board about a year after Morris Jeff opened. Dusk was lowering outside the windows of the school's bright and spacious library where the board meetings are held. Morris Jeff, Perkins told the board, would be adding eleven new teachers, the result of both attrition and new positions becoming available due to the school's expansion. She made a point of emphasizing that the school had succeeded in hiring "several veteran" teachers who would "expand the diversity" of the school's teaching force.[274]

"The culture of this city has to be represented and it's deeply rooted in African American culture," said Perkins after the board meeting. "We're teaching African American children. And we have to have African American mentors, not just for children but for the rest of us who aren't African American. Just like we have to have white teachers to help African American teachers." The whole idea of diversity "continues to become more and more complex the bigger the school gets."[275]

Perkins also noted that NSNO had renewed a grant for $20,000 earmarked for "personalized learning." The school would use the funds, Perkins said, to buy technology.

Three years after its founding, Morris Jeff had received no funding via NSNO. In fact, NSNO had twice turned the school down. Early on, Patricia Perkins asked NSNO to do a school review—one of NSNO's self-described missions. At the time, Perkins was the only administrator in the building who wasn't also teaching. "I knew right away that we weren't being fully understood," Perkins says. "We didn't fit their model. We were too understaffed at the top. Not enough administrators; just me and 210 kids."[276]

It wasn't until 2014 that Morris Jeff's third grant application was finally accepted. "In the last year to year and a half, they are trying to find out how to support us," said Krebs in 2015.[277]

It's unclear what has prompted NSNO's turnaround. Did the gatekeeper realize that the school, with its diverse students and teachers, represented the rare answer to growing criticism over the lack of community voice in New Orleans schools? Did Morris Jeff's growing waitlist compensate for its teachers' contract? Or, perhaps, it was Morris Jeff's relatively strong performance by Louisiana's measures—in the 2014–2015 school year, Morris Jeff was awarded a "B" grade for its 84.3 SPS, making it one of the highest-rated RSD schools, ahead of most of the city's KIPP schools.[278]

CARELESS DISREGARD

While Morris Jeff and MLK prevailed as rare examples of community schools in New Orleans, the takeover of local schools by outside CMOs was much more typical and often resulted in unhappy outcomes. Consider the poignant stories of John McDonogh, which had pioneered the DNA lab and Creole cottage programs in the 1990s, and Frederick Douglass High School, the post-*Brown* rebranding of the Nicholls School from which Leona Tate had graduated. In her mostly optimistic book about New Orleans charters, *Hope Against Hope*, Sarah Carr describes the fate of Frederick Douglass, which had been named after the self-educated, self-liberated slave. The school had suffered during the 1980s and 1990s from a "lack of resources and chronic churn of principals and teachers as the district superintendency rapidly changed hands, increasing drug and gun violence in the surrounding neighborhood and competition for strong students posed by citywide magnet programs."

Yet, amid such chaos, a small group of educators at the school ran "a nationally recognized writing program called Students at the Center," which worked with community groups to revitalize the flailing school from the ground up. With a special needs population at 20 percent, one of the highest in the city, the writing program not only inspired young people to express themselves, but also trained and empowered students to serve as reading and writing coaches for other students.

But after the storm, writes Carr, "when the RSD operated Douglass, it quickly became clear that Superintendent Paul Vallas intended to hand the building over to a charter school operator, most likely KIPP. During the 2009–2010 school year, the last before Douglass closed, the RSD treated the schools' remaining students and staff with callous disregard. After waffling all school year on whether Douglass would stay open . . . RSD officials decided to close Douglass completely. Some parents and students with intense special needs did not receive word of the decision until the summer and scrambled to find new schools at the last minute."[279]

John McDonogh fared worse. The school also fell on hard times in the years before Hurricane Katrina, and after the storm it was turned over to Steve Barr, a successful charter entrepreneur from Los Angeles, and his new dystopian-sounding Future Is Now group, who promised—in a familiar refrain—to bring kids, most of whom lagged academically, up to grade level within just a year. Once again, state superintendent John White promised community involvement, which never materialized, and Barr's takeover was met with vociferous local opposition.[280] And that was before Barr turned John Mac into the set of a reality TV show called *Blackboard Wars*, produced by Oprah Winfrey (who had also financed Sci Academy). The show was introduced with a trailer that called the school "one of the most dangerous schools in America," a reference to a fatal 2003 shooting inside the high school's gym. What was seen as crass exploitation of the school, its children, and a painful historical moment infuriated the local community. "The reality show preyed on students with mental illness, a gay student, and a pregnant student, and epitomized the injustice and ineffectiveness of putting an inexperienced and incompetent Teach for America 21-year-old in a classroom with students with the highest needs," wrote Kari Dequine Harden in the *Louisiana Weekly*.[281]

Barr and "charter board members begged everyone to stop focusing on the show and start focusing on the students. But education-watchers throughout the city cringed."[282]

Blackboard Wars faded from view, and the McDonogh takeover quickly unraveled. Instead of the stellar performance Barr had promised, the school featured single-digit performance scores and an "F" grade in its first year, close to a million-dollar deficit, and enrollments that fell "through the floor." By the end of its second year, the school would close. "NSNO, the RSD and Future Is Now made a commitment and promise to that community about the level of academic achievement we would deliver—and we haven't," conceded Neerav Kingsland, then the head of NSNO. The organization will "learn from the experience to make sure future investments work at the highest levels."[283]

Kingsland's mea culpa in the case of John Mac came in 2014, the same year NSNO finally gave Morris Jeff its first grant.

On Saturday, October 15, 2016, the NAACP's board of directors, at a meeting in Cincinnati, endorsed a strict moratorium on new charter schools, citing the need for greater school "transparency and accountability."[284]

In its 2016 education resolutions, the NAACP also noted the "disproportionately high use of punitive and exclusionary discipline" policies in charter schools, private boards that didn't represent the public, missing charter funds totaling close to half a billion dollars nationally, weak charter school oversight, and co-locations that siphoned resources from public schools. Finally, the NAACP resolved that it "opposes the privatization of public schools."[285]

In the lead-up to the vote, charter school supporters in New Orleans and elsewhere had been quick to accuse the NAACP of pandering to the teachers union, an ironic charge for a host of reasons, including the large numbers of African American parents who send their children to charter schools, as well as the moratorium's timing, more than two decades after charter schools began to take root and more than a decade after New Orleans began to transform itself into the nation's first all-charter city. Shavar Jeffries, president of Democrats for Education Reform, a leading pro-charter organization, declared that W.E.B. DuBois was "rolling in his grave" and suggested that the NAACP might have narrowed its moratorium target by excluding charter schools with a strong record of sending students to college. Eva Moskowitz, the doyen of Success Academy in New York City, which had recently become known for its got-to-go lists and public shaming of students, chastised the NAACP for having "turned its back" on students. The *Wall Street Journal* headline blared: "The NAACP's Disgrace," its editorial dripping with disdain for the "civil-rights outfit" that was "trapping poor minority children in failure factories."[286]

In fact, despite the good work of some charters and the fact that a number of charters are good for *some* children, the mainstream charter movement is plagued with problems that it and its supporters rarely acknowledge. A month before the NAACP moratorium, the U.S. Department of Education's Inspector General's Office published an audit report finding "financial risk," "program risk," and "lack of accountability" among two-thirds of the charter schools it had reviewed.[287] "Whatever position one takes on charters, there is no denying that the charter sector in a number of states is severely troubled, with little or virtually no oversight, leading to numerous financial and other scandals."[288]

Indeed, the NAACP's call for a moratorium came after many reports of fiscal mismanagement had cast the charter sectors of entire states, such as Ohio, as well as large swaths of online and for-profit charter organizations, in a felonious light. It came after a report by the American Civil Liberties Union of Southern California found that the enrollment policies of more than 20 percent of all California charter schools violated state and federal law. It came after the New Orleans SPLC consent decree.[289]

In New Orleans, the established charter industry has been working to fix the problems exposed by the SPLC lawsuit. It has attempted to level the playing field by creating a unified expulsion system throughout the city's schools and by establishing a common enrollment system that encompasses the RSD and many OPSB schools—though as recently as 2016, seven of the city's most selective schools still did not participate. And while there have been examples of theft and cheating among New Orleans's charter schools, and many charter executives are, by public-education standards, overpaid (Barr's salary was $250,000—and that was in addition to the six-figure salaries earned by his principals),[290] the biggest problem in New Orleans has not been corruption.[291]

Rather, the problem in New Orleans has been hubris and overreach. Since 2006, the average renewal rate of charter schools has been 64.8 percent. That means well over one-third of the charter schools launched since Hurricane Katrina have failed so badly that they have either been taken over or closed.[292]

Nor have the serial school closings improved the lot of the kids in the lowest-performing schools. A 2016 study by the Education Research Alliance shows that "mobility"—i.e., kids changing schools—in the relatively low-performing RSD occurs at a rate three to four times higher than that for children who attend the relatively high-performing OPSB schools, a pattern consistent with the idea that families in a "choice" environment will shop around for better options. Yet ERA concedes that its findings "reinforce prior research that market-based school reform increases stratification between schools. Low-performing students are less likely to move from lower-performing schools to higher-performing schools."[293]

Joseph S. Clark High School, one of the RSD's last traditional public schools to be "taken over"—and widely perceived as a dumping ground for students who couldn't get in elsewhere—demonstrates how school churn in an atomized system with few controls can leave kids out in the cold. Indeed, rather than the conventional takeover approach in which a CMO builds "a high school one grade level at a time," Clark was to be the first high school to be taken over in its entirety.[294] Yet most of Clark's 366 students declined to reenroll when it reopened under new management in the fall of 2011. During its first year under FirstLine, Clark had only 117 "persisters," or returning students, according to a study by Stanford University's Center for Research on Education Outcomes (CREDO). FirstLine could not account for where the students went after they left Clark. However, Jay Altman, its chief executive, said in an email that before FirstLine took over, a similarly low proportion of students, about 35 percent, were returning. (The school district did not respond to my queries about Clark.)

One problem is that in the decentralized New Orleans charter system, no agency was responsible for keeping track of all kids. Belatedly, the Recovery School District acknowledged that it was "worried" about high school attrition and began assigning counselors to help relocate the sizable population of students from schools it was closing.[295]

Leona Tate's granddaughter Deanna, who attended three high schools, was one of the lucky ones. She attended Clark, most likely before it was taken over by FirstLine; it was rated "F" then and now. She also attended Sojourner Truth, which closed in her junior year. She finally enrolled in McDonogh 35—which received a "C" rating—and graduated.[296]

It was the struggles of Tate's grandson Omari, who has special needs, that sparked Tate's interest in charter governance. She began attending charter board and BESE meetings and watching the people on panels with the "no-care looks" on their faces. (That, she adds, usually changed when they found out who she was.) Finally, Omari landed at RENEW, an "F"-rated school that has been part of a network under a state-appointed monitor following charges that its CMO fraudulently used $300,000 in special-education funds to close a budget gap, as well as charges that it had state-testing violations.[297]

Several other Tate grandchildren and adoptive grandchildren attend one of two Carver schools, both no-excuses institutions run by Sci Academy's CMO, Collegiate Academies. The CMO took over the historic George Washington Carver High School in the Upper Ninth Ward; the high school was phased out and replaced with two new schools, Carver Collegiate and Carver Prep. In 2013, the first year of a centralized, more transparent expulsion system, Collegiate Academies' new schools had among the city's highest expulsion rates, leading to at least one civil rights complaint, though no judgment.[298]

Sarah Carr referred to "careless disregard" in describing the case of the Frederick Douglass takeover. That disregard for both children and the truth was still on display in 2015 at the tenth-anniversary conference hosted by the Education Research Alliance when Paul Vallas returned to New Orleans and boasted that only 7 percent of the city's students attended failing schools, down from 62 percent before Katrina, a feat accomplished "with no displacement of children."[299]

A decade after Hurricane Katrina, among open-admissions RSD schools there were still no "A"-rated schools, and about 40 percent of RSD schools were graded "D," "F," or "T"—the schools that are so bad they have been taken over by a new charter operator.[300]

The local charter establishment had presented the takeover of the city's schools as a binary choice—the mismanagement and corruption of the old OPSB of the pre-Katrina years or the shiny, efficient, technocratic charter schools run by mostly white out-of-towners and funded by white, mostly out-of-town money and muscle.

The city's education technocrats took an idea that was meant to foster grassroots teacher- and parent-led schools—a laudable goal—and made it part of a national crusade. It is a crusade led by far-flung CMOs and funded by deep-pocketed interests whose aims are as much financial and ideological—transforming school districts into "portfolio" districts, submitting them to the rigors of competition, and freeing them from the evils of collective bargaining—as educational. In their haste to put up schools like so many tract houses, they seized on a one-size-fits-all model featuring no-excuses discipline, replaceable teachers, and narrow test-prep curricula. They built schools to which, ten years after the experiment began, the vast majority of CMO leaders, funders, and teachers—the rare ones who found time to start families while working grueling charter school hours—still virtually never sent their own children.

They introduced new terminology—creaming, counseling out, cherry picking, and got-to-go lists—that have no place in open-enrollment public schools.

They paid lip service to the idea of community, but rarely made good on the promise. In a stunning example of how far the ideals of community involvement have receded in New Orleans, in 2016 the Lycée Français became the first charter in the city to *explicitly ban* both parents and grandparents from serving on its school board.[301] In New Orleans, school boards are typically selected from a central pool of volunteers who often have little connection to individual schools.

In the process, too often, they ran roughshod over the city's most traumatized and vulnerable children.

During the ERA's tenth-anniversary conference in 2015, Michael Stone, then the chief of NSNO, in a display of humility remarkable for how rare it is in the industry, conceded how far the New Orleans charter experiment still has to go to address the inequities of the system. He said:

- *On cherry picking:* "This is a real issue you have to deal with in a decentralized system . . . how do you make sure schools aren't just willy-nilly excluding kids and doing it in soft ways and hard ways." Stone suggested that the new centralized enrollment system, OneApp, held the answer to solving that problem.
- *On "access" to the "best" schools:* "This is a real problem, it's an information problem for families that are the lowest-income families. In part it's a problem because we have seven or eight or nine 'A' schools, a number of them are charter schools that are part of OPSB, that refuse to participate in the open-enrollment process." Actually, every "A" school in New Orleans for the past decade has been a selective-admission OPSB school. Stone goes on to concede that "until every school is participating in [the central enrollment] process, we aren't really providing access to every family."
- *Also on access:* By law, "every school is required to provide transportation," but not all OPSB schools provide busing. And many ask for fees, "even though they're charter schools and technically public schools."
- *On the test-score gains of New Orleans charters:* "We have to be careful because we're trumpeting these gains that are getting us to the state average for a state that's forty-ninth in the country. . . . What we call mastery everyone else calls proficient—and we're only at 18 percent" proficient.[302]

Yet Stone's comments on how NSNO and the city's charters were tackling the special-education challenge belied the earnest humility suggested by his earlier remarks. In the near future, he explained, "what we hope is that when we look back at the last three years we'll see the impact of a huge effort around opportunities for special education." NSNO, he explained, had for the first time "invested $5 million in creating supports for special education coordinators to help them do their jobs better, to build out high-quality programs. . . . This is all initiated by charters saying 'yes, our responsibility is to take care of all these kids.'"[303]

No mention of the SPLC consent decree. It was as though, convicted of a crime and sentenced to community service, Stone was congratulating himself for meeting the demands of the court.

New Orleans's special-education problem wasn't just about charter schools' not being *willing* to accept special-needs kids—though there was plenty of that too. The city's mishandling of this matter raised fundamental questions of whether an all-charter system of independent LEAs (local education agencies)—essentially each school an island unto itself, required to meet all the needs of its students—was sustainable in the long run. As the New Orleans experiment loses its novelty and as the general supply of philanthropic dollars inevitably dwindles, where will a single school or even a small CMO find the resources, year after year, to serve all the special needs in a community?

Part of that answer might be found in the new "return" legislation. As the charter revolution begins its second decade, the Louisiana State Legislature voted, in 2016, to move the RSD schools back to the jurisdiction of the OPSB—though the independent charter "mini-kingdoms"—the CMOs—will retain their autonomy. How that will work, no one knows. Under the law, the OPSB will retain, primarily, the power to grant and revoke charters, while the unelected charter boards will continue to control curriculum, contracts, and personnel decisions. The OPSB supported an alternative bill sponsored by Rep. Joseph Bouie that would have vested the OPSB with greater oversight authority. Some local educators assume that the "return" won't impinge on the independence of charters. Others believe that in giving the OPSB the power to determine the terms under which it will grant and revoke charters, the board will regain some of its earlier powers.[304]

A perpetual question is what the OPSB, so troubled in the years before Katrina, will do with its power to oversee the schools and clamp down on abuses. And what of the few efforts—like a centralized expulsion system—that were developed by the RSD? Will those "expertise" and systems disappear with the RSD, or will they be transferred in some fashion to the OPSB?

Back at Sci Academy, the school remained, as of 2015, a year before the "return legislation, one of only eight "B" schools in the RSD (though it had slipped to a "C" rating in 2014). Sci Academy also says it is moving in a more progressive direction, "towards projects, creativity, dialogue." Even the red lines are said to be gone.[305]

Eddie Barnes, who had been a star at Sci in its 2012 graduating class, spent a year and a half at Middlebury College. In February 2014, his sophomore year, Eddie dropped out.

The reasons are complicated. There was the homesickness and culture shock, the vast physical distance between rural Vermont and New Orleans, the alien food, the snow—weeks and weeks of it—and having to trudge to an 8 a.m. psychology class through the cold and wet.[306]

There were the academic challenges. At college, Eddie discovered, and became fascinated by, the Russian language and Russian literature, but he dropped at least one course because it was too hard. At Sci Academy, the teachers had helped him with time management, but at Middlebury he was "surprised"—and unprepared for—how much free time he had. Eddie eventually took a time-management class at the Middlebury library.[307]

There were also financial difficulties. He was a finalist for a POSSE Foundation scholarship, but ended up with a full academic scholarship from Middlebury. Yet, with incidental expenses, Eddie ran up $2,000 to $2,500 in college debt.[308]

And there was the pull of family. When his mother was scheduled for knee surgery, Eddie felt that, as the oldest child and with three younger brothers still at home, he needed to return to New Orleans. By then, Eddie also had a young son at home.[309]

Back in New Orleans, Eddie has worked as a valet at a parking garage and was recently promoted to a doorman position at the St. Christopher Hotel, an elegant boutique hotel on Magazine Street where the tips are said to be good. (Eddie demurs when asked about his income.)[310]

He also hopes to return to college, and has set his sights on Southern University at New Orleans or the University of New Orleans. But, so far, his college debt has been a deterrent.[311]

Meanwhile, Eddie's younger brother J'Remi inherited his brother's and his mother's aspirations and is now in college, hoping to avoid the obstacles that derailed Eddie. In 2015, he too graduated from Sci Academy near the top of his class. J'Remi got a POSSE scholarship and, after carefully weighing his options, decided to attend the prestigious Grinnell College in Iowa. J'Remi also applied for and received additional grants to help cover his living expenses. Travel to Iowa is a lot easier than to Vermont; the family has already driven to Iowa a few times to see J'Remi.[312]

To be sure, Iowa also led to culture shock. "Going from crawfish to corn is not ideal," he says. Then, too, he no longer enjoys Sci's close monitoring of his work and study habits. In college, he adds, "It's on you."[313]

But J'Remi has enjoyed a more robust college-support network. The POSSE organization keeps tabs on him, as does his Sci Academy adviser, Jon Bogard. J'Remi also can turn to family friends in Cedar Rapids.[314]

Anya Barnes is now thinking about moving the family to Atlanta. But if she stays in New Orleans, she plans to move her youngest sons, Arnold and J'Miri, to Sci Academy.[315]

Lawrence Melrose remains incarcerated for an armed robbery in the French Quarter, a murky incident involving a forty-year-old man who had just left a bar when he happened upon Lawrence and a friend. Lawrence was accused of pulling a gun and driving off with the man's car, while his buddy got off "scot-free." Lawrence's uncle Shelton Joseph, who says he often had trouble reaching Lawrence's court-appointed lawyer, was convinced that Lawrence should take his chances on a trial.[316]

Instead, Lawrence, alone in Orleans Parish Prison—Joseph had severe health problems and went long stretches without seeing him—took a deal: ten years in state penitentiary for a crime committed when he was seventeen, one that resulted in injury to no one.[317]

Sometime between 2016 and 2017, Lawrence was transferred to David Ward Correctional Center in Homer, Louisiana, which had recently become the subject of a federal lawsuit charging abuse of mentally ill inmates. According to Joseph, Lawrence had neither graduated from high school nor received the mental-health services he needed in prison. Having gotten into at least one prison fight, his uncle doubts that Lawrence's sentence will be reduced.[318]

Trevon, meanwhile, is believed to have dropped out of Southern University of New Orleans and was seen, most recently, working in a coffee shop on Magazine Street. Sci Academy has lost touch with him.[319]

As for Leona Tate, she has created the Leona Tate Foundation for Change and is working to transform the abandoned McDonogh 19 building into a "civil rights museum" and education center so that "no one will forget." That's surely something New Orleans could use.

John Kuhn, superintendent of the Perrin-Whitt School District in Texas, recently identified a host of publications that are seeking to write the history of charter school success, including *Education Next*, Edexcellence.net, and *The 74*, which in 2016 published *The Founders: Inside the Revolution to Invent (and Reinvent) America's Best Charter Schools*, a hagiography of the movement.[320]

But it is also important to envision the history that never was: a post-Katrina rebuilding—even one premised on a sizable charter sector, albeit with better oversight and coordination of vital services like those for special-needs students—that sought to engage the community in a way that would have helped preserve, even enhance, its stake in their children's education. What if, instead of raising the performance scores so as to lasso the vast majority of New Orleans charters into the RSD, the city had taken control of the worst schools while encouraging community groups like MLK and Morris Jeff to lead by example. What if it had made a concerted effort to enlist dedicated, respected educators and involved citizens and parents—people like

Hicks and Sanders, Weishaupt and Bagert, Harper Royal and Bigard—in the school-design and chartering process?

What if New Orleans had offered a broad range of charter school choices for its poorest students—ones that sought to nurture creativity and a love of learning and to foster restorative justice in lieu of harsh discipline. What if New Orleans had embraced a robust technical-education option from the beginning so that kids with low ACT scores did not have to go into debt to attend community colleges from which they stood little chance of graduating? And what if, instead of being the exceptions, schools like MLK and Morris Jeff had been the rule?

This chapter was made possible with funding from the Investigative Fund at the Nation Institute and from the New World Foundation's Civic Opportunities Initiative Network.

CONCLUSION

A Civic Action: How Schools—and Society—Benefit from Real Democracy

In November 2016, America shocked the nation and the world by electing Donald Trump as president of the United States. The selection of a man whose candidacy, at least initially, was very likely an extension of his reality TV persona and a bad-boy publicity stunt for the Trump brand became, instead, a frightening symbol of the state of American culture and civic life. To be sure, Hillary Clinton won the popular vote. There was also the misogyny against Clinton; the dirty tricks of FBI director James Comey (though his reputation benefited from his firing by Trump) and the hacking of Russia's Vladimir Putin, both of whom helped undermine Clinton's candidacy. And there was the "largely uncritical and mostly unmediated" media coverage Trump received—worth an estimated *$1.9 billion*, six times the value of the coverage of Ted Cruz, who was the number-two G.O.P. candidate with the most free media, and *ten times* as much as Clinton; as well as latent white rage over Barack Obama's presidency. These factors all provided, in the topsy-turvy rationale of the 2016 election, a perverse logic for the selection of a man whose campaign was fueled by hate and racism.[1]

Yet the election of this larger-than-life Chucky demagogue, with his multiple bankruptcies and divorces, his sexual predations and business malfeasance, his hate-filled speeches and tweets, also represented a failure of corporate-style education reform as it has taken shape over more than twenty years. Among an electorate that often favors "ordinary" people they can identify with, Trump, the consummate philistine—unread and uninterested, crude, unthinking, and disdainful of facts and any attempt at rational truth—holds up a dystopian mirror of the electorate.

A president who declared his love for the uneducated, his base, and who not only derided, but seems ignorant of, key tenets of our constitutional democracy, including the rights of minorities, checks and balances, and freedom of press and of religion, likely has little interest in making American education more robust or our democracy more, well, democratic. Nor does the G.O.P. leadership, which has enabled the Trump presidency and, as one conservative commentator has conceded: "imported the spirit of thuggery, crookedness and dictatorship into the very core of the American state."[2]

Corporate education reformers cannot be directly blamed for the ascendance of Trump. However, over two decades of an ed-reform apparatus that has emphasized the production of math and ELA test scores over civics and learning for learning's sake has helped produce an electorate that is ignorant of constitutional democracy and thus is more vulnerable to demagoguery.

This book has argued that continuous improvement is a must for public education, especially in an advanced technological age. It has shown that schools can learn from the philosophy of systems thinkers and the grassroots participative ideas associated with the open-source software movement and the most successful twenty-first-century business practices—ideas that share traits with some "radical" political movements such as SNCC. And it endorses the idea that schools offer an arena for practicing and learning about democratic governance.

But the examples in this book—New York's progressive movement, the Massachusetts education reforms, the Demingite district of Leander, Texas, and educator-led experiments among myriad public schools and some charters—are swimming against the powerful currents of the mainstream education-reform movement. As of this writing, Trump has named Betsy DeVos, a philanthropist and crusader for charter schools, vouchers, and deregulation, as his secretary of education. DeVos's extreme positions, including support for funding religious schools via vouchers and the deregulation of even for-profit charters, have put mainstream reformers in an ideological bind. Thus, Shavar Jeffries, the head of Democrats for Education Reform, a leading ed-reform organization backed by hedge-fund operators and other philanthro-capitalists, declared, in the wake of Trump's election, that no Democrat should accept a Trump appointment, because doing so would make them "an agent for an agenda that both contradicts progressive values and threatens grave harm to our nation's most vulnerable kids." Yet, following DeVos's appointment, Jeffries congratulated Trump's education nominee and applauded "Mrs. DeVos's commitment to growing the number of high-quality public charter schools," making no mention of her support for vouchers.[3]

Jeffries's about-face is not surprising given the ties between DeVos and DFER, which has received at least $145,000 (via its 501(c)(3) nonprofit, Education Reform Now) in funding from American Federation for Children (AFC), a DeVos lobbying nonprofit (501(c)(4)).[4] But it also underscores how little daylight there is between Democratic "reformers" and those on the far right like DeVos, as well as the corrupting influence of big-money donors.

The rise of Trump marks an inflection point for public education and the mainstream education-reform movement. While the bulk of education funding comes from state and local governments, the education-reform era has demonstrated how influential federal policy and incentives can be; seven years after the start of the Great Recession, thirty-one states were still providing less state funding per student than they had during the 2008 school year—and half of those states suffered double-digit cuts. That's a key reason Race to the Top grants—with their controversial (and dubious) incentives for test-based teacher evaluations, performance pay, privatization, and the Common Core—held such allure.[5]

The chaos that is likely to be unleashed as the Trump administration seeks to make public education ever more fertile ground for privatization, freed from the constraints of oversight, will, no doubt, help lay waste to school budgets—and entire schools—across the country as "money follows each child." Given the hard-right turn the country has taken, it is likely—should our democracy survive in its current form—that the pendulum will swing leftward again and create a friendlier climate for public education. And, as the progressives discovered in New York City during the fiscal crisis of the 1970s, chaos may create pockets of opportunity for educators and policymakers savvy enough to exploit the cracks in the cheap asphalt of Trump's educational constructions. For educators and policymakers interested in creating a robust post-Trump public school system, this book offers a template for a more collaborative, generative approach to school improvement—one based on the solid edifice of systems thinkers like W. Edwards Deming and the experience of educators who have embraced a philosophy of continuous improvement.

As this book winds to a close, it is important to underscore that K–12 education in the twenty-first century cannot be framed as a battle between preparing young people for a competitive global marketplace, on the one hand, versus a democratic society, on the other. That's a false dichotomy; schools must do both.

It's also useful to review the foundation on which the modern "accountability-based" education-reform movement has been built—and against which many of the examples in this book have struggled. Rather than nurturing American citizens capable of creatively navigating a global economy, schools have become factories for test-score production and rote learning. Since the administration of George W. Bush, accountability has been based on top-down mandates, fear, and testing. Decades of business-minded reforms have resulted in a shrunken education vision that focuses on the utilitarian demands of the marketplace, accountability via a dizzying area of low-quality tests, and education goals that stray far from the lofty aims envisioned by John Adams's conception of an educated populace. At the same time, the education reformers have ignored the most important business lessons about how systems work and the ecosystems needed to foster a culture of organizational improvement.

There's nothing wrong with accountability itself—accountability to children, parents, and community—nor with public transparency. Nor is there anything wrong with assessments that measure student learning, as long as there's a direct feedback loop to improvement and as long as fear doesn't distort the mission of the test. Pasi Sahlberg, the much-heralded Finnish educator, has extolled the virtues of small data, including "students' self-assessments, teachers' notes, external school surveys, and observations made of teaching and learning situations."[6] Finland even requires a battery of standardized tests—a high school exit exam that all students must take in order to graduate from high school.[7] Indeed, the entire quality movement was built on the importance of knowing which processes to measure and how to measure them, as well as understanding that the most important factors are, as Deming said, "unknown and unknowable."

But standardized testing can be a blunt instrument. And the folly of the modern testing regimes has been made manifest by the fact that a tsunami of tests—dozens over the course of each student's education—are used to rate children, teachers, and schools even though standardized tests are almost never used for the only legitimate purpose for regular testing—to help teachers improve their practice and better tailor lessons to the needs of students.

In a modern technological age, American schools that were built for an earlier industrial era, and especially in light of the challenges of the urban inner city, surely needed improvement. But instead of scouring the world for the best education practices, America embraced testing and the disruptions of the market. For business-minded Americans, tests have all the benefits of an easy-to-digest profit-and-loss statement. When scores go up, education is deemed to be improving; when scores go down, schools are labeled failures. But like quarterly earnings reports, tests have the nasty habit of distorting and manipulating production in order to generate the desired numbers. The absurdity of this outlook was underscored by one education reformer, an "accountability hawk," who recently took to task New York City's private schools, which are arguably among the best in the country, for not doing more testing. How are parents to know how much their children have actually learned, he asked? (Ironically, in recent years this education reformer has sought to temper his hawkish support of testing, saying recently that the nation is "increasingly hard-nosed" about accountability measures and "looking—probably too much—at test scores and graduation rates and such.")[8]

In fact, private-school parents have a pretty good idea of what their children have learned, but not because of the schools' near-perfect graduation rates or students' high SAT and ACT scores and admissions to the best colleges in the country. They know because they see what their children produce at science fairs, at dramatic productions, in their school essays, during dinner-table conversations in which they demonstrate the ability to hone opinions and arguments as well as their knowledge of world events.

HOW TEST SCORES WAGGED THE DOG

The groundwork for the nation's testing frenzy was laid, of course, in Texas, where George W. Bush was, until Trump's election, the last businessman president and, perhaps, the second-least-qualified president in the modern era. A mediocre student himself, Bush introduced an assessment regime that led to miraculous test-score growth in Texas, which helped propel him to the presidency. Even as Texas developed the testing regimes that would become a basis of No Child Left Behind, researchers were already uncovering the lie that was Bush's "Texas Miracle." Writes Anya Kamenetz, author of *The Test*, about what happened in Houston:

> 40 to 45 percent of African American and Latino students—those who failed any core course—were being held back in the ninth grade. . . . They could take sophomore classes, but they were officially reclassified as freshmen, meaning the lowest performers would sit out the tenth grade accountability test. Larger numbers of students were classified as English-language learners and/or special ed, exempting them from the tests as well. When it came to eleventh grade, the tactics got more insidious. The State of Texas eventually changed its reporting rules when evidence emerged that students were being "pushed out," advised to take the GED, then counted as transfer students rather than dropouts.[9]

The majority of high schools in Houston had, in fact, falsified their dropout rates.[10]

NCLB, meanwhile, "enshrined" the demand for high test scores via the "Adequate Yearly Progress" designation for evaluating schools. Then, the

Obama administration's Race to the Top initiative tightened the screws, "pushing states to tie their teacher evaluations to test scores. Administrators were expected to deliver extreme improvements, including an impossible mandate that every single student score proficient in reading and math by 2014. Schools that failed to make the grade could be—and were—shut down or taken over by private charter-school operators."[11]

The United States spent about $1.7 billion annually on standardized testing, according to a 2012 study by the Brookings Institution, much of it linked to the new Common Core State Standards.[12] But federal testing was just the tip of the iceberg. Standardized tests at the state and district levels have proliferated since NCLB. Students took as many as twenty standardized tests per year and an average of ten standardized tests in grades three through eight, according to a 2014 study by the Center for American Progress, which looked at urban and suburban districts in seven states. "[A] culture has arisen in some states and districts that places a premium on testing over learning," concludes the study, which also finds "some districts and states may be administering tests that are duplicative or unnecessary; they may also be requiring or encouraging significant amounts of test preparation."[13]

As fraudulent testing miracles abounded, they confirmed Campbell's Law that "the more any quantitative social indicator is used for social decision-making, the more subject it will be to corruption pressures and the more apt it will be to distort and corrupt the social processes it is intended to monitor." Policy makers ignored Deming's warning that real improvement requires organizations to "drive out fear" instead of fomenting it.[14]

There was Atlanta, where in 2015 educators were convicted and jailed in one of the nation's most high-profile cheating scandals. The Atlanta school superintendent, Betsy L. Hall, who died of cancer shortly before the verdict, had been accused of creating "a culture of fear, intimidation and retaliation" that had allowed "cheating—at all levels—to go unchecked for years."[15] (Readers might well ask why teachers were prosecuted and jailed under a federal racketeering statute meant for organized crime, while the financial executives responsible for the mortgage collapse that led to the Great Recession went largely untouched. But that's another book.)

In Philadelphia, several educators were charged with cheating after they told investigators that, "under 'intense' pressure to have their schools meet state standards, they changed answers on students' Pennsylvania System of School Assessment (PSSA) tests."[16]

New Orleans also experienced its share of testing shenanigans—though, as I noted in chapter 5, other problems in the Crescent City dwarf problems with cheating.

Meanwhile, in Washington, D.C., cheating allegations dogged the much-heralded Michelle A. Rhee. The broom-wielding edupreneur, who posed witch-like in her *Time* cover photo and who presaged Trump by firing an employee in front of the news media, perhaps represents, more than anyone but Success Academy's Eva Moskowitz, the test-or-else approach to education reform. The D.C. cheating allegations stemmed from at least three sources: a *USA Today* investigation of too-good-to-be-true test-score gains, a highly respected principal-turned-whistleblower, and a "long-buried" data analysis by Rhee's own data consultant, which found a raft of "'wrong to right' erasures" on the students' answer sheets, a red flag for "cheating by adults," in seventy D.C. districts.

Savvy educators knew the testing regimes were a game, but it took the bravest ones, like Adell Clothorne, a respected principal, to blow the whistle on the cheaters. Clothorne had been hired by Rhee to run D.C.'s Noyes Education Campus and to build on the test-score improvements of her predecessor, who had boasted miraculous gains, including 2008 math scores that showed 58 percent of students scoring proficient or above, up from just 10 percent in 2006. In the process, Noyes had earned a designation as a National Blue Ribbon School from the federal government, and Rhee had rewarded the school's teachers and its principal with cash incentives ranging from $8,000 to $10,000 for each of two straight years. During her tenure, Rhee had disbursed $1.5 million in such bonus payments.[17]

Clothorne herself was expected to further raise test scores or risk getting fired. But when Clothorne sat in on the school's classes at the beginning of her tenure, she didn't find "blue ribbon"–quality work; instead, she suspected that Noyes's test scores had been inflated by cheating because she "saw students who were struggling to read" and "a lack of instruction across the board" that didn't line up with the data she was given.[18]

The situation Clothorne described had the makings of a test-score pyramid scheme. Carrots and sticks (bonuses and firings) were used to "incentivize" principals to raise test scores. If the principal was successful, hosannas and promotion followed. A new principal was brought in to replace the departing hero principal and was similarly incentivized to raise test scores still further. Or else. The only way to do so—if the departing principal's baseline test scores were the result of cheating—was to keep cheating. Instead, Clothorne, who, working late one night, caught teachers changing test scores, blew the whistle.[19]

Rhee ultimately resigned; the cheating allegations were never fully investigated.[20] Rhee went on to found Students First, an organization dedicated to disseminating her test-or-else approach to holding teachers accountable and to breaking teachers unions. The organization was backed by the Broad and Walton foundations.[21] Rhee, however, once again moved on quickly, and Students First was merged with Can50, another national reform organization dedicated to "accountability."

Indeed, Rhee, who once asserted that "[n]obody makes a thirty-year or ten-year commitment to a single profession," exemplifies the dilettantish approach to education that is embedded in so many reform efforts.[22]

As bad as cheating are the districts and institutions that have turned test taking, not genuine educational achievement, into the primary goal of schooling. The testing mania at flagship New Orleans schools like Sci Academy, which has spent $1,000 per pupil on test prep, is just one obvious distortion. Test taking was demonstrably the focus for the Edison for-profit charter chain, which distilled the market-focused hopes of the education-reform movement until the experiment withered. Consider the performance of students at Edison-run schools in Philadelphia—Edison's single largest client until the city terminated its contract in 2008—where the company ran twenty-two schools at its peak. An analysis of Edison's Philadelphia test scores showed that students performed much better on reading and math assessments, which determined schools' annual yearly progress, than they did on writing and science, which Pennsylvania began testing in 2006, but which did not carry high-stakes consequences.

"If reading scores exceeded writing scores—and math scores exceeded science scores—for Edison's schools in Philadelphia to a greater degree than they did for other schools in the district with similar student demographics, then it is fair to consider the distinction as evidence of the implicit danger of privatizing a complex service like education: the provider has every reason to concentrate on prominent metrics and otherwise shortchange the customer," hypothesized Samuel Abrams in *Education and the Commercial Mindset*.[23]

Indeed, while the average proficiency rates for reading were comparable between Philadelphia public schools and Edison schools with similar demographics, Edison writing scores were *far inferior* to its reading scores, as well as the writing scores of Philadelphia public schools.[24]

The Edison project was a disaster for investors, for the cities where it operated, and for its students. Yet it is also noteworthy for the army of education reformers who seized on the experiment as the future of a market-based makeover for public education.

The unvarnished (or unerased) reality is that, after decades of evermore intensive standardized testing, the performance of U.S. students on international comparison tests like the PISA has not changed.[25] And while the NAEP scores of black and Latino students have edged up since 1971 (though they have yet to reach parity with their white classmates, and in many cases the gap has remained stubbornly fixed between 2008 and 2012), the aggregated scores of all seventeen-year-olds haven't budged in the close to forty years leading up to 2012.[26]

Diane Ravitch, the noted education historian and, most recently, crusader against corporate-style education reform, has long argued that the United States has always performed poorly on international tests and that doing so has not hurt the country's economic standing. Mediocre performance on international tests, however, is nothing to crow about. Indeed, in a shrinking global world, some countries arguably are catching up to—if not surpassing—the United States in their economic output and standard of living.[27]

Ravitch is certainly correct that income inequality and segregation are largely responsible for the country's relatively poor performance on international tests. The United States has among the greatest income disparities of any industrialized nation—disparities that also are reflected in how public schools are funded; and while white and Asian students score at or above the OECD average, black and Latino students do significantly worse.[28] Indeed, perhaps the most important recent trend in American public education is that the number of students attending "high poverty" schools where 75 to 100 percent of the students are black or Latino has soared from 10 percent to 17 percent between 2000 and 2014; meanwhile, the number of students in "low poverty" schools where no more than 25 percent of the students are black or Latino has plunged from 33 percent to 17 percent.[29]

But there is also reason to fear that testing mania has dumbed down education in key respects and that the education-reform cure—accountability via a diet full of high-stakes testing—has been worse than the disease. Certainly, untested subjects like science and social studies, especially in elementary schools, have been given short shrift. Meanwhile, the reformers' insistence on college-for-all and producing test scores that can get even the weakest students into college—any college—has resulted in the neglect of robust vocational alternatives, which have been a source of well-paying jobs in countries like Germany. The decline in vocational opportunities, in turn, has been aided by the disappearance of unions, which long provided important vocational training.

By 2014, even the most ardent proponents of accountability via standardized testing were having second thoughts. "I believe testing issues today are sucking the oxygen out of the room in a lot of schools," blogged Secretary of Education Arne Duncan in August 2014. And in New York State, where some districts had developed tests solely for the purpose of evaluating teachers, John King, then New York's education commissioner, who would soon succeed Duncan at the Department of Education, offered incentives for districts to pare down the number of tests they gave.[30] Meanwhile, parents across the ideological spectrum were joining the opt-out movement, rebelling against Common Core testing, which had spawned the latest high-stakes testing regimes.

Yet up to the present day, education reformers have used accountability-by-test-score to take over the poorest public schools and replace them with charters that often serve a different population of students (less poor and less needy) and are, ironically, often far less accountable than public schools. Take Success Academy, with its much-vaunted elementary-school test scores. Of the seventy-three students who began at Success Academy Harlem I as first graders, only seventeen would be part of the CMO's first graduating class in spring 2018; four-fifths of the class had disappeared in the intervening years.[31] How many changed schools voluntarily? How many were forced out? No one knows.

Even a charter proponent like Richard Whitmire, author of *The Founders*, a charter hagiography, concedes that there is no "apples to apples" comparison between traditional public schools and CMOs, such as Success Academies. Writes Whitmire: "People, and I have been guilty of this, have compared Success' scores to traditional public schools and they're apples and oranges. . . . It would be totally unfair to compare Success to a traditional New York public school that's in the same building because Success doesn't fill up its classes. It doesn't backfill after fourth grade. There's no apples to apples there."[32]

BETSY DEVOS'S CHOICE

If Michigan, the home state of Betsy DeVos, Trump's education secretary, is any guide, market distortions in K–12 education are likely to proliferate. Michigan has become a case study for what may be the nation's most disastrous reform strategy, and much of that failure can be traced directly to DeVos.

Both Michigan and Massachusetts passed education-reform laws in 1993. The historic Massachusetts legislation helped propel—and keep—the Bay State at number one in the nation, based on NAEP scores. The Michigan law was, by contrast, epic in its failure: more than twenty years after its passage, Michigan ranks in the bottom third of the country on fourth-grade reading and ELA and eighth-grade math. While Michigan's NAEP scores on every test outperformed the national average as recently as 1998, by 2015, the state lagged the nation in every test except eighth-grade reading, where its performance equaled the national average.[33]

In June 2016, the *New York Times* published a scathing investigation of Detroit schools, which found the city with "lots of choice," but "no good choice." The article by Kate Zernike concluded: "Michigan leapt at the promise of charter schools 23 years ago, betting big that choice and competition would improve public schools. It got competition, and chaos." Shortly before the 2016 election, John King, newly ensconced as Obama's secretary of education and himself an ardent charter supporter, conceded: "There are a lot of schools that are doing poorly and charter authorizers do not seem to be taking the necessary actions to either improve performance or close those underperforming charters."[34]

Much of the problem can be laid directly at the feet of DeVos and her husband, Dick, who played a key role in the passage of Michigan's 1993 charter school law and who have worked, ever since, to protect charters from additional regulation. The DeVos money and influence is "one reason that Michigan's charter sector is among the least regulated in the country," despite the fact that about 80 percent of the state's charters are run by private companies, "far more than in any other state."[35] Notes *Politico*:

> All told, the DeVoses have contributed at least $7 million to lawmakers and the state Republican Party in recent years, and their influence can be seen in just about every major piece of education-related legislation in Michigan since the 1990s. That includes the 1993 law that permitted charters in the state and a 2011 vote to lift a cap on the number of charter schools in the state.
>
> Michigan permits practices barred by some other states, such as for-profit charter operators, virtual charter schools and multiple charter-authorizing bodies. Along the way, fraud and waste has been a problem.[36]

In March 2016, the problems of Detroit charters attracted the attention of the state senate, which voted for additional oversight and quality control under a plan "endorsed and promoted" by Republican governor Rick Snyder. DeVos backed some additional accountability efforts, including a measure requiring automatic closure of charters that ranked in the bottom 5 percent of schools for three consecutive years.

But something happened when the senate bill moved to the state house of representatives. Lawmakers "gutted" the new oversight rules. Notes the *Detroit Free Press*: when the bill was returned to the senate, it "preserved the free-for-all charter environment that has locked Detroit in an educational morass for two decades. After less than a week of debate, the senate caved.[37] Even then, several legislators complained that the influence of lobbyists, principally charter school lobbyists, was overwhelming substantive debate. The effort was intense, they said, and unrelenting."

And the source of this unrelenting push for continued deregulation was the DeVos family. Just days after the Michigan senate bill was gutted, "several members of the DeVos family made maximum allowable contributions to the Michigan Republican party, a total of roughly $180,000.

"The next day, DeVos family members made another $475,000 in contributions to the party.

"It was the beginning of a spending spree that would swell to $1.45 million in contributions to the party and to individual candidates by the end of July, according to an analysis by the Michigan Campaign Finance Network."[38]

Many of the nation's charter advocates choose to view cases like Michigan's as the bug in an otherwise well-functioning charter project. But the selection of DeVos, and the havoc wreaked in Michigan education, demonstrates that the bug is, in fact, the system, and likely to become ever more so. The DeVos ideology of unfettered competition of schools and of authorizers, with virtually no regulation, is a logical extension of both a system in which private operators are handed public moneys with little or no oversight and the assumption—stated or unspoken—that the invisible hand will regulate the market.

By contrast, it's worth noting that where states have made consistent efforts to increase funding of the poorest school districts and have invested in proven pedagogical strategies, such as preschool, student achievement has increased—as measured by NAEP scores and graduation rates. New Jersey, for example, where a controversial series of judicial rulings, beginning in 1990—the so-called Abbott decisions—resulted in significant increases in public school spending, is now, Linda Darling-Hammond argues, "the highest-achieving state in the U.S. if student demographics are taken into account." (With 45 percent minority students, New Jersey has far more non-white students than Massachusetts.)[39]

DeVos could turn out to be the mainstream charter movement's worst nightmare. Just days after the 2016 election, Doug Harris, the leader of the Education Research Alliance in New Orleans, issued a devastating critique of DeVos: "As one of the architects of Detroit's charter school system, she is partly responsible for what even charter advocates acknowledge is the biggest school reform disaster in the country."[40]

Harris's op-ed suggests that Michigan and others could learn from New Orleans's track record. In fact, both New Orleans and Detroit have conducted massive social experiments without the testing, controls, and feedback that legitimate experiments require, and, in both cities, mostly white policymakers have conducted these social experiments on mostly black children. Indeed, fans of the New Orleans reforms have insisted from the beginning that these experiments emerged fully formed and beautiful, like Athena from the head of Zeus. In reality, it took a class-action lawsuit, local activism, and investigations by academics and journalists before New Orleans began to address the myriad problems in its charter system, including sky-high suspension rates, shortchanging special-needs students, blatant creaming (though subtle creaming continues), and lack of vocational opportunities, to name only a few. Meanwhile, opaque reporting at the state level by a pro-charter administration has made it impossible to confirm how many of the state's poorest and neediest students have been squeezed out of the city's charter system.

Seven months after Trump's election, policy analysts at the Manhattan Institute and the Center for Education Reform issued an extraordinary manifesto that amounted to an insider's attack on the charter industry using most of the anti-privatization arguments of charter school opponents. Exposing a growing rift in the school-privatization movement, the manifesto charges that charters have become cookie-cutter test-production mills that stifle innovation; that major charter school funders—the report singles out the Walton Family Foundation—"encourage" the industry to speak with "one voice" rather than offering "competing perspectives"; that the funders impose "top-down" uniform policies, such as "no excuses" discipline, while deliberately squeezing out "mom and pop" charters. The report even claims the New Orleans charter experiment has fallen victim to "creeping bureaucratization."[41]

Rather than serving as a clarion call for improved oversight, however, the manifesto calls for further massive deregulation of all education sectors (nonprofit and for-profit charters as well as private schools that receive vouchers). Winking at DeVos and the Trump administration, the study calls for greater "freedom" from regulation while conceding that the unregulated market it extols will result in more failing schools: "We accept that more freedom might mean that more schools fail than would in a more regulated environment, but we believe that failure is necessary for success."[42]

No one knows for sure what the impact will be if unregulated charter competition is allowed to proliferate under a Trump administration. Behavioral economics suggests that the results aren't likely to be pretty. Shopping for schools, after all, isn't the same as shopping for consumer goods; $150 wasted on brand-name sneakers is unlikely to have long-lasting consequences. And most major purchases offer far more information than charter schools do. Even shopping for a secondhand car, buyers can rely on *Blue Book* values and detailed ratings. And a clever consumer can always take a car for a test drive and drop it off at a trusted mechanic.

Samuel Abrams draws on the important work of behavioral economists Kenneth Arrow and Oliver Williamson to show that "information asymmetry" makes schools much more like medical services than consumer goods. "Because medical knowledge is so complicated, the information possessed by the physician as to the consequences and possibilities of treatment is necessarily very much greater than that of the patient, or at least so it is believed by both parties," writes Arrow. Thus, doctors are not expected to act like businesspeople.[43]

In other words, shopping for a school is like a patient with a back problem in search of the right medical treatment. The patient might benefit from expensive surgery, much less expensive physiotherapy, or just bed rest. But the patient—like the parent searching for a school—has only the most limited way to determine the right course of treatment and the best practitioner. At the end of the day, she must *trust* her doctor.

Taken to its logical extreme, a spate of unfettered and unregulated privatization unleashed by DeVos could see the proliferation of fly-by-night operators, the K–12 equivalent of predatory Trump Universities. It may even loosen the grip of the most lauded CMOs like KIPP, siphoning off students as advertising wars (funded by philanthropists and public dollars) lure kids to charters named after their favorite sports or rap stars, regardless of quality. (Agassi Prep in Las Vegas, which was founded by tennis star Andre Agassi, is one of the worst-performing schools in Nevada, yet Agassi has raised $300 million to open charters around the country. And SLAM, the Sports Leadership and Management charter school, was opened in Miami in 2013 by the rapper and self-described former drug dealer and drunk driver Pitbull.[44])

Such an unregulated free-for-all would further tarnish an industry that has recently suffered setbacks via the NAACP and both Massachusetts and Georgia voters, to name only a few. Dog-eat-dog competition, meanwhile, risks escalating the test-score wars and creating new incentives for cheating. In the process, they might suck what little oxygen is left from mom-and-pop charters such as New York City's Amber and New Orleans's Morris Jeff.

Public schools, which still educate over 85 percent of American kids, are likely, meanwhile, to suffer death by a thousand cuts. (Charter schools educate only about 5 percent of U.S. children, while private schools enroll about 10 percent.[45]) "Competition" from charters and vouchers is likely to continue siphoning off the highest-achieving students; inadequate and unpredictable budgets will careen up and down as school funding "follows each child"; and the resulting test-score declines will engender further attacks on public schools.

But first, schools will endure the unraveling of the most sweeping, top-down mandate of the last few years—the Common Core State Standards. A common curriculum may well be a laudable goal for the nation, and the Common Core was arguably an improvement over the standards in many—though not all—states. Yet in an America often divided along rigid red-state/blue-state lines, developing a single set of academic standards was, in all likelihood, doomed from the start—as it is hard to imagine states like Louisiana and Mississippi and Massachusetts and New York agreeing on a common curriculum via a democratic, collaborative process.

Indeed, the Common Core represents the last major example of education overreach and an ill-conceived testing regime imposed top-down by the money and influence of the Gates Foundation and President Obama's education department (with roots forged during the administration of George W. Bush).[46] The architects of the Common Core not only escalated the feeding frenzy of accountability via test scores, they also inadvertently served to *narrow* school curricula, dealing a death blow to untested subjects like civics and social studies. First, the new standards focused almost entirely on math and ELA—though not the teaching of literature. Second, the rush to build a new testing regime around the Common Core spurred nonsensical state policies, exemplified by New York State's rush to impose "Common Core–aligned" tests *before* either teacher training or curriculum were available for the new standards, creating a tsunami of new tests—some faux–Common Core, others for the sole purpose of rating teachers. In the process, John King, then the secretary of education for New York, and Governor Andrew Cuomo not only set both teachers and kids up for failure, they also added fuel to a growing backlash against state testing.

Worse, the ELA standards hurt kids by squeezing out the teaching of literature and overemphasizing nonfiction while at the same time giving social studies and science little time or attention. Theoretically, students could marshal their knowledge of nonfiction in classes like science and social studies. But because the test is all powerful and only ELA teacher evaluations were subject to the test, two things happened: ELA teachers felt they had to add nonfiction texts and reduce their teaching of fiction. The Common Core "makes it impossible for English teachers to construct a coherent literature curriculum," charged Sandra Stotsky, a professor emerita of education at the University of Arkansas in Fayetteville and an architect of the Massachusetts curriculum standards.[47]

Meanwhile, the teaching of nontested subjects like science and social studies were deemphasized or cut altogether, especially at the elementary school level.

CIVICS DISAPPEARS

It is difficult to draw a direct line between the gradual disappearance of civics and social studies and the election of Donald Trump. But the proliferation of fake news, the apparent inability of many Americans to distinguish between fake- and high-quality news sources, as well as the general ignorance of democratic traditions almost certainly made Americans more susceptible to Trump-like demagoguery.

Richard Kahlenberg and Clifford Janey, in a searing critique of civics curriculum, in the aftermath of the 2016 election opened their study for the Century Foundation with a useful reminder of the connection between education and democracy:

> [P]ublic education in the United States was also meant to instill a love of liberal democracy: a respect for the separation of powers, for a free press and free religious exercise, and for the rights of political minorities. In this way, demagogues who sought to undermine those institutions would themselves be suspect among voters. Educating common people was the answer to the oligarchs who said the average citizen could not be trusted to choose leaders wisely.[48]

There may be no greater story of political rivalry and friendship than that of Thomas Jefferson and John Adams; yet, despite their considerable disagreements over the role of the then-new federal government, the one thing they could agree on was the central role of education in a democracy. While Adams had helped father public education in Massachusetts, Jefferson tried, with limited success, to establish a public education system in Virginia. Writing a letter to Thaddeus Kosciusko, Jefferson stated his belief that "general education" was needed "to enable every man to judge for himself what will secure or endanger his freedom." Without such education, he continued, "no republic can maintain its strength."[49]

On the cusp of World War II and the fight against fascism, Franklin D. Roosevelt echoed those sentiments:

> Democracy cannot succeed unless those who express their choice are prepared to choose wisely. The real safeguard of democracy, therefore, is education. It has been well said that no system of government gives so much to the individual or exacts so much as a democracy. Upon our educational system must largely depend the perpetuity of those institutions upon which our freedom and our security rest. To prepare each citizen to choose wisely and to enable him to choose freely are paramount functions of the schools in a democracy.[50]

Al Shanker, the noted labor leader and son of immigrants, held that it is schools—public schools, to be specific—that are tasked with instilling the "common values and shared culture" that make us all Americans. Or as David E. Campbell wrote in a paper for the conservative American Enterprise Institute: "[P]ublic schools have been a leading institution for creating unum out of pluribus."[51]

Despite this rich history, the accountability era has stripped American education of social studies and civics. In 2010, the New York State Board of Regents eliminated the testing of social studies in grades five and eight as a "cost reduction" measure; the "culture wars" may also have played a role. Indeed, not long thereafter, New York embarked on a new round of test development, including a faux–Common Core test in advance of the actual Common Core test and, in New York City, *two* teacher-evaluation tests—the so-called MOSL and the baseline MOSL.[52] As of 2012, only twenty-one states required a civics exam, a "dramatic reduction" from the thirty-four states that conducted regular assessments on social studies subjects in 2001.[53] "We know from report after report that social studies is not being tested and is therefore not being taught," says Peggy Altoff, a social studies consultant for Colorado and a past president of the National Council for the Social Studies. "States may have strong standards, but without strong legislation to back the teaching of it, I don't think it's happening."[54]

Even NAEP has deemed social studies and civics to be expendable. In 2014, the NAEP governing board dropped fourth- and twelfth-grade civics and American history, beginning in 2014, even while it added a new computer-based technology and engineering literacy test in 2015.[55]

It would be a mistake to view the stripping of civics and social studies as merely an inadvertent consequence of budget cuts. The problem, as the *Washington Post*'s Valerie Strauss puts it, is "a system that favors a largely automated accounting of a narrow slice of students' capacity and then attaches huge consequences to that limited information."[56] Then, too, there is the contempt for small "d" democracy that is baked into the education-reform movement itself. Leading the way were John Chubb and Terry Moe, whose book *Politics, Markets and America's Schools* argued that "direct democratic control" over public education appears to be "incompatible with effective schooling."

Moe and Chubb's book became the bible of the privatization movement and, by proxy, of education reformers, even though it makes several clear arguments against testing and tying teacher evaluations to test scores and acknowledges the "real-world imperfections" of markets: "consumers may be too poorly informed to make choices that are truly in their best interests."[57]

But these shortcomings are nothing as compared with Moe and Chubb's arguments for why democratically controlled public schools *cannot* work. The most important characteristic of *effective* schools is "autonomy," argue Moe and Chubb. Yet public education "inhibits the emergence of effective organizations . . . because its institutions of democratic control function naturally to limit and undermine school autonomy."[58]

In fact, *grassroots* democratic decision making was instrumental in crafting the improvement strategies of the public schools, as well as the handful of charter schools, portrayed in this book.

Equally important, unwieldy bureaucracies, loss of teacher voice and influence, lack of responsiveness to students and parents, and counterproductive testing are the hallmarks of many charter-management organizations, especially those of the no-excuses variety, as well as the corporate education-reform movement.

Bureaucracy is, indeed, a problem, both via the ever-more dominant accountability regimes imposed at the state and federal levels, as well as those of large central education departments in cities like New York. However, it's also the case that the CMOs that have achieved the greatest fame—those in New Orleans and at Success Academy in New York City—are almost perfect examples of the problems reform proponents decry about *democratically controlled* public schools: they squelch teacher voice and professionalism and promote high teacher turnover. Their cookie-cutter no-excuses operations make a mockery of the promise of "market choice" and can hardly be considered broadly responsive to children or parents. Too often, in charter school–heavy areas, parents are invited to "choose" a school, but not to make any changes to said school—it's a take-it-or-leave-it proposition.

Meanwhile, competition for a limited pot of philanthropic funding has led both CMOs and the education-reform movement to promote the proliferation of standardized tests, which have further eviscerated teacher voice and professionalism as well as school autonomy.

Many education reformers see suburban schools as "lucky" and exceptional: "It is important to stress that the capacity of some public schools to develop reasonably healthy, effective organizations does not imply that all public schools can somehow do so. . . . They are more likely to be blessed with relatively homogenous, problem-free environments, and, when they are, their organizations should tend to benefit in all sorts of ways as a result."[59]

Thus, democratic control is for middle-class white suburban families, but *not* poor urban people of color. Maybe they are correct that democratic control is *easier* in relatively homogenous well-educated communities. However, what this book has shown is that from Bloomberg's New York to New Orleans, the elites who control the education-reform agenda have absorbed a deep distrust of democratic decision making both at the school-board level and in schools themselves.

Moe and Chubb, along with other backers of privatization and corporate-style education reform, completely ignore the successes of New York City's progressive movement, even though their book was published *three years after* Debbie Meier became the first educator to win the MacArthur prize for her work in urban schools and *two years after* Tony Alvarado became New York City school superintendent based largely on his work in District Four, with its focus on small autonomous schools. It's like disparaging the computer industry for its clunky design and technological incompatibilities in 1984 while ignoring the emergence of Apple.

Indeed, there are many more examples of public school successes that have been largely ignored, while flashy but short-lived corporate-style reform experiments have been heaped with accolades and cash. For example, the fly-by-night experiment in Newark, New Jersey, in which then mayor Cory Booker promised to leverage $100 million dollars of Mark Zuckerberg's money into a transformed school system, imposed from above, never went anywhere. Much of Zuckerberg's money was wasted on consultants; the consultants and the superintendent alienated parents; tenure rules were weakened, turning off teachers; and a focus on charter schools gave short shrift to public schools, which still educate the majority of kids in the city. Before the five years was up, Cory Booker rode the Newark reform narrative into the Senate (and Governor Chris Christie, Booker's partner in the reforms, moved on to the Trump campaign). Yet by that time, in Newark, "there was at least as much rancor as reform," contributing to the election of Ras Baraka, a former public school teacher and principal, as the next mayor, as well as the decision to return control to the schools from the state to the Newark school district.[60]

Amid all the turmoil in Newark, there had been a much less heralded, and more successful, reform alternative that had been quietly taking root not far away, for *more than twenty-five years*—the steady and systematic transformation of the Union City, New Jersey, public schools. Like Newark, Union City's public schools were once deemed in need of a state takeover. But Union City got a reprieve; and as David Kirp describes in his thoughtful book *Improbable Scholars*, the district pursued a deliberate, inclusive, and entirely homegrown approach to reform, rallying schools, rank-and-file teachers, and even parents in a grassroots effort at continuous improvement—one that benefited from increased funding. And the schools soon saw an increase in enrollment. In Union City, the number of eighth graders who passed the eighth-grade math test soared to 71 percent in 2008 from 42 percent in 1999.[61] The graduation rate at Union City High School, where 94 percent of kids are economically disadvantaged and 99 percent are minorities, was 87 percent in 2015.[62] (It's noteworthy that in the aftermath of the Newark debacle, Baraka has won widespread praise for his policies, including establishing "community schools," which provide onsite health care and social services, and for working with Christopher Cerf, who took over as Newark schools superintendent after the "tumultuous tenure" of his protégé Cami Anderson, one of the architects of Newark's reform strategy. Cerf has since resigned.)[63]

Contrary to education-reform dogma, the examples in this book suggest that *restoring* democracy, participative decision making, and the training needed to make both more effective can be a key to school improvement and to imbuing children—especially poor minority children—with the possibilities of citizenship and power in a democracy. A commitment to democratically led continuous improvement transformed largely poor urban areas—in Brockton and in New York City, for example—where schools were once failing.

Significantly, two studies conducted nearly fifty years apart suggest that, *especially for the neediest students*, education in civics plays a key role in increasing both knowledge of democratic institutions and civic engagement. A seminal study of civic education in 1965 found that while courses in civics didn't make much of an impact on white students, the "civics curriculum is an important source of political knowledge for Negroes and . . . appears in some cases to substitute for political information gathering in the media." More importantly, civics education *increased* the sense of agency felt by African American students—that is, the "political efficacy" or their sense of trust in government and their belief that they can understand and influence political outcomes. Although African American students at all levels of parental education felt less empowered than their white counterparts did, the authors note that "without the civics curriculum the gap would be even greater."[64]

More recently, a study by the conservative American Enterprise Institute of young people aged eighteen to twenty-four in the twenty-one states that gave a civics assessment in 2012 found that knowledge of civics increased among African Americans, Hispanics, and immigrants—and especially Hispanic immigrants—though not much among whites. (However, the AEI study did not find a link between voting or party affiliation and civics assessments.)[65]

Perhaps no one has expressed the importance of civics for the poor as well as Denise Dodson, the incarcerated woman who learns about the role of American government during a decades-long prison sentence, and to whom Anna Deavere Smith gives poignant voice in her latest play, *Notes from the Field*:

> I learned how the government works. Like I didn't—I never understood what was the governor for, or what is the mayor for. I don't get it. I don't understand. Understand that they are important people, but to what degree of importance, what are they there for. And I really never got that in my history classes. So to get that now, as a grown woman, is like—woah.
>
> Finding out what this world really all about, how it revolves, what's expected of you as a citizen . . .[66]

Indeed, Debbie Meier's dictum that a school should be "a community where kids could see the complexity of democracy, and fall in love with it"—has, in the Trump era, never been more important. Trump's triumph should serve as a "Sputnik moment" for both civics education and an expanded, more robust approach to democratic governance.[67]

Rather than accept, à la Moe and Chubb and the corporate reformers, that public school systems cannot be governed democratically, we must find ways to renew and strengthen a *positive* role for democratic governance in schools; give new voice to educators and provide the training they need to be effective participants in collaborative improvement strategies; and breathe new life into the teaching of civics.

Let us look at some of the key lessons learned from this quiet revolution.

The Massachusetts education reforms were the largest-scale, most-promising reforms in the country. They were based on restoring funding equity to the schools, including providing major cash infusions for the poorest schools—though that equity has eroded in recent years. The trade-off for extra funding was increased accountability and oversight based on both a robust curriculum crafted by educators and the MCAS exit exam, which also was periodically and systematically improved by educators. For Brockton High, the combination of extra funding and accountability—and also enough time to allow for meaningful and thoughtful change—provided an important spur for a demoralized faculty and resulted in the key cornerstone for its success: a highly local, collaboratively developed improvement strategy. In part because in the early 1990s Brockton was seen as a virtually lost cause, in part because a small cadre of educators took the initiative, the Brockton school bureaucracy gave Brockton High teachers leeway to see what they could do. And the teachers, spurred on by both the opportunity to reshape the school's destiny and the new impending exit exam, took extraordinary measures. The results were stunning.

Massachusetts, and Brockton in particular, demonstrates the key ingredients necessary for meaningful school reform, especially among the poorest districts:

- Teacher voice and local decision making that include both educators and the local community
- Equitable funding
- Strong leadership
- Development of a clear and widely embraced strategy for improvement—in Brockton's case, a comprehensive literacy strategy
- Accountability within a coherent framework and with room and time to innovate—though recent changes in the testing regime and increasing focus on test-based teacher evaluations have proven to be more of an impediment than an aid to improvement

This book has demonstrated that given leadership *and* grassroots democratic improvement efforts—and some protection from onerous bureaucratic requirements—school districts, indeed, an entire state, can rise to the challenge of educational innovation. New York City's progressive movement, both during the Debbie Meier/Tony Alvarado era and under the Bloomberg administration, demonstrated that school leaders who are inclined to lead collaboratively can achieve remarkable improvement across a range of indicators. A combination of extra funding and control over their budgets enabled principals like Chrystina Russell and, later, David Baiz at new small schools like Global Tech to emulate the innovative spirit of their progressive forebears and to offer students benefits often associated with the most-lauded charters, including an extended-day program through a partnership with Citizen Schools, as well as laptops for every child. Local collaboration and consensus building, leadership, extra funding, and a protective umbrella also helped transform the Julia Richman campus.

But the importance of constructive democratic collaboration cannot be overemphasized: even during the cash-strapped years of the New York City financial crisis, Debbie Meier and like-minded educators achieved more with less *because* they were given the space to maneuver and innovate.

There is no doubt that unions must be seen—and see themselves—as partners in improvement efforts. Many reforms were enabled by enlightened union leadership. *Significantly, however, at no point did unions prove to be a significant impediment to any of the reform efforts examined in this book.* In New York City's small schools, strong teacher–leaders led their schools collaboratively; the schools in this book thrived on collegial relationships. Even at Brockton, Sue Szachowicz, who sometimes battled the union and often chaffed against strict union rules, acknowledged that the union also served as an important resource. Equally important, in a world with fewer and fewer opportunities for democratic engagement, unions can provide an important opportunity for voice and grassroots decision making.

Throughout U.S. history, American industry has cultivated a confrontational relationship with organized labor even though some of the most enlightened thinkers—from Walter Reuther to Al Shanker—were union men. As Peter Drucker liked to say: if it hadn't been for the circumstances that had kept Reuther laboring in a factory instead of giving him a chance to go to college, he could have been president of GM instead of the head of its union. Wrote Drucker: "The corporation simply cannot afford to deprive itself of the intelligence, imagination and initiative of ninety per cent of the people who work for it, that is, the workers."[68]

Teacher professionalism and the intimate setting of the classroom demand a more collaborative approach to teachers unions.

Modeling constructive democratic decision making in both schools and school-district governance, is a must.

- Democracy is messy and time consuming. So increasing teacher and community voice will also mean providing funding for *grassroots-led* training of educators, school-board members, and communities in how to be active and productive participants in collaborative educational improvement. This almost certainly means combining, in some way, the continuous-improvement teachings of the quality movement, as defined by Deming, and the community organizing and training efforts of a Saul Alinsky or SNCC. Drawing on such diverse ideas would have the added benefit of cutting across political, philosophical, and racial traditions. Leander's approach to training, which was both *voluntary* and modeled by district management, was successful over the long term because it gave educators at all levels of the district useful, practical tools for collaboration and improvement and because it gave everyone in the district a common language for understanding the goals and principles of improvement. At the Julia Richman complex in New York City, training and consensus building have helped the facility maintain autonomy—and protection from bureaucratic meddling—in one of the city's most successful reform efforts.

- Providing robust training for school boards—both in the issues faced by schools and in continuous-improvement strategies—is also key. Local governance via school boards was vital to maintaining Leander's Deming-infused philosophy for over thirty years. At Brockton and in the grassroots fight against the 2016 charter referendum in Massachusetts, cohesive action by community groups, teachers, and families have kept democratic action in schools alive.
- Imbuing teachers' contracts with greater flexibility, as with New York City's so-called PROSE contracts (Progressive Redesign Opportunity Schools for Excellence) and the "thin contracts" used by some charter schools, would serve to foster greater collaboration among teachers' and administrators. It would also open opportunities for innovation and encourage teachers to become better problem solvers while also affording them the protection they need to act in the best interests of their students. The schools that encourage teacher voice, as seen in Leander, Brockton, and New York City, and as documented in Kahlenberg and Potter's *A Smarter Charter*, produce better, richer educational opportunities for children.[69] Today "it's imperative to be a union reformer," argues Adam Urbanski, the longtime teachers union leader and founder of the Teachers Union Reform Network (TURN). "As the experience of the private sector shows, you can't have a successful union in a failing enterprise. The way for a union to thrive is to

worry about the success of the enterprise as well as the success of the membership" and to devote as much time to its "professional work" as to "bread-and-butter" economic issues. In 2017 TURN ended its national organization, establishing instead a network of grassroots regional organizations; the aim—to develop chapters "within easy driving distance of every teacher in America."[70]

- It means greater efforts at both racial and economic integration so that children from diverse backgrounds interact, such as at schools like Julie Zuckerman's Castle Bridge school in New York City, a member of the progressive coalition, where 10 percent of the seats are reserved for children with an incarcerated parent and where outspoken (often middle-class) parents can model participation for (often poorer) parents who are hesitant to speak up.

Meanwhile, larger districts will have to find ways to keep large bureaucracies at bay. This may be the greatest challenge for educators. As noted in chapter 2, the best principals in New York City whipsawed between their admiration for and detestation of Bloomberg's education regime. But, ultimately, because he had never tried to make allies out of educators, Bloomberg's reforms unraveled as quickly as it took his successor, Bill de Blasio, to unpack his bags in Gracie Mansion. Had more of New York City's principals, as well as the teachers unions, rallied to defend some of Bloomberg's innovations, such as the network structure described in chapter 2, it would have been much harder for his successor to eliminate them.

The best schools need protection from giant vampire squid bureaucracies. Finding the right balance between oversight and protection is a key challenge, especially for large school districts, and is likely to depend on experimentation. Here are some ideas for providing public schools with the kind of cover for innovation that schools need.

- The *concept* of network structure, one both relatively independent of the education bureaucracy and accountable to the schools that selected the networks, showed promise in Bloomberg's New York. For a brief time, the networks served as an important support for principals and a check against the power of superintendents. And as Eric Nadelstern, former progressive educator turned right-hand man to Joel Klein, explained, the leaner network structure saved hundreds of thousands of dollars that could go directly to schools, not the bureaucracy.

Such a network structure would have an added advantage. The self-selecting nature of the networks could result in the creation of groups like the Empowerment Zone, in which strong schools with strong leaders gravitate together. Such networks could earn the right to free themselves from much bureaucratic oversight. This could have three benefits. First, it would free the bureaucracy to focus on the schools and networks that needed the most help. Second, it would create organic spaces for innovation, as well as incubators for fostering new education leaders—much the way Alvarado's District Two did; the new leaders, in turn, could help seed new schools much as Ann Cook had originally proposed to the Gates Foundation and Joel Klein. Third, nongeographic networks could help promote integration.

- Much more attention must be paid to culture—how to develop, reinforce, and protect it. Leander's three-decade effort to infuse an entire district of forty thousand students by planting metaphorical plugs of St. Augustine's grass and fostering a *voluntary* continuous-improvement culture—reinforced by hiring practices, Culture Day, trainings, improvement systems, and myriad other methods—surely deserves greater study. A similar focus on culture—small schools, teacher–leaders, collaboration, training, and improvement—suffused Alvarado's districts in New York City.
- While the Leander, Massachusetts, and New York City progressive movements shared a common regard for democratic principles, participative improvement, a commitment to training, and respect for teachers, they each have profoundly different cultures. Each developed its own model. There is no One Best Way.

Long-term efforts to increase democratic involvement are likely to depend on policies that reach far beyond school-district governance.

- It's time to recognize that the widespread disparagement of public institutions—and the increasing segregation of American society—has tracked the growing diversity of our electorate, making it more important than ever to reinvest in public institutions, especially public schools. As public schools have seen a sharp decline in white students and a rise in poor black and Latino students, too many Americans have asked *sotto voce*: "Why should *we* be paying for the education of *their* children?" California, where the majority of public school students are now Latino, represents a textbook example of the abandonment of public education. While the Golden State once boasted the best-funded schools in the nation, it now ranks forty-seventh. At the same time, California has more kids in charter schools than any other state; about a quarter of the students in Oakland and Los Angeles now attend charter schools, a circumstance that has contributed to the travails of public schools in those cities.[71]

Nikole Hannah-Jones won a MacArthur "genius" award in 2017 for "chronicling the demise of racial integration efforts and persistence of segregation in American society, particularly in education."[72] She reminds us:

> Early on, it was this investment in public institutions that set America apart from other countries. Public hospitals ensured that even the indigent received good medical care. . . . Public parks gave access to the great outdoors not just to the wealthy who could retreat to their country estates but to the masses in the nation's cities. Every state invested in public universities. Public schools became widespread in the 1800s . . . with the understanding that shuffling the wealthy and working class together (though not black Americans and other racial minorities) would create a common sense of citizenship and national identity, that it would tie together the fates of the haves and the have-nots and that doing so benefited the nation. A sense of the public good was a unifying force because it meant that the rich and the poor, the powerful and the meek, shared the spoils—as well as the burdens—of this messy democracy. . . . As black Americans became part of the public, white Americans began to pull away.[73]

This may be Trump's America for now, but no matter what his backers (particularly the G.O.P.) may wish, the country is not getting any whiter. The future depends on, once again, coming together.

- Similarly, the widespread demonization of unions—not just teachers unions—must end; a robust capitalist democracy requires the countervailing power of organized labor—in schools and beyond. Compared to many European countries, the United States has a history of exceptionally acrimonious management-labor relations, an antagonism that dates back to the late nineteenth century as well as the foundations of Taylorism. That even Democratic proponents of corporate-style education reform have backed antiunion policies is a sign of how embedded antilabor sentiments are in American culture. Although they represented a minority view in American industry, some of the country's greatest management thinkers, including Mary Parker-Follet, Chester Barnard, Deming, and Drucker, all recognized the importance of tapping the know-how of rank-and-file employees and developing a partnership, which can only be meaningful if the employees have the standing union membership provides. At the same time, the economic fluidity and uncertainty of globalism demand both a much more robust safety net and worker protections for America's capitalist democracy to flourish.

Restoring unions also would help resolve a serious gap in vocational education while at the same time helping to strengthen the middle class and civil society. "High school vocational programs were often aligned with organized labor: students learned a skill in the classroom and qualified for their union card, and went to work in a union shop," notes Peter Cappelli, of the Wharton School, in *Why Good People Can't Get Jobs*. Beyond economics, "unions were also once a primary vehicle for social cohesion and civic engagement. . . . Membership in a union brought with it a shared identity and sense of commitment."[74]

The precipitous drop in union membership from close to 28 percent in 1968 to just 11 percent in 2014 has corresponded with a comparable drop in middle-class incomes; during the same time period the percentage of income going to the middle class—the middle 60 percent of income earners—dropped to 46 percent from 53 percent. Apprenticeships, meanwhile, dropped by nearly a half to 288,000 between 2003 and 2013. Today the United States ranks dead last among OECD countries in the amount of vocational training offered in schools. The so-called skills gap, Cappelli explains, is largely a product of the decline in unionization and the failure of companies to pick up the slack; corporations, he points out, prefer to hire employees trained elsewhere, rather than to invest the time and money to develop their own training programs.[75]

- The creation of mandatory service—in a national service program or in the military—for every young person, after she completes high school, would not only "reinforce the idea of a mutual obligation" and common purpose, but serve as a vital glue for our diverse society. The abolition of the military draft and the creation of an all-volunteer army have "ended an institution that was effective at breaking down the divides of region, race, and class."[76]

Charter schools should return to their roots as vehicles of teacher-led innovation, not public school substitution.

One major problem with large CMOs is the inevitable edge they enjoy in grabbing ever larger slices of a finite pie of philanthropic funding, which only escalates the test-score arms race. This reality not only has helped sustain testing regimes that have sucked the joy and purpose out of learning, but also has marginalized neighborhood charters, which have met ever increasing demands for higher test scores by narrowing their own curricular offerings in a Sisyphean attempt to meet the test-score gains of mightier CMOs. Similarly, as in New Orleans, young men like Lawrence and Trevon are subjected to endless test prep in the misguided belief that everyone should, or can, attend college—another metric used by philanthropists to fund CMOs. (Only belatedly are charters beginning to address the nation's desperate need for vocational training.)

Here are some suggestions both for increasing diversity and innovation among charters and for reviving the role of the charter sector as a source of innovation, rather than as a fight-to-the-death zero-sum game:

- Reducing the total number of schools that any CMO can control in a single market would promote diversity among types of schools and reduce the clout of any single charter provider or charter model. Charter authorizers might require new charters to demonstrate that they are filling a pedagogical void—thus encouraging schools to experiment with different educational models and reducing the prevalence of no-excuses schools in the inner city.
- Authorizers should also work on developing richer accountability measures—a process that is likely to happen if testing as a whole is reduced.
- Parents who are happy with their charter schools will be loath to give them up. Yet policymakers must address the tipping-point problem and seek to assess the point at which a preponderance of charters begins to hurt public schools in the same neighborhood.

> So doing, they will have to either curtail the growth of charters, mitigate the disadvantages that open-admissions public schools face in poor neighborhoods with a large number of charters, or develop other policies that seek to prevent turning open-admissions public schools into dumping grounds for the hardest-to-teach children.

Policymakers should consider making an innovative civics project a high school exit requirement.

Modeling the practice of small "d" democracy is more important than ever. Imbuing children, especially poor minority kids, with a sense of civic purpose and possibility at a time when many states are imposing voter-registration rules that aim to keep their parents away from the ballot box will be difficult. But it is crucial. Notes TURN's Urbanski: "You cannot teach what you do not model."[77]

Educating young people for democratic citizenship is so important that education reformers might want to consider tackling its civics problem and the nation's penchant for test-prep with a novel solution: scrap most annual testing and replace it with a two-part civics project that students will need to complete in order to get a high school diploma. The first part might be a high-quality warts-and-all citizenship test that tests students' knowledge of the nation's founding fathers, institutions, and documents, as well as the darker side of our republic—*Dred Scott*, the long and oft-delayed fight for women's suffrage, Japanese internment camps, and so forth. Such a test should include graphs and charts of economic and political trends, as well as maps, that students must interpret, providing a test of their basic numeracy skills. In an ideal world, Part 1 would also include a news-and-how-to-use-it component that requires students to analyze and differentiate between "quality" news sources, opinion, and fake news. It should also include an essay component; this would have the benefit of testing the ability to read nonfiction and write.

If done right, such a robust civics test could have the added benefit of eliminating the need for much—if not all—other standardized testing.

The second, and equally important, part of the project should involve citizenship in action, with students required to undertake a rigorous, self-designed, collaborative civics project that would be evaluated by a team that included *local outsiders*—one that could demonstrate both civic engagement and the ability to produce a narrative explanation in written or multimedia form. Such a project should be evaluated by a panel of teachers from at least two or three schools, as well as local civic leaders ranging from lawyers and lawmakers to members of the nonprofit sector. The projects could be modeled on New York State's Performance Standards Consortium. Civics projects could run the gamut from West Side Collaborative's challenge-based assessments, such as the one based on the Pacific Trash Vortex, to the anti-bullying efforts at Leander ISD in Texas; the goal would be to encourage students to take on a meaningful effort at civic engagement—one that involves hands-on exploration and goal setting, but *not* rote learning.

Accountability needs to be radically rethought with a view toward educating young people who are ready to function in both the twenty-first century economy and as active citizens in a democracy.

Much damage has been done by the accountability movement, which must be curtailed. While unraveling the testing regimes may be difficult given our accountability-obsessed culture, at the very least, testing key subjects should be reduced to a maximum of two grades in K–8, with a high-quality MCAS-like test in high school. Less testing should mean higher-quality tests. And all tests—and the curricula they are based on—should be developed and improved upon by a diverse board of educators, including classroom teachers.

Diversity, divisions, and local pride will make it very unlikely that the Common Core will ever be successful across all fifty states—even without the backlash that followed the top-down imposition of the standards on the states. This is actually a good thing, for the Common Core was just one stab at creating One Best Way in education, and it is very likely as elusive a project as was Taylor's pursuit of an optimal scientific approach to manufacturing. By contrast, diverse efforts at educational improvement across the states might serve to develop a number of useful models and an opportunity for states to learn from one another. Thus, federal policy might be aimed at highlighting the most promising innovations.

Consider radically different arrangements for improving both schools and community services.

- Debbie Meier once suggested that new libraries should be embedded in public school buildings. A library-cum-school structure would create multiple benefits: it would avoid duplication—schools wouldn't need dedicated "school libraries" if the public library was downstairs, right next to the school's administrative offices or the gymnasium; the shared maintenance costs would benefit both schools and libraries; the library could provide a cost-effective, safe, and educational after-school space and, potentially, programming that both kids and working parents need; and it would revitalize the role of libraries in a community.

- Community schools, which emphasize bringing social services into schools and making public schools more of a community hub, are a similar idea.

At the dawn of the Internet age, during the advent of distributed processing and flat organizations, which helped unleash the power of collaborative networks of knowledge workers, education reformers reached back to a failed Taylorite model of reform. While the decidedly geeky systems thinkers and quality pioneers of the late twentieth century had painstakingly demonstrated that training and collaboration, as well as understanding processes, are the keys to engaging employees in continuous improvement, the reformers, in their rush to innovate now and think later, blamed teachers and imposed a reign of fear. In a harrowing echo of stopwatch-wielding factory inspectors with their bogeys and quotas, the twenty-first-century technocrats, led by Bush, Gates, and Duncan, made a fetish of data collection, testing, Value Added Measurement, and teacher rankings—many of them of dubious validity. Meanwhile, the new testing mania, combined with the push for privatization, transformed the inspiring idea of charter schools as laboratories for grassroots innovation into an industry dominated—at least in the inner city—by no-excuses CMOs run and financed by (mostly) well-meaning edupreneurs who would never choose such education for their own children.

The CMOs, in turn, sought to feed their appetite for philanthropic funding with a test-score arms race. Driven partly by free-market ideology and in part by contempt for low-wage educators, they have even sought to dismantle some of the most successful education reform efforts—such as those of Massachusetts and the progressive movement in New York City. And as income inequality grew nationwide, armies of nouveaux riches who knew next to nothing about K–12 education and, in most cases, had never seen the inside of a public school classroom declared their collective shock at the state of the nation's schools and poured ever more money and energy into the reform machine.

Civics and the idea that a love of learning must be nurtured like desert flowers were, at best, dismissed as quaint, outdated luxuries. Whatever the failings of the public school system, which were, in some places, considerable, children and educators suffered mightily under the new cure. And

America is now paying the piper, at least in part thanks to a two-decade-long guerrilla war that has further hollowed out public education—whatever its original shortcomings—and debased any notion of knowledge exploration for its own sake, as well as imposed—or reinforced, depending on the school or school district—a joyless utilitarian approach to schooling.

The pioneers of the quiet revolution stand out against this tide of opportunism and dilettantism. Importantly, they have not resisted change or declared public education to be without flaws or fault. Rather, they have sought to deepen professionalism among ordinary teachers, inspiring and harnessing their passion and know-how in pursuit of continuous improvement. And they have reached out to—and enlisted the help of—the broader school community. They have used meaningful training, collaboration, peer pressure, and old-fashioned leadership to build communities of like-minded and engaged educators. They have borrowed best practices wherever they can find them, including charter schools and even businesses. They have innovated. While most of these schools and districts continue to administer standardized tests—in most cases they have to—their leaders understand that test scores often say more about the system than about individual teachers; instead, they seek to devise assessments that will improve their practice. And they have petitioned for, and often found, protection from onerous mandates among enlightened policymakers and bureaucrats.

They also have cultivated unique school cultures that, even while they share a common philosophy of continuous improvement and democratic engagement, make each distinct from the other. Thus, the quiet revolution provides a useful template for improvement. However, it is also a reminder that real improvement is not quick and dirty, but rather comes from study, hard work, commitment, collaboration, and trial and error over the medium to long term.

One of the biggest challenges facing these innovators has been to strike the right balance between local democratic control and oversight by city, state, or federal governments. This is an ongoing project, but one well worth pursuing. Both the country and one of its greatest companies, General Motors, once thrived under just such a federalist system. While many of our institutions suffer from gridlock and dysfunction today, it is time to renew the struggle to regain the proper balance between central and local control, both in our government and in our schools.

Harvard's Jal Mehta notes that the systemic innovations that are most likely to improve schools, such as providing training to principals to become better instructional leaders, teacher residencies, and development of master teachers, "are probably things that would happen more at the state and sometimes the district level than at the federal level. All that is too complex to do as a one-size-fits-all."[78]

America has entered a dystopian dark age, one fueled by bigotry and a celebration of ignorance. Schools must become institutions of both deeper learning and constructive resistance. They must promote the love of knowledge and intellectual exploration over hate and philistinism. They must become practitioners of *both* continuous improvement and creative noncompliance. And they must relight the flame of democracy via classroom curricula and their governance structures.

Amid dark and stormy waters, the pioneers of the quiet revolution offer a beacon toward which schools, districts, and educators can—and must—steer their craft.

ACKNOWLEDGMENTS

I am very grateful to my agent, Jim Levine, and my editor, Tara Grove, who were willing to take a risk on this education book, as well as to Emily Albarillo, Brian Ulicky, and Sarah Swong at The New Press, who helped midwife this book. I'm also grateful to my many colleagues at Baruch College/CUNY—especially Josh Mills and my compatriots in the journalism department—who have always been supportive of my work, including this book. And thank you to Doug Muzzio for his counsel on all manner of subjects.

This project has been in the works, on and off, for over a decade. So I write these acknowledgments with trepidation and the near certainty that I will forget to recognize someone whose thoughts, advice, or contributions I will inadvertently omit. Nevertheless, I write with great appreciation to Jackie Pryce-Harvey, Chrystina Russell, David Baiz, and all the teachers at Global Tech who allowed me to sit in on their meetings and classes, beginning in 2010. Thank you to the Global Tech students, including Kaira, Franklin, Raven, Tabitha, and many others. Numerous other educators welcomed me into their schools and classrooms and patiently answered my questions, including Ann Cook, Herb Mack, Avram Barlowe, and the teachers and students at Urban Academy; Jeanne Rotunda and her colleagues at West Side Collaborative; Alisa Berger and Mary Moss and the faculty and students at the iSchool; Julie Zuckerman at the Castle Bridge School; Anna Allenbrooke and her colleagues at Brooklyn New School; Chris Aguirre and Jeanne Lavalle from City Polytechnic High School; and Rose Kerr, Mathew Valia, and Michael Parise at Civic Leadership school on Staten Island. Thank you to Joe Negron and the teachers at KIPP Infinity, as well as to Monique Bryan and her family. Thank you to Vasthi Acosta at the Amber charter school, as well as the many teachers at Citizens Schools, including Meg Lembo. Thank you also to Kaliris Salas-Ramirez and the parents at Central Park East.

I am also grateful for numerous education experts, writers, and others who helped me to refine my own thinking. Thank you to Kaiser Fung who helped me analyze the CREDO studies and to Art Kleiner whose assignments, thinking, and energy always served as an inspiration. Valerie Strauss's *Answer Sheet* has been an invaluable source of education news. Similarly, Diane Ravitch's blog has become an indispensable "pro-public education town square." Thank you to Debbie Meier. Thank you also to the folks at Teaching Matters, including Lynette Guastaferro, William Heller, and Nick Siewert, and to those at the NY Principals Leadership Academy, including Kathleen Nadurak and Irma Zardoya and their colleagues. Thanks to Jacqueline Ancess, Richard Barth, Sanaya Beckles, Julian Cohen, Rudy Crew, Beverly Donohue, Sy Fliegel, Beth Leif, Jim Lengel, Anthony Lombardi, Gene Longo, Steve Mancini, Nancy Mann, Eric Nadelstern, Susan Ochshorn, Susan Patrick, Stephen Phillips, Shael Polakow-Suransky, Sophie Sa, Pasi Sahlberg, Avi Tropper, Adam Urbanski, and Ann Wiener. Thank you also to countless other educators affiliated with the New York City Department of Education who asked not to be identified.

Thank you to the Bay Staters, especially, those at Brockton High, and most especially Sue Szachowicz, Sharon Wolder, Bob Perkins, and their students, including Daniela Belice, as well as numerous teachers. Thank you Chris Cooney; John Merian and his family; as well as Kathleen Smith, Ethan Cancell, Aldo Petronio, and Michael Thomas. A special thanks to Jennifer Berkshire for her advice and work, which always left me with new insights and better questions. Thank you also to Tom Birmingham, Russ Davis, Maurice Cunningham, Jamie Gass, Tracy Novick, Bob Pearlman, Paul Reville, Mark Roosevelt, Senator Stan Rosenberg, Sandra Stotsky, and Peggy Wiesenberg.

With great appreciation to Monta Akin at Leander ISD, Sarah Ambrus, Terry Ballard, Bret Champion, Tom Glenn, Greg Graham, Sharon Hejl, Eric Haug, Ron Lafevers, Kellie Lambert, David Langford, Chris Simpson, and countless other educators, staff, and students who were helpful with my chapter on Leander. Thank you also to Patricia Linares and Skip Meno.

I am grateful to the Nation Institute's Investigative Fund, especially Sarah Blustain and Esther Kaplan, and to the New World Foundation's Civic Opportunities Initiative Network, especially Noah Bernstein and Colin Greer, for helping to underwrite my early research in New Orleans. And thanks to Marilyn Neimark and Alisa Solomon for urging me to apply to the Nation Institute.

In New Orleans, thank you especially to Katy Reckdahl, who helped with some follow-up reporting, as well as the countless New Orleans students and families whom I met over the course of five years, many of whom welcomed me into their homes. I'm grateful to Raynard Sanders and Ashana

Bigard for showing me around the neighborhoods, schools, and landmarks that bore witness to New Orleans's civil rights struggles. Thank you to Chaseray Griffith and Eden Heilman at the Southern Poverty Law Center; Barbara Ferguson and Charles Hatfield with Research on Reforms; Doug Harris at the Educational Research Alliance; and Jill Zimmerman, formerly of the Cowen Institute. Thank you also to the many schools that let me visit, often multiple times, including Doris Hicks at Martin Luther King; Ben Marcovitz at Sci Academy, as well as Allie Levey and other teachers and administrators; Jay Altman of the FirstLine schools, as well as the CMO's students and teachers; Elizabeth Ostberg of The Net along with her students and colleagues; Mark Burton of Kipp McDonogh 15 and his teachers; and Patricia Perkins of Morris Jeff and her colleagues. I am also grateful to Donald E. DeVore and Joseph Logsdon, whose book *Crescent City Schools* helped fill vital historical gaps and provided important context for my chapter on New Orleans.

Thank you also to Broderick Bagert, Anya Barnes, Eddie Barnes and J'Remi Barnes, Representative Joseph Bouie, Katie Cenance-Jones, Deirdre Johnson Burel, Michael Deshotels, Danielle Dreilinger, Bob Ferris, Lance Hill, Elizabeth Jeffers, Shelton Joseph, Darryl Kilbert, Neerav Kingsland, Margaret Lang, Celeste Lofton, LaQuanta McKay, Lori Mince, Alysson Mills, Lawrence Melrose, Chris Meyer, Andre Perry, George Paitich, Stefin Pasternak, Jim Randel, Derek Raguski, Tony Recasner, Karran Harper Royal, Mercedes Schneider, Rowan Schaeffer, Leona Tate, and Jennifer Weishaupt.

In Los Angeles, thank you to Rafe Esquith and his many former students. Thank you also to Josh Leibner and Stuart Magruder.

I owe a great debt to those who read early versions of the manuscript—Sam Abrams, Brian Beabout, Jennifer Berkshire, Bryan Cole, Nick Siewert, Sandra Stotsky, and Ann Wiener. Their insights were invaluable. Any errors are entirely my own.

Thank you to my friend Alan Kopp, a skilled photographer. Alas, artistry can do only so much . . .

Last, but not least, hugs for Jose—for his support and for his astute last-minute copy editing. Thank you to my girls, Sarah and Annie, who have tolerated, with good humor, the endless conversations about schools and education reform; you are my inspiration, my role models.

NOTES

Introduction: The Quiet Revolution

1. Stephen Phillips, interview with the author, May 2016.
2. Robert Kanigel, *The One Best Way: Frederick Winslow Taylor and the Enigma of Efficiency* (Cambridge, MA: MIT Press, 2005), 12–13.
3. https://www.consciouscapitalism.org/about/credo.
4. Joseph Schumpeter coined the seemingly paradoxical term *creative destruction*, which has since become a mantra for some business people.
5. Elizabeth Green, *Building a Better Teacher: How Teaching Works (and How to Teach It to Everyone)* (New York: W.W. Norton & Company, 2015), 175–81. *SLANT* stands for: Sit up, Listen, Ask and answer, Nod your head, and Track the speaker.
6. Terry M. Moe and John E. Chubb, *Liberating Learning: Technology, Politics, and the Future of American Education* (San Francisco: Jossey Bass, 2009), 1–2, 63–64.
7. Andrea Gabor, "Lessons for Chicago from the Labor Wars of the Industrial Era," *Andrea Gabor*, September 12, 2012, https://andreagabor.com/2012/09/12/lessons-for-chicago-from-the-labor-wars-of-the-industrial-era.
8. Phillips, interview.
9. Richard D. Kahlenberg and Halley Potter, *A Smarter Charter: Finding What Works for Charter Schools and Public Education* (New York: Teachers College Press, 2014), 99.
10. The Cowen Institute for Public Education Initiatives, *The State of Public Education in New Orleans* (New Orleans, LA: Tulane University, 2013); Nichole Dobo, "DeVos Praises Virtual Schools, but New Research Points to Problems," *Hechinger Report*, February 22, 2017, http://hechingerreport.org/devos-praises-virtual-schools-new-research-points-problems.
11. Steven F. Wilson, "Success at Scale in Charter Schooling," *The Future of American Education: An AEI Working Group and Project to Commission, Discover, and Disseminate New Research on K–12 School Reform* (Washington, D.C.: American Enterprise Institute, 2008), http://www.aei.org/wp-content/uploads/2011/10/20081021-Wilson-FAEP-Rev.pdf.
12. Linda Darling-Hammond, Beverly Falk, and Jacqueline Ancess, *Authentic Assessment in Action: Studies of Schools and Students at Work* (New York: Teachers College Press, 1995), 5.

13. United States National Commission on Excellence in Education, *A Nation at Risk: The Imperative for Educational Reform: A Report to the Nation and the Secretary of Education* (Washington, D.C.: United States Department of Education, 2013).
14. Maris A Vinovskis, *From a Nation at Risk to No Child Left Behind: National Education Goals and the Creation of Federal Education Policy* (New York: Teachers College Press, 2009), 15–16.
15. Sarah Reckhow, *Follow the Money: How Foundation Dollars Change Public School Politics* (New York: Oxford University Press, 2012), 21.
16. "Primary Sources 2012: America's Teachers on the Teaching Profession" (Bill & Melinda Gates Foundation, Scholastic Inc., 2012), 65; Matthew G. Springer, Dale Ballou, Laura Hamilton, Vi-Nhuan Le, J.R. Lockwood, Daniel F. McCaffrey, Matthew Pepper, and Brian M. Stecher, "Teacher Pay for Performance: Experimental Evidence from the Project on Incentives in Teaching" (Nashville, TN: National Center on Performance Incentives at Vanderbilt University, 2010); Joan Brasher, "Teacher Merit Pay Has Merit: New Report" (Nashville, TN: Vanderbilt University), April 11, 1970, https://news.vanderbilt.edu/2017/04/11/teacher-merit-pay-has-merit-new-report.
17. Howard Fuller, "What Does All This Mean for Urban School Reform and Public Policy?" Remarks at *The Urban Education Future*? (New Orleans, LA: Tulane University, June 20, 2015).
18. Weldon Beckner, *The Case for the Smaller School* (Bloomington, IN: Phi Delta Kappa Educational Foundation, 1983); Reckhow, *Follow the Money*, 15.
19. Jal Mehta, *The Allure of Order* (New York: Oxford University Press, 2013), 88–89.
20. Mike Klonsky, "An Interview with Deborah Meier on the Small-Schools Movement," *Huffington Post*, May 11, 2011.
21. Reckhow, *Follow the Money*, 28.
22. Ibid., 29.
23. "Presenter Bios," https://docs.gatesfoundation.org/documents/imagineconveningbios.pdf; Valerie Strauss, "New Book: Obama's Education Department and Gates Foundation Were Closer Than You Thought," *Washington Post*, August 15, 2016.
24. Strauss, "New Book."
25. Bill Gates, *Strengthening American Competitiveness for the 21st Century News Center, Before the United States Senate Committee on Health, Education, Labor, and Pensions*, March 7, 2007, https://news.microsoft.com/2007/03/07/bill-gates-u-s-senate-committee-hearing-on-strengthening-american-competitiveness.
26. Walter Isaacson, *Steve Jobs* (New York: Simon & Schuster, 2011), 506, PDF e-book.
27. Ibid., 527.

1: Big Dreams, Small Schools: How Entrepreneurial Rebels Built a Movement in New York City

1. Frank McCourt, *Teacher Man: A Memoir* (New York: Scribner, 2005), 136.
2. Sam Roberts, "Infamous 'Drop Dead' Was Never Said by Ford," *New York Times*, December 28, 2006.
3. Ibid.
4. Diane Ravitch, *The Great School Wars: A History of the New York City Public Schools* (Baltimore, MD: Johns Hopkins University Press, 2000), 263–72, 291.
5. Ibid., 309–10.
6. Kim Phillips-Fein, "The Legacy of the 1970s Fiscal Crisis," *The Nation*, April 16, 2013, http://www.thenation.com/article/legacy-1970s-fiscal-crisis.
7. Arthur Tobier, "Alice Seletsky: 1929–2009," *NDSG Oral History Project*, September 2005, http://www.ndsg.org/oralhistory/aseletsky/index.html.
8. Vasthi Acosta, interview with the author, January 2016.
9. McCourt, *Teacher Man*, 12.
10. Daniel Perlstein, "Teaching Freedom: SNCC and the Mississippi Freedom Schools," *History of Education Quarterly* 30, no. 3 (Autumn 1990): 297–324. As David Rogers points out in *110 Livingston Street*, during the 1960s the New York City education bureaucracy went to great lengths to thwart any attempts at desegregation, even its own stated desegregation policies. David Rogers, *110 Livingston Street* (New York: Random House, 1968), 298–99, 305–23.
11. Perlstein, "Teaching Freedom."
12. Deborah Meier, *In Schools We Trust* (Boston: Beacon Press, 2002), 59.
13. Linda Darling-Hammond, Jacqueline Ancess, and Susanna Wichterle Ort, "Reinventing High School: Outcomes of the Coalition Campus Schools Project," *American Educational Research Journal* 39, no. 3 (2002): 639–73. doi:10.3102/0002831 2039003639.
14. Ann Wiener manuscript notes.
15. Mike Klonsky, "An Interview with Deborah Meier on the Small-Schools Movement," *Huffington Post*, May 11, 2011.
16. Eric Nadelstern, "To Be Strong Leaders, More Principals Need to Share Authority," *WNYC School Book*, November 4, 2011, http://www.wnyc.org/story/303228-to-be-strong-leaders-more-principals-need-to-share-authority.
17. Ann Bradley, "Open to Innovation," *Education Week*, April 21, 1999, https://www.edweek.org/ew/articles/1999/04/21/32open.h18.html.
18. Meier, *In Schools We Trust*, 50.
19. Brenda S. Engel, "Introduction: Oral History Project North Dakota Study Group," http://ndsg.org/online_registration/2012/engel_reading_2012.pdf.
20. Meier, *In Schools We Trust*, 26.
21. Ann Cook, interview with the author, December 2015.
22. David Bensman, *Quality Education in the Inner City: The Story of Central Park East Schools* (New York: Desktop Publishing by Kramer Communications, 1987), 7.

23. Joseph P. McDonald, *American School Reform: What Works, What Fails, and Why* (Chicago: University of Chicago Press, 2014), 45.
24. Suzanne Daley, "Alvarado Tailors Schools to Students," *New York Times*, April 30, 1983; McDonald, *American School Reform*, 144.
25. Alvarado would resign under a cloud of financial improprieties, including disclosures that he had borrowed from subordinates and lied on mortgage applications. (Lynda Richardson, "A Superintendent's Stormy History Repeats Itself," *New York Times*, March 20, 1992.)
26. Michael A. Goldstein, "St. Anthony," *New York Magazine*, October 13, 1997.
27. Daley, "Alvarado Tailors Schools to Students"; Ann Cook, Jan. 29 interview; Goldstein, "St. Anthony."
28. Goldstein, "St. Anthony."
29. Deborah Meier, interview with the author, January 29, 2016.
30. Seymour Fliegel, "Debbie Meier and the Dawn of Central Park East," *City Journal*, Winter 1994, https://www.city-journal.org/html/debbie-meier-and-dawn-central-park-east-12572.html; Tobier, "Alice Seletsky: 1929–2009."
31. Bensman, *Quality Education*, 2.
32. Fliegel, "Debbie Meier"; Meier, interview.
33. Meier, interview.
34. Engel, "Introduction: North Dakota Study Group Oral History Project."
35. Meier, interview; Fliegel, "Debbie Meier"; David Bensman, *Quality Education*, 10; Meier, *In Schools We Trust*, 63.
36. Meier, interview; Fliegel, "Debbie Meier."
37. Fliegel, "Debbie Meier."
38. Goldstein, "St. Anthony."
39. Ibid.
40. John Merrow, book proposal: "A Definitive History of the Charter School Movement," sent via email January 4, 2018. Also Ted Kolderie, "Ray Budde and the Origins of the 'Charter Concept,'" *Education Evolving*, June 2005.
41. Klonsky, "Interview with Deborah Meier."
42. Fliegel, "Debbie Meier."
43. Cook, interview, January 29; Fliegel, "Debbie Meier."
44. Fliegel, "Debbie Meier."
45. Ibid.
46. Meier, interview.
47. Fliegel, "Debbie Meier."
48. Ibid.
49. Deborah Meier, "Thoughts on Japan & Julia Richman," *Education Week* (blog), January 19, 2010, http://blogs.edweek.org/edweek/Bridging-Differences/2012/01/blog_-_thursday_the_19th.html.
50. Ibid.
51. Meier, interview.

52. Deborah Meier, *The Power of Their Ideas: Lessons for America from a Small School in Harlem* (Boston: Beacon Press, 2005), 6; Meier, interview.
53. Meier, interview.
54. Winston Churchill, speech, House of Commons, November 11, 1947, *Winston S. Churchill: His Complete Speeches, 1897–1963*, ed. Robert Rhodes James, vol. 7, p. 7566 (1974), http://www.bartleby.com/73/417.html.
55. Meier, interview; Cook, interview; Thomas Toch, "Divide and Conquer," *Washington Monthly*, May 1, 2003.
56. Meier, *The Power of Their Ideas*, 108.
57. Meier, *In Schools We Trust*, 59.
58. Meier, interview.
59. Meier, *In Schools We Trust*, 73–74.
60. Fliegel, "Debbie Meier."
61. Bensman, *Quality Education*, 53; Fliegel, "Debbie Meier."
62. Fliegel, "Debbie Meier."
63. Meier, *In Schools We Trust*, 28.
64. Deborah Meier, "Timeline," *Save CPE1*, http://www.savecpe1.org/timeline; Kathleen Teltsch, "MacArthur Awards of $150,000 to $375,000 Go to 'Outstandingly Talented' 32," *New York Times*, June 16, 1987.
65. Stephen Phillips, interviews with the author, May 2015 and May 2016; The Aaron Diamond Foundation, *The Aaron Diamond Foundation Final Report 1993–1996*, http://philanthropy.org/seminars/documents/ADFFinalReportExtract1996.pdf.
66. Stephen Phillips, email to the author, June 3, 2016; Sean Kirst, "Historic Role in Syracuse, Historic Resting Place: Sidney L. Johnson to Be Interred Today at Arlington," *Syracuse.com*, September 22, 2014, http://www.syracuse.com/kirst/index.ssf/2014/09/sid_johnson_and_arlington_and_syracuse.html.
67. Phillips, interview, 2016; McDonald, *American School Reform*, 119.
68. Phillips, interview, 2016.
69. Mary Anne Raywid, Gil Schmerler, Stephen E. Phillips, and Gregory A. Smith, *Not So Easy Going: The Policy Environments of Small Urban Schools and Schools-within-Schools* (Charleston, WV: ERIC Clearinghouse on Rural Education and Small Schools, 2003), http://files.eric.ed.gov/fulltext/ED474653.pdf.
70. Stephen Phillips, email to the author, October 26, 2017.
71. Ibid.
72. Ibid. (Norm Fruchter would not agree to an interview.)
73. Stephen Phillips, email to the author, June 4, 2016; Diane Ravitch and Joseph P. Viteritti, eds., *City Schools Lessons from New York* (Baltimore: Johns Hopkins University Press, 2000), 66.
74. Phillips, interview, 2016.
75. Ibid.; Ravitch and Viteritti, *City Schools*, 67.
76. Hammond, Ancess, and Wichterle Ort, "Reinventing High School," 639.

77. Ibid., 639–73; Ann Wiener manuscript notes; McDonald, *American School Reform*, 120.
78. Phillips, interview, 2016.
79. Emma Graves Fitzsimmons, "Florence Scala: 1918–2007: 'Heroine' Led Fight Against City Hall in '60s," *Chicago Tribune*, August 29, 2007, http://articles.chicagotribune.com/2007-08-29/news/0708281426_1_hull-house-city-hall-studs-terkel; Studs Turkel, *Division Street: America* (New York: New Press, 2006); Clarence N. Stone, Robert P. Stoker et al., *Urban Neighborhoods in a New Era: Revitalization Politics in the Postindustrial City* (Chicago: University of Chicago Press, 2015), 99–100.
80. Ann Cook, interview with the author, February 2016.
81. Ibid.; Engel, "Introduction."
82. Dolores Mei, Jan Rosenblum, John Berman, and Linda Solomon, *Inquiry Demonstration Project 1988–89* (Brooklyn, NY: New York City Board of Education Office of Research, Evaluation and Assessment, 1990), http://files.eric.ed.gov/fulltext/ED322277.pdf.
83. Ibid.
84. McCourt, *Teacher Man*, 187.
85. Theodore Sizer, *Horace's Compromise* (New York: Houghton Mifflin, 1984), 126.
86. Hammond, Ancess, and Wichterle Ort, "Reinventing High School," 639.
87. Ibid.
88. Today, alternative schools are nontraditional schools offering, say, block scheduling or minimal standardized testing. Transfer high schools, by contrast, are for overage and undercredited students who are not on track to graduate within five years.
89. Dani Gonzalez, interview with the author, February 2016.
90. Ibid.; Avram Barlowe, email to the author, June 2, 2016.
91. Mei et al., *Inquiry Demonstration Project 1988–89.*
92. Hammond, Ancess, and Wichterle Ort, "Reinventing High School," 639.
93. Avram Barlowe, interview with the author, October 2015; Emma Sokoloff-Rubin, "At a Few City Schools, an Old Course Speaks to New Standards," *Chalkbeat*, April 14, 2014, http://ny.chalkbeat.org/2014/04/14/at-a-few-city-schools-an-old-course-speaks-to-new-standards/#.VpprY1IYVG0.
94. Annette Fuentes, "Report from Lockdown High: Fear vs. Facts on School Safety," *City Limits*, March 11, 2011, http://citylimits.org/2011/03/11/report-from-lockdown-high-fear-vs-facts-on-school-safety.
95. Hammond, Ancess, and Wichterle Ort, "Reinventing High School," 639–73.
96. Phillips, interview, 2016.
97. Ibid.
98. McDonald, *American School Reform*, 122.
99. United Federation of Teachers, "PROSE," http://www.uft.org/teaching/prose; Ann Cook, interview with the author, June 6, 2016.; Randi Weingarten, "Randi Weingarten's Response to a Critic," *Education Week*, November 6, 2014, http://www.edweek.org/ew/articles/2014/11/06/12weingarten.h34.html.

100. Jacqueline Ancess and Suzanna Wichterle Ort, "How the Coalition Campus Schools Have Re-imagined High School: Seven Years Later," *The National Center for Restructuring Education, Schools, and Teaching (NCREST)* (New York: Teachers College, Columbia University, 1999).
101. Toch, "Divide and Conquer"; Phillips, interview, 2016.
102. Dani Gonzalez, school tour, February 2016; Toch, "Divide and Conquer."
103. *Dept. of Labor, Health, and Human Services, Education and Related Agencies Appropriations for 2002: Hearings Before a Subcommittee of the Committee on Appropriations, House of Representatives*, 107th Cong. (2002) (testimony of Dr. Renee Jenkins, Professor and Chairman, Department of Pediatrics and Child Health, Howard University College of Medicine), https://www.gpo.gov/fdsys/pkg/CHRG-107hhrg77408/html/CHRG-107hhrg77408.htm.
104. Ann Cook, interview with the author, December 2015.
105. Ibid.
106. Ibid.
107. Ibid.
108. Terry Weber, conversation at Urban Academy, February 2016.
109. Elissa Gootman, "Small Schools Show Concern Over Proposal to Swap Land," *New York Times*, June 28, 2006; Toch, "Divide and Conquer."
110. Toch, "Divide and Conquer."
111. Ibid.; Ancess and Wichterle Ort, "How the Coalition Campus Schools Have Re-imagined High School."
112. Hammond, Ancess, and Ort, "Reinventing High School."
113. "Vanguard High School," https://insideschools.org/school/02M449; "Urban Academy Laboratory High School," https://insideschools.org/school/02M565; "Manhattan International High School," https://insideschools.org/school/02M459; "Talent Unlimited High School," https://insideschools.org/school/02M519.
114. Avram Barlowe, interview with the author, October 12, 2015; Abbie Fentress Swanson, "The South Bronx: Where Hip Hop Was Born," *WNYC*, August 2, 2010, http://www.wnyc.org/story/89709-south-bronx-hip-hop-year-zero.
115. Avram Barlowe, interview.
116. Ibid.
117. Ibid.
118. Ibid.
119. Rubin, "At a Few City Schools, an Old Course Speaks to New Standards"; Barlowe, interview.
120. Barlowe, interview.
121. Herb Mack, interview with the author, February 2016.
122. Ibid.
123. Ibid.
124. Ibid.
125. Ibid.
126. Ibid.

127. Student shout-out during Urban Academy visit, February 2016.
128. Urban Academy Laboratory High School, review, http://insideschools.org/component/schools/school/108.
129. Mei, "Inquiry Demonstration Project 1988–89"; Opening Brief, *New York Performance Standards Consortium v. The New York State Education Department*, August 16, 2001, http://performanceassessment.org/activism/pdf/openingbrief.pdf.
130. McCourt, *Teacher Man*, 107.
131. Vito Perrone, Monographs by the North Dakota Study Group on Evaluation, http://www.ndsg.org/monographs.html; Paul Vitello, "Vito Perrone Sr., Who Fought Standardized Tests, Dies at 78," *New York Times*, September 16, 2011.
132. Vito Perrone, *A Report to the Rockefeller Brothers Fund* (North Dakota: North Dakota Study Group on Evaluation, University of North Dakota, June 1975).
133. Ann Cook and Herb Mack, "The Word and the Thing: Ways of Seeing the Teacher" (North Dakota: NDSGE, University of North Dakota, December 1975), 1, http://www.ndsg.org/monographs/NDSG_1975_Cook_and_Mack_The_Word_and_the_Thing.pdf; Engel, "Introduction."
134. Ann Cook and Phyllis Tashlik, "Making the Pendulum Swing: Challenging Bad Education Policy in New York State," *Coalition of Essential Schools*, December 9, 2005; Sam Roberts, "Thomas Sobol, 83, Dies; Education Advocate as New York State Commissioner," *New York Times*, September 4, 2015.
135. Ann Cook, interview with the author, February 2016.
136. Opening Brief, *New York Performance Standards Consortium v. The New York State Education Department.*
137. Sarah Reckhow, *Follow the Money: How Foundation Dollars Change Public School Politics* (New York: Oxford University Press, 2012), 54–55; Frederick M. Hess, "Retooling K–12 Giving," *Philanthropy Magazine*, September/October 2014; Peter Appleboome, "Annenberg School Grants Raise Hopes, and Questions on Extent of Change," *New York Times*, April 30, 1995; McDonald, *American School Reform*, 122.
138. Meier, interview; Reckhow, *Follow the Money*, 54.
139. Reckhow, *Follow the Money*, 54.
140. Ibid.
141. Eric Nadelstern, *Ten Lessons from New York City Schools* (New York: Teachers College Press 2013), 14; Meier, interview.
142. Leanna Steifel, Patrice Iatarola, Norm Fruchter, and Robert Berne, "The Effects of Size of Student Body on School Costs and Performance in New York City High Schools" (study, Institute for Education and Social Policy, New York University, April 1998), http://files.eric.ed.gov/fulltext/ED420464.pdf.
143. Opening Brief, *New York Performance Standards Consortium v. The New York State Education Department.*
144. Ibid.; Phillips, interview, 2016.
145. Opening Brief, *New York Performance Standards Consortium v. The New York*

State Education Department; Phillips, interview, 2016; Raywid et al., "Not So Easy Going."

146. McDonald, *American School Reform*, 123.
147. Interview with the author, December 2017.
148. Geoff Decker, "Chancellor's District Architect Says His School Improvement Model Is 'Dead Wrong,'" *Chalkbeat*, November 6, 2014, https://www.chalkbeat.org/posts/ny/2014/11/06/chancellors-district-architect-calls-his-model-for-school-improvement-flawed.
149. Meier, "Timeline"; Meier, interview; MacArthur Foundation, "Deborah Meier, Education Class Leader | Class of 1987," Last updated Jan. 1, 2005, https://www.macfound.org/fellows/308/#sthash.E82WhrtT.dpuf; Fliegel, interview with the author.
150. Fliegel, interview.
151. Anemona Hartocollis, "Principals of Alternative High Schools Are Ordered to Increase the Schools' Enrollments," *New York Times*, February 13, 1998; Somini Sengupta, "Superintendent of New Schools Is Resigning," *New York Times*, July 9, 1997; Deborah Meier and Dianne Suiter, "Sustaining Change: The Struggle to Maintain Identity at Central Park East Secondary School," *Horace*, December 2, 2009, http://essentialschools.org/horace-issues/sustaining-change-the-struggle-to-maintain-identity-at-central-park-east-secondary-school.
152. McDonald, *American School Reform*, 123.
153. Ibid.
154. Bill & Melinda Gates Foundation, New York City Department of Education, "$51 Million Grant from the Bill & Melinda Gates Foundation to Support Small Dynamic High Schools to Boost Student Achievement," News release, September 17, 2003, https://www.gatesfoundation.org/Media-Center/Press-Releases/2003/09/New-York-City-Department-of-Education-Receives-Grant; Janice M. Hirota, "Reframing Education: The Partnership Strategy and Public Schools" (Report to the Carnegie Corporation of New York, Youth Development Institute, Fund for the City of New York, September 2005), https://www.chapinhall.org/sites/default/files/old_reports/281.pdf.
155. Hirota, "Reframing Education"; Maureen Kelleher, "New York City's Children First: Lessons in School Reform, American Progress" (report, Center for American Progress, January 2014), https://www.americanprogress.org/wp-content/uploads/2014/03/NYCeducationReport.pdf.
156. Kelleher, "New York City's Children First."
157. Opening Brief, *New York Performance Standards Consortium v. The New York State Education Department.*
158. Phillips, interview, 2016.
159. Carol Siri Johnson, "History of New York State Regents Exams" (paper, December 31, 2009), http://files.eric.ed.gov/fulltext/ED507649.pdf.
160. Jennifer Medina, "New Diploma Standard in New York Becomes a Multiple-Question Choice," *New York Times*, June 28, 2010.

161. Johnson, "History of New York State Regents Exams"; Time Out from Testing, "Timeline of New York State Regents Fiascoes," http://timeoutfromtesting.org/timeline.php.
162. Linda Darling-Hammond, sworn affidavit, Stanford University, signed July 3, 2001, http://performanceassessment.org/activism/pdf/darlinghammond.pdf.
163. Ann Cook, interview with the author, December 2015.
164. New York Supreme Court Appellate Division–Third Department In The Matter of the Application of The New York Performance Standards Consortium Petitioners-Appellants, against The New York State Education Department; and Richard Mills, as Commissioner of Education of the State of New York, Respondents Appellants' Brief, http://performanceassessment.org/activism/pdf/nypscbrief.pdf.
165. Ibid.; Michael Hill, "Schools Sue State Over Portfolios," AP, August 16, 2001 (via Factiva); "Summary of the NY Performance Standards Consortium Lawsuit," Performance Assessment.org, http://performanceassessment.org/activism/alegal.html; Ancess and Wichterle Ort, "How the Coalition Campus Schools Have Re-imagined High School."
166. Opening Brief, *New York Performance Standards Consortium v. The New York State Education Department.*
167. Ibid.
168. Brian McGuire, "Legislators Consider Bill to Alter Graduation Requirements," *New York Sun*, June 9, 2005.
169. Ibid.
170. Michael Winerip, "New York City Student Testing Over the Past Decade," *New York Times*, December 19, 2011.
171. Ibid.
172. Ibid.
173. Ibid.
174. McCourt, *Teacher Man*, 157.
175. Tom Vander Ark, "Tom Vander Ark, Executive Director, Education, Bill & Melinda Gates Foundation," interview by Kevin Kinsella, *Philanthropy News Digest*, October 15, 2003, http://philanthropynewsdigest.org/newsmakers/tom-vander-ark-executive-director-education-bill-melinda-gates-foundation.
176. Anna M. Phillips, "Tom Vander Ark's New York–Area Charter Schools Falter," *New York Times*, July 14, 2011; Cathleen P. Black, "The Proposed Temporary Co-Location of Brooklyn City Prep Charter School" (New York Department of Education, February 5, 2011), http://schools.nyc.gov/NR/rdonlyres/26767179-A349-4E3D-B4E1-05B87B03ECD8/98437/PEP_Notice_Brooklyn_City_Prep_vfinal7.pdf.
177. *Dept. of Labor, Health, and Human Services, Education and Related Agencies Appropriations for 2002: Hearings Before a Subcommittee of the Committee on Appropriations, House of Representatives*, 107th Cong. (2002) (testimony of Tom Vander Ark), https://www.gpo.gov/fdsys/pkg/CHRG-107hhrg77408/html/CHRG-107hhrg77408.htm.
178. Ibid.

179. Opening Brief, *New York Performance Standards Consortium v. The New York State Education Department.*
180. Cook, interview.
181. Tom Vander Ark, phone interview with the author, December 2015.
182. Ibid.
183. Cook, interview.
184. Amy McIntosh, *LinkedIn* (profile page), https://www.linkedin.com/in/amy-mcintosh-b278b.
185. Ibid.
186. Cook, interview.
187. Ibid.
188. Mack, interview.
189. Alyson Klein, "Staffer Heads to U.S. Department of Education," *Education Week*, December 3, 2013. McIntosh, *LinkedIn* (profile page).
190. New Visions for Public Schools Press Release: "Robert Hughes to Join the Bill and Melinda Gates Foundation as K–12 Director," https://www.newvisions.org/blog/entry/robert-hughes-to-join-the-bill-and-melinda-gates-foundation-k-12-director.
191. New York City Department of Education, "About Us," http://schools.nyc.gov/AboutUs/default.htm.

2: Testing Power: When Is Disruption Just . . . Disruptive?

1. Andrea Gabor, "Leadership Principles for Public School Principals," *Strategy + Business*, May 23, 2005, https://www.strategy-business.com/article/05207?gko=669d4.
2. Ibid.
3. Ibid.; David Chai, "Schools Chancellor Joel I. Klein Announces Nationally Renowned Business Leaders and Educators to Head Leadership Academy" (NYC Department of Education, January 14, 2003), http://schools.nyc.gov/press/02-03/n52_03.htm.
4. Philissa Cramer and Rachel Cromidas, "In a Change, City Is Steering Aspiring Principals off the Fast Track," *Chalkbeat*, November 15, 2012, http://ny.chalkbeat.org/2012/11/15/in-a-change-city-is-steering-aspiring-principals-off-the-fast-track/#.Vv6gl3oXtks; Elissa Gootman and Robert Gebeloff, "New York City Principals Are Younger and Freer, but Some Raise Doubts," *New York Times*, May 25, 2009; Robert E. Knowling Jr,. *LinkedIn* (profile page), https://www.linkedin.com/in/robert-e-knowling-jr-11a18b11; Andrew Wolf, "Sharpton Group Flays Ferrer on Diallo; Signs of Flexibility on School Reform," *New York Sun*, April 12, 2005.
5. Peter Senge et al., *Schools That Learn* (New York: Crown Business Books, 2012), 510–11.
6. Sy Fliegel, interview with the author, March 2016.
7. Off-the-record interview with the author, December 2017.
8. Joseph McDonald, "Autonomy and Accountability in New York City School

Reform" (paper presented at the American Educational Research Association Annual Meeting, April 2009).

9. Ibid.
10. Joseph P. McDonald, *American School Reform: What Works, What Fails, and Why* (Chicago: University of Chicago Press, 2014), 138; Joel I. Klein, "Empowerment Schools FAQ, June 15," 2006, http://schools.nycenet.edu/region6/midwood/empowerment.html.
11. McDonald, *American School Reform*, 126.
12. Andrea Gabor, notes from Sunday brunch, Summer 2009; Jacqueline Pryce-Harvey, interview with the author, July 2009.
13. Andrea Gabor, notes from Sunday brunch.
14. Ibid.
15. Ibid.; Chrystina Russell, email message to author, May 2016.
16. Andrea Gabor, "A Harlem Middle School Bets on Technology," *Gotham Gazette*, April 26, 2010, http://www.gothamgazette.com/index.php/city/504-a-harlem-middle-school-bets-on-technology; Kate Taylor, "Public Schools Fund, Under de Blasio, Is Struggling to Lure Wealthy Donors," *New York Times*, May 13, 2015.
17. Gabor, "Harlem Middle School"; Chrystina Russell interview with author.
18. Jackie Pryce-Harvey, interview with author, July 2017.
19. Ibid.
20. Ibid.
21. Ibid.
22. Andrea Gabor, "A Signature Bloomberg-Era Education Innovation Is at a Crossroads," *Gotham Gazette*, April 21, 2013, http://www.gothamgazette.com/index.php/education/4227-in-the-waning-months-of-bloombergs-tenure-a-signature-education-innovation-is-at-a-crossroads-.
23. Ibid.; Beth Fertig, "In One NYC School, a Snapshot of Bloomberg's Education Legacy," *NPR*, December 18, 2013.
24. Gabor, "Signature Bloomberg-Era Education Innovation."
25. Andrea Gabor, "City Schools Gamble on Going Digital," *Gotham Gazette*, September 18, 2008, http://www.gothamgazette.com/index.php/city/609-city-schools-gamble-on-going-digital.
26. School visit and interviews, September 2010; James G. Lengel, "Case Study: The NYC iSchool," *Education 3.0*, http://lengel.net/ed30/ischool.html.
27. Cisco, "NYC iSchool and iZone," https://www.cisco.com/c/dam/en_us/about/citizenship/socialinvestments/docs/NYCiSchoolBrief.pdf.
28. Gabor, "City Schools Gamble;" Senge et al., *Schools That Learn*, 512–13.
29. Senge et al., *Schools That Learn*, 512–13.
30. Ibid.; Gabor, iSchool, and Global Tech visit and interviews, May 2010.
31. Gabor, "City Schools Gamble."
32. Ibid.
33. Gene Longo, "NYC iSchool: Rethinking School for the 21st Century," *Cisco Blogs*,

May 15, 2009, http://blogs.cisco.com/news/nyc_ischool_rethinking_school_for_the_21st_century.

34. Andrea Gabor, "Education Technology Lessons from the School of One and an Old Tracy–Hepburn Film," *Andrea Gabor*, August 11, 2011, https://andreagabor.com/2011/08/11/education-technology-lessons-from-school-of-one-and-an-old-tracy-hepburn-film%e2%80%a6.
35. Ibid.; iZone, "School of One," http://iZonenyc.org/initiatives/school-of-one.
36. "History," NewClassrooms.org, www.newclassrooms.org/about/history. Gary Rubinstein "School of One" *Gary Rubinstein's Blog,* July 24, 2012, https://garyrubinstein.wordpress.com/2012/07/24/school-of-one.
37. Eric Nadelstern, interview with author, November 2012; Rachel Monahan, "Klein's Clever School of One Project a Pricey Reject," *New York Daily News*, September 4, 2012, http://www.nydailynews.com/new-york/education/nyc-chancellor-joel-klein-highly-touted-school-math-project-dropped-2-3-schools-pilot-program-article-1.1152131.
38. CityPathways, "Who We Are," http://www.citypathways.org/who-we-are.
39. Senge, *Schools That Learn*, 515–16; Andrea Gabor, "School Reform for Realists," *Strategy+business*, August 28, 2012, http://www.strategy-business.com/article/00126?gko=d3afd.
40. Claire Jellinek, "Leading the Charge in Digital Learning," *Homeroom: The Official Blog of the U.S. Department of Education*, January 11, 2012, http://blog.ed.gov/2011/09/leading-the-charge-in-digital-learning.
41. Chrystina Russell, interview with author, September 26, 2011.
42. Ibid.
43. Ben Chapman and Corinne Lestch, "Money for Charter Schools Balloons During Mayor Bloomberg's Tenure," *New York Daily News*, July 14, 2013; Corinne Colbert and Jennifer Petrie, "Deborah Meier: The Importance of Democracy in Public Schools Today," Institute for Democracy in Education.
44. Monique Bryan, interviews with author, September and October 2012.
45. Ibid.
46. Ibid.
47. Ibid.
48. Ibid.
49. Andrea Gabor, "A Demographic Divide in Harlem: The Neediest Kids Go to Public Schools, Not Charters," *Andrea Gabor* (blog), May 13, 2014, http://andreagabor.com/2014/05/09/a-demographic-divide-in-east-harlem-the-neediest-kids-go-to-public-schools-not-charters.
50. Kahlenberg and Potter, *A Smarter Charter*, 1, 54.
51. Julie Zuckerman, interview with author, May 2015.
52. The problems go well beyond technical quibbles and suggest that any generalizations drawn from the study about the quality of traditional public schools relative to charter schools would be a big mistake. For example, the method used for selecting charter and public school students in the study introduced,

in many cases, an anti–public school bias. In at least one case, the findings on New Orleans, Raymond admits that CREDO violated its own methodology, a fact not disclosed in either the study or its accompanying technical documents; since there are few public school students left in New Orleans, the study compared charter students to public school students *outside* the city. In other cities, the study excludes public schools that do NOT send students to charters, thus introducing a bias against the best urban public schools, especially small public schools that may send few, if any, students to charters. Kahlenberg and Potter, *A Smarter Charter*, 68; Andrea Gabor, "New CREDO Study, New Credibility Problems," *Andrea Gabor* (blog), April 28, 2015, https://andreagabor.com/2015/04/28/new-credo-study-new-credibility-problems-from-new-orleans-to-boston.

53. J. Murray, "Ohio Charters Fall Short on the Nation's Report Card," *Ohio Gadfly Daily* (blog), The Thomas B. Fordham Institute, November 13, 2013, http://edexcellence.net/commentary/education-gadfly-daily/ohio-gadfly-daily/ohios-charters-fall-short-on-the-nations-report; Audrey Amrein-Beardsley, "Charter v. Public School Students: NAEP 2013 Performance," *VAMboozled!* (blog), December 15, 2015, http://vamboozled.com/charter-v-public-school-students-naep-2013-performance.
54. Andrea Gabor, "More Breathless Praise for Success Academy; and Why We Should Be 'Terrified,'" *Andrea Gabor* (blog), December 9, 2017, https://andreagabor.com/2017/12/09/new-endorsements-for-success-academy-and-why-we-should-be-terrified.
55. Andrea Gabor, "Charter School Refugees," *New York Times*, April 4, 2014; Marlene Kennedy, "Charter School Claims State Can't Audit It," courthousenews.com, July 11, 2013, https://www.courthousenews.com/charter-school-claims-state-cant-audit-it; Kate Taylor, "At Success Academy School, a Stumble in Math and a Teacher's Anger on Video," *New York Times*, February 12, 2016; Eliza Shapiro, "In a Memo, Success Academy Lawyers Warn Staff of 'Mistakes,'" *Politico New York*, March 23, 2016, http://www.capitalnewyork.com/article/city-hall/2016/03/8594332/memo-success-academy-lawyers-warn-staff-mistakes.
56. Sy Fliegel, phone interview with author, March 2016.
57. Ibid.
58. Nancy Hass, "Scholarly Investments," *New York Times*, December 5, 2009; Vasthi Acosta, interview with the author, January 2016.
59. Andrea Gabor, "Inside Success Academy: Nose Pressed to the Window Pane," *Andrea Gabor* (blog), December 27, 2015, http://andreagabor.com/2015/12/09/inside-success-academy-nose-pressed-to-the-window-pane.
60. Ibid.
61. Eliza Shapiro, "Success Academy Documents Point to 'Possible Cheating' Among Challenges," *Politico New York*, May 10, 2016, http://www.politico.com/states/new-york/city-hall/story/2016/05/success-academy-documents-point-to-possible-cheating-among-challenges-101595.
62. Vasthi Acosta, interview; Amber Charter School, Kingsbridge, https://www.ambercharter.org/domain/59.

63. Vasthi Acosta, interview.
64. Ibid.
65. Carey Goldberg, "Boston Study: What Higher Standardized Test Scores Don't Mean," *Wbur's Commonhealth*, December 11, 2013, http://commonhealth.wbur.org/2013/12/standard-test-fluid-skills.
66. Javier C. Hernández and Susanne Craig, "Cuomo Played Pivotal Role in Charter School Push," *New York Times*, April 3, 2014.
67. Off-the-record interview with charter-industry source.
68. Gabor, "Charter School Refugees."
69. Ibid.
70. Andrea Gabor, "What a New IBO Study on Special-Needs Kids in NYC Says About Charter v. Public School Comparisons," *Andrea Gabor* (blog), January 11, 2014, https://andreagabor.com/2014/01/11/what-a-new-ibo-study-on-special-needs-kids-says-about-charter-v-public-school-comparisons.
71. Chrystina Russell, interview with author, September 2011.
72. Ibid.
73. Chrystina Russell and David Baiz, interviews with author. Russell interceded on Franklin's behalf, and Franklin is now living in Boston and attending Southern New Hampshire University, where Russell is vice president of global development.
74. Kaira Batiz, interview with author, May 6, 2015.
75. Ibid.
76. Ibid.
77. Ibid.
78. Ibid.
79. Ibid.
80. David Baiz, interview with author, June 2016.
81. Andrea Gabor, "When Making a Great Teacher Is a Team Effort," *Huffington Post*, May 8, 2012, http://www.huffingtonpost.com/andrea-gabor/when-making-a-great-teach_b_1332388.html.
82. Ibid.
83. Ibid.
84. Chrystina Russell, David Baiz, and Valerie Miller, interviews with author, December 2010.
85. Gabor, "When Making a Great Teacher Is a Team Effort."
86. Julie Zuckerman, phone interview with author, November 2013.
87. Fliegel, interview.
88. McDonald, "Autonomy and Accountability"; Patrick Wall, "How a Few School Support Groups Created Under Bloomberg Survived Farina's Overhaul," *Chalkbeat*, February 13, 2015, https://www.chalkbeat.org/posts/ny/2015/02/13/how-a-few-school-support-groups-created-under-bloomberg-survived-farinas-overhaul.
89. Ann Cook, interview with author, June 2016.
90. Peter Goodman, "The Network for International High Schools: Islands of Excellence in the Turbulent World of Public Schools," *Ed in the Apple* (blog), April 30,

2015, https://mets2006.wordpress.com/2015/04/30/the-network-for-international-high-schools-islands-of-excellence-in-the-turbulent-world-of-public-schools; "Here We Go Again," *NYC Rubber Room Reporter and ATR CONNECT* (blog), January 21, 2010, http://nycrubberroomreporter.blogspot.com/2010/01/here-we-go-again.html; McDonald, "Autonomy and Accountability"; Fernanda Santos, "A Top Overseer of City Schools Plans to Retire," *New York Times*, January 21, 2011.

91. Andrea Gabor, "A Bloomberg-Era Reform Worth Saving?," *Andrea Gabor* (blog), https://andreagabor.com/2013/11/25/a-bloomberg-era-reform-worth-saving; Eric Nadelstern, *Ten Lessons from New York City Schools* (New York: Teachers College Press, 2013), 17.
92. Nancy Mann, interview with author, 2012.
93. McDonald, *American School Reform*, 48; off-the-record interview.
94. Russell, phone interview.
95. Ibid.
96. Jackie Pryce-Harvey, interview with author, July 2017.
97. Nick Siewert, interview with author, May 2016.
98. Chrystina Russell and David Baiz, interviews with author, December 2010.
99. Russell, interview.
100. Russell and Baiz, interviews.
101. Global Tech Quality Review 2013–2014.
102. NY State Senate, "Senate Passes Bill Reforming the Board of Regents Selection Process," News release, March 14, 2014, New York State Senate, https://www.nysenate.gov/newsroom/press-releases/senate-passes-bill-reforming-board-Regents-selection-process.
103. Saul B. Cohen, email to members of the New York State Standards Review Initiative and the ELA/ESL Standards Panel, May 4, 2010.
104. Maura Walz, "New York Loses in First Round of Race to the Top; Will Reapply," *Chalkbeat*, March 29, 2010; Jennifer Medina, "New York Wins Race to the Top Grant," *New York Times*, August 24, 2010.
105. Ibid.
106. Andrea Gabor, "Unwrapping New York State's Latest Common Core Tests," *Andrea Gabor* (blog), June 11, 2014, http://andreagabor.com/2014/06/11/unwrapping-new-york-states-latest-common-core-tests.
107. Elizabeth Phillips, "We Need to Talk About the Test," *New York Times*, April 9, 2014.
108. Leonie Haimson, "The Pineapple and the Hare: Pearson's Absurd, Nonsensical ELA Exam, Recycled Endlessly Throughout Country," *NYC Public School Parents* (blog), April 19, 2012, http://nycpublicschoolparents.blogspot.com/2012/04/pineapple-and-hare-pearsons-absurd.html.
109. Andrea Gabor, "New York City Principals Mount Campaign Against 'Unfair' Tests, Target New High-Stakes 'Common Core' Assessment," *Andrea Gabor* (blog), May 15, 2013, https://andreagabor.com/2013/05/15/round-two-new-york-city-principals-mount-a-campaign-against-unfair-testing.

110. Michael Winerip, "Regents Pay a Political Price for Their Free Advisers, Dissenters Warn," *New York Times*, August 14, 2011; Kate Taylor, "Cuomo, in Shift, Is Said to Back Reducing Test Scores' Role in Teacher Reviews," *New York Times*, November 25, 2015.
111. Andrea Gabor, "New Education Mandates Hindered by Red Tape," *Al Jazeera*, December 12, 2013, http://america.aljazeera.com/articles/2013/12/18/new-education-mandateshinderedbyredtape.html.
112. Ibid.
113. Ibid.
114. Ibid.
115. Rachel Monahan, "New York City Principals Boo Bloomberg; Want de Blasio's Overhauls," *New York Daily News*, December 16, 2013, http://www.nydailynews.com/new-york/education/nyc-school-principals-boo-bloomberg-overhauls-article-1.1548867.
116. Zuckerman, interview.
117. Tovah Klein, Marcia Sells, Peter Rubie, and Amy Monegro, "The System Flunked, We Didn't," *New York Times*, November 11, 2007.
118. Zuckerman, interview; Andy Newman, "Hearst Official to Replace Klein at Helm of City Schools," *New York Times*, November 9, 2010; Elissa Gootman and Michael Barbaro, "Cathleen Black Is Out as City Schools Chancellor," *New York Times*, April 7, 2011.
119. Sharon Otterman, "Experienced, Homegrown Educator Leaves City Schools," *New York Times*, April 4, 2011.
120. Nadelstern, interview.
121. Patrick Wall, "Top State Education Official Criticizes City's School Support Networks," *Chalkbeat*, October 29, 2013, https://www.chalkbeat.org/posts/ny/2013/10/29/top-state-education-official-criticizes-citys-school-support-networks-2.
122. Andrea Gabor, "A Bloomberg-Era Reform Worth Saving?" *Gotham Gazette*, November 25, 2013, http://www.gothamgazette.com/education/4742-a-bloomberg-era-reform-worth-saving.
123. Patrick Wall, "How a Few School-Support Groups Created Under Bloomberg Survived Fariña's Overhaul," *Chalkbeat*, February 13, 2015.
124. Andrea Gabor, "Requiem for a School That Works," *Gotham Gazette*, April 7, 2017, http://www.gothamgazette.com/opinion/6858-requiem-for-a-school-that-works.
125. Ibid.
126. Ibid.
127. Ibid.; David Baiz, interview with author, June 13, 2017; Pryce-Harvey, interview.
128. Gabor, "Requiem."
129. Ibid.
130. Baiz, interview; "Our Team," *Hamilton Grange School*, https://www.thehamiltongrangeschool.org/our-team.
131. Gabor, "Requiem."
132. "Esperanza Preparatory Academy," *InsideSchools*, https://insideschools.org

/school/04M372; Off-the-record interview with teacher at Esperanza Preparatory Academy; Norm Scott, "District 4 Alexandra Estrella, Rumored to Being Bumped Upstairs, Hosts Inappropriate Drag Show at School Talent Show," *Ed Notes Online* (blog), June 3, 2017, https://ednotesonline.blogspot.com/2017/06/district-4-alexandra-estrella-rumored.html.

133. Off-the-record interview.
134. Andrea Gabor, "Death of a Bloomberg Era School Roils East Harlem," *Gotham Gazette*, January 30, 2018. http://www.gothamgazette.com/opinion/7449-death-of-bloomberg-era-school-roils-east-harlem.
135. Alex Zimmerman, "New York City Closes the Door on Mayor Bloomberg's Boot Camp for Principals, Marking End of an Era," *Chalkbeat*, August 31, 2017, https://www.chalkbeat.org/posts/ny/2017/08/31/new-york-city-closes-the-door-on-mayor-bloombergs-boot-camp-for-principals-marking-end-of-an-era.

3: State of Reform: The Not-So-Quiet Revolution in Massachusetts

1. Vivek Rao, "So Ordered? Scrutinizing the Massachusetts Judiciary's Role in the State's Sweeping Education Reform Plan," April 29, 2011, https://www.law.berkeley.edu/files/So_Ordered_Rao.pdf.
2. Ibid.; http://www.doe.mass.edu/finance/chapter70/McDuffy_report.pdf.
3. Rao, "So Ordered?"
4. Ibid.
5. Ibid.
6. Ibid.; L.E. Crowley, "FootJoy Closing Ends an Era," *Boston Globe*, March 22, 2009, http://archive.boston.com/news/local/articles/2009/03/22/footjoy_closing_ends_era.
7. "Every Child a Winner!: A Proposal for a Legislative Action Plan for Systemic Reform of Massachusetts' Public Primary and Secondary Education System" (Worcester, MA: Massachusetts Business Alliance for Education), D2.
8. Rao, "So Ordered?"
9. Anthony Flint, "Saving a System Mired in Mediocrity," *Boston Globe*, December 15, 1991, A21.
10. Patricia Nealon, "In Brockton, a Case Study of Crisis Students," *Boston Globe*, November 24, 1991.
11. Ibid.
12. "Charter Schools' Early Days in Massachusetts," *CommonWealth*, March 8, 2016, http://commonwealthmagazine.org/education/charter-schools-early-days-in-massachusetts.
13. "April 14, 1642: Massachusetts Passes First Education Law," *Mass Moments*, https://www.massmoments.org/moment-details/massachusetts-passes-first-education-law.html.

14. John Adams, "Thoughts on Government," 1776, http://www.heritage.org/initiatives/first-principles/primary-sources/john-adams-thoughts-on-government.
15. Mark Roosevelt, phone interview with author, November 2015.
16. Massachusetts Constitution, https://malegislature.gov/Laws/Constitution.
17. Rao, "So Ordered?"
18. Ibid.
19. Paul Reville, interview with author, November 2015.
20. "Every Child a Winner!"
21. Jordana Hart, "New Chief Known as Critic of Public Schools," *Boston Globe*, March 4, 1999, City Edition A; Editorial, "Rennie's Achievement" *Boston Globe*, January 18, 2001.
22. Jerry Taylor, "Crusade for Schools Puts CEO in Limelight He Shuns," *Boston Globe*, May 2, 1993; Cara Feinberg, "Martin Met Coretta," *Boston Globe*, January 22, 2003.
23. "Every Child a Winner!"
24. Ibid.; Rao, "So Ordered?"
25. Rao, "So Ordered?"
26. Tom Birmingham, interview with author, December 16, 2014.
27. Rao, "So Ordered?"
28. Ibid.
29. Craig Lambert, "The Welds of Harvard Yard: History Through a Family Lens," *Harvard Magazine*, November 1998, https://harvardmagazine.com/1998/11/welds.html.
30. Rich Rubino, "Political Family Feuds: The Good, the Bad, and the Really Ugly," *Huffington Post*, November 16, 2013.
31. Don Aucoin, "When Wits Collide State House Trio Parades IQs," *Boston Globe*, March 18, 1997.
32. Howie Carr, *The Brothers Bulger* (New York: Grand Central Publishing, 2006), 315; Rao, "So Ordered?"
33. Roosevelt, interview.
34. Achieve, "Taking Root: Massachusetts' Lessons for Sustaining and the College- and Career-Ready Agenda," 2009, https://www.achieve.org/publications/taking-root-massachusetts-lessons-sustaining-college-and-career-ready-agenda; Ann Bradley.
35. Michael Jonas, "High-Stakes Test," *Commonwealth*, June 5, 2008, http://commonwealthmagazine.org/education/mark-roosevelt-makes-the-transition-from-education-policymaker-to-practitioner.
36. Paul Reville, phone interview with author, November 2015.
37. Sarah Rimer, "Massachusetts Governor Cruises Election Road," *New York Times*, September 7, 1994.
38. Paul Reville, interview with author, December 15, 2014.
39. Jerry Taylor, "Crusade for Schools Puts CEO in Limelight He Shuns," *Boston Globe*, May 2, 1993; Frank Phillips, "Leaders Sort Out School Plans Weld Offers Cap,

Delay on Choice," *Boston Globe*, May 7, 1993; Editorial, "A 'Charter School' Loophole," *Boston Globe*, April 3, 1993; Peter J. Howe, "Wider School Choice Proposal Is Promised," *Boston Globe*, February 24, 1993.

40. Joan Vennochi, "Dangerous Liaisons," *Boston Globe*, March 12, 1993.
41. Patricia G. Anthony and Gretchen B. Rossman, "The Massachusetts Education Reform Act: What Is It and Will It Work?," *Viewpoints*, 1994.
42. Remedial programs help students who have fallen behind catch up academically.
43. Peter J. Howe, "Questions on Extent of School Reform," *Boston Globe*, June 7, 1993; Birmingham, interview; Achieve, "Taking Root."
44. Phil Oliff and Iris J. Lav, "Hidden Consequences: Lessons from Massachusetts for States Considering a Tax Cap," *Center on Budget and Policy Priorities*, May 21, 2008, http://www.cbpp.org//archiveSite/5-21-08sfp.pdf.
45. Birmingham, interview.
46. Abbreviated Working Draft for the Massachusetts Board of Elementary and Secondary Education, November 17, 2017, https://www.google.com/url?sa=t&rct=j&q=&esrc=s&source=web&cd=3&ved=0ahUKEwimusCk4KDYAhXhg-AKHXb2AAQQFgguMAI&url=http%3A%2F%2Fwww.doe.mass.edu%2Fbese%2Fdocs%2FFY2018%2F2017-11%2Fitem8a-workingdraft.docx&usg=AOvVaw0oMUUUK2nFUXv72NTfHm2p.
47. Andrea Gabor, "Round Two in the Bay State's Battle over the Common Core," *Andrea Gabor* (blog), April 8, 2015, https://andreagabor.com/2015/04/08/round-two-in-the-bay-states-battle-over-the-common-core.
48. Patricia Smith, "Needed: A Good Dose of Reality," *Boston Globe*, January 3, 1997; Carolyn Thompson, "John Silber's Reputation Precedes Him to Education Post," *Associated Press*, November 6, 1995; Trudy Tynan, "State Board of Education Still Struggling with History Curriculum," *Associated Press*, April 14, 1997.
49. Charles Glenn, "High Standards for Teachers," *Boston Globe*, October 6, 2007, http://archive.boston.com/news/globe/editorial_opinion/oped/articles/2007/10/06/high_standards_for_teachers.
50. Achieve, "Taking Root."
51. Sue Szachowicz, email communication, May 8, 2016.
52. Chris Cooney, interview with author, May 2014.
53. Sue Szachowicz, *Transforming Brockton High School: High Standards, High Expectations, No Excuses* (Rexford, NY: International Center for Leadership in Education, 2013), 1.
54. Sue Szachowicz, interview with author, October 2011; "Whatever Happened to Former BHS Principal Eugene Marrow?" *Enterprise News*, July 31, 2013, http://www.enterprisenews.com/article/20130731/NEWS/307319779.
55. Szachowicz, email.
56. "How High Schools Become Exemplary," The Achievement Guide Initiative at Harvard University, AGI Conference Report, 2009, http://www.agi.harvard.edu/events/2009Conference/2009AGIConferenceReport6-30-2010web.pdf.
57. Andrea Gabor, "Is Politics—Not School Improvement—Behind Brockton's

New Charter?," *Andrea Gabor* (blog), February, 27, 2016, https://andreagabor.com/2016/02/27/is-politics-not-school-improvement-behind-brocktons-new-charter; "2015 MCAS Scores for Each School in Massachusetts," *The Enterprise*, September 25, 2015, http://www.enterprisenews.com/article/20150925/NEWS/309309971.

58. Birmingham, interview.
59. Szachowicz, *Transforming Brockton High School*, 20–21.
60. Ibid., 21.
61. Ibid., 21–22.
62. Ibid., 22.
63. Ibid., 25.
64. Ibid., 22; Szachowicz, interview, November 2013.
65. Cooney, interview.
66. Alice Dembner, "Silber's No. 1 Job: Reading Skills Named to Board, He Plans 'Reform Schools,'" *Boston Globe*, November 5, 1995.
67. Szachowicz, *Transforming Brockton High School*, 26.
68. Ibid.
69. Szachowicz, interview, May 2014.
70. Szachowicz, *Transforming Brockton High School*, 26.
71. Szachowicz, interview, May 2014.
72. Andrea Gabor, "How a Decade-Long Literacy Obsession Transformed Brockton High," *Andrea Gabor* (blog), September 30, 2011, https://andreagabor.com/?s=Brockton+literacy.
73. Andrea Gabor, "Schools Caught in Red Tape Generated by New Education Mandates," *Al Jazeera America*, December 18, 2013, http://america.aljazeera.com/articles/2013/12/18/new-education-mandateshinderedbyredtape.html.
74. Cooney, interview.
75. Ibid.
76. Andrea Gabor, "How a Decade-Long Literacy Obsession Transformed Brockton High," *Andrea Gabor* (blog), September 30, 2011, https://andreagabor.com/2011/09/30/a-school%e2%80%99s-decade-long-literacy-obsession-and-how-it-transformed-brockton-high.
77. Szachowicz, *Transforming Brockton High School*, 29.
78. Szachowicz, interview, May 2014
79. Ibid.
80. Ibid.
81. Ibid.
82. Ibid.
83. Ibid.
84. Cooney, interview.
85. John Merian, interview with author, May 2014.
86. Ibid.
87. Ibid.; Alyce Reizian, interview with author, May 2014.

88. Merian, interview.
89. Merian, interview.
90. Peter Kilborn, "Another Tumble in the Decline of Main Street," *New York Times*, November 4, 1993.
91. Merian, interview.
92. Reizian, interview.
93. Maria Papadopoulos, "Hundreds Turn Out for Brockton's Santa Hat Challenge," *The Enterprise*, November 24, 2013, http://www.enterprisenews.com/x1069226640/Hundreds-turn-out-for-Brockton-s-Santa-Hat-Challenge; Carla Gualdron, "Brockton to Hold 26th Annual Holiday Parade Saturday," *The Enterprise*, November 23, 2012, http://www.enterprisenews.com/x459326454/Brockton-s-holiday-parade-to-honor-returning-Veterans; MetroSouth Chamber of Commerce Action Report, March 2015, http://www.metrosouthchamber.com/pdf/march15ar.pdf; "Edgar Department Stores," *Revolvy*, http://www.revolvy.com/main/index.php?s=Edgar%20Department%20Stores&uid=1575.
94. Merian, interview.
95. "US Demography 1790 to Present," Social Explorer, http://www.socialexplorer.com/6f4cdab7a0/explore; Szachowicz, interview.
96. Szachowicz, interview.
97. Gerald Beals, "Be Enlightened . . . The 'Brockton Operation,'" 1999, http://www.thomasedison.com/enlightened.html; Bradford Kingman, *History of Brockton, Plymouth County, Massachusetts, 1656–1894* (Salem, MA: Higginson), https://archive.org/stream/historyofbrockto00king/historyofbrockto00king_djvu.txt.
98. Merian, interview.
99. Andrea Gabor, "Will Brockton High's Principal Succeed Where Mayor Bloomberg Failed?" *Andrea Gabor* (blog), October 29, 2012, https://andreagabor.com/2012/10/29/will-brockton-highs-principal-succeed-where-mayor-bloomberg-failed.
100. Alex Bloom, "New Principal Looks to Build on Success of Brockton High," *Patriot Ledger*, July 9, 2013, http://www.patriotledger.com/article/20130709/NEWS/307099837. Wolder was moved to another position in the district in 2017.
101. Kerry A. White, "Silber Resigns as Mass. Board Head; Ends Standoff over New State Chief," *Education Week*, March 10, 1999, http://www.edweek.org/ew/articles/1999/03/10/26mass.h18.html.
102. Lyndsey Layton, "How Bill Gates Pulled Off the Swift Common Core Revolution," *Washington Post*, June 7, 2014.
103. Ibid.
104. Reville, interview; Andrea Gabor, "Round Two."
105. "Public School Funding in Massachusetts: Where We Are, What Has Changed, and How We Compare to Other States," *Massachusetts Budget and Policy Center*, September 1, 2011, http://massbudget.org/report_window.php?loc=Annual_Census_Education_paper_FY09_data_Sept_2011_release_v04.html.

106. Ricki Morell, "Massachusetts Wonders if Race to the Top Is Worth It," *Hechinger Report*, June 1, 2010, http://hechingerreport.org/massachusetts-wonders-if-race-to-the-top-is-worth-winning.
107. "Public School Funding in Massachusetts."
108. Jamie Gass, "National Poetry Month Showcases the Need for Higher-Quality English Standards," *Mass Live*, April 23, 2015, http://www.masslive.com/opinion/index.ssf/2015/04/national_poetry_month.html.
109. Birmingham, interview.
110. Sandra Stotsky, *Testimony Before Texas State House of Representatives on House Bill No. 2923*, April 15, 2011, http://parentsacrossamerica.org/sandra-stotsky-on-the-mediocrity-of-the-Common Core-ela-standards/#sthash.KOrBgVhA.dpuf.
111. Ibid.
112. Ibid.
113. Ibid.
114. Jacob Hall, "Sandra Stotsky: Common Core Gets Things Backward," *State Journal*, August 28, 2014.
115. Sue Desmond-Hellman, "What If . . . : Lessons in U.S. Education," *Bill & Melinda Gates Foundation*, http://www.gatesfoundation.org/2016/ceo-letter#section4.
116. Valerie Strauss, "How Hard Would It Be to Replace the Common Core with Something Better?," *Washington Post*, January 1, 2015.
117. Charles Chieppo and Jamie Gass, "Gates' Money at Core of Support," *Boston Herald*, April 7, 2015, http://www.bostonherald.com/news_opinion/opinion/op_ed/2015/04/gates_money_at_core_of_support.
118. Ibid.
119. Andrea Gabor, "Round Two."
120. Jeremy C. Fox, "Education Board Votes to Adopt Hybrid MCAS-PARCC Test," *Boston Globe*, November 17, 2015, https://www.bostonglobe.com/metro/2015/11/17/state-education-board-vote-whether-replace-mcas/aex1nGyBYZW2sucEW2o82L/story.html.
121. Andrea Gabor, "Round Two."
122. George Scott et al., "Race to the Top: States Implementing Teacher and Principal Evaluation Systems Despite Challenges," *United States Government Accountability Office*, September 2013, http://www.gao.gov/products/GAO-13-777.
123. Andrea Gabor, "Schools Caught in Red Tape Generated by New Education Mandates," *Al Jazeera*, December 18, 2013, http://america.aljazeera.com/articles/2013/12/18/new-education-mandateshinderedbyredtape.html.
124. Szachowicz, interview; Cooney, interview; Nancy Bloom, "Straight Outta Brockton," *Edushyster*, January 8, 2013, http://edushyster.com/straight-outta-brockton.
125. Ibid.; Alex Bloom, "Brockton Residents, Officials Show Up to Support or Oppose Charter School," *The Enterprise*, December 19, 2012, http://www.uscharters.org/2012/12/brockton-residents-officials-show-up-to.html.

126. Andrea Gabor, "Is Politics—Not School Improvement—Behind Brockton's New Charter?" *Andrea Gabor* (blog), February 27, 2016, https://andreagabor.com/2016/02/27/is-politics-not-school-improvement-behind-brocktons-new-charter.
127. Bloom, "Straight Outta Brockton."
128. "Brockton Educators Rip Charter School Proposal," *The Enterprise*, January 12, 2015, http://www.enterprisenews.com/article/20150112/News/150119422/?template=printart.
129. Bloom, "Straight Outta Brockton."
130. "Would the Proposed Charter School in Brockton Be a Benefit to the City?" *The Enterprise*, November 9, 2011; John Laidler, "Would the Proposed Charter School in Brockton Be a Benefit to the City?" *Boston Globe*, November 9, 2014, https://www.bostonglobe.com/metro/regionals/south/2014/11/09/two-views-merits-proposed-charter-school-brockton/B8Rvh8MTN8ltaS32VQyKeJ/story.html.
131. "Brockton Educators Rip Charter School Proposal."
132. Andrea Gabor, "Update: Brockton's Charter Fiasco Continues as Controversial School Prepares to Leave Town," *Andrea Gabor* (blog), September 3, 2016, https://andreagabor.com/2016/09/03/update-brocktons-charter-fiasco-continues-as-controversial-school-prepares-to-leave-town.
133. Ibid.
134. Ibid.
135. Ibid.
136. Ibid.
137. Ibid.
138. Andrea Gabor, "Is Politics."
139. Mark Larocque, "Attendance Lags Behind Expectations at New Heights Charter School of Brockton," *The Enterprise*, September 9, 2018, http://www.enterprisenews.com/news/20160909/attendance-lags-behind-expectations-at-new-heights-charter-school-of-brockton; also Andrea Gabor, "Bay State Charter Campaign Gets a Black Eye in Brockton: New Heights Charter Unlikely to Open on Main St.," *Andrea Gabor* (blog), August 12, 2016 https://andreagabor.com/2016/08/12/bay-state-charter-campaign-gets-a-black-eye-in-brockton-new-heights-charter-unlikely-to-open-on-main-st.
140. "Our Opinion: Just Say No to Charter Schools," *The Enterprise*, February 20, 2016, http://www.enterprisenews.com/article/20160220/NEWS/160229526/0/SEARCH.
141. Szachowicz, interview; Cooney, interview.
142. Ibid.
143. Ibid.
144. Ibid.
145. Bob Pearlman, "Pilot Schools," http://www.bobpearlman.org/Strategies/Pilots.htm; Tracy Jan, "High-Flying Pilot Schools Study Points to Range of Successes in Boston's Experimental Program," *Boston Globe*, November 9, 2007, http://archive.boston.com/news/education/k_12/mcas/articles/2007/11/09/high_flying_pilot_schools.

146. Sarah R. Cohodes, Elizabeth M. Setren, Christopher R. Walters, Joshua D. Angrist, and Parag A. Pathak, *Charter School Demand and Effectiveness: A Boston Update* (Boston, MA: The Boston Foundation, 2013), https://seii.mit.edu/wp-content/uploads/2013/10/Charter-School-Demand-and-Effectiveness.pdf.
147. "New Study of Massachusetts' Charter Schools Finds Urban Charter Schools Boost Achievement Sharply, but Results for Nonurban Charters Are Mixed," *Harvard University Center for Education Policy Research*, February 4, 2011, https://cepr.harvard.edu/news/new-study-massachusetts-charter-schools.
148. Andrea Gabor, "New CREDO Study, New Credibility Problems: From New Orleans to Boston," *Andrea Gabor* (blog), April 28, 2015, https://andreagabor.com/2015/04/28/new-credo-study-new-credibility-problems-from-new-orleans-to-boston; "Problems with CREDO's Charter School Research: Understanding the Issues," National Education Policy Center, June 2015, http://nepc.colorado.edu/newsletter/2015/09/problems-credos-research.
149. The Boston Opportunity Agenda, *Fourth Annual Report Card*, 2015, http://www.tbf.org/tbf/81/~/media/5C473FE62FFB4914A6513139077E2D26.pdf; The Boston Opportunity Agenda, *Fifth Annual Report Card*, 2016, https://www.tbf.org/~/media/TBFOrg/Files/Reports/BOA%20Annual%202016_FinalREV15th2.pdf.
150. "Charter Cap 'n Gown II: The College Years," *Edushyster*, January 26, 2015, http://edushyster.com/charter-cap-n-gown-ii-the-college-years.
151. Birmingham, interview.
152. Andrea Gabor, "Is Deval Patrick's 'Miracle School' the Best Example of Mass. Ed Reform?," *Andrea Gabor* (blog), September 6, 2012, https://andreagabor.com/2012/09/06/is-deval-patricks-miracle-school-the-best-example-of-mass-ed-reform/; Akilah Johnson, "A 'Dream' Trip and Visit with President Obama," *Boston Globe*, January 20, 2013, https://www.bostonglobe.com/metro/2013/01/21/second-graders-roxbury-talk-obama-inauguration-and-martin-luther-king/scyookevIOoSVZPhaZKMLK/story.html.
153. Jeremy C. Fox, "Walsh Taking Heat over School Agenda," *Boston Globe*, December 4, 2015.
154. Jeremy R. Levine and William Julius Wilson, "Poverty, Politics, and a 'Circle of Promise': Holistic Education Policy in Boston and the Challenge of Institutional Entrenchment," *Journal of Urban Affairs* 35, no. 1 (2013): doi:10.1111/juaf.12001.
155. *Public School Mama*, https://publicschoolmama.com/2015/11.
156. Andrea Gabor and Peggy Wiesenberg, "Update: How Long-time Charter Funders Are Upping the Ante in Their Bid to Blow the Bay State's Charter-School Cap," *Andrea Gabor* (blog), November 7, 2016, https://andreagabor.com/2016/11/07/update-how-long-time-charter-funders-are-upping-the-ante-in-their-bid-to-blow-the-bay-states-charter-school-cap; "Gov. Patrick Signs Landmark Education Bill," *Massachusetts Municipal Association*, January 18, 2010, https://www.mma.org/gov-patrick-signs-landmark-education-bill.
157. Andrea Gabor and Peggy Wiesenberg, "Record Fine for Campaign-Finance Violation Sheds Light on Dark Money Donors to Bay State Charter Referendum,"

Andrea Gabor (blog), September 26, 2017, https://andreagabor.com/2017/09/26/record-fine-for-campaign-finance-violation-sheds-light-on-dark-money-contributors-to-charter-referendum.

158. James Vaznis, "Struggling Brockton Schools May Sue the State," *Boston Globe*, March 17, 2018.

4: No Lone Stars: How Trust and Collaboration in One Texas School District Have Created Lasting Reform

1. Lisa Napper, email to Monta Akin, November 9, 2015.
2. "Cedar Chopping in Central Texas," Williamson County Historical Commission, http://www.williamson-county-historical-commission.org/Round_rock/Cedar_Chopping_in_Central_Texas_Cedar_Park_Texas.html.
3. Monta Akin, interview with author, January 2015, and email.
4. Ibid.
5. Ibid.
6. Bret Champion, Leander Culture Day interview, January/February 2015.
7. Ibid.
8. Ibid.
9. Rhonda Bliss, Culture Day interview, January/February 2015.
10. Gloria Vela, Culture Day interview, January/February 2015.
11. Joe E. Robinson, *Continuous Improvement in the Leander ISD: A Quantitative and Qualitative Assessment of Culture and Core Values* (Dissertation, Texas A&M, October 21, 2011), 482.
12. Ibid., 306.
13. Ibid., 270.
14. Ibid., 271.
15. Ibid.
16. "Historical Overview of Assessment in Texas," *Technical Digest 2010 to 2011*. https://www.google.com/url?sa=t&rct=j&q=&esrc=s&source=web&cd=1&ved=0ahUKEwjjhb7V_uTYAhViluAKHfV4BugQFggnMAA&url=https%3A%2F%2Ftea.texas.gov%2FWorkArea%2FDownloadAsset.aspx%3Fidb%3D2147506146&usg=AOvVaw1OPv_pEZhbaPr_yWrKxJ0O.
17. Ben Davis, *Examining Teacher Performance Incentives*, Report no. 78-17 (Texas: House Research Organization, 2004).
18. Ibid.
19. Nate Blakeslee, "Crash Test," *Texas Monthly*, May 2013, http://www.texasmonthly.com/politics/crash-test/#sthash.qEtx5IPb.dpuf.
20. Ibid.
21. Monta Akin, interview with the author, February 2015.
22. Ibid.
23. Ibid.

24. Tom Glenn, interview with the author, March 2014; Akin, interview; David Langford, phone interview with the author, March 2017.
25. Akin, interview; Langford, phone interview, March 2017.
26. David Langford, W. Edwards Deming Institute Podcasts, 2014.
27. Andrea Gabor, *The Man Who Discovered Quality: How W. Edwards Deming Brought the Quality Revolution to America: The Stories of Ford, Xerox, and GM* (New York: Times Books, 1990), 15, 40.
28. MacKenzie Hird, Richard Larson, Yuko Okubo, and Kanji Uchino, "Lesson Study and Lesson Sharing: An Appealing Marriage," *Creative Education*, June 2014.
29. Gabor, *The Man Who Discovered Quality*, 127.
30. Ibid., 238.
31. Ibid., 125, 126, 131, 138.
32. Langford, phone interview, March 2017.
33. Kathleen Cotton, "Applying Total Quality Management Principles to Secondary Education: M. Edgecumbe High School, Sitka, Alaska," School Improvement Research Series, November 1994, http://educationnorthwest.org/sites/default/files/ApplyingQualityManagementPrinciples.pdf; Langford, phone interview, March 2017; Dean Fosdick, "'Far East' at Center of Alaska Boarding School's Curriculum," *Associated Press*, January 12, 1986.
34. David Langford, interview with author, March 2013.
35. Cotton, "Applying Total Quality Management Principles to Secondary Education."
36. Langford, phone interview, March 2017.
37. Ibid.; David Langford, W. Edwards Deming Institute Podcasts, 2014.
38. Langford, phone interview, March 2017.
39. Cotton, "Applying Total Quality Management Principles to Secondary Education."
40. Ibid.
41. Ibid.
42. Robinson, *Continuous Improvement*, 249.
43. Akin, interview; Tripp Babbitt, W. Edwards Deming Institute podcast with Monta Akin, January 9, 2015, http://podcast.deming.org/monta-akin-discusses-leander-independent-school-districts-transformation-to-happyville.
44. Bret Alan Champion, "The Effects of High-Stakes Testing on Central Office Organizational Culture: Changes in One School District" (DEd diss., University of Texas at Austin, 2007), https://www.lib.utexas.edu/etd/d/2007/championd49134/championd49134.pdf.
45. Akin, interview.
46. Teresa Palomo Acosta, "Edgewood ISD v. Kirby," *Texas State Historical Association*, June 12, 2010, https://tshaonline.org/handbook/online/articles/jre02.
47. Stephen Phillips, email to author, June 3, 2016; Kirst, "Historic Role in Syracuse."
48. Debbie Graves, "Nominee for Education Chief Doesn't Like to Go by the Book," *Austin American-Statesman*, February 9, 1991.
49. Ibid.

50. Ibid.; "New York Educator Selected as Texas' Next Education Chief," *Victoria Advocate* (Austin), February 17, 1991.
51. Harley Johnson, "An Educator's Valedictory," *Cox News Service*, June 8, 2007.
52. John Hunter, "Deming Today: Leander Texas Independent School District," *The W. Edwards Deming Institute Blog*, September 18, 2014, https://blog.deming.org/2014/09/deming-today-leander-texas-independent-school-district.
53. Akin, interview.
54. Johnson, "An Educator's Valedictory."
55. Akin, interview with author.
56. Akin, email to author, October 18, 2015.
57. Lisa Napper, email to Monta Akin.
58. Glenn, interview.
59. Champion, "The Effects of High-Stakes Testing on Central Office Organizational Culture."
60. "Leander ISD," *Texas Tribune*, https://schools.texastribune.org/districts/leander-isd.
61. Akin, interview with author, August 2015.
62. "Seven Student Learning Behaviors Drive DI and Robotics Competitions," Leander ISD, Superintendent's Column (Archive), February 27, 2012, http://www2.leanderisd.org/default.aspx?name=abt.supertndnt.column2&a=122.
63. Monta Akin, interview with author, August 2015.
64. Sharon Hejl, interview with author, August 2015.
65. David Langford, *Tool Time for Education, Langford International*, 2015, 48.
66. Hejl, interview, August 2015.
67. Ibid.; Christina A. Samuels, "An Instructional Approach Expands Its Reach," *Education Week*, March 2, 2011, http://www.edweek.org/ew/articles/2011/03/02/22rti-overview.h30.html.
68. Hejl, interview.
69. Ibid.
70. Susan Combs, "Public School Construction Costs," Texas Comptroller of Public Accounts: Data Services Division, July 2014, http://www.texastransparency.org/Special_Features/Reports/School_Construction/pdf/Public_School_Construction_Costs.pdf.
71. Aman Batheja, "Swelling School Districts Find Costly Way to Put Off the Pain," *New York Times*, August 28, 2014.
72. Donnie Hisle, interview with author, August 2015.
73. Glenn, interview.
74. Cobby Caputo for Leander ISD Board of Trustees, February 15 at 5:00pm Edited, https://www.facebook.com/Cobby4LISD/posts/410408875803824 Major Issue No.1-District Long-Term Debt.; Hisle, interview.
75. Hisle and Skoviera interviews, August 2015.
76. Ibid.
77. Akin, interview, January 2015.

78. Parkside Scholar video, http://mediacast.leanderisd.org/inventivex/mediaresources/checkout_clean.cfm?ContentID=181842&TransactionID=158337&Checksum=%20%20764720&RepServerID=&JumpSeconds=0.
79. Team interviews and photos at Parkside, January 2015.
80. Hejl, interview with author, January 2015.
81. Ibid.
82. Sarah Ambrus and Christine Simpson, *Riding Shotgun: Empowering Students to Lead Change* (Raleigh, NC: Lulu Press, 2012), 3.
83. Terry Ballard, phone interview with author, August 2014.
84. Christine Simpson and Sarah Ambrus, interviews with author, January 2015.
85. Mike Parker, "Simpson New LMS Principal," *Cedar Park-Leander Statesman*, June 12, 2012, http://www.leanderisd.org/default.aspx?name=dis.news2&a=578.
86. Simpson and Ambrus, interviews, January 2015.
87. Greg Graham, interview with author, January 2015; Ballard, interview.
88. "Campus," FCA Austin, http://fcaaustin.org/campus.
89. Simpson, interview, January 2015.
90. Ambrus and Simpson, *Riding Shotgun*, 10.
91. Ambrus and Simpson, interview.
92. Ambrus and Simpson, *Riding Shotgun*, 11.
93. Ibid., 3.
94. Ambrus and Simpson, interview.
95. Ibid.
96. Ibid.
97. Ambrus and Simpson, *Riding Shotgun*, 73.
98. Ambrus, interview, January 2015.
99. Ballard, phone interview.
100. Ibid.
101. Terry Ballard, LinkedIn profile, https://www.linkedin.com/in/htballard.
102. Simpson, interview with author, January 2015.
103. Kase 101 radio interview.
104. Ballard, phone interview.
105. Akin, interview, January 2015.
106. "Leander High School in Leander, Texas," StartClass.com, http://public-schools.startclass.com/l/88410/Leander-High-School-in-Texas.
107. Eric Haug, phone interview, July 2017; Graham, interview.
108. Graham, interview.
109. Leander Continuous Improvement Conference, January/February 2015.
110. Ibid.
111. Ibid.
112. Akin, interview, August 2015.
113. Ibid.
114. Ibid.

115. Ibid.
116. Haug, interview.
117. Ibid.
118. Leander teacher, phone interview with author, August 2017.
119. Akin, interview, August 2017.

5: The Hurricane and the Charters

1. Andrea Gabor, "Post-Katrina, The Great New Orleans Charter School Tryout," *Newsweek*, September 20, 2013.
2. Nick Anderson, "Education Secretary Duncan Calls Hurricane Katrina Good for New Orleans Schools," *Washington Post*, January 30, 2010.
3. Gabor, "Post-Katrina."
4. Ibid.
5. Ibid.
6. Ibid.
7. Andrea Gabor, "The Myth of the New Orleans School Makeover," *New York Times*, August 23, 2015.
8. Ibid.
9. "2014–2015 Louisiana ACT 12th Grade Results," *Louisiana Department of Education*, http://media.nola.com/education_impact/other/EMBARGOED%202014-2015%20Louisiana%20ACT%2012th%20Grade%20Results.pdf; Danielle Dreilinger, "New Orleans ACT Results Mixed for 2016," *Times-Picayune*, July 25, 2016.
10. Doug Harris, interview with the author, August 24, 2016; Doug Harris, email message to the author, October 29, 2016.
11. Gabor, "The Myth."
12. Brian R. Beabout, "Community Leadership: Seeking Social Justice While Recreating Public Schools," *International Handbook on Social (In)Justices and Educational Leadership*, Springer International Handbooks of Education (New York: Springer, 2013), 543–70.
13. Harold Meyerson, "How the Charter School Lobby Is Changing the Democratic Party," *Los Angeles Times*, August 26, 2016, http://www.latimes.com/opinion/op-ed/la-oe-meyerson-charter-school-democrats-20160826-snap-story.html.
14. Gabor, "Post-Katrina."
15. Ibid.
16. Ibid.
17. The Cowen Institute for Public Education Initiatives, *The State of Public Education in New Orleans* (New Orleans: Tulane University, 2013).
18. Ibid.
19. Ibid.
20. "The Edible Schoolyard New Orleans," http://docshare.tips/the-edible-schoolyard-new-orleans_575bf1cfb6d87f62248b48ed.html.
21. Dawn Ruth, "Why Should You Know About FirstLine?" *New Orleans Magazine*,

January 2012, http://www.myneworleans.com/New-Orleans-Magazine/January-2012/Why-should-you-know-about-FirstLine; Gabor, "Post-Katrina."

22. Gabor, "Post-Katrina"; "History," *Edible Schoolyard New Orleans*, http://www.esynola.org/history.html.
23. Raynard Sanders, interview with the author, August 2016.
24. Sarah Carr, *Hope Against Hope* (New York: Bloomsbury, 2015), 100.
25. Paul Arce-Trigatti, Jane Arnold Lincove, Douglas N. Harris, and Huriya Jabbar, *Is There Choice in School Choice?: School Program Offerings in the New Orleans Public School Market* (New Orleans: Educational Research Alliance for New Orleans, 2016).
26. "PK–8 Performance," Louisiana Department of Education, https://www.louisianabelieves.com/resources/library/test-results.
27. "Nola By the Numbers: High Stakes Testing 2010–2011," *The Cowen Institute*, June 2011 http://www.coweninstitute.com/wp-content/uploads/2011/06/NBTN-LEAP-and-GEE-2011-CORRECTED.pdf; Danielle Dreilinger, "New Orleans High School Exam Results, Graduation Rate Near State Average," *Times-Picayune*, July 11, 2014.
28. Doug Harris, "The New Orleans OneApp," *EducationNext* 15, no. 4, http://educationnext.org/new-orleans-oneapp.
29. Gabor, "Post-Katrina."
30. Ibid.
31. Ibid.
32. Ibid.
33. Ibid.
34. Ibid.
35. Ibid.
36. Ibid.
37. Ibid.
38. Ibid.
39. Ibid.; Alison Burciaga, email message to author, November 28, 2016.
40. Gabor, "Post-Katrina."
41. Ibid.
42. Allen Grove, "Southern University at New Orleans Admissions: ACT Scores, Acceptance Rate, Financial Aid & More," *ThoughtCo*, July 23, 2017, https://www.thoughtco.com/southern-university-at-new-orleans-profile-786807.
43. Gabor, "Post-Katrina."
44. Ibid.
45. Ibid.
46. Bob Warren, "Louisiana Education Superintendent John White Pitches Diploma Revamp in Mandeville," *Times-Picayune*, June 24, 2013; Danielle Dreilinger, "'Career Diploma' Promises Louisiana High School Graduates Good Jobs—Without Four Years of College," *Times-Picayune*, March 6, 2014.
47. "Raising the Bar: Louisiana Type 2, 4, and 5 Charter Schools, 2014–15 Annual

Report," *Louisiana Department of Education*, https://www.louisianabelieves.com/docs/default-source/school-choice/2014-2015-charter-annual-report.pdf.

48. Gabor, "Post-Katrina."
49. "Raising the Bar."
50. Collegiate Academies Form 990, June 30, 2014, http://990s.foundationcenter.org/990_pdf_archive/800/800601507/800601507_201406_990.pdf?_ga=1.262722959.2093656780.1476134204; Gabor, "Post-Katrina."
51. Gabor, "Post-Katrina."
52. Ibid.
53. Ibid.
54. Ibid.
55. Ibid.
56. Ibid.
57. Ibid.
58. Ibid.
59. Ibid.
60. Carr, *Hope Against Hope*, 239.
61. Eden Heilman, phone interview with author, September 2, 2016
62. Eden Heilman, email message to author, September 26, 2016; "2015 Y.T.D. Stats (School Related Incidents)."
63. Heilman, interview.
64. Off-the-record interview.
65. "Q.B.V. Jefferson Parish Public School System," *Southern Poverty Law Center*, January 10, 2012, https://www.splcenter.org/seeking-justice/case-docket/qb-v-jefferson-parish-public-school-system.
66. Heilman, interview.
67. Cowen Institute, Tulane University, Reconnecting Opportunity Youth, May 2012 http://www.thecoweninstitute.com.php56-17.dfw3-1.websitetestlink.com/uploads/Reconnecting-Opportunity-Youth-Reference-Guide-1506029488.pdf.
68. Katy Reckdahl, "Ashes of Federal Marshal Who Helped Integrate New Orleans Schools Returning to City," *Times-Picayune*, September 29, 2012, http://www.nola.com/education/index.ssf/2012/09/ashes_of_federal_marshal_who_h.html.
69. Leona Tate, interview with author, August 25, 2016.
70. Drew Cristopher Joy, *Contextualizing Katrina: Resources on New Orleans History and Culture for Visiting Activists and Confronting Racism Resources for White Activists* (New Orleans: Tulane University, 2009), https://organizingforpower.files.wordpress.com/2009/06/cg-anti-racism-reading-packet.pdf.
71. Sanders, interview.
72. Brian R. Beabout, *Principals' Perceptions of School Leadership in Post-Katrina New Orleans* (State College, PA: Pennsylvania State University Graduate School Department of Learning and Performance Systems, 2008), 78.
73. Ibid., 78–80.

74. Sanders, interview.
75. Patricia Perkins, interview with author, June 2016.
76. Tate, interview.
77. Davison M. Douglas, "Bush v. Orleans Parish School Board and the Desegregation of New Orleans Schools," prepared for inclusion in the project Federal Trials and Great Debates in United States History, Federal Judicial Center, Federal Judicial History Office, 2005, 6, https://www.fjc.gov/sites/default/files/trials/bush.pdf.
78. Tate, interview.
79. Ibid.
80. Ibid.
81. Ibid.
82. Ibid.
83. Ibid.
84. Ibid.
85. Donald E. DeVore and Joseph Logsdon, *Crescent City Schools: Public Education in New Orleans 1841 to 1991* (New Orleans: OPSB, The Center for Louisiana Studies, University of Southwestern Louisiana, 1991), 2–3.
86. Ibid.
87. Ibid.
88. Ibid., 41.
89. Ibid., 60; "Historic Inequities in New Orleans Public Education: A Legacy of Struggle," *New Orleans Tribune*, http://id3410.securedata.net/theneworleanstribune/publiceducation.htm.
90. DeVore and Logsdon, *Crescent City Schools*, 62, 70–71, 73, 81.
91. Ibid., 33, 103; Danielle Dreilinger, "McDonogh No. 35, New Orleans' 1st Black Public High School, Gets New Home," *Times-Picayune*, September 23, 2015, http://www.nola.com/education/index.ssf/2015/09/first_black_high_school_mcdono.html.
92. DeVore and Logsdon, *Crescent City Schools*, 20, 52, 64, 103.
93. Ibid., 92.
94. Ibid., 103, 105.
95. Ibid., 90.
96. Ibid., 94.
97. Ibid., 118; State Constitution of Louisiana, 1898, Suffrage and Elections, Article 197; Leonard P. Ayres, *Laggards in Our Schools* (New York: Russell Sage Foundation, Charities Publication Committee, 1909), 176.
98. Ayres, *Laggards*, 56.
99. Ibid.
100. Ibid., 63, 97.
101. Ibid., 138.
102. DeVore and Logsdon, *Crescent City Schools*, 172.
103. Ibid., 141, 172.

104. Ibid., 136 to 140, 143; Jones L. Wallas, "A History of Compulsory School Attendance and Visiting Teacher Services in Louisiana," Louisiana State University Historical Dissertations and Theses, 1967, 88.
105. DeVore and Logsdon, *Crescent City Schools*, 162.
106. Ibid., 146.
107. Ibid., 147, 163.
108. Ibid., 163–64.
109. Ibid., 167, 182; John Smith Kendall, *History of New Orleans, vol. 3* (Chicago: Lewis Publishing Company, 1922), 1158–59.
110. DeVore and Logsdon, *Crescent City Schools*, 168, 361.
111. Ibid., 170.
112. Ibid., 191.
113. Ibid.; The Cowen Institute for Public Education Initiatives, *New Orleans Public School History: A Brief Overview* (New Orleans: Tulane University, 2007); Della Hasselle, "RSD Scraps Plans to Move Cohen to Booker T. Washington Site," *Louisiana Weekly*, October 26, 2015.
114. DeVore and Logsdon, *Crescent City Schools*, 182–83; Beabout, *Principals' Perceptions*, 85.
115. Cowen Institute, "New Orleans Public School History."
116. DeVore and Logsdon, *Crescent City Schools*, 211; "Historic Inequities in New Orleans Public Education: A Legacy of Struggle," *New Orleans Tribune*, http://id3410.securedata.net/theneworleanstribune/publiceducation.htm; "Journey for Justice: The A.P. Tureaud Story," *Louisiana Public Broadcasting*, http://www.lpb.org/index.php?/site/programs/journey_for_justice_the_a.p._tureaud_story.
117. Douglas, "Bush v. Orleans Parish School Board," 2.
118. Liva Baker, *The Second Battle of New Orleans* (New York: Harper Collins, 1996), 305.
119. Crain, *The Politics of School Integration* (New York: Routledge, 2017), 245. DeVore and Logsdon, *Crescent City Schools*, 232.
120. DeVore and Logsdon, *Crescent City Schools*, 235.
121. Ibid., 241.
122. Baker, *The Second Battle*, 423.
123. Cowen Institute, "New Orleans Public School History."
124. Ibid.
125. A.J. Liebling, "The Great State-I," *New Yorker*, May 28, 1960.
126. Ibid.
127. Editorial, "The Need for Ladies on the School Board," *Daily Picayune*, August 1, 1895.
128. "Louisiana Most Corrupt State in the Nation, Mississippi Second, Illinois Sixth, New Jersey Ninth?," *Corporate Crime Reporter* 40, October 8, 2007, http://www.corporatecrimereporter.com/corrupt100807.htm.
129. Brian Thevenot, "Jefferson Case Shows Meltdown of Orleans Parish School

Board," *Times-Picayune*, August 28, 2009, http://www.nola.com/politics/index.ssf/2009/08/jefferson_case_shows_meltdown.html; "Anthony Amato, Former New Orleans Public Schools Superintendent, Dies at 66," *Times-Picayune*, December 2, 2013, http://www.nola.com/education/index.ssf/2013/12/school_superintendent_anthony.html.

130. Thevenot, "Jefferson Case."
131. Ibid.
132. Ibid.
133. Ibid.
134. Cindy Chang, "Ellenese Brooks-Simms Gets Sentence Reduced as Reward for Helping Prosecutors," *Times-Picayune*, March 11, 2010, http://www.nola.com/crime/index.ssf/2010/03/ellenese_brooks-simms_got_sent.html.
135. Reasons for Judgment, Civil District Court for the Parish of Orleans, State of Louisiana, *Eddy Oliver, Et Al. Versus Orleans Parish School Board, Et Al.*, May 20, 2012.
136. Brian Thevenot, "New Orleans' School System Flunks; Superintendent Amato Resigns," *Times-Picayune*, April 13, 2005.
137. Ibid.
138. Nancy Picard, "Louisiana's Great Education Giveaway," *Louisiana Voice*, April 26, 2013, https://louisianavoice.com/2013/04/26/guest-column-metairie-attorney-dissects-the-post-katrina-politicalization-patronage-of-louisiana-public-education; The Cowen Institute for Public Education Initiatives, *The Recovery School District of Louisiana* (New Orleans: Tulane University, 2010).
139. *Eddy Oliver v Orleans Parish School Board et al*, Reasons for Judgment, Civil District Court for the Parish of Orleans, State of Louisiana, "Division N," June 20, 2012; Picard, "Louisiana's Great Education Giveaway."
140. *Eddy Oliver, Et Al. Versus Orleans Parish School Board, Et Al*, Reasons for Judgment.
141. Picard, "Louisiana's Great Education Giveaway"; Gary Rivlin, "Why the Lower Ninth Ward Looks Like the Hurricane Just Hit," *The Nation*, August 13, 2015.
142. The Cowen Institute for Public Education Initiatives, *The State of Public Education in New Orleans Five Years After the Storm* (New Orleans: Tulane University, 2010); Thevenot, "New Orleans' School System Flunks."
143. Dan Baum, "The Lost Year: Letter from New Orleans," *New Yorker*, August 21, 2006.
144. Beabout, *Principals' Perceptions*, 87.
145. Louisiana Legislative Auditor, "Financial Audit Services Management Letter," December 21, 2015, https://www.lla.la.gov/PublicReports.nsf/E3B5A06799FE3E5586257F1F006F1199/$FILE/0000B9BC.pdf; Jessica Williams, "Louisiana Education Department Ineffectively Audited Programs, Report Says," December 1, 2014, *Times Picayune*, http://www.nola.com/education/index.ssf/2014/12/louisiana_education_department_3.html; Gabor, "Post-Katrina."
146. "Graduation Exit Code Pre-Reviews: 2012–2013 Graduation Cohort," *Louisiana*

Department of Education, http://www.louisianabelieves.com/docs/default-source/data-management/final-exit-code-pre-reviews.pdf?sfvrsn=2.

147. Danielle Dreilinger, "School Transfer Data Raises Questions About Accuracy of Louisiana Dropout Rates," *Times-Picayune*, October 3, 2014.
148. Michael Deshotels, "100% Error Rate on Student Transfers," July 14, 2014, http://louisianaeducator.blogspot.com/2014/07/100-error-rate-on-student-transfers.html; Michael Deshotels, interview with author, June 2015.
149. *Louisiana Education Department v. Michael R. Deshotels, Et Al.*, 19th Judicial District Court Parish of East Baton Rouge, State of Louisiana, Division D, C647953, https://deutsch29.wordpress.com/2016/10/07/la-supt-john-white-loses-lawsuit-he-filed-against-citizens.
150. Walter Isaacson, "Go Southeast, Young Man," *New York Times*, June 8, 2006.
151. Walter Isaacson, "The Greatest Education Lab," *Time*, June 17, 2007, 47–79.
152. Samuel Abrams, *Education and the Commercial Mindset* (Cambridge, MA: Harvard University Press, 2016), 37, 136.
153. Ibid., 158 of 1362.
154. Ibid., 278, 417; "Edison Schools Settles SEC Enforcement Action," U.S. Securities and Exchange Commission, May 14, 2002, https://www.sec.gov/news/press/2002-67.htm.
155. Jessica Williams, "Wilson Charter, Edison Learning Blaming One Another for $400,000 Shortfall," *The Lens*, March 29, 2013, http://thelensnola.org/2013/03/29/andrew-wilson-charter-school-edisonlearning-blame-one-another-for-400000-shortfall.
156. Danielle Dreilinger, "InspireNOLA Will Take Over Andrew Wilson Charter School in New Orleans," *Times-Picayune*, February 28, 2015; Danielle Dreilinger, "New Board, Management Recommended for Andrew Wilson Charter; Broadmoor Board Fights Back," *Times-Picayune*, January 3, 2015.
157. Jacob Cohen, "Eastern New Orleans, Land of Educational Uncertainty," *Times-Picayune*, December 28, 2012.
158. Isaacson, "The Greatest Education Lab."
159. Campaign Finance Reports, Louisiana Ethics Administration Program, http://ethics.la.gov/CampaignFinanceSearch/SearchResultsByContributions.aspx.
160. Andrew Vanacore, "Orleans Parish School Board Candidate Sarah Usdin Laps the Field in Fund-raising," *Times-Picayune*, October 10, 2012; Campaign Finance Reports, Louisiana Ethics Administration Program; Karran Harper Royal, Twitter Direct Message to author, October 11, 2016.
161. Campaign Finance Reports, Louisiana Ethics Administration Program.
162. Isaacson, "The Greatest Education Lab."
163. Ibid.; "Scaling the New Orleans Charter Restart Model," https://www2.ed.gov/programs/innovation/2010/narratives/u396b100118.pdf.
164. *New Schools for New Orleans*, www.newschoolsforneworleans.org.
165. *Accelerating Academic Gains in New Orleans* (New Orleans: New Schools for New Orleans, 2012), http://www.newschoolsforneworleans.org/wp-content/uploads/2015/08/NSNO-Annual-Update-2012.pdf; "Donors," *New Schools for New Orleans*, http://www.newschools.org/about-us/team/donors.

166. Sarah Reckhow, *Follow the Money: How Foundation Dollars Change Public School Politics* (New York: Oxford University Press, 2012), 37–41.
167. Ibid., 41–42.
168. "School Investments," *New Schools for New Orleans*, http://www.newschools.org/what-we-do/charter-school-investments; "About KIPP New Orleans," *KIPP: New Orleans Schools*, https://www.kippneworleans.org/about-careers.
169. Jessica Williams, "Tulane's Cowen Institute retracts New Orleans Schools Report, Apologizes," *Times-Picayune*, October 10, 2014.
170. Huriya Jabbar, "How Do School Leaders Respond to Competition? Evidence from New Orleans," *Education Research Alliance*, March 26, 2015, http://educationresearchalliancenola.org/files/publications/ERA-Policy-Brief-How-Do-School-Leaders-Respond-To-Competition.pdf; Also http://econ.tulane.edu/vitae/harris.pdf.
171. Ibid.; Arce-Trigatti et al., *Is There Choice in School Choice?*
172. Jabbar, "How Do School Leaders Respond to Competition?"
173. Doug Harris, phone interview with author, May 2017.
174. "Notice of Proposed Class Action Settlement," *P.B., by and through his next friend, Cassandra Berry, et al. vs. John White, et al.*, United States District Court for the Eastern District of Louisiana, Civil Case 2:10-cv-04049, Section A, https://www.splcenter.org/sites/default/files/d6_legacy_files/downloads/case/pb_v_white_-_notice_of_proposed_class_action_settlement.pdf.
175. Harris, interview.
176. Ibid.
177. Peter Cook, "JUST SAY NO: @aagabor is coming to #NOLAed & wants interviews. Don't talk to her: http://pcook.me/9ZQ0 #LaEd," Twitter, August 24, 2016.
178. *New Schools for New Orleans.*
179. Ibid.
180. "Black Community Alliances," *Teach for America*, https://www.teachforamerica.org/about-us/our-initiatives/african-american-community-initiative.
181. Ashana Bigard, interview with author, June 2015; Ashana Bigard, "*I Went to the National Charter Conference & All I Got Was This Lousy Responsibility Bracelet*," *Edushyster*, June 30, 2015, http://haveyouheardblog.com/charter-gras-2015/#more-6947.
182. Bigard, "National Charter Conference."
183. The Cowen Institute for Public Education Initiatives, "Transforming Public Education in New Orleans: The Recovery School District 2003 to 2011," http://www.coweninstitute.com/wp-content/uploads/2011/12/History-of-the-RSD-Report-2011.pdf.
184. Kristen L. Buras, "Race, Charter Schools, and Conscious Capitalism: On the Spatial Politics of Whiteness as Property (and the Unconscionable Assault on Black New Orleans)," *Harvard Education Review* 91, no. 2 (2011).
185. Ibid.
186. Andrew Vanacore, "Group to Study Charter Process; Some Fear Schools Won't Reflect Culture," *Times-Picayune*, February 24, 2012.

187. Bob Peterson, *Keeping the Promise?: The Debate over Charter Schools* (Milwaukee, WI: Rethinking Schools, Ltd., 2008), 23.
188. Peter Dreier and John Atlas, "The Missing Katrina Story," *Tikkun*, January 1, 2007.
189. Leslie A. Maxwell, "Commitment, Charter Status, Brought School Back," *Education Week*, August 29, 2007.
190. "Performance Scores," Louisiana Department of Education, https://www.louisiana believes.com/resources/library/performance-scores.
191. Gary Rivlin, "Why the Lower Ninth Ward Looks Like the Hurricane Just Hit," *The Nation*, August 13, 2015.
192. Beabout, *Principals' Perceptions*, 9.
193. Shari Fink, "The Deadly Choices at Memorial," *New York Times*, August 25, 2009.
194. Rivlin, "Lower Ninth Ward."
195. Ibid.
196. Baum, "The Lost Year."
197. Ibid.
198. Ibid.
199. Rivlin, interview; Doris Hicks, interview with author, August 2012.
200. Hicks, interview.
201. Daniela Rible, "First School in Lower 9th Ward Reopened," *New America Media*, August 30, 2007.
202. Rivlin, "Lower Ninth Ward."
203. Rible, "First School in Lower 9th Ward Reopened."
204. Rivlin, "Lower Ninth Ward."
205. Ibid.; "MLK Charter School to Open Monday in New Orleans," *New Orleans CityBusiness*, September 11, 2006.
206. Rivlin, "Lower Ninth Ward."
207. Ibid.
208. Rible, "First School in Lower 9th Ward Reopened"; http://organizingforpower.org /about/about-lisa.
209. Jennifer Weishaupt, interview with author, August 2016.
210. Ibid.
211. Broderick Bagert, interview with author, June 24, 2015; Eileen Loh Harrist, "The Challenger," *The Gambit*, December 3, 2002. https://www.bestofneworleans.com /gambit/the-challenger/Content?oid=1240950.
212. Broderick Bagert, email message to author, October 16, 2016.
213. Beabout, "Community Leadership."
214. Ibid.
215. Ibid.
216. Ibid.
217. Ibid.
218. Bagert interview.
219. Ibid.

220. Bagert interview; Beabout, "Community Leadership."
221. Ibid.
222. "The Rebirth of Morris Jeff Community School," *New Orleans Tribune*, n.d., http://id3410.securedata.net/theneworleanstribune/morrisjeff.htm.
223. Beabout, "Community Leadership."
224. Ibid.
225. Ibid.; Bagert, interview.
226. Ibid.
227. Ibid.; Weishaupt, interview.
228. Weishaupt, interview.
229. Ibid.
230. Ibid.
231. Beabout, "Community Leadership."
232. Weishaupt, interview; Bagert, interview.
233. Bagert, email.
234. Ibid.
235. Valerie Faciane, "Public Hearing Tonight on $1.8 Billion Master Plan for New Orleans Public Schools," *Times-Picayune*, September 18, 2008.
236. Bagert, email (attached presentation).
237. Ibid.
238. Ibid.
239. Michael Homan, "Mid City Charter Schools," December 12, 2006, *Mid-City Neighborhood Organization*, http://mhoman1.rssing.com/browser.php?indx=69146368&item=1.
240. Michael Homan, "Charter Schools and New Orleans," March 14, 2007, *Michael Homan* (blog), http://michaelhoman.blogspot.com/2007/03/charter-schools-and-new-orleans.html?m=0.
241. Ibid.
242. Peterson, *Keeping the Promise?*, 23.
243. Michael and Susan Klonsky, *Small Schools: Public School Reform Meets the Ownership Society* (New York: Routledge, 2008), 5.
244. Danielle Dreilinger, "Jefferson Charter School Dispute: SABIS, Milestone Argue over Cause of Break," *Times-Picayune*, June 6, 2014, http://www.nola.com/education/index.ssf/2014/06/sabis_definitely_out_at_milest.html
245. John Dibert Community School, Charter Application Binder, August 29, 2009, 79; Marta Jewson, "Editor's Note: FirstLine Renames Dibert School with Move to New Wheatley Campus," *The Lens*, October 26, 2015.
246. Bagert, email.
247. Weishaupt, interview.
248. Bagert, interview.
249. Beabout, "Community Leadership."
250. Isaacson, "The Greatest Education Lab."

251. Michael Homan, "The Two Pauls," May 11, 2007, *Michael Homan* (blog), http://michaelhoman.blogspot.com/2007_05_01_archive.html.
252. Bagert, interview.
253. Kahlenberg and Potter, *A Smarter Charter*, 157.
254. Morris Jeff Community School, "Type V Charter School Application," August 24, 2009, http://s3.documentcloud.org/documents/242526/morris-jeff-community-school-application.pdf.
255. Bagert, interview.
256. Off-the-record interview, November 2016.
257. Ibid.
258. Laura Krebs, interview with author, June 2015; Beabout, "Community Leadership."
259. Krebs, interview.
260. Kahlenberg and Potter, *A Smarter Charter*, 156.
261. John Pope, "Morris Jeff Community School Is a Microcosm of New Orleans Diversity," *Times-Picayune*, November 14, 2010, http://www.nola.com/education/index.ssf/2010/11/morris_jeff_community_school_i.html.
262. Ibid.
263. Jessica Williams, "Use of Seclusion Rooms Remains Focus of Debate at Morris Jeff Charter School," *The Lens*, September 12, 2011.
264. Ibid.
265. Ibid.
266. Ibid.
267. Bagert, interview; Rasheed could not be reached despite repeated efforts.
268. Williams, "Seclusion Rooms."
269. Krebs, interview.
270. Danielle Dreilinger, "Morris Jeff Teachers, Board Ratify Union Contract," *Times-Picayune*, June 21, 2016.
271. Ibid.
272. Ibid.
273. Ibid.
274. Morris Jeff, board meeting, June 2015.
275. Perkins, interview.
276. Ibid.
277. Krebs, interview.
278. Louisiana Department of Education, "Raising the Bar."
279. Carr, *Hope Against Hope*, 100.
280. Andrew Vanacore, "School Reform Legend Prepares to Take Over Wayward John McDonogh High School," *Times-Picayune*, March 18, 2012, http://www.nola.com/education/index.ssf/2012/03/school_reform_legend_steve_bar.html.
281. Kari Dequine Harden, "OPSB Wants to Take Over John McDonogh," *Louisiana Weekly*, July 28, 2014, http://www.louisianaweekly.com/opsb-wants-to-take-over-john-mcdonogh.

282. Danielle Dreilinger, "John McDonogh High School, 'Blackboard Wars' Focus, Will Close in June," *Times-Picayune*, October 7, 2014.
283. Ibid.; Jarvis DeBerry, "John McDonogh Reality Show May Have Kept It a Little Too Real: Jarvis DeBerry," *Times-Picayune*, October 24, 2013, http://www.nola.com/opinions/index.ssf/2013/10/john_mcdonogh_reality_show_may.html.
284. "Statement Regarding the NAACP's Resolution on a Moratorium on Charter Schools," *NAACP*, October 15, 2016, http://www.naacp.org/latest/statement-regarding-naacps-resolution-moratorium-charter-schools.
285. "Standard Grading Policies," https://www.naacp.org/wp-content/uploads/2017/08/Charter_School_Resolution.2016.pdf.
286. *Wall Street Journal*, Editorial, October 18, 2016.
287. *Nationwide Assessment of Charter and Education Management Organizations, Final Audit Report* (Washington, D.C.: U.S. Department of Education, Office of Inspector General, September 2016), https://www2.ed.gov/about/offices/list/oig/auditreports/fy2016/a02m0012.pdf.
288. Valerie Strauss, "NAACP Ratifies Controversial Resolution for a Moratorium on Charter Schools," *Washington Post*, October 15, 2016.
289. Ibid.; American Civil Liberties Union, *Unequal Access: How Some California Charter Schools Illegally Restrict Enrollment*, April 25, 2017, https://www.aclusocal.org/sites/default/files/field_documents/report-unequal-access-080116.pdf.
290. Harden, "OPSB Wants to Take Over John McDonogh."
291. Danielle Dreilinger, "How 3 Top New Orleans Public Schools Keep Students Out," *Times-Picayune*, December 8, 2016; Kari Dequine Harden, "New Orleans Nearing a 'Privatized' Public School System," *Louisiana Weekly*, June 2, 2014.
292. Whitney Bross and Doug Harris, "The Ultimate Choice: How Charter Authorizers Approve and Renew Schools in Post-Katrina New Orleans," *Education Research Alliance*, September 12, 2016; Doug Harris, email message to author, October 29, 2016.
293. Spiro Maroulis, Robert Santillano, Douglas N. Harris, and Huriya Jabbar, "What Happened to Student Mobility After the New Orleans's Market-Based Reforms," *Education Research Alliance*, May 17, 2016.
294. Andrew Vanacore, "Charter Group Poised to Take Over Joseph S. Clark High School," *Times-Picayune*, March 26, 2016.
295. Andrea Gabor, "The Myth of the New Orleans School Makeover," *New York Times*, August 23, 2015.
296. Tate, interview; "Performance Scores," Louisiana Department of Education, https://www.louisianabelieves.com/resources/library/performance-scores.
297. Ibid.
298. Kari Harden, "N.O. Charter School Ranks Second Among La. Schools," *Louisiana Weekly*, May 5, 2014, http://www.louisianaweekly.com/n-o-charter-school-ranks-second-among-la-schools; Danielle Dreilinger, "New Orleans Schools Expel More Students, but Are More Accountable," *Times-Picayune*, August 23, 2013, http://

www.nola.com/education/index.ssf/2013/08/post_197.html; Danielle Dreilinger, "Civil Rights Complaint Targets New Orleans Charter Group Collegiate Academies," *Times-Picayune*, November 20, 2014, http://www.nola.com/education/index.ssf/2014/04/civil_rights_complaint_filed_a.html; Alison Burciaga, email communication with author, December 2, 2016.

299. Gabor, "The Myth of the New Orleans School Makeover."
300. Ibid.
301. Education Research Alliance for New Orleans, "Lycee Francais Votes to Ban Parents from School's Governing Board," *Uptown Messenger*, June 28, 2016.
302. "The Urban Education Future?: Michael Stone," *Education Research Alliance for New Orleans*, June 18, 2015, https://educationresearchalliancenola.org/conferences/the-urban-education-future/participants/michael-stone.
303. Ibid.
304. Danielle Dreilinger, "New Orleans' Katrina School Takeover to End, Legislature Decides," *Times-Picayune*, April 7, 2017, http://www.nola.com/education/index.ssf/2016/05/new_orleans_schools_reunify.html.
305. Danielle Dreilinger, "2 New Orleans Charter Schools Walk a Progressive Path," *Times-Picayune*, August 8, 2017.
306. Eddie Barnes, interview with author, 2013; Eddie and Anya Barnes, interview with Katy Reckdahl, October 2016.
307. Ibid.
308. Ibid.
309. Ibid.
310. Ibid.
311. Ibid.
312. Ibid.; Arianna Prothero, "Some Charters Help Alumni Stick with College," *Education Week*, April 19, 2016.
313. Prothero, "Some Charters."
314. Eddie and Anya Barnes, interview.
315. Ibid.
316. Shelton Joseph, phone interview with author, October 27, 2016.
317. Ibid.
318. Ibid.; David Kunzelman, "'Alarming' Allegations in Lawsuit: Louisiana Prisoners Forced to Bark for Food," *The Advocate*, July 20, 2017, http://www.theadvocate.com/baton_rouge/news/article_7190a9d6-6d95-11e7-9de5-e3acb4de53e1.html.
319. Katy Reckdahl, reporting, October and November 2016; Alison Burciaga, email communication with author, December 1, 2016.
320. Tim Furman, "John Kuhn at SOS March," filmed July 30, 2011, YouTube, 5:55.

Conclusion: A Civic Action: How Schools—and Society—Benefit from Real Democracy

1. E.J. Dionne Jr., Norman J. Ornstein, and Thomas E. Mann, *One Nation Under Trump* (New York: St. Martins Press, 2017), 63–65 and 115.
2. David Frum, *Trumpocracy*, (New York: Harper Collins Publishers, 2018), 168
3. Mercedes Schneider, "Why DFER's Shavar Jeffries Must Support Ed Sec Betsy DeVos," *deutsch29: Mercedes Schneider EduBlog*, November 27, 2016, https://deutsch29.wordpress.com/2016/11/27/why-dfers-shavar-jeffries-must-support-ed-sec-betsy-devos; Whitney Tilson, email to mailing list, November 17, 2016.
4. Schneider, "Support Ed Sec Betsy DeVos."
5. Michael Leachman, Nick Albares, Kathleen Masterson, and Marlana Wallace, "Most States Have Cut School Funding, and Some Continue Cutting," *Center on Budget and Policy Priorities*, revised January 25, 2016, http://www.cbpp.org/research/state-budget-and-tax/most-states-have-cut-school-funding-and-some-continue-cutting; "Race to the Top: States Implementing Teacher and Principal Evaluation Systems despite Challenges," U.S. Government Accountability Office, (Report to the Chairman, Committee on Education and the Workforce, House of Representatives, September 2013).
6. C.M. Rubin, "The Global Search for Education: Would Small Data Mean Big Change?" *CMRubin World* (blog), December 5, 2016, http://www.cmrubinworld.com/the-global-search-for-education-would-small-data-mean-big-change.
7. Valerie Strauss, "The Brainy Questions on Finland's Only High-Stakes Standardized Test," *Washington Post*, March 24, 2014.
8. Notes from a private event.
9. Anya Kamenetz, *The Test: Why Our Schools Are Obsessed with Standardized Testing—But You Don't Have to Be* (New York: PublicAffairs, 2015), 87.
10. Ibid.
11. Daniel Denvir, "Why Were Atlanta Teachers Prosecuted Under a Law Meant for Organized Crime?" *The Nation*, April 22, 2015, https://www.thenation.com/article/why-were-atlanta-teachers-prosecuted-under-law-meant-organized-crime.
12. Matthew M. Chingos, "Strength in Numbers: State Spending on K–12 Assessment Systems," Brown Center on Education Policy at Brookings, policy paper, 2012, https://www.brookings.edu/wp-content/uploads/2016/06/11_assessment_chingos_final_new.pdf.
13. Melissa Lazarin, "Testing Overload in America's Schools," Center for American Progress, October 2014, https://cdn.americanprogress.org/wp-content/uploads/2014/10/LazarinOvertestingReport.pdf.
14. Tony Waters, "Campbell's Law and the Fallacies of Standardized Testing," *Ethnography.com* (blog), May 14, 2013, http://www.ethnography.com/index.php?s=Campbell%27s+Law.
15. Alan Blinder, "Mistrial for South Carolina Officer Who Shot Walter Scott," *New*

York Times, December 5, 2016, https://www.nytimes.com/2016/12/05/us/walter-scott-michael-slager-north-charleston.html.

16. Kirsten A. Graham, "2 More Phila. Educators Charged in Cheating Probe," *Philly.com*, September 26, 2014, http://www.philly.com/philly/education/20140926_2_more_Philly_principals_charged_in_cheating_probe.html.
17. John Merrow, "Meet Adell Clothorne," *Taking Note*, January 9, 2013, http://takingnote.learningmatters.tv/?p=6070; Jack Gillum and Marisol Bello, "When Standardized Test Scores Soared in D.C., Were the Gains Real?" *USA Today*, March 30, 2011, https://usatoday30.usatoday.com/news/education/2011-03-28-1Aschooltesting28_CV_N.htm.
18. Merrow, "Meet Adell Clothorne."
19. Ibid.
20. Valerie Strauss, "Why Not Subpoena Everyone in D.C. Cheating Scandal—Rhee Included? (update)," *Washington Post*, April 12, 2013.
21. Daniel Denvir, "Michelle Rhee's Right Turn," *Salon*, November 17, 2012, https://www.salon.com/2012/11/17/michele_rhees_right_turn.
22. Rachael Brown, "Crusader of the Classrooms," *The Atlantic*, November 2008, https://www.theatlantic.com/magazine/archive/2008/11/crusader-of-the-classrooms/307080.
23. Samuel Abrams, *Education and the Commercial Mindset* (Cambridge: Harvard University Press, 2016), 161.
24. Ibid., 162–64.
25. Jennifer C. Kerr, "Internationally, U.S. Students Are Falling," *U.S. News & World Report*, December 6, 2016, https://www.usnews.com/news/politics/articles/2016-12-06/math-a-concern-for-us-teens-science-reading-flat-on-test.
26. *NAEP 2012: Trends in Academic Progress*, National Center for Education Statistics 18, 40, https://nces.ed.gov/nationsreportcard/subject/publications/main2012/pdf/2013456.pdf.
27. Diane Ravitch, "Mike Petrilli and I Have a Brief Exchange About International Test Scores," *DianeRavitch* (blog), November 6, 2015.
28. Linda Darling-Hammond, "How Can We Close the Achievement Gap?," Stanford Center for Opportunity Policy in Education, blog, https://edpolicy.stanford.edu/library/blog/295.
29. Andrew Ujifusa, "Share of High-Poverty, Racially Isolated Schools Rising, GAO Report Says," *Education Week*, May 17, 2016, http://blogs.edweek.org/edweek/campaign-k-12/2016/05/high_poverty_racially_isolated_schools_GAO.html.
30. Lazarin, "Testing Overload"; Motoko Rich, "States Given a Reprieve on Ratings of Teachers," *New York Times*, August 21, 2014.
31. Rebecca Mead, "Success Academy's Radical Educational Experiment," December 11, 2017, *New Yorker*, https://www.newyorker.com/magazine/2017/12/11/success-academys-radical-educational-experiment.
32. Jennifer Berkshire, "Apples to Apples," *Edushyster*, October 17, 2016, http://edushyster.com/apples-to-apples/.

33. The Nation's Report Card, "State Profiles," https://www.nationsreportcard.gov/profiles/stateprofile?chort=1&sub=RED&sj=AL&sfj=NP&st=MN&year=2015R3.
34. Kate Zernike, "A Sea of Charter Schools in Detroit Leaves Students Adrift," *New York Times*, June 28, 2016; Andrea Gabor, "Will Massachusetts Learn from Michigan's Charter Calamity?," *Andrea Gabor*, July 25, 2016, https://andreagabor.com/2016/07/25/will-massachusetts-learn-from-michigans-charter-calamity.
35. Philissa Cramer, "What You Should Know About Betsy Devos, Trump's Education Secretary Pick—and What Her Choice Might Tell Us About His Plans," *Chalkbeat*, November 22, 2016, https://www.chalkbeat.org/posts/us/2016/11/22/what-a-betsy-devos-appointment-would-tell-us-about-donald-trumps-education-plans.
36. Caitlin Emma, Benjamin Wermund, and Kimberly Hefling, "DeVos' Michigan Schools Experiment Gets Poor Grades," *Politico*, December 9, 2016, http://www.politico.com/story/2016/12/betsy-devos-michigan-school-experiment-232399.
37. Ibid.; Steven Henderson, "DeVos Family Showers GOP with Contributions After DPS Vote," *Detroit Free Press*, September 3, 2016, http://www.freep.com/story/opinion/columnists/stephen-henderson/2016/09/03/charter-devos-money-michigan/89774760.
38. Ibid.
39. Hammond, "How Can We Close the Achievement Gap?"; David Kirp, *Improbable Scholars* (New York: Oxford University Press, 2013), 85.
40. Doug Harris, "Betsy DeVos and the Wrong Way to Fix Schools," *New York Times*, November 25, 2016.
41. Jeanne Allen, Cara Candel, and Max Eden, eds., *Charting a New Course: The Case for Freedom, Flexibility & Opportunity Through Charter Schools*, Center for Education Reform, June 2017, https://www.edreform.com/wp-content/uploads/2017/06/Charting-a-New-Course.pdf.
42. Ibid.
43. Abrams, *Education and the Commercial Mindset*, 171.
44. Claudio Sanchez, "Is Pitbull 'Mr. Education'? Rapper Opens Charter School in Miami," NPR, October 15, 2013; Diane Ravitch, "Andre Agassi: Raising Hundreds of Millions as His Own Charter Is One of the Worst Schools in Nevada," *Diane Ravitch's blog*, November 7, 2016, https://dianeravitch.net/2016/11/07/andre-agassi-raising-hundreds-of-millions-as-his-own-charter-is-one-of-the-worst-schools-in-nevada; "National Charter Schools Conference Features Sexist Lyricist Pitbull," *Jersey Jazzman* (blog), June 29, 2013, http://jerseyjazzman.blogspot.com/2013/06/national-charter-schools-conference.html.
45. Public Charter School Enrollment, National Center for Education Statistics, last updated March 2017, http://nces.ed.gov/programs/coe/indicator_cgb.asp.
46. Allie Bidwell, "The History of Common Core State Standards," *U.S. News & World Report*, February 27, 2014, https://www.usnews.com/news/special-reports/articles/2014/02/27/the-history-of-common-core-state-standards.
47. Andrew Ujifusa, "Pressure Mounts in Some States Against Common Core,"

Education Week, February 2, 2013, https://www.edweek.org/ew/articles/2013/02/06/20commoncore_ep.h32.html.

48. Richard D. Kahlenberg and Clifford Janey, "Putting Democracy Back in Public Education," *The Century Foundation*, November 10, 2016, https://tcf.org/content/report/putting-democracy-back-public-education.
49. "Reading 1: Education as the Keystone to the New Democracy," National Park Service, https://www.nps.gov/nr/twhp/wwwlps/lessons/92uva/92facts1.htm.
50. Kahlenberg and Janey, "Putting Democracy Back"; Franklin D. Roosevelt, "124—Message for American Education Week, September 27, 1938," *The American Presidency Project*, http://www.presidency.ucsb.edu/ws/?pid=15545.
51. David E. Campbell, "Putting Civics to the Test: The impact of State-Level Civics Assessments on Civic Knowledge," *American Enterprise Institute*, September 17, 2014, https://www.aei.org/publication/putting-civics-to-the-test-the-impact-of-state-level-civics-assessments-on-civic-knowledge.
52. David Abrams, "New York State Testing Program Cost Reduction Strategies" (memo to District Superintendents, State Education Department, July 2010), http://www.p12.nysed.gov/assessment/ac-general/archive/cost-reductions-10.pdf.
53. "New CIRCLE Fact Sheet Describes State Laws, Standards, and Requirements for K–12 Civics," *The Center for Information & Research on Civic Learning and Engagement*, Jonathan M. Tisch College of Civic Life, Tufts University, October 10, 2012, http://civicyouth.org/new-circle-fact-sheet-describes-state-laws-standards-and-requirements-for-k-12-civics.
54. Sarah D. Sparks, "Students Lose Way in NAEP Geography Test," *Education Week*, July 19, 2011, www.edweek.org/ew/articles/2011/07/19/37naep.h30.html.
55. Sarah D. Sparks, "Board Cuts Back on Several NAEP Tests in Response to Budget Cuts," *Education Week*, August 2, 2013, www.blogs.edweek.org/edweek/inside-school . . . /08/board_nixes_naep_trend_test_ad.htm.
56. Strauss, "Did No Child Left Behind's Test-Based Reforms Fail? Or Not?"
57. John E. Chubb and Terry M. Moe, *Politics, Markets and America's Schools* (Washington, D.C.: The Brookings Institution, 1990), 34.
58. Ibid., 23.
59. Ibid., 65.
60. Dale Roussakoff, *The Prize* (New York: Houghton Mifflin Harcourt, 2015), 210; David W. Chen, "After More Than 20 Years, Newark to Regain Control of Its Schools," *New York Times.*
61. Kirp, *Improbable Scholars*, 83, 88.
62. "Best High Schools," *U.S. News & World Report* https://www.usnews.com/education/best-high-schools/new-jersey/districts/union-city-school-district/union-city-high-school-12783.
63. Jeffrey C. Mays, "Newark Schools Chief Resigns Early to Ease Transition to Local Control," *New York Times*, December 26, 2017; Chen, "After More Than 20 Years, Newark to Regain Control of Its Schools."

64. Kenneth P. Langton and M. Kent Jennings, "Political Socialization and the High School Civics Curriculum in the United States," *The American Political Science Review*, vol. 62, no. 3 (September 1968), 852–67.
65. Campbell, "Putting Civics to the Test."
66. Anna Deavere Smith, *Notes from the Field: Doing Time in Education*, theater performance, New York City, 2016. Confirmation of wording via Alisa Solomon email, December 27, 2016.
67. Kahlenberg and Janey, "Putting Democracy Back"; Klonsky, "An Interview with Deborah Meier on the Small-Schools Movement."
68. Andrea Gabor, *The Capitalist Philosophers: The Geniuses of Modern Business* (New York: Times Business, 2000), 312.
69. Patrick Wall, "Contract's Plan to Fuel School Experimentation Sparks Debate," *Chalkbeat*, May 15, 2014, https://www.chalkbeat.org/posts/ny/2014/05/15/contracts-plan-to-fuel-school-experimentation-sparks-debate.
70. Adam Urbanski, interview with author.
71. "Charters & Consequences," *The Network for Public Education*, November 2017; Kirp, *Improbable Scholars*, 6.
72. Nikole Hannah-Jones, Class of 2017, MacArthur Fellows Program, https://www.macfound.org/fellows/988.
73. Nikole Hannah-Jones, "Have We Lost Sight of the Promise of Public Schools?," *New York Times Magazine*, February 21, 2017.
74. Peter Cappelli, *Why Good People Can't Get Jobs: The Skills Gap and What Companies Can Do About It* (Philadelphia: Wharton Digital Press, 2012), 75–77; Dionne, Ornstein, and Mann, *One Nation Under Trump*, 240.
75. Cappelli, *Why Good People Can't Get Jobs*, 75–80; David Madland and Alex Rowell, "Unions Help the Middle Class, No Matter the Measure," Center for American Progress Action Fund, June 9, 2016, https://www.americanprogressaction.org/issues/economy/reports/2016/06/09/139074/unions-help-the-middle-class-no-matter-the-measure.
76. Dionne, Ornstein, and Mann, *One Nation Under Trump*, 239.
77. Richard Kahlenberg and Clifford Janey, "Is Trump's Victory the Jump-Start Civics Education Needed?," *The Atlantic*, November 10, 2016, https://www.theatlantic.com/education/archive/2016/11/is-trumps-victory-the-jump-start-civics-education-needed/507293.
78. "74 Interview: The Rigorous, Not-Easily-Defined Education Reform Philosophy of Harvard's Jal Mehta," *The 74 blog*, November 3, 2017, https://www.the74million.org/article/74-interview-the-rigorous-not-easily-defined-education-reform-philosophy-of-harvards-jal-mehta.

SELECTED BIBLIOGRAPHY

Books

Abrams, Samuel. *Education and the Commercial Mindset.* Cambridge, MA: Harvard University Press, 2016.

Ambrus, Sarah, and Christine Simpson. *Riding Shotgun: Empowering Students to Lead Change.* Raleigh, NC: Lulu Press, 2012.

Anrig, Greg. *Beyond the Education Wars.* New York: Century Foundation Press, 2013.

Arce-Trigatti, Paul, Jane Arnold Lincove, Douglas N. Harris, and Huriya Jabbar. *Is There Choice in School Choice?: School Program Offerings in the New Orleans Public School Market.* New Orleans: Educational Research Alliance for New Orleans, 2016.

Ayres, Leonard P. *Laggards in Our Schools.* New York: Russell Sage Foundation, Charities Publication Committee, 1909.

Baker, Liva. *The Second Battle of New Orleans.* New York: Harper Collins, 1996.

Beckner, Weldon. *The Case for the Smaller School.* Bloomington, IN: Phi Delta Kappa Educational Foundation, 1983.

Bensman, David. *Quality Education in the Inner City: The Story of Central Park East Schools.* New York: Desktop Publishing by Kramer Communications, 1987.

———. *Central Park East and Its Graduates.* New York: Teachers College Press, 2000.

Cappelli, Peter. *Why Good People Can't Get Jobs.* Philadelphia: Wharton Digital Press, 2012.

Carr, Howie. *The Brothers Bulger.* New York: Grand Central Publishing, 2006.

Carr, Sarah. *Hope Against Hope.* New York: Bloomsbury, 2015.

Chubb, John E., and Terry M. Moe, *Politics, Markets and America's Schools.* Washington, D.C.: The Brookings Institution, 1990.

Crain, Robert. *The Politics of School Integration.* New York: Routledge, 2017.

Darling-Hammond, Linda, Beverly Falk, and Jacqueline Ancess. *Authentic Assessment in Action: Studies of Schools and Students at Work.* New York: Teachers College Press, 1995.

Deming, W. Edwards. *The New Economics.* Cambridge, MA: Massachusetts Institute of Technology, Center for Advanced Engineering Study, 1993.

DeVore, Donald E., and Joseph Logsdon. *Crescent City Schools: Public Education in New Orleans 1841 to 1991.* New Orleans: OPSB, Center for Louisiana Studies, University of Southwestern Louisiana, 1991.

Dionne, E.J., Jr., Norman J. Ornstein, and Thomas E. Mann. *One Nation After Trump*. New York: St. Martins Press, 2017.

Esquith, Rafe. *Real Talk for Real Teachers*. New York: Viking Penguin, 2013.

Ferris, Robert. *Flood of Conflict*: The New Orleans Free School Story.

Fliegel, Seymour. *Miracle in East Harlem*. New York: Manhattan Institute Book, Times Books, 1993.

Frum, David. *Trumpocracy*. New York: Harper Collins Publishers, 2018.

Gabor, Andrea. *The Capitalist Philosophers: The Geniuses of Modern Business*. New York: Times Business, 2000.

———. *The Man Who Discovered Quality: How W. Edwards Deming Brought the Quality Revolution to America: The Stories of Ford, Xerox, and GM*. New York: Times Books, 1990.

Goldstein, Dana. *The Teacher Wars*. New York: Doubleday, 2014.

Green, Elizabeth. *Building a Better Teacher: How Teaching Works (and How to Teach It to Everyone)*. New York: W.W. Norton & Company, 2015.

Hirsch, E.D., Jr. *Why Knowledge Matters*. Cambridge, MA: Harvard Education Press, 2016.

Isaacson, Walter. *Steve Jobs*. New York: Simon & Schuster, 2011.

Joy, Drew Cristopher. *Contextualizing Katrina: Resources on New Orleans History and Culture for Visiting Activists and Confronting Racism Resources for White Activists*. New Orleans: Tulane University, 2009.

Kahlenberg, Richard D. *Tough Liberal*. New York: Columbia University Press, 2007.

———. and Halley Potter. *A Smarter Charter: Finding What Works for Charter Schools and Public Education*. New York: Teachers College Press, 2014.

Kamenetz, Anya. *The Test: Why Our Schools Are Obsessed with Standardized Testing—But You Don't Have to Be*. New York: PublicAffairs, 2015.

Kanigel, Robert. *The One Best Way: Frederick Winslow Taylor and the Enigma of Efficiency*. Cambridge, MA: MIT Press, 2005.

Kendall, John Smith. *History of New Orleans*, vol. 3. Chicago: Lewis Publishing Company, 1922.

Kirp, David. *Improbable Scholars*. New York: Oxford University Press, 2013.

Klein, Joel. *Lessons of Home*. New York: Harper Collins, 2014.

Klonsky, Michael, and Susan Klonsky. *Small Schools: Public School Reform Meets the Ownership Society*. New York: Routledge, 2008.

Langford, David. *Tool Time for Education*. Langford International, 2015.

Mathews, Jay. *Work Hard, Be Nice*. Chapel Hill, NC: Algonquin Books of Chapel Hill, 2009.

McCourt, Frank. *Teacher Man: A Memoir*. New York: Scribner, 2005.

McDonald, Joseph P. *American School Reform: What Works, What Fails, and Why*. Chicago: University of Chicago Press, 2014.

Mehta, Jal. *The Allure of Order: High Hopes, Dashed Expectations, and the Troubled Quest to Remake American Schooling*. New York: Oxford University Press, 2013.

Meier, Deborah. *The Power of Their Ideas: Lessons for America from a Small School in Harlem*. Boston: Beacon Press, 2005.

———. *In Schools We Trust*. Boston: Beacon Press, 2002.

Moe, Terry M., and John E. Chubb. *Liberating Learning: Technology, Politics, and the Future of American Education*. San Francisco: Jossey Bass, 2009.

Nadelstern, Eric. *Ten Lessons from New York City Schools*. New York: Teachers College Press, 2013.

Noguera, Pedro. *The Trouble with Black Boys*. New York: Jossey Bass, 2008.

Peterson, Bob. *Keeping the Promise?: The Debate over Charter Schools*. Milwaukee, WI: Rethinking Schools, Ltd., 2008.

Rasheed, Aesha, ed. *New Orleans Parents' Guide to Public Schools*, Spring 2015, https://www.scribd.com/document/289832665/New-Orleans-Parents-Guide-2015-New.

Ravitch, Diane. *Reign of Error*. New York: Alfred E. Knopf, 2013.

———. *The Death and Life of the Great American School System*. New York: Basic Books, 2010.

———. *The Great School Wars: A History of the New York City Public Schools*. Baltimore, MD: Johns Hopkins University Press, 2000.

———, and Joseph P. Viteritti, eds. *City Schools: Lessons from New York*. Baltimore: Johns Hopkins University Press, 2000.

Reckhow, Sarah. *Follow the Money: How Foundation Dollars Change Public School Politics*. New York: Oxford University Press, 2012.

Rogers, David. *110 Livingston Street*. New York: Random House, 1968.

Roussakoff, Dale. *The Prize*. New York: Houghton Mifflin Harcourt Publishing, 2015.

Senge, Peter M., Nelda Cambron-McCabe, Timothy Lucas, Bryan Smith, and Janis Dutton. *Schools That Learn*. New York: Crown Business Books, 2012.

Sizer, Theodore. *Horace's Compromise*. New York: Houghton Mifflin, 1984.

Smith, Anna Deavere. *Notes from the Field: Doing Time in Education*, theater performance, New York City, 2016.

Stone, Clarence N., and Robert P. Stoker. *Urban Neighborhoods in a New Era: Revitalization Politics in the Postindustrial City*. Chicago: University of Chicago Press, 2015.

Szachowicz, Sue. *Transforming Brockton High School: High Standards, High Expectations, No Excuses*. Rexford, NY: International Center for Leadership in Education, 2013.

Tough, Paul. *How Children Succeed*. New York: Houghton Mifflin Harcourt Publishing, 2012.

———. *Whatever It Takes*. New York: Houghton Mifflin Harcourt Publishing, 2008.

Vinovskis, Maris A. *From a Nation at Risk to No Child Left Behind: National Education Goals and the Creation of Federal Education Policy*. New York: Teachers College Press, 2009.

Articles, Papers, and Reports

Accelerating Academic Gains in New Orleans. New Orleans: New Schools for New Orleans, 2012. http://www.newschoolsforneworleans.org/wp-content/uploads/2015/08/NSNO-Annual-Update-2012.pdf.

Achieve, "Taking Root: Massachusetts' Lessons for Sustaining and the College- and

Career-Ready Agenda," 2009. https://www.achieve.org/publications/taking-root-massachusetts-lessons-sustaining-college-and-career-ready-agenda.

Allen, Jeanne, Cara Candel, and Max Eden, eds. *Charting a New Course: The Case for Freedom, Flexibility & Opportunity Through Charter Schools.* The Center for Education Reform, June 2017. https://www.edreform.com/wp-content/uploads/2017/06/Charting-a-New-Course.pdf.

American Civil Liberties Union. *Unequal Access: How Some California Charter Schools Illegally Restrict Enrollment.* April 25, 2017. https://www.aclusocal.org/sites/default/files/field_documents/report-unequal-access-080116.pdf.

Ancess, Jacqueline, and Suzanna Wichterle Ort. "How the Coalition Campus Schools Have Re-imagined High School: Seven Years Later." The National Center for Restructuring Education, Schools, and Teaching (NCREST). New York: Teachers College, Columbia University, 1999.

Anderson, Nick. "Education Secretary Duncan Calls Hurricane Katrina Good for New Orleans schools." *Washington Post*, January 30, 2010.

Babbitt, Tripp. W. Edwards Deming Institute podcast with Monta Akin, January 9, 2015. http://podcast.deming.org/monta-akin-discusses-leander-independent-school-districts-transformation-to-happyville.

Baum, Dan. "The Lost Year: Letter from New Orleans." *New Yorker*, August 21, 2006.

Beabout, Brian R. "Community Leadership: Seeking Social Justice while Recreating Public Schools." *International Handbook on Social (In)Justices and Educational Leadership*, Springer International Handbooks of Education. New York: Springer, 2013.

———. *Principals' Perceptions of School Leadership in Post-Katrina New Orleans.* State College, PA: The Pennsylvania State University Graduate School Department of Learning and Performance Systems, 2008.

"Best High Schools," *U.S. News & World Report.* https://www.usnews.com/education/best-high-schools/new-jersey/districts/union-city-school-district/union-city-high-school-12783.

Blakeslee, Nate. "Crash Test." *Texas Monthly*, May 2013. http://www.texasmonthly.com/politics/crash-test/#sthash.qEtx5IPb.dpuf.

Bross, Whitney, and Doug Harris. "The Ultimate Choice: How Charter Authorizers Approve and Renew Schools in Post-Katrina New Orleans." *Education Research Alliance*, September 12, 2016.

Buras, Kristen L. "Race, Charter Schools, and Conscious Capitalism: On the Spatial Politics of Whiteness as Property (and the Unconscionable Assault on Black New Orleans)." *Harvard Education Review* 91, no. 2 (2011).

Campbell, David E. "Putting Civics to the Test: The Impact of State-Level Civics Assessments on Civic Knowledge." *American Enterprise Institute*, September 17, 2014. https://www.aei.org/publication/putting-civics-to-the-test-the-impact-of-state-level-civics-assessments-on-civic-knowledge.

Champion, Bret Alan. "The Effects of High-Stakes Testing on Central Office Organizational Culture: Changes in One School District." DEd diss., University of Texas at

Austin, 2007. https://www.lib.utexas.edu/etd/d/2007/championd49134/championd 49134.pdf.

Chingos, Matthew M. "Strength in Numbers: State Spending on K–12 Assessment Systems." Brown Center on Education Policy at Brookings, 2012. https://www.brookings.edu/wp-content/uploads/2016/06/11_assessment_chingos_final_new.pdf

Combs, Susan. "Public School Construction Costs." Texas Comptroller of Public Accounts: Data Services Division, July 2014. http://www.texastransparency.org/Special_Features/Reports/School_Construction/pdf/Public_School_Construction_Costs.pdf.

Cook, Ann, and Herb Mack. "The Word and the Thing: Ways of Seeing the Teacher." North Dakota: NDSGE, University of North Dakota, December 1975. http://www.ndsg.org/monographs/NDSG_1975_Cook_and_Mack_The_Word_and_the_Thing.pdf.

Cook, Ann, and Phyllis Tashlik. "Making the Pendulum Swing: Challenging Bad Education Policy in New York State." Coalition of Essential Schools, December 9, 2005.

Cotton, Kathleen. "Applying Total Quality Management Principles to Secondary Education: M. Edgecumbe High School, Sitka, Alaska." School Improvement Research Series, November 1994. http://educationnorthwest.org/sites/default/files/ApplyingQualityManagementPrinciples.pdf.

The Cowen Institute for Public Education Initiatives. *New Orleans Public School History: A Brief Overview.* New Orleans: Tulane University, 2007.

The Cowen Institute. *Nola by the Numbers: High Stakes Testing 2010–2011.* June 2011 http://www.coweninstitute.com/wp-content/uploads/2011/06/NBTN-LEAP-and-GEE-2011-CORRECTED.pdf.

The Cowen Institute for Public Education Initiatives. *The State of Public Education in New Orleans.* New Orleans: Tulane University, 2013.

The Cowen Institute for Public Education Initiatives. *The State of Public Education in New Orleans Five Years After the Storm.* New Orleans: Tulane University, 2010.

The Cowen Institute for Public Education Initiatives. *Transforming Public Education in New Orleans: The Recovery School District 2003 to 2011.* http://www.coweninstitute.com/wp-content/uploads/2011/12/History-of-the-RSD-Report-2011.pdf.

Darling-Hammond, Linda. Sworn affidavit, Stanford University, signed July 3, 2001. http://performanceassessment.org/activism/pdf/darlinghammond.pdf.

———, Jacqueline Ancess, and Susanna Wichterle Ort. "Reinventing High School: Outcomes of the Coalition Campus Schools Project." *American Educational Research Journal* 39, no. 3 (2002): 639–73. doi:10.3102/00028312039003639.

Denvir, Daniel. "Why Were Atlanta Teachers Prosecuted Under a Law Meant for Organized Crime?" *The Nation,* April 22, 2015. https://www.thenation.com/article/why-were-atlanta-teachers-prosecuted-under-law-meant-organized-crime.

Deshotels, Michael. "100% Error Rate on Student Transfers." July 14, 2014. http://louisianaeducator.blogspot.com/2014/07/100-error-rate-on-student-transfers.html

Devlin, Paula. "Jefferson Case Shows Meltdown of Orleans Parish School Board."

Times-Picayune, August 28, 2009. http://www.nola.com/politics/index.ssf/2009/08/jefferson_case_shows_meltdown.html.

Engel, Brenda S. "Introduction: Oral History Project North Dakota Study Group." http://ndsg.org/online_registration/2012/engel_reading_2012.pdf.

"Every Child a Winner!: A Proposal for a Legislative Action Plan for Systemic Reform of Massachusetts' Public Primary and Secondary Education System." Worcester, MA: Massachusetts Business Alliance for Education.

Gabor, Andrea. "Charter School Refugees," *New York Times*, April 4, 2014.

———. "A Demographic Divide in Harlem: The Neediest Kids Go to Public Schools, Not Charters." *Andrea Gabor* (blog), May 13, 2014. http://andreagabor.com/2014/05/09/a-demographic-divide-in-east-harlem-the-neediest-kids-go-to-public-schools-not-charters.

———. "Is Politics—Not School Improvement—Behind Brockton's New Charter?" *Andrea Gabor* (blog), February 27, 2016. https://andreagabor.com/2016/02/27/is-politics-not-school-improvement-behind-brocktons-new-charter.

———. "The Myth of the New Orleans School Makeover," *New York Times*, August 23, 2015.

———. "New CREDO Study, New Credibility Problems." *Andrea Gabor* (blog), April 28, 2015. https://andreagabor.com/2015/04/28/new-credo-study-new-credibility-problems-from-new-orleans-to-boston.

———. "A Signature Bloomberg-Era Education Innovation Is at a Crossroads." *Gotham Gazette*, April 21, 2013. http://www.gothamgazette.com/index.php/education/4227-in-the-waning-months-of-bloombergs-tenure-a-signature-education-innovation-is-at-a-crossroads-.

———. "Post-Katrina, The Great New Orleans Charter School Tryout," *Newsweek*, September 20, 2013. http://www.newsweek.com/2013/09/20/post-katrina-great-new-orleans-charter-tryout-237968.html.

———. "Unwrapping New York State's Latest Common Core Tests." *Andrea Gabor* (blog), June 11, 2014. http://andreagabor.com/2014/06/11/unwrapping-new-york-states-latest-common-core-tests.

———, and Peggy Wiesenberg. "Record Fine for Campaign-Finance Violation Sheds Light on Dark Money Donors to Bay State Charter Referendum." *Andrea Gabor* (blog), September 26, 2017. https://andreagabor.com/2017/09/26/record-fine-for-campaign-finance-violation-sheds-light-on-dark-money-contributors-to-charter-referendum.

Gillum, Jack, and Marisol Bello. "When Standardized Test Scores Soared in D.C., Were the Gains Real?" *USA Today*, March 30, 2011. https://usatoday30.usatoday.com/news/education/2011-03-28-1Aschooltesting28_CV_N.htm.

Goldstein, Michael A. "St. Anthony." *New York*, October 13, 1997.

Julie Hancock and others v. David P. Driscoll. Commonwealth of Massachusetts. http://www.doe.mass.edu/finance/chapter70/McDuffy_report.pdf.

Harris, Doug. "Betsy DeVos and the Wrong Way to Fix Schools." *New York Times*, November 25, 2016.

———. "The New Orleans OneApp." *EducationNext* 15, no. 4. http://educationnext.org/new-orleans-oneapp.

"Historic Inequities in New Orleans Public Education: A Legacy of Struggle." *New Orleans Tribune*. http://id3410.securedata.net/theneworleanstribune/publiceducation.htm.

Henderson, Steven. "DeVos Family Showers GOP with Contributions After DPS Vote." *Detroit Free Press*, September 3, 2016. http://www.freep.com/story/opinion/columnists/stephen-henderson/2016/09/03/charter-devos-money-michigan/89774760.

Hird, MacKenzie, Richard Larson, Yuko Okubo, and Kanji Uchino. "Lesson Study and Lesson Sharing: An Appealing Marriage." *Creative Education*, June 2014.

Hirota, Janice M. "Reframing Education: The Partnership Strategy and Public Schools." Report to the Carnegie Corporation of New York, Youth Development Institute, Fund for the City of New York, September 2005. https://www.chapinhall.org/sites/default/files/old_reports/281.pdf

Isaacson, Walter. "Go Southeast, Young Man." *New York Times*, June 8, 2006.

———. "The Greatest Education Lab." *Time*, June 17, 2007, 47–79.

Jabbar, Huriya. "How Do School Leaders Respond to Competition? Evidence from New Orleans." Education Research Alliance, March 26, 2015. http://educationresearchalliancenola.org/files/publications/ERA-Policy-Brief-How-Do-School-Leaders-Respond-To-Competition.pdf.

Johnson, Carol Siri. "History of New York State Regents Exams." Paper, December 31, 2009. http://files.eric.ed.gov/fulltext/ED507649.pdf.

Kahlenberg, Richard D., and Clifford Janey. "Putting Democracy Back in Public Education." The Century Foundation, November 10, 2016. https://tcf.org/content/report/putting-democracy-back-public-education.

Kelleher, Maureen. "New York City's Children First: Lessons in School Reform, American Progress." Report, Center for American Progress, January 2014. https://www.americanprogress.org/wp-content/uploads/2014/03/NYCeducationReport.pdf

Langton, Kenneth P., and M. Kent Jennings. "Political Socialization and the High School Civics Curriculum in the United States." *American Political Science Review*, vol. 62, no. 3, September 1968.

Layton, Lindsey. "How Bill Gates Pulled Off the Swift Common Core Revolution." *Washington Post*, June 7, 2014.

Lazarin, Melissa. "Testing Overload in America's Schools." Center for American Progress, October 2014. https://cdn.americanprogress.org/wp-content/uploads/2014/10/LazarinOvertestingReport.pdf.

Leachman, Michael, Nick Albares, Kathleen Masterson, and Marlana Wallace. "Most States Have Cut School Funding, and Some Continue Cutting." Center on Budget and Policy Priorities, revised January 25, 2016. http://www.cbpp.org/research/state-budget-and-tax/most-states-have-cut-school-funding-and-some-continue-cutting.

Liebling, A.J. "The Great State-I." *New Yorker*, May 28, 1960.

Maroulis, Spiro, Robert Santillano, Douglas N. Harris, and Huriya Jabbar. "What

Happened to Student Mobility After the New Orleans' Market-Based Reforms." *Education Research Alliance*, May 17, 2016.

McCaffrey, Daniel F., Matthew Pepper, and Brian M. Stecher. "Teacher Pay for Performance: Experimental Evidence from the Project on Incentives in Teaching." Paper, Nashville, TN: National Center on Performance Incentives at Vanderbilt University, 2010.

McDonald, Joseph. "Autonomy and Accountability in New York City School Reform." Paper presented at the American Educational Research Association Annual Meeting, April 2009.

Mead, Rebecca. "Success Academy's Radical Educational Experiment." *New Yorker*, December 11, 2017. https://www.newyorker.com/magazine/2017/12/11/success-academys-radical-educational-experiment.

Mei, Dolores, Jan Rosenblum, John Berman, and Linda Solomon. "Inquiry Demonstration Project 1988–89." Brooklyn, NY: New York City Board of Education Office of Research, Evaluation and Assessment, 1990. http://files.eric.ed.gov/fulltext/ED322277.pdf.

Merrow, John. "Meet Adell Clothorne." *Taking Note*, January 9, 2013. http://takingnote.learningmatters.tv/?p=6070.

Meyerson, Harold. "How the Charter School Lobby Is Changing the Democratic Party." *Los Angeles Times*, August 26, 2016.

NAACP. "Statement Regarding the NAACP's Resolution on a Moratorium on Charter Schools." October 15, 2016. http://www.naacp.org/latest/statement-regarding-naacps-resolution-moratorium-charter-schools.

NAEP 2012: Trends in Academic Progress. National Center for Education Statistics. https://nces.ed.gov/nationsreportcard/subject/publications/main2012/pdf/2013456.pdf.

Nationwide Assessment of Charter and Education Management Organizations, Final Audit Report. Washington, D.C.: U.S. Department of Education, Office of Inspector General, September 2016. https://www2.ed.gov/about/offices/list/oig/auditreports/fy2016/a02m0012.pdf.

"Notice of Proposed Class Action Settlement." *P.B., by and through his next friend, Cassandra Berry, et al. vs. John White, et al.*, United States District Court for the Eastern District of Louisiana, Civil Case 2:10-cv-04049, Section A. https://www.splcenter.org/sites/default/files/d6_legacy_files/downloads/case/pb_v_white_-_notice_of_proposed_class_action_settlement.pdf.

Oliff, Phil, and Iris J. Lav. "Hidden Consequences: Lessons from Massachusetts for States Considering a Tax Cap." Center on Budget and Policy Priorities, May 21, 2008. http://www.cbpp.org//archiveSite/5-21-08sfp.pdf.

Perlstein, Daniel. "Teaching Freedom: SNCC and the Mississippi Freedom Schools." *History of Education Quarterly* 30, no. 3, Autumn 1990.

Perrone, Vito. "Monographs by the North Dakota Study Group on Evaluation." http://www.ndsg.org/monographs.html.

———. "A Report to the Rockefeller Brothers Fund." North Dakota: North Dakota Study Group on Evaluation, University of North Dakota, June 1975.

Pham, Lam D., Tuan D. Nguyen, Matthew G. Springer. "Teacher Merit Pay and Student Test Scores: A Meta-Analysis." Vanderbilt University, April 3, 2017. https://s3.amazonaws.com/vu-my/wp-content/uploads/sites/868/2013/02/05145950/Pham-Nguyen-Springer-2017.pdf.

Phillips, Elizabeth. "We Need to Talk About the Test." *New York Times*, April 9, 2014.

"Problems with CREDO's Charter School Research: Understanding the Issues." National Education Policy Center, June 2015. http://nepc.colorado.edu/newsletter/2015/09/problems-credos-research.

"Public School Funding in Massachusetts: Where We Are, What Has Changed, and How We Compare to Other States." Massachusetts Budget and Policy Center, September 1, 2011.

"Race to the Top: States Implementing Teacher and Principal Evaluation Systems despite Challenges," United States Government Accountability Office. September 2013. http://www.gao.gov/products/GAO-13-777.

Rao, Vivek. "So Ordered? Scrutinizing the Massachusetts Judiciary's Role in the State's Sweeping Education Reform Plan." Unpublished manuscript, April 29, 2011. https://www.law.berkeley.edu/files/So_Ordered_Rao.pdf.

Raywid, Mary Anne, Gil Schmerler, Stephen E. Phillips, and Gregory A. Smith. "Not So Easy Going: The Policy Environments of Small Urban Schools and Schools-Within-Schools." Charleston, WV: ERIC Clearinghouse on Rural Education and Small Schools, 2003. http://files.eric.ed.gov/fulltext/ED474653.pdf.

Reasons for Judgment. Civil District Court for the Parish of Orleans, State of Louisiana, *Eddy Oliver, Et Al. Versus Orleans Parish School Board, Et Al.*, May 20, 2012.

Rivlin, Gary. "Why the Lower Ninth Ward Looks Like the Hurricane Just Hit." *The Nation*, August 13, 2015.

Robinson, Joe E. *Continuous Improvement in the Leander ISD: A Quantitative and Qualitative Assessment of Culture and Core Values.* Dissertation, Texas A&M, October 21, 2011.

Steifel, Leanna, Patrice Iatarola, Norm Fruchter, and Robert Berne. "The Effects of Size of Student Body on School Costs and Performance in New York City High Schools." Study, Institute for Education and Social Policy, New York University, April 1998. http://files.eric.ed.gov/fulltext/ED420464.pdf

Toch, Thomas. "Divide and Conquer." *Washington Monthly*, May 1, 2003.

United States National Commission on Excellence in Education. *A Nation at Risk: The Imperative for Educational Reform: A Report to the Nation and the Secretary of Education.* Washington, D.C.: United States Department of Education, 2013.

Wallas, Jones L. "A History of Compulsory School Attendance and Visiting Teacher Services in Louisiana." Louisiana State University Historical Dissertations and Theses, 1967.

Wilson, Steven F. "Success at Scale in Charter Schooling." The Future of American Education: An AEI Working Group and Project to Commission, Discover, and Disseminate New Research on K–12 School Reform. Washington, D.C.: American Enterprise Institute, 2008.

Winerip, Michael. "New York City Student Testing Over the Past Decade." *New York Times*, December 19, 2011.

Zernike, Kate. "A Sea of Charter Schools in Detroit Leaves Students Adrift." *New York Times*, June 28, 2016.

Blogs

Berkshire, Jennifer. *Have You Heard* (formerly *Edushyster*). http://haveyouheardblog.

Crazy Crawfish. https://crazycrawfish.wordpress.com.

Deshotels, Michael. *Louisianaeducator*. http://louisianaeducator.blogspot.com.

Education Next. http://educationnext.org/edblog.

Haimson, Leonie. *Class Size Matters*. https://www.classsizematters.org.

Greene, Peter. *Curmudgucation*. http://curmudgucation.blogspot.com.

Ravitch, Diane. www.dianeravitch.net.

Rubinstein, Gary. https://garyrubinstein.wordpress.com.

Schneider, Mercedes. https://deutsch29.wordpress.com.

The 74million. https://www.the74million.org/blog.

Tilson, Whitney. E-letter. wtilson@kaselearning.com.

Weber, Mark. *Jersey Jazzman*. http://jerseyjazzman.blogspot.com.

INDEX

ABOUT THE AUTHOR

Andrea Gabor, the Bloomberg chair of business journalism at Baruch College/CUNY, is a former staff writer and editor at *U.S. News & World Report* and *Businessweek*. Gabor has written for the *New York Times*, *Los Angeles Times*, *Smithsonian* magazine, *Harvard Business Review*, *Fortune*, and the *Village Voice*. She lives in New York City.